THE LOST WHITE TRIBE

THE LOST WHITE TRIBE

Explorers, Scientists,
and the Theory that
Changed a Continent

Michael F. Robinson

OXFORD
UNIVERSITY PRESS

Oxford University Press is a department of the University of Oxford.
It furthers the University's objective of excellence in research, scholarship,
and education by publishing worldwide. Oxford is a registered trade mark of
Oxford University Press in the UK and certain other countries.

Published in the United States of America by Oxford University Press
198 Madison Avenue, New York, NY 10016, United States of America

© Michael F. Robinson 2016

All rights reserved. No part of this publication may be reproduced,
stored in a retrieval system, or transmitted, in any form or by any means,
without the prior permission in writing of Oxford University Press,
or as expressly permitted by law, by license, or under terms agreed with
the appropriate reproduction rights organization. Inquiries concerning
reproduction outside the scope of the above should be sent to the
Rights Department, Oxford University Press, at the address above.

You must not circulate this work in any other form,
and you must impose this same condition on any acquirer.

Library of Congress Cataloging-in-Publication Data
Robinson, Michael F. (Michael Frederick), 1966– author.
The lost white tribe : explorers, scientists, and the theory that changed a continent /
Michael F. Robinson.
    pages   cm
Includes bibliographical references and index.
ISBN 978-0-19-997848-9—ISBN 978-0-19-997849-6—ISBN 978-0-19-997850-2
1. Africa—Discovery and exploration—European.
2. Africa—Colonization—History—19th century.
3. Ethnology—Africa—History. 4. Whites—Africa—History. I. Title.
DT3.R63 2016
960.23—dc23   2015015102

1 3 5 7 9 8 6 4 2

Printed in the United States of America
on acid-free paper

To Michele

CONTENTS

Acknowledgments ix

Introduction 1

PART I: STANLEY'S LOST STORY

   1. Gambaragara   13
   2. Another World   23
   3. Early Encounters   36
   4. The Story Breaks   47
   5. The Curse of Ham   55
   6. Oriental Jones   64
   7. The Beautiful Skull   75
   8. The Hypothesis Revised   85
   9. King Mutesa   95
  10. Great Zimbabwe   108
  11. At the Summit   120

PART II: A WORLD GONE WHITE

12. The Dynastic Race   137
13. The Aryan Tidal Wave   147
14. Blond Eskimos   162
15. Tribes of the Imagination   175
16. The White Psyche   188
17. Cracks in the Theory   199
18. The Roof of the World   211
19. Colored by War   224
20. Kennewick Man   235

Epilogue: What Did Stanley See?   245
Notes   257
Select Bibliography   279
Index   289

ACKNOWLEDGMENTS

This project began in 1998 when I read Vilhjalmur Stefansson's essay about his encounter with "Blond Eskimos." It was a strange story. At the time, it didn't follow the direction of my research on Arctic exploration, and I left it out of the book I was writing on this subject, *The Coldest Crucible: Arctic Exploration and American Culture*. Something about the "Blond Eskimos" story stayed with me, though, so I held on to the essay. Soon I began finding more white-encounter stories and set them aside in a file cabinet. By the time I started working on this project seriously in 2008, the cabinet was stuffed with accounts of long-lost Caucasians, Hamites, and Aryans, reviews of lost race literature, Nazi expeditions, and research articles on skulls.

If this project succeeds in being something more than a cabinet of strange stories, it is because I have been helped by many people. Jason Anthony, Valerie Olson, Katharine Owens, Avi Patt, Laurel Clark Shire, Bryan Sinche, Richard Troy, and Robin Troy read early proposals of *The Lost White Tribe* and sharpened its focus. Kathleen Sheppard, Neil Kodesh, Michele Troy, and Dane Kennedy read portions of my manuscript and offered valuable expertise. Rand Richards Cooper read this manuscript from beginning to end, and then, because he is gracious and thorough, read it again. His suggestions made it a stronger book.

At the Royal Museum for Central Africa in Belgium, Dr. Mathilde Leduc-Grimaldi guided me through the collections of the Stanley Archive. At Makerere University in Kampala, professor Mahmood Mamdani, director of the Makerere Institute of Social Research, and

Arthur Syahuka Muhindo, professor of history, freely gave their time to answer my questions about the Hamitic hypothesis and its links to the peoples of the Ruwenzori.

My weeks in Kampala were happy ones because of a network of friends that stretched from Connecticut to East Africa: Jake and Alicia Fournier, Eddy Odet, Christine Nalubega, Christine Nabachwa, and John Ssebyoto. In the Ruwenzoris, it was my good fortune to have William Kiminywa guide me to the top of Mount Stanley and John Hunwick, founder of Ruwenzori Trekking Services, to welcome me at the bottom. Stanley would have loved my view of the mountain from the back of Hunwick's motorcycle.

In writing *The Lost White Tribe*, I benefitted from a Connecticut NASA Space Grant, the Belle K. Ribicoff Junior Faculty Prize, and a Vincent P. Coffin grant. Research in Belgium and Uganda was supported by the University of Hartford's International Travel Center and funds provided by the University of Hartford Sabbatical Committee. I owe special thanks to David Goldenberg, dean at Hillyer College, and Anthony Rauche, chair of the college's Humanities Department, both of whom cleared me time and helped find me resources for writing, research, and travel. Students in two seminars—*The Search for Authentic Experience* and *Living on the Edge: Exploration, Technology, and Extreme Environments*—gave me a lot to think about as I started my research.

My agent, Wendy Strothman, found a home for this book at Oxford University Press where it was welcomed by Tim Bent, Alyssa O'Connell, and Joellyn Ausanka. Richard Ring, Head Curator and Librarian at the Watkinson Library at Trinity College, and Christy Bird, Interlibrary Services Coordinator at the University of Hartford, helped me track down important documents and images.

Thanks to the Robinson and Troy clans—especially Mark, Maryann, Colleen, Robbie, and Molly Robinson as well as Bart and Penny Troy—for their comments, encouragement, and support. Thanks also to my kids—Tess, Isabella, and Theodore—who had no choice in selecting this project but still had to endure it, or rather, me: the silent, blue-lit figure working at his laptop. Greatest thanks go to Michele Troy. She knows the lie of acknowledgment pages: they are cheerful, tidy things. But they hide the chaos and disorientation of writing a book. To begin a book project is to commit to a voyage that is guaranteed to go off course. Eventually you lose your way. When I did, she was there to guide me to shore. This book is for her.

ptitle
THE LOST WHITE TRIBE

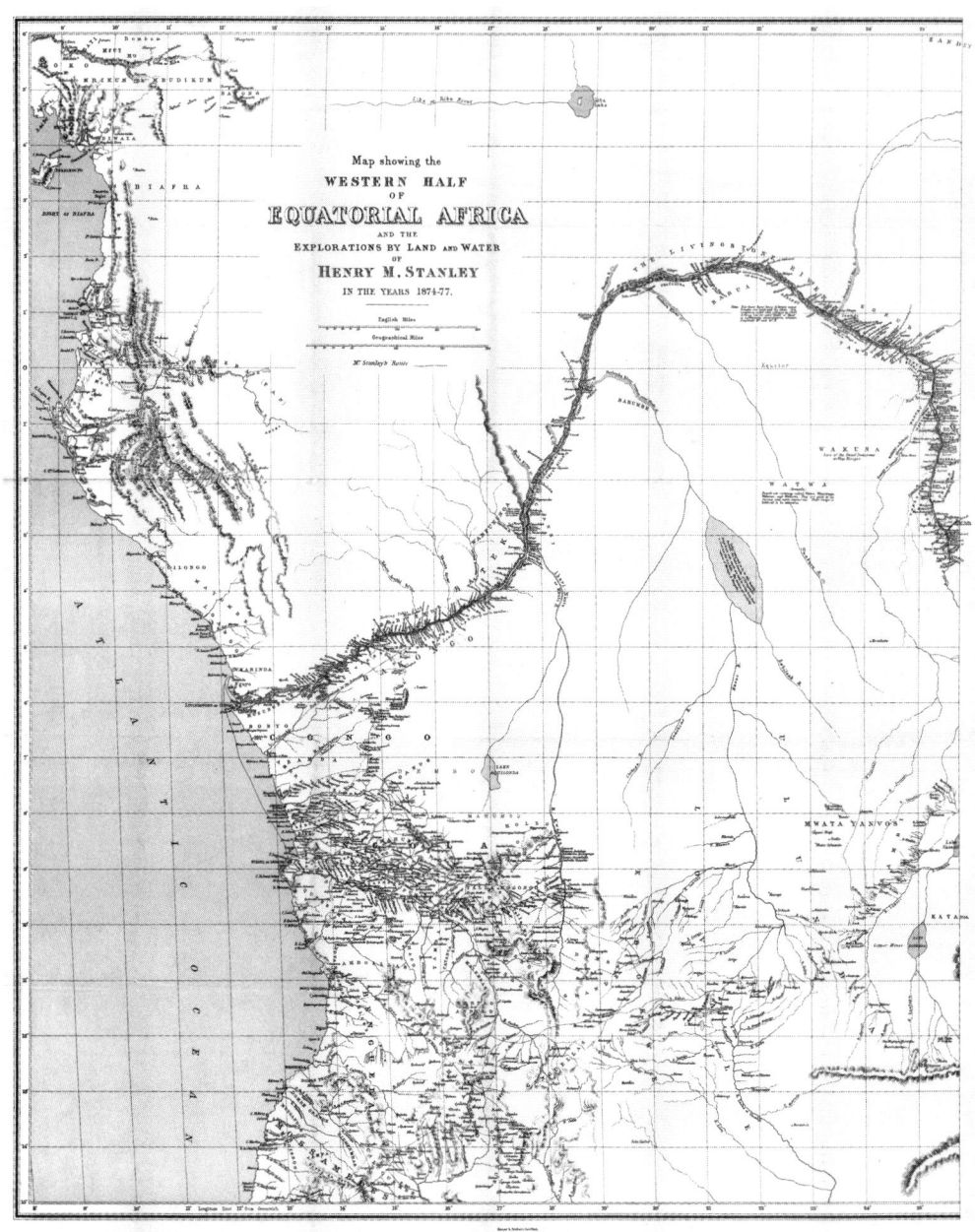

Historic Maps Collection, Princeton University Library. HMC01.246.

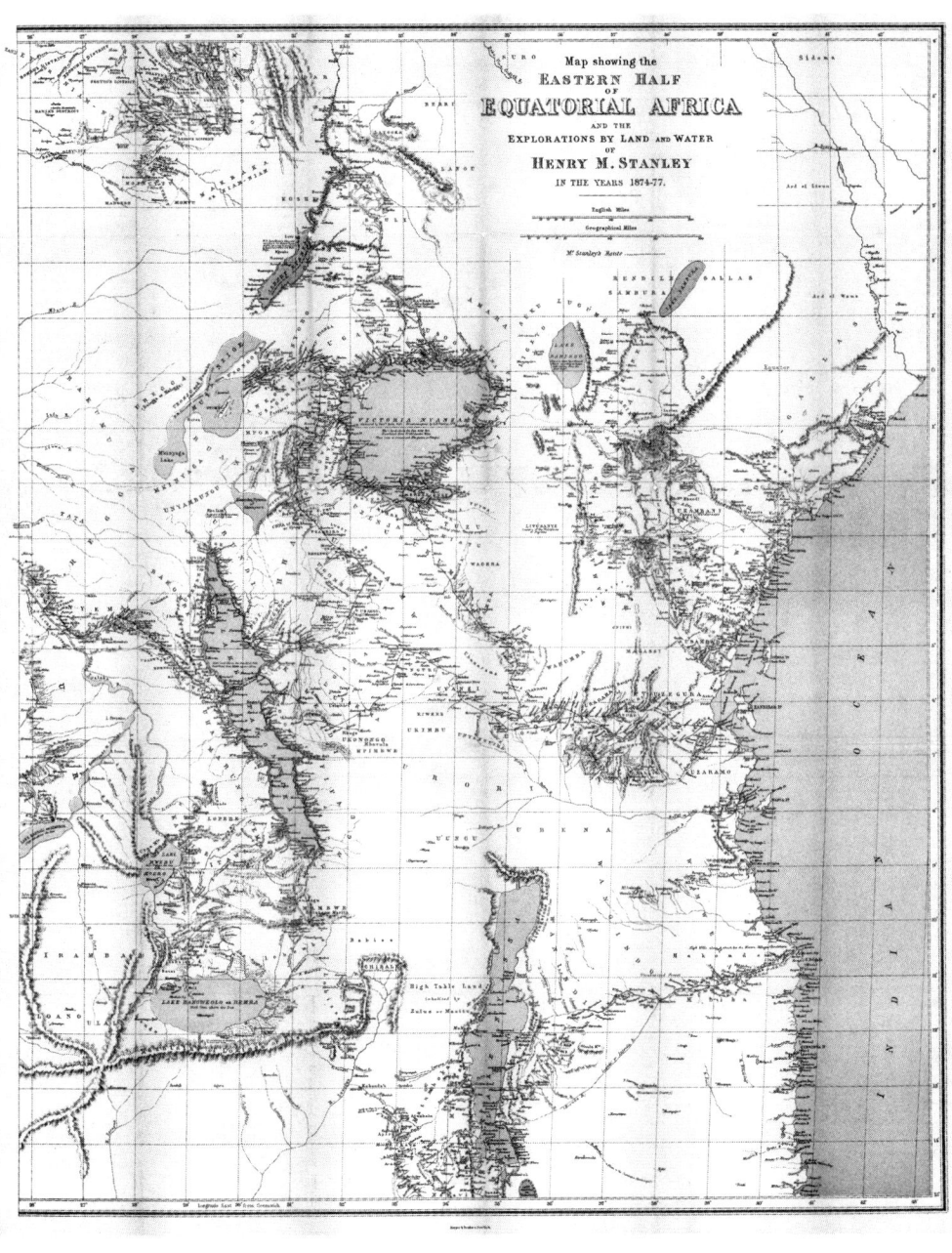

INTRODUCTION

Late-nineteenth-century Bond Street passed through the poshest part of London, its grand houses and art galleries not far from the bustle of Piccadilly and Regent Street. Yet in the fall of 1885 a reporter named David Ker found it a dark corridor of tall, grim buildings of which Henry Morton Stanley's mansion was the "tallest and grimmest of all." Nothing about the place suggested to Ker that it belonged to the world's most famous explorer, a man who had crossed the African continent, charted the Congo, and found the British missionary David Livingstone. Ker pushed through the bustle of "splashed pedestrians" and rang at Stanley's door, which was opened by a butler. He gave his card and was ushered upstairs to the study. Here he found traces of the explorer's feats: a magnificent tiger skin sprawled across the carpet and a large map of the lower Congo River covering the table.

After a few minutes Stanley entered. He was a small, compact man, serious in demeanor. He had "stern thoughtful eyes," Ker observed. While he had lost the "gladiator slimness" of his years on the Congo, his skin was deeply tanned. His hair looked "utterly changed" from when Ker had seen him years before. Even his speech seemed peculiar to Ker. Having lived so long outside of the English-speaking world, Stanley now had an accent. In the plush, quiet interior of his

Henry Morton Stanley. Credit: National Portrait Gallery, London. Reference Number: Ax9169.

Bond Street mansion, the only thing that seemed out of place was Stanley himself. He resided in London but, in truth, he lived nowhere: a man more comfortable at the edges of the empire than in the center of it.[1]

And yet Stanley's life at the edges had brought him to the center of world attention. Finding Livingstone in 1871 had made him an instant international celebrity, his own fame dramatically raising interest in Africa in the process. By the 1880s, the great powers of Europe had turned their eyes to the great southern continent: its gold and ivory, its vast reserves of rubber and cotton, and its command over the world's vital sea routes. Africa, the world's least-known inhabited continent, had suddenly become the most-prized object of conquest. Britain, France, and Germany were making claims to tracts of land from the Nile delta to the Cape of Good Hope, setting off what the *London Times* described as a "scramble for Africa" that was carving up the continent into a patchwork of colonial possessions. Even tiny Belgium had entered the fray, eager for the wealth and prestige accorded bigger powers. It had set its sights on the 2900-mile-long Congo River and its basin, a region seventy-six times bigger than Belgium itself.[2]

For five years, Belgium's ambition had been Stanley's project: assisting King Leopold in his effort to bring the Congo under European control. With a small company of Africans and Europeans, he had established a series of river stations on the lower Congo, negotiating treaties with the clans who lived on its banks. Ker asked Stanley about the details of this massive project as they looked over the large map on Stanley's table: the heat and humidity of the jungle, the geography of the river, and the status of the railroad that Stanley hoped to build along its southern bank.

The fate of the Congo was a matter of towering importance, to both Stanley and the future of Africa, but Ker had other reasons for coming to Bond Street. Near the end of the hour, he began a new line of questioning. It was about an incident that had occurred years before, during Stanley's trans-African expedition of 1874–77, when he was traveling through the East African kingdom of Buganda, domain of the powerful king Mutesa. When Stanley happened to mention Mutesa in the course of conversation, Ker seized his chance: "It was in Mutesa's country that you met those white Africans from Gambaragara, wasn't it? Do you really think there are a whole nation of them in the interior, as some people say?"

"Indeed I do," Stanley replied.

Some ten years earlier he had encountered what he called the "white race of Gambaragara," in the mist-shrouded mountains of East

Africa. In August 1876, his dispatch about the discovery had appeared in the pages of the *New York Herald* and then raced around the world: reprinted, paraphrased, and excerpted by dozens of newspapers across the United States and Europe. The *Hartford Courant* ran the story under the title "White People in Africa." Chicago's *Daily Inter Ocean* printed it under the heading "A New Race of Light-Colored People in the African Mountains." The *Albany Evening Journal* reported it as "one of the most remarkable discoveries that Stanley has made." The story continued to circulate after Stanley's return. He frequently spoke about the "white Africans" in his public lectures and wrote about them in his expedition narrative *Through the Dark Continent*.

The "white race" of Africa soon became a subject of interest for scientists as well. They debated Stanley's discovery in scientific journals on both sides of the Atlantic, from the *American Naturalist* to the *Journal of the Royal Society*. By the time Stanley met with Ker in 1885, his expedition account was taken so seriously that efforts were under way to confirm it. In 1884, the Portuguese explorer Manuel Iradier made plans to reach the mysterious mountains of East Africa and "visit the race of white men who inhabit them." Soon the story of Gambaragara was supported by the reports of other Westerners—anthropologists, archaeologists, and other explorers—who had confirmed the existence of white people living in other regions of the African interior.[3]

Meanwhile, explorers in other parts of the globe—northern Japan, the jungles of the Philippines and Central America, and the frozen wastes of the Canadian Arctic—were also returning to Europe and United States with stories of white tribes. Were these discoveries somehow linked? Many scientists thought so. In the last decades of the nineteenth century, they sifted through the reports of anomalous encounters—flaxen-haired Indians, blue-eyed Inuit, round-eyed Japanese—in hopes of connecting the dots of racial geography to form a picture of the white racial past. Out of these efforts came a theory of human evolution and migration, an attempt to create a prehistory of the human species that might explain the existence of pale-skinned peoples by tracing their trajectories into the darker-skinned regions of the world. This was one reason why Stanley's story of Gambaragara was taken seriously. It appeared to be a clue in a much bigger mystery, one that in the solving promised answers to fundamental questions: Where did the human species originate? Why had it split into separate races? And how had these races come to settle the different regions of the planet?

It was almost 5 p.m. and a young African man entered Stanley's study and served tea. The interview was winding to a close. Ker had enough material for his article, which would focus mainly upon the political jockeying over Africa in general and the Congo in particular making his interview with Stanley both timely and newsworthy. Yet when the *New York Times* published the interview a few weeks later, it was the story of tribes, not territory, that led the headline—"White Africans and the Congo." Even as Africa became the stage for a geopolitical contest among the European powers, then, this strange story of a white race continued to kindle special interest.

———

TWO YEARS LATER, IN 1887, Stanley would return to East Africa and glimpse, from a distance, the mountain homeland of the light-skinned Africans he had met years before. Meanwhile, Ker would publish a novel titled *Lost Among White Africans*, a project made possible, as he acknowledged, "wholly to the kindness of Mr. Stanley himself." It would be one of dozens of works of fiction to appear in at the end of the nineteenth century focusing on the discovery of lost white tribes. By now, the story of the "white race of Gambaragara" had not only become the inspiration for fiction, but it was also increasingly treated as an anthropological fact. Stanley's report was one of a growing corpus of white tribe encounters that filled the pages of newspapers and science journals in the 1800s and early 1900s. It is not surprising then, that Australian writer L. E. Neame wrote the following in an article called "Mysterious White Races" in *Chambers's Journal* in 1905: "The idea that in remote parts of the tropics, amidst the dark skinned races, there exist mysterious isolated white tribes bearing a strong resemblance to Europeans has long possessed a curious fascination." This fascination—kindled by so many different reports—continued well into the century.[4]

Yet it has not continued to the present. Gambaragara has been forgotten. Despite the widespread interest in the story at the time and its influence on a number of important historical figures, historians have been largely silent on Stanley's white tribe. Early Stanley biographers mentioned Gambaragara specifically, but more recent books about Stanley have said little on the topic, and none talks of his encounters with the "white people living in the heart of Africa." Richard Hall's *Stanley*, published in 1974, gives the discovery of Mount Gambaragara two sentences, a high-water mark. Since then Gambaragara has disappeared from the Stanley literature. Even James Newman's excellent *Imperial Footprints* (2004), which re-creates each of Stanley's expeditions "with attention paid to why Stanley made it, what transpired along the way, and what happened afterward as a result," makes no mention of these episodes.[5]

This is surprising, given the enormous attention that has been paid to so many aspects of Stanley's life and travels. He was the most famous explorer in the world when he reported on Gambaragara in 1876 and remained so until his death in 1903. Since then he has remained a celebrated figure, even as recent portraits have taken stock of his complexities and contradictions. Amid the generation of explorers who followed in his wake—the test pilots, aquanauts, and astronauts that have come to define the twentieth and twenty-first centuries—Stanley has held his own. A bibliography of literature on Stanley published in 1943, the centenary of the explorer's birth, listed 123 published books, articles, and lectures. The pace has only increased since then. There has been a fairly constant stream of articles, conference panels, and expedition histories related to Stanley. By my count there are at least forty full biographies that chronicle the explorer's life and works. In short, Stanley has become one of the great meridians of Victorian exploration, a line that frames such subjects as the scramble for Africa, the rise of newspaper publishing, and the growth of popular culture. Yet the story of Gambaragara has disappeared.[6]

It's easy to understand why. The explorer's story has proven daunting for biographers, encompassing too much for the constraints of a single volume. The material about his life and exploits (as soldier, correspondent, author of ten books, and leader of seven expeditions) fills hundreds of cubic feet of space at the Stanley Archives in Belgium. Tracking him across Africa, and then across the wider arc of the Victorian age, are complicated enough tasks without also having to track coverage in the press and public writings. In the 1870s and 1880s, stories about his expeditions continually appeared in the news, the subject of both praise and controversy. In short, Stanley's commanding presence within popular culture was Nile-sized, generating a never-ending current of stories that flowed from the dailies of Europe and the United States. With so many episodes, incidents, and controversies, it would be natural that Gambaragara might get lost.

Yet it was nonetheless a major part of Stanley's own writings: appearing in his diary, field dispatch, newspaper reports, expedition narrative, autobiography, and even in his 1904 eulogy. It seems unlikely that it has been the victim of a collective act of inattention. Rather, it's more probable that the discovery of white tribes doesn't fit the stories we want to tell about Stanley and the exploration of Africa. Most accounts of his expeditions focus on their geographical feats as well as their human cost. Both were considerable. Stanley led four major expeditions to Africa between 1871 and 1889. At times it seemed as if he was bludgeoning rather than exploring his way across the continent, cutting a series of bloody swaths that left hundreds dead and injured. While early biographers admired Stanley for his bravery and tenacity, later writers and scholars have taken him to task for the brutality of his campaigns, which some have plumbed, seeking a deeper explanation of Stanley's psychology. Other have projected the violence outward, looking at Stanley's expeditions as the first salvo of the "scramble for Africa": the conversion of African kingdoms into European colonies, a process that led to yet more violence, the massive disruption of African cultures, and the destruction of political systems from which the continent has yet to fully recover. In the process, however, aspects that do not fit within these narratives, such as the story of Gambaragara and its white inhabitants, have been ignored.[7]

Stanley's white tribe seems peripheral to the themes of empire building and geographical discovery. If anything, it seems like a relic from a different age, a return to the medieval world, when maps portrayed Africa as a place of one-footed monsters and dog-faced men. Stanley's talk of a white tribe does not mesh with the ostensibly scientific qualities of his narrative—the measurements of latitude and longitude, the lists of native vocabulary, the detailed description of plants and animals—that were the hallmarks of the Victorian explorer. White Africans seem by contrast like some flight of fancy, a vision that Stanley must have had while in the grip of yellow fever or, less charitably, yellow journalism.

We have also lost track of the Gambaragara story because it makes us uncomfortable. For four hundred years, Westerners placed white people at the center of their accounts of Africa. The story of the continent emerged from the logs of slave ships, the reports of colonial officers, and the accounts of explorers like Stanley. Since the continent's independence from colonial rule in the 1960s, Africans have tried to recover the voices of people silenced in the history of Atlantic slavery and the century of European occupation that followed. It is understandable, then, why twenty-first century scholars would be reluctant to examine this legend of an African white tribe, perhaps in fear of reviving it. The white invaders are gone, but their shadows remain, no longer seeking Africa's people or gold, but its history.

Why then revive the ghosts of empire for a story that cannot be true? The reason is that Stanley's white tribe story had profound consequences for the history of Africa and its relationship with the West. The story of Gambaragara may have seemed innocuous, but it contained a dangerous idea—black Africa was a world flecked with white—and as such offered new justification for the conquest and settlement of Africa. If white tribes had their own history in Africa, it followed that the Europeans who followed Stanley into African were not settling, but *resettling*, lands that had been conquered by fair-skinned invaders centuries before. As such, the white-complexioned Gambaragarans provided supporting evidence to an argument that redefined Africa's past, and more importantly set its course for the century ahead: the so-called Hamitic hypothesis, which informed and was advanced by Stanley's expeditions.

This book is a biography, not of Stanley, but of this idea. The Hamitic hypothesis argued that fair-skinned tribes had invaded Africa long ago. Born from ancient myth, the theory evolved over time became by the late 1800s the darling of scientists, subject to their most sophisticated instruments and most prized analytical techniques, all in hopes of solving the mysteries of the human racial past. In following the life story of the Hamitic hypothesis, this book moves across centuries and continents to seek out its source. It is a story that cuts through many different fields and disciplines—anthropology, archaeology, linguistics, and biology—following those who were committed to this theory and developing tools to establish that it was a living reality. If Stanley's discovery struck a chord among Victorian audiences, it was one chord in a larger symphony of ideas that composed the Hamitic hypothesis.

Introduction

To tell its story, this book conducts its own expedition, one beginning with the ancient origins of the hypothesis in the Hebrew Bible, and moving from the legends of East African clans to the grammars of British linguists and the skull-collecting safaris of Victorian anatomists. The mystery of Gambaragara and other reports of white African tribes raised questions that most explorers were ill-equipped to answer. Stanley, for example, had come to Africa to solve the mystery of the Nile's source. He was prepared to chart the tributaries of rivers, not to trace the branches of family trees. Yet even had he known what genealogical mysteries lay waiting for him in the interior of East Africa, he would not have been able to solve them. Human ancestry is not directly observable. It does not resolve with the same clarity as bright lakes and rushing rivers; it cannot be sketched within the gridlines of an explorer's map.

As a result, the Hamitic hypothesis had to be pieced together by other means. For Western scientists, skin color was an obvious, but inconclusive, indicator of race. They also scoured for traces—native myths, artifacts, speech, and traditions—that might link living peoples like the Gambaragarans with their racial ancestors. These traces were observable, measurable, and verifiable. Yet history—as any good historian or archaeologist will admit—does not only require fact gathering but also story making. As careful as the scholar might be in letting these traces speak for themselves, they are held together by the scaffolding we create for them: a framework of inference, comparison, and extrapolation that are organized according to our beliefs about the world. The creators of the Hamitic hypothesis built their theory out of a combination of facts and judgments, of measurable traces as well as assumptions. To find why it exerted such influence on the Western imagination, we need to explore the naturalist's study as much as the equatorial rainforest—for it is in these different places that artifacts and arguments became knitted together.

Ultimately, the story of the Hamitic hypothesis helps explain not merely the mystery of white tribes, but also the modern world. It anchored a global theory of human origins and migration that, when combined with the Aryan race theory, predicted the existence of white tribes all over the globe. These predictions seemed to come true. From the 1870s through the 1930s, explorers found native peoples that they identified as white across the farthest reaches of planet: from the Arctic wastes of Victoria Island to the mountains of Tibet to the jungles of Panama. These discoveries are a part of this story, too. Yet unlike the Aryan race theory—which most people associate only with the short, violent history of the Third Reich in Germany—the Hamitic theory continues to live on into the twenty-first century. It has taken root in the soil of modern African culture, shaping attitudes about race in ways that do not receive much attention in the West, even when they are implicated in acts of exceptional violence, such as the Rwandan genocide of 1994.

The Hamitic hypothesis has proven amazingly durable—adapting itself to all sorts of environments, converting Africans to its cause, captivating—in a sense capturing—Europeans for centuries. The idea that native clans descend from ancient ancestors—called by various names, from European, Caucasian, and Aryan, to Hamitic—may have been forgotten in the West, but remains established among peoples from India to East Africa. Yet the mark of its Western heritage remains. This story begins, then, with Europeans, exploring the world and finding, in its wildest and remotest places, a mirror in which they saw themselves reflected.

PART I

STANLEY'S LOST STORY

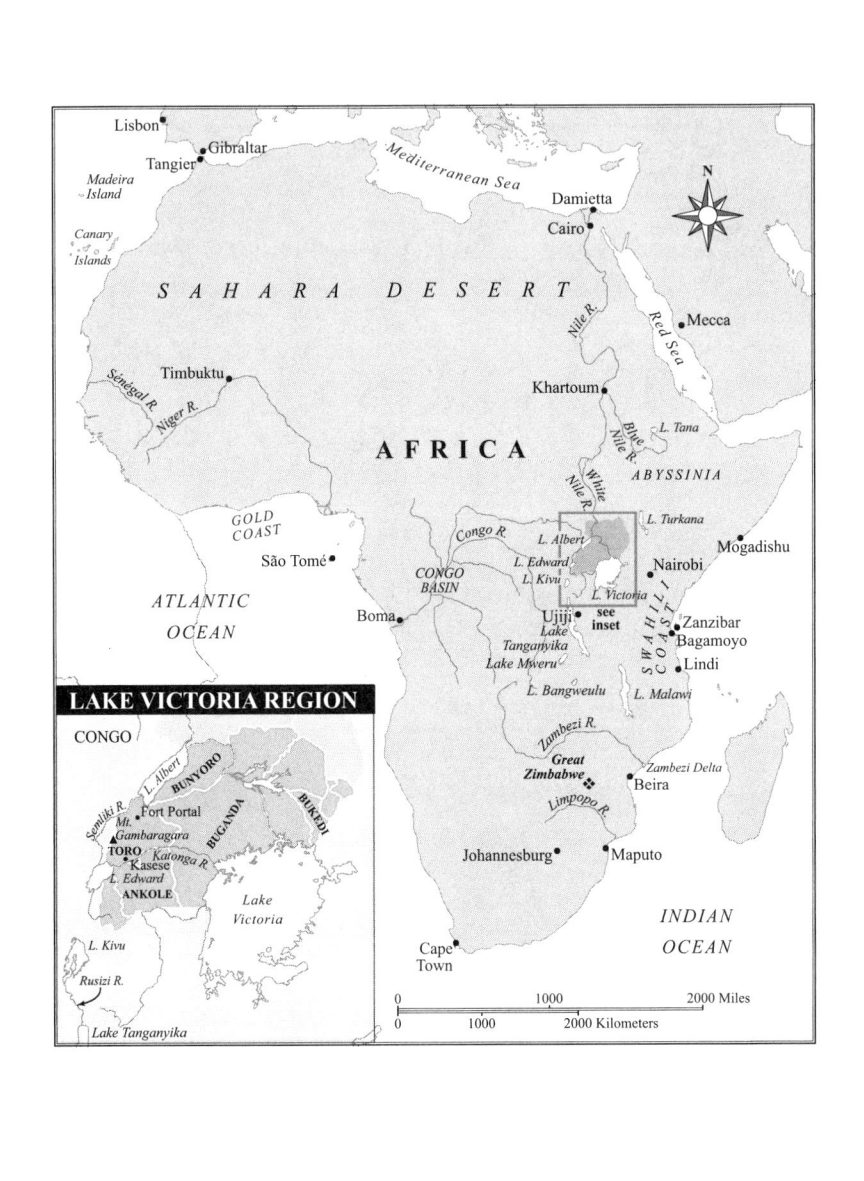

1

GAMBARAGARA

THE FOUR MEN WERE SO light in complexion, so European in their features, that if Stanley hadn't known better he would have thought them, as he put it, "Greeks in white shirts." Yet he also knew that this was absurd. What would Europeans be doing west of Lake Victoria? Only a handful of Westerners had ever set foot in this region of East Africa, a broad plateau of rolling grasslands and gnarled Euphorbia trees. The men were soldiers in a 2000-strong force escorting Stanley into the interior where the ravages of clan warfare and slave trading had sowed deep mistrust of outsiders. In appearance, the four men looked nothing like the other Ganda warriors, who were from Lake Victoria and reddish-brown in complexion. Nor did they look like the Zanzibari porters who, along with their families, had traveled with Stanley 700 miles from the Swahili Coast. The contrast went deeper than skin color, however. The men "differed altogether in habits and manners from the Waganda," Stanley observed. As they made their camp, he noted that they ate or drank little except for the milk from cows that they brought with them.

Despite the imminent danger of attack from unfriendly tribes, the light-skinned soldiers absorbed Stanley's attention. "My curiosity," he wrote in his journal on December 3, 1875, "was roused to the highest pitch." While the men were "extremely uncommunicative," Stanley

Stanley marching through East Africa in 1875 with Mount Gambaragara in the background. Credit: Henry Stanley, *Through the Dark Continent*, 1878.

spent time learning about them from their Ganda commander, Colonel Sekajugu. The men were not from Lake Victoria, Sekajugu informed him, but from the mountain country to the west. There, villages of people with the same pale complexion and European features lived on the slopes of the highest mountain, Gambaragara. The mountain rose to such a great height, Sekajugu told Stanley, that even though situated at the equator its summit was covered in snow year round. Its slopes were terraced and coursed with waterfalls. The Gambaragarans themselves were a pastoral people, the subjects of King Nyika; they dwelled in villages located on the base and slopes of the great mountain, herding cattle and living mostly on a diet of milk and bananas. When threatened by outsiders, they retreated to Gambaragara's snowy summit, where high walls of rock surrounded a crater lake hundreds of yards in diameter.[1]

Even to nineteenth-century ears, Colonel Sekajugu's story had the ring of the fantastic about it. Since the Middle Ages, Africa had inspired marvelous tales. Despite Europe's ruthlessly practical interests in Africa—the flow of sub-Saharan gold that gave liquidity to its markets and the millions of slaves that, for centuries, had powered its

New World colonies—it remained a place of Western fantasy, a dreamland of the weird and monstrous. On medieval maps, cannibals and dog-faced men were depicted wandering its shores while one-eyed giants lurked in the interior. Africa made Europe—ravaged by plague, religious warfare, and revolution—appear paradisiacal by comparison. If it was a land of riches, it was also a place of marvels and horrors.[2]

Yet by the time Stanley arrived in Africa in the 1870s, stories involving the weird and the monstrous had fallen out of favor. Victorian scholars had no tolerance for tales of magic and miracles. New maps revealed the change in thinking: monsters were slowly disappearing from the corners of the world, replaced by wind charts, isothermal lines, and graphs on the comparative heights of mountains. For educated readers, reports of strange races in strange places now required more than the author's credibility to be taken seriously. Nineteenth-century explorers had to approach secondhand stories in the same manner as they would wild animals: warily and deliberately. Before they filled in the blank regions of map, they were expected to use their reason, senses, and scientific instruments to drive off myths that dwelled there. As a newspaperman and an explorer, Stanley was familiar with the dangers of unconfirmed reports. He was particularly wary of stories about Africa that he called "the haunt of the light-headed fable."[3]

Like most African explorers of his era, however, Stanley was more interested in geographical questions than anthropological ones. First among these was the source of the Nile. The location of the headwaters of the great river had been debated for two thousand years by scholars, clerics, and emperors. "No object has more excited my spirit." Julius Caesar reportedly asked the Egyptian priest Acoreus, "Tell me what spring feeds the famous river?" By the second century CE, the Alexandrian geographer Ptolemy had formulated an answer to Caesar's question. The Nile, he wrote in *Geographia*, flowed from two lakes near the equator, both nestled at the base of a great snow-capped range that he called *Lunae Montes*, the "Mountains of the Moon." Ptolemy based his theory on rather weak foundations—hearsay of merchants and travelers—but it was enough to convince cartographers. They inscribed the twin lakes and the Mountains of the Moon on their maps of Africa for more than a thousand years.[4]

As European explorers began advancing into the African interior in the 1800s, expectations that they would discover the source of the

Nile grew. It seemed only a matter of time before they reached the southern limits of the great watershed. Though rarely men of science, explorers often symbolized the methodical march of science into the hidden corners of the world. Through their efforts, reason would replace myth, and observation would triumph over legend. Discovering the source of the Nile had little practical value, but this was not the point. It would liberate the Nile from its long legacy of rumor and conjecture and transform it into the very symbol of human progress, accessible to anyone studying a geography primer or thumbing through a family atlas. In this sense, what the Nile quest would yield was less important than what it represented: the triumph of careful observation over conjectural stories.

In this spirit, a generation of explorers—mostly but not exclusively British—set off to resolve the mystery in the 1850s and 1860s. Under the aegis of the Royal Geographical Society, British expeditions surveyed the Nile watershed from the north, south, and east. In 1856, Richard Burton and John Hanning Speke, both of whom served as soldiers in British India, trekked inland from the East African coast, reaching the shores of a vast lake, Tanganyika, in 1857. Shortly thereafter, Speke reached another great lake to the north of Tanganyika, which he named Victoria in honor of the British queen. Another expedition, led by Samuel and Florence Baker, approached the Nile's source from the north in 1862. Arriving at the confluence of the Nile's two great tributaries—the Blue Nile and the White Nile—the couple set off up the uncharted White Nile until they came across yet another massive lake, "a sea of quicksilver," which they named Albert, after the queen's consort. Capping this series of discoveries, David Livingstone found more lakes south of Tanganyika, including Lake Bangweulu. Over the course of twenty years, British explorers had completed a vast reconnaissance of East Africa, whose lakes and rivers had been revealed, forming the pieces of a great hydrographic puzzle. Now they needed only to be fitted together, the lines of the great watershed connected, and the mystery of the Nile would be solved.[5]

Unfortunately, explorers and geographers could not agree about *what* they had solved. Burton, who had stood upon the vast shores of Lake Tanganyika in 1858, believed that it was the Nile's source. His former partner Speke argued for Lake Victoria. Livingstone, on the other hand, claimed that the Nile's watershed originated southwest of

Lake Tanganyika, possibly Lake Bangweulu. Of course the lake put forward as the source of the Nile by each man also happened to be the one for which he claimed discovery. The feuding became public. As geographers took sides in the controversy, the British Association for the Advancement of Science scheduled a debate among the explorers at its annual meeting in 1864. On the eve of the meeting, Speke went shooting partridges with his cousin, and while climbing over a low wall used his shotgun to brace himself. The trigger got snagged on a branch and the shotgun went off, firing a round into Speke's chest, killing him. Speke's death was ruled accidental by a coroner's inquest, a ruling corroborated by his cousin and other witnesses, but this did not stop Burton from suggesting that Speke had shot himself to avoid defending his false claims about Victoria as the Nile's source.[6]

The rancor over the Nile mystery laid bare a Victorian myth about exploration. Geographical discovery was not a dispassionate process, nor were explorers disinterested parties. While courage and tenacity could, with the assistance of scientific instruments, extend the explorer's reach into the unknown, they did not eliminate bias, emotion, or self-interest. The pictures of the African interior taking shape in the geographical journals of the day, including maps ornamented with lakes, rivers, and coordinate lines, still had to be fashioned by human hands. Science had not delivered a method for shearing the perceptions of the observer from the observations themselves. Explorers were not merely the agents of geography, but landscape artists, whose views of the unknown were filtered, embellished, and sometimes imagined.

The question of the Nile's source remained in doubt into the 1870s. This provided Stanley with a reason to return to Africa in 1874, only three years after his celebrated discovery of David Livingstone. Because so few of the East African lakes had been fully surveyed, it remained unclear how the tributary waters circulated among them, linking them together. Stanley's trans-African expedition, funded jointly by the *New York Herald* and the *Daily Telegraph* of London, would clear up the uncertainty by circumnavigating Lake Victoria and Lake Tanganyika, and then tracing the massive Lualaba River to its mouth, which would be either the Congo River to the west or the Nile River to the north.

Stanley left the coast of East Africa on November 17, 1874, with 3 British men, 228 Zanzibari men and women, an assortment of donkeys, and 5 dogs. Most of the porters carried forty- to sixty-pound packs, filled with cloth and beads, intended for barter with peoples of the interior. Others carried sections of the forty-foot-long boat, *Lady Alice*, named after Stanley's young fiancée, in which he planned to survey Lake Victoria and Lake Tanganyika. On February 27, 1875, the expedition reached Lake Victoria, having trekked 720 miles in 103 days, an extraordinary rate of speed for a party of that size traveling by foot over difficult terrain in the intense equatorial heat.[7]

It was even more impressive given the hardships endured en route. One of Stanley's British men, Edward Pocock, died of smallpox on the trek from the coast. Another, Frederick Barker, was sick with fever and would die shortly after reaching Lake Victoria. Many in the party were weakened by hunger, had succumbed to fever, or were killed in clashes with local villagers, the Nyamwezi, who lived south of Lake Victoria. Stanley portrayed these clashes as unprovoked attacks, but the villagers had reason to be hostile to outsiders. In recent years, the lands south of Lake Victoria had become a battlefield between local Nyamwezi and Swahili Arabs from the Eastern coast over the control of the ivory trade. In the resulting chaos, bands of marauders and mercenaries from the south, known as *ruga-ruga*, harassed villagers and took many for slaves. As a result, Africans throughout the lakes regions often mistook Stanley's expedition for a raiding party. That his men routinely pilfered food from villages didn't help. When some of his porters stole milk from a Nyaturu village, the resulting battle left twenty-two of his party dead or missing. By the time the trans-African expedition reached Lake Victoria, it had lost sixty-two of its members, a quarter of its original number.[8] Having arrived at the lake, however, the survey party proceeded more smoothly. They assembled the sections of *Lady Alice*, which was made of lightweight cedar, and loaded the boat with cloth, flour, dried fish, and other provisions. Stanley set sail with a crew of ten men in March 1875, leaving the rest of his party on Victoria's southern shore, to launch the first attempt to corroborate Speke's claim about the lake's being the source of the Nile.

Paddling and sometimes sailing eastward, the crew began a great counterclockwise circumnavigation of Victoria. On the lake's northern shore, Stanley entered the kingdom of Buganda, ruled by a powerful king—or *Kabaka*—named Mutesa. Stanley already knew of Mutesa from earlier reports. Speke's account of his journey depicted him as a murderous and vainglorious tyrant. Stanley found him to be eccentric and autocratic but intelligent as well as helpful. With the help of a royal canoe escort provided by Mutesa, Stanley completed his circumnavigation of the lake in fifty-seven days. The results supported Speke's claim. Lake Victoria, located at an altitude of 4185 feet above sea level, covered an area the size of Ireland. Its waters flowed north out of the lake at Ripon Falls, either toward Lake Albert or directly into the Nile. However the other lakes of the region—Albert, Edward, and the Tanganyika—were connected to this watershed, this much seemed clear: from the high plateau of East Africa, the waters of Lake Victoria coursed across swamps and pastureland, over cataracts and the arid Sahel, covering a thousand miles of the Sahara before fanning out into the vast lotus of the Nile delta, 3500 miles to the north.

Stanley had thus begun to write the triumphant final chapter of the epic exploration of the Nile, assembling the clues provided by earlier explorers. Yet it was a triumph that revealed the depths of European ignorance about the African interior, for it highlighted that this colossal lake—the third largest in the world—had been known to the outside world for a mere fifteen years. The vast region surrounding it still remained shrouded in mystery, known only from the reports of Speke, Burton, and Baker. With an escort of two thousand men provided by Mutesa, Stanley set off to complete his survey of the watershed to the west, first to Lake Albert, then to Lake Tanganyika, and finally to the Lualaba River beyond.

This large force of men, entrusted with protecting Stanley as he pushed deep in the interior, introduced him to the Gambaragarans. Comprised of many different East African clans, the force presented a spectrum of physical variations, a broad array of heights, facial types, skin colors, and complexions that showed the diversity of African peoples. Even amid this diversity, however, the Gambaragarans stood out, conspicuously different from the rest of the escort party. As he headed west toward Lake Albert, seeking other sources of the Nile, Stanley was also approaching the source of a new mystery.

Stanley was in high spirits. Marching west through the grasslands and rolling hills of East Africa, he found that the pleasures of exploration outweighed its dangers. While he cast himself as a champion of the West, he had never really been at home in either Europe or America. He had been raised in a Welsh workhouse and then immigrated to the United States at the age of eighteen. Hardship had honed Stanley's toughness and tenacity, but also left scars. He remained sensitive about his origins and evasive about his personal history. While he had basked in the fame of finding Livingstone in 1871 and was eager to represent European civilization in his explorations of Africa, he often felt ill at ease among the British upper classes, unable to overcome his insecurities. He was slow to make friends and quick to take offense at perceived slights. As much as he sought out the approval of polite society, he rejoiced at leaving behind Europe, a place of "sordid interests and petty fears." In such a place as Africa, the mind "frees itself and soars into higher altitudes unrestrained, and imperceptibly changes the whole man."[9]

Events brought Stanley quickly back to earth. The expedition party was leaving Buganda and entering the mountainous frontier of Bunyoro (what is today western Uganda) ruled by Mutesa's rival, Kabba Rega. The rolling grasslands gave way to a fierce landscape, one he described in his history of the expedition: "Peaks, cones, mountain humps and dome-like hills shot up in every direction, while ice-cold streams rolled over torn and dismantled rocks, or escaped beneath rough natural bridges of rock with furious roar." The severity of the landscape augured other challenges. Relations between Buganda and Bunyoro were poor. Ganda warriors had invaded Bunyoro only a few years earlier, and it was unlikely that Kabba Rega would distinguish between Stanley's geographical expedition and a full-scale military invasion, especially since both involved the incursion of thousands of Ganda soldiers.

Nonetheless, a few days after he asked Colonel Sekajugu about the light-skinned soldiers in his escort, Stanley became absorbed by elements of the colonel's story, which seemed to be coming together. On January 7, 1876, as the expedition approached Lake Edward, Stanley climbed a small mountain near the Katonga River. From its heights, he "caught a passing glimpse of the king of mountains Gambaragara," its peak reaching thirteen thousand to fifteen thousand feet. At a distance of twenty miles, Gambaragara appeared to Stanley as "an enormous blue mass" still too far away to see any waterfalls, terraces, or crater lakes, let alone strange-looking inhabitants. Before he could investigate further, however, Kabba Rega threatened to attack the expedition party. Stanley wanted to push on, but Sekajugu and the other African leaders of his party resisted. Unable to negotiate safe passage with Kabba Rega, and unwilling to proceed without his African escort, Stanley's party headed south, back toward the safety of Buganda. He would not see the mountains again for twelve years.[10]

Stanley would accomplish his goals. In the course of his expedition, he would confirm Lake Victoria as the source of the Nile, connect Lake Tanganyika and the Lualaba River to the Congo watershed, and chart the course of the Congo River from its quiet tributaries in the Lakes Region to the great leviathan of water that emptied into the Atlantic Ocean. In the process, he would also traverse Africa from east to west. The years ahead would be filled with projects—lectures and interviews, books and articles, plans for future expeditions—that grew out of the 1874–77 trans-African expedition. Amid these mountains of work, both literary and geographical, Gambaragara seemed an insignificant oddity, consisting of a small collection of observations and anecdotes gathered over the course of a month in the winter of 1876. Compared with the search for the Nile's source and the mapping of the Congo River, it was a trifle.

Yet, Stanley continued to think about the white-skinned men, returning to their subject in his books, articles, and lectures, despite his failure to reach their mountain in 1876. Or, perhaps, because of it. He was a man of exceptional drive, someone who had achieved fame for exploring a world that had defeated most other Europeans. In later years, while overseeing the construction of a road on the Congo River, Stanley would be called "Bula Matari" by the Congolese, "the breaker of rocks." The name appealed to him. The determination he exhibited while traversing Africa gave Stanley a way of compensating for his insecurities in the salons of Europe. Self-discipline was a theme that weaves through all of his expeditionary writings. Rather than education or social pedigree, he believed that willpower was the engine that drove geographical discovery. It was the key to unlocking Africa and opening it to the West. Yet even willpower had its limits. Twenty miles from the snow-capped mountains, he could go no farther. Gambaragara became Stanley's North Pole—the ultimate point along the axis of the undiscovered.[11]

In truth, Gambaragara should have been far more accessible than the North Pole. It lay within a continent connected to Europe and the Middle East by trade, whose contours had been charted by mariners from Portugal to China, and which had been crisscrossed by trading routes for more than a thousand years. The trans-African expedition nonetheless confirmed only how little was known about the interior of Africa. In particular, the broad plateau of East Africa, rising four thousand feet from the shores of the Indian Ocean, represented a fortress that, like Gambaragara itself, seemed almost impossible to scale. Of all the riddles involving Africa, this was the most puzzling one of all: why had the West remained so ignorant of this continent for so long?

2

ANOTHER WORLD

When Columbus sailed the shores of this continent, he observed strange things: lumbering manatees, palm trees, and large rivers. He also made note of things he expected to happen but didn't: the water did not boil when his ship had passed over the equator, as some medieval philosophers had predicted. This was, after all, the region of the earth that Aristotle had labeled the "torrid zone." "I am a good witness," Columbus wrote his Spanish sovereigns in 1495, "that it is not uninhabitable." The explorer Alvise Cadamosto also marveled at the strangeness of these lands. It was as if he had traveled to a different planet. "Our customs and lands," he wrote, "in comparison with those seen by me, might be called another world."[1]

Mapmakers attempted to make sense of this new world, or at least make space for it, by revising the maps that had been used since antiquity. They drew in land where water had been and extended its coastlines southward. As fresh reports arrived from returning ships, they revised their maps again, extending coastlines farther down the lines of latitude, a limitless plunge that seemed destined to connect the continent with the South Pole. Knowledge of these shores brought swagger to Spain and Portugal, the new powers of the Atlantic in the fifteenth century. Yet it brought anxieties too. While cartographers wrestled with maps, philosophers struggled to shoehorn the new information into the boot of medieval knowledge, to reconcile it all with scriptures and classical sources. Voyagers were testing not only the limits of geography, but of ideas too. As explorers sailed from Europe, they left behind the ancient texts that had long anchored their thought. The poet Luís Vaz de Camões captured the excitement and disorientation of these discoveries in his poem "The Lusiads":

> Now, pressing onward, past the burning zone,
> Beneath another heaven and stars unknown,
> Unknown to heroes and to sages old,
> With southward prows our pathless course we hold.[2]

Moving south, past the burning zone, explorers surveyed the edges of this vast landmass. It was another world, as Cadamosto had called it, one barely glimpsed in the chronicles of travelers or the texts of ancient scholars. It was the continent of Africa.

Stanley would arrive in this world filled with many of the same questions that had challenged Camões and others since antiquity. Africa had occupied the attention of scholars for two thousand years, but it remained a mystery nevertheless, one even more enigmatic than the other great continent that Columbus had reported lay to the west. It remained unexplored in large part because of the difficulties of travel within the African interior, difficulties that would not be overcome until the end of the nineteenth century. As Stanley made his way across Africa in 1876, a trek that would take three years, a transcontinental express train reached San Francisco from New York in eighty-three hours. Africa was a place that yielded more slowly to discovery, and as a result left more room for speculation and interpretation—about its geography as well as its peoples.[3]

The importance of Africa is often overlooked in Age of Discovery, that period between 1400 and 1600 when European mariners first traced the broad contours of the world. With its riches of tea, silk, and spices, Asia appeared to be Europe's chief object of desire. Africa, by contrast, was the spoiler: a giant obstacle to Asia that needed to be mapped so that it could be avoided, as Columbus did in 1492, or circumnavigated, as Vasco da Gama did in 1498. According to this view, only the demand for African slaves brought the continent to the Europe's attention in the 1500s.

Fifteenth-century world map modeled on fifth-century writings of Macrobius.

In truth, European explorers coveted Africa above all other prizes, even before the Atlantic slave trade began to grow. It was the promise of African riches that drew European mariners into the more dangerous waters of the Atlantic Ocean in the early 1400s, a program of exploration that lasted for a century as Portuguese explorers slowly surveyed the entire African coast. No one yet knew how far Africa extended to the south. European mapmakers had consistently placed the three recognized continents—Europe, Africa, and Asia—in the Northern Hemisphere. The southern shores of Africa, geographers presumed, ended north of the equator, where a long band of seething water belted the earth and separated the *Ecumene*, "the known world," from southern lands, the *Antipodes*. The result was an Africa that was about the size of Europe and tightly bound to the other continents. On the maps made by Macrobius and other medieval cartographers, Africa scarcely appears to be a continent at all, existing instead as the southern flank of a single landmass that stretches from Britain to China. Only slender filaments of water, the Mediterranean Sea and Red Seas, define Africa as a distinct region.[4]

By placing the continents of Africa and Europe so close together, medieval cartographers were expressing an idea about Africa itself. In their vision of the world, Africa was a Mediterranean land, the southern edge of a northern realm that was connected to Europe by culture, history, and trade. This vision flourished because Europeans knew best the continent's northern edges, the Mediterranean coast that stretched over 2800 miles from the Nile delta to the western port of Tanger. Along this long littoral, Europeans saw landscapes—the forests of Morocco, the snow-capped mountains of Algeria, the wheat fields of the Nile delta—that did not seem so different from those in Europe. They were also reminded of settings from the Scriptures. North Africa was one of the great stages of the Old Testament, the land where Moses confronted Pharaoh and led the Jews out of slavery. It carried more recent meanings too. After the Roman emperor Constantine converted to Christianity in the fourth century CE, these African shores became Christian. Indeed, if medieval Europeans had been asked to identify an African, they would probably have given the name Augustine of Hippo, who grew up near the city of Carthage and became a celebrated bishop in late antiquity.[5]

Still, there were mysterious aspects to Africa that would have been apparent to anyone walking through a souk in Alexandria in the early 1400s and seen sacks of guinea pepper, also known as "grains of paradise," used for flavoring food and wine; bags of African alum, the quartz-like mineral used for fixing dyes; or massive tusks that lay stacked, waiting to be loaded onto galleys bound for Europe, where they would be carved into crucifixes, croziers, and Madonnas for church altars. Most of these items arrived in Alexandria on ships coming down the Nile from Cairo and ports farther south. The question was where they originated. The Nile itself also raised questions: many wondered how a river could flow through hundreds of miles of the desert without replenishment by tributaries or rain. As much as Europeans conceived of Africa as a Mediterranean world, they saw hints of another Africa, one located south of the Sahara and that looked nothing like its northern coast.[6]

Knowledge about this other Africa was difficult to obtain. The Sahara presented an imposing barrier to travel as well as information. The desert spanned three thousand miles from east to west and two thousand miles from north to south, comprising an area larger than the contiguous United States. During the Roman Empire, traders moved across the Sahara on chariot routes, some of which were protected by forts and outposts. Yet horses were not ideally suited for this kind of travel. By the second century CE, Berber traders who lived in North

Africa began using camels for long-distance journeys southward, relying on oases as way stations. The journey across the desert was expensive and dangerous, and took months to complete. Traders lowered the risk and cost of these treks by expanding the size of their caravans. By the Middle Ages, caravans of a thousand or more camels were common along the Sahara routes, bringing spices, ivory, and dyestuffs to the markets of the Mediterranean coast.[7]

Still, information about Africa south of the Sahara was slow to percolate north. In addition to the challenges of geography, there were political and religious obstacles that would hinder travelers well into the Victorian Age. North Africa, under Muslim control since the 700s, was hostile territory for the Christian kingdoms of Europe. In the west, Spanish Christians fought a long *Reconquista* to drive Muslim forces off of the Iberian Peninsula, while in the east, Muslim caliphs fought Christian crusaders for control of the Holy Land. Warfare did not halt contact between Christians and Muslims in the Mediterranean; ships leaving Venice and Genoa continued to reach port in Egypt, Tripoli, and Muslim Spain. Yet this trade came with restrictions. Muslim authorities prohibited trade with the ships from *Dar al-Harb*, "Land of War," except in certain coastal cities on the delta such as Alexandria and Damietta. Even when permitted into these cities, Europeans were required to stay in *funduks*, special residence areas, for foreign residents.[8]

Information about sub-Saharan Africa therefore flowed toward the Middle East and Asia rather than to Europe. The Muslim conquest of North Africa gradually brought Islam to the southern regions of the Sahara and its semi-arid borderlands, the Sahel. As a result, these regions became linked to the Middle East through trade as well as faith. The pilgrimage of African Muslims to Mecca in Arabia, known as the *Hajj*, also reinforced these eastern networks. The geographer Mohammed Al Idrisi relied on information from Muslim traders and travelers when he drew up his magisterial 1154 world map, the *Tabula Rogeriana*, which would represent the most accurate map of Africa for the next three hundred years. In the 1300s, the Moroccan explorer Ibn-Battuta contributed vivid descriptions of African lands in his accounts of travels down the Swahili Coast (East Africa) and across the Sahara. These texts were written in Arabic, however, which limited their influence on European geographical knowledge. Barriers in language, then, combined with those posed by religion, politics, and geography conspired to limit European knowledge about sub-Saharan Africa, though it didn't diminish dreams of its treasures.

For Europeans, the greatest African treasure was gold. West African gold had been making its way north to Europe since antiquity. The people of the West African Sahel traded gold to Berber merchants in exchange for such goods as salt, wool, and textiles. In the 1300s, the gold trade became more organized due to the rise of the Mali Empire in West Africa. When the king of this empire, Mansa Musa, made his pilgrimage to Mecca in 1324, his camels carried a full ton of gold in their saddlebags. He spent this gold so profligately that it caused an inflation in prices and a crash in the gold market along the route. He "flooded Cairo with his benefactions," wrote the Arab historian Al-Umari, who arrived in Cairo a few years after Mansa Musa's visit. "He left no court, emir, nor holder of a royal office without the gift of a load of gold."[9] This caravan of gold made a lasting impression. European maps of North Africa showed the *mansa* sitting on a throne in the Mali desert, contemplating a fist-sized nugget of gold in his right hand. Demand for gold intensified in Europe as Christian merchants used it as a form of currency. By the 1370s, Genoa alone was importing almost a ton of the metal each year to use in its mints.[10]

Supply could not keep up with demand. Desire in the West for Eastern spices, cotton, and silks outmatched the market for Western wool and timber in the East. A trade deficit developed between Europe and Asia. In the early 1400s, Venice was exporting a ton of gold to the East each year to pay for goods in the Levant. As gold and silver left Europe in exchange for Eastern luxuries, currency supplies in Europe dwindled. European mints began to close from the lack of precious metals. Portugal minted its last gold coin in 1383 and did not produce another one until 1435. Gold and silver mines in Transylvania, Germany, and Sardinia tried to keep up, providing metal for European mints, but they could not make up the shortfall. In France and Burgundy, local economies returned to barter, and cathedrals started dispersing lead coins to parishioners. As gold and silver grew scarce, the value of the metals increased beyond the nominal value of coins. Unwilling to part with money that was worth more as metal than as currency, Europeans began to horde their coins. As money was taken out of circulation, the crisis deepened. To make matters even worse, the Mali

Empire fell into disarray, disrupting the flow of gold across the Sahara. Europe found itself in the middle of a "bullion famine."[11]

Desperate, European powers considered ways of accessing Africa's goldfields directly. The most promising route lay down the west coast of Africa, where a "River of Gold" was believed to empty into the Atlantic Ocean west of the Sahara. Obtaining gold from its source in Mali would allow European merchants to avoid paying the high transportation costs attached to bringing gold across the Sahara. It would also make Christian kingdoms less dependent on Muslim powers for their economic survival. It did not escape attention in Europe that the wood, iron, and pitch its merchants traded for gold was being used to build Muslim warships in the Mediterranean. The trans-Saharan gold trade was not only expensive, therefore, but dangerous, giving military muscle to Europe's Muslim rivals.[12]

From this mixture of religious angst and economic worry grew Europe's impulse to explore sub-Saharan Africa. Voyaging down Africa's western coast promised not only a means of getting gold but also gaining intelligence about the extent of the Muslim world, particularly its expansion south of the Sahara. Europeans also hoped that they might find Christian allies in these lands. This hope grew from a series of encounters between Europeans and Africans. When Christian crusaders completed their bloody conquest of Jerusalem in 1099, they were surprised to encounter a number of Ethiopian monks and pilgrims, members of Christian Orthodox monasteries such as the Jacobites at the Church of the Holy Sepulchre. This was only the first of many contacts between Christian Europe and Christian Africa during the Middle Ages. In 1306, a delegation of thirty Ethiopians traveled to Rome, Genoa, and Avignon in hopes of forging an alliance against the Muslim forces of the Levant. By the early 1400s, the Ethiopians had even established an embassy in Venice.[13]

Contact with Christian Africans breathed life into a legend that had circulated through Europe for hundreds of years: the existence of Prester John. The story of a powerful Christian monarch, ruling a kingdom in the East or in Africa, had deep roots, and gained life in 1165, when the Byzantine emperor Manuel I Komnenos received a letter allegedly written by John in which he described his wealthy kingdom and his eagerness to engage in battle with the Muslims to defend the Holy Land (Crusader-occupied Jerusalem would fall to Saladin in 1187). As

Europe learned of the existence of Christians in Ethiopia, the realm of Prester John increasingly became a feature on European maps of Africa that began to locate his kingdom on them, usually near the source of the Nile.[14]

By the 1400s, Europeans saw Africa as a place of potential wealth and Christian power, a region that would liberate Europe from its bullion crisis and emancipate the Holy Land from its Muslim occupiers. Under the direction of Prince Infante Dom Henrique (Henry the Navigator), Portugal, small as it was, led the effort to explore Africa's west coast. Facing the Atlantic Ocean, Portugal already had considerable experience sailing the waters of the "Near Atlantic." Still, the exploration of the African coast proceeded slowly because of its dangers, none of which were obvious from the charts of the Mediterranean. While the Atlantic shores of Africa were close to Lisbon, a fraction of the distance to Alexandria, traditional Mediterranean ships proved no match for Atlantic storms. Their "clinker-built" hulls, hollow shells of overlapping planks, broke to pieces in rough seas. Nor were square-sailed cogs and galleys well suited for the Atlantic's powerful winds and currents. The north-east trades, which blew southeast out of Europe and down the African coast, gave ships an excellent following wind, but made the return trip almost impossible. As a result, expeditions to the west coast of Africa usually ended in disaster. The Vivaldi brothers of Genoa, for example, sailed down the coast of Africa in 1291, seeking a route to Asia. They were followed in 1346 by Jaume Ferrer of Majorca, who sought Africa's River of Gold. Neither expedition returned. So established became these perils that the Portuguese identified a point of no return on the African coast—Cape Bojador at 26° N. While no European mariner in the 1400s believed the world was flat (that they did was a myth propagated by Washington Irving in the nineteenth century), Cape Bojador was, figuratively speaking, the point in the Atlantic where ships fell off the edge of the world. Beyond this sandy, wind-swept bluff lay death.[15]

Cape Bojador did not stop Prince Henry, who pushed forward with his plans, aided by advances in technology. The new "caravel" ships possessed hulls joined to internal skeletons, making them sturdier. These ships also used two or three masts, which could hang a variety of sails: square sails for following winds and lateen (triangular) sails for sailing close to the wind, making the return against the north-east trades easier. Employing compasses and sextants to determine their direction and latitude, Iberian mariners grew adept at navigating out of sight of land. Once freed from the coast, they soon discovered the *Volta do mar*, "return from the sea," where the Canary current and northeast trades ended and counter winds, the westerlies, blew ships back toward Europe. By 1435, the Portuguese mariner Gil Eanes "doubled" Cape Bojador. Within ten years, the Portuguese reached the mouth of the Senegal River at 16° N at the southern edge of the Sahara. Here, Berber traders exchanged gold for European goods such as cloth, wheat, and horses. The Portuguese had found their river of gold, or at least its tributary.[16]

In the process, they discovered other riches, too. As Iberian ships ventured farther south into the Atlantic, they found a number of islands and archipelagos, including the Canaries, Madeira, the Azores, and Cape Verdean Islands. These volcanic islands served as way stations, supporting merchant ships as they explored the African coast. They also offered an excellent climate for growing sugar cane. For Europeans, whose experience of sweetness was limited to ripe fruit, sugar was highly prized. As it became more available in Europe, it launched a taste revolution. Europeans began to spike tea and coffee, jams and jellies, marmalades and candies with the stuff. Using the native people of the Canaries, the Guanches, as slave laborers, the Portuguese created a forced-labor system of sugar agriculture that was as brutal as it was profitable. It was soon imitated by other European powers. From these small island plantations grew the roots of a colossal system, the Atlantic slave trade, that soon expanded beyond the sugar trade and, with the discovery of the West Indies by Columbus in 1492, would knit together—by profit and by force—the peoples of Europe, Africa, and the Americas.[17]

When the Portuguese first captured Africans on the Saharan coast in the 1440s, it seemed almost easy. Returning with its cargo of Berber slaves in 1442, the slave ship became the talk of Lisbon. As the Portuguese official Gomes Eanes de Zurara wrote, "When these people saw the wealth that the ships had brought back, acquired in so short a time, and seemingly with such ease, some asked themselves in what manner they too could acquire a share of these profits."[18] Yet slave raids quickly became more difficult. Once aware of the threat posed by Europeans, Arab and Berber peoples of the Saharan coast moved inland. As a result,

Portuguese ships had to raid lands farther south in the more densely populated regions of the Senegal River where, Cadamosto reported, "all men are very black."[19]

Slaving in these southern lands was a different proposition. In the sparsely populated areas of the Saharan coast, raiding parties easily overwhelmed poorly defended villages. The African towns south of the Senegal River, however, were larger and better organized. Portuguese merchant Nuno Tristam discovered this, to his regret, when he attempted to make a slave raid in 1444. Anchoring his caravel at the mouth of a river, he led a party of twenty-two men in two boats upriver. They were met by eighty African men, armed with bows, who attacked them with poisoned arrows. Tristam's party retreated to the caravel, but the poison had already taken its toll. Four men died in their boats, and sixteen more died after reaching the ship, including Tristam himself.[20]

The African interior presented other deadly hazards to Europeans. Malaria, yellow fever, and sleeping sickness were endemic to the savannahs and rain forests of Central Africa. Arriving in Africa from an entirely different disease environment, Europeans had no immunity to these pathogens and, as a result, were decimated when they tried to travel inland.[21]

Francisco Barreto's 1569 expedition to the kingdom of Mutapa (from Zimbabwe to the Mozambique coast) demonstrated the power of diseases to cut down European explorers. Hearing of fabulous gold mines in the South African interior, Barreto led a force of hundreds of soldiers up the Zambezi River. When his men and horses began to succumb to a strange illness, he suspected poisoning by local Muslim traders.[22] The suspected men were arrested, "condemned, and put to death by strange inventions," wrote Jesuit Francisco Monclaro, who accompanied the party:

> *Some were impaled alive; some were tied to the tops of trees, forcibly brought together, and then set free, by which means they were torn asunder; others were opened up the back with hatchets; some were killed by mortars, in order to strike terror into the natives; and others were delivered to the soldiers, who wreaked their wrath upon them with arquebusses.*[23]

This carnival of atrocities ravaged the local community of Swahili Muslims, but did nothing to stop the sickness afflicting Barreto's party. Hundreds of soldiers fell ill and died on the journey to Mutapa. The expedition slowly disintegrated. Barreto led the remnants of his party back to the coast, but, even there, pestilence followed them. Eight days after his return, Barreto began to experience colic and vomiting. He died the following day. When Monclaro brought Barreto's remains to St. Marcal for burial, there was no place to put him. The church had become a morgue. "The building was full of fresh corpses so that there was no room for him, it was necessary to make him a grave crossways along the altar."[24]

By the late 1500s, Europeans began to understand that they could not safely explore the African interior. African kingdoms were too powerful, and the climate too deadly, for conquest and colonization. As a result, the Portuguese largely confined themselves to the coast, building *feitorias*, fortified trading posts, where they purchased or traded for gold, slaves, and ivory with African merchants. Other European powers followed suit, competing with the Portuguese and one another for the control of coastal forts and access to African trade networks. Even with these precautions, Europeans approaching the coast took their lives in their hands. By the early 1700s, 150 years after Barreto's expedition to Monomatapa, one out of three British men in Guinea with the Royal Africa Company died within four months of their arrival. Three of five men died in the first year. The slow progress dismayed British geographers who assembled the African Association in 1788 with the goal of exploring the African interior. Their man in the field, the American John Ledyard, died before leaving Cairo. The next explorer, Simon Lucas, was turned back in the Libyan Desert. Over the next fifteen years, the African Association sent five more explorers to fill in the blanks on the African map. All of them died. In the early 1800s, explorers marched, sailed, and sledged their way to the farthest corners of the globe, but they did not yet reach—or, more precisely, return from—the African interior, now grimly known as "the White Man's Grave."[25]

When Columbus and Cadamosto marveled at the equatorial coast of Africa in the late 1400s, it had seemed "another world" to them, so different was it from the continent's Mediterranean coast. By the early 1500s, however, the outlines of this world had come into focus. The Sahara, the Gold, Slave, and Ivory Coasts of the Bight, the Niger and Congo deltas, the Cape of Good Hope, and the long Swahili Coast of East Africa were now known to the West, described in travel accounts, ships logs, and ledgers of trade. Trading forts dotted the African coast, funneling the riches of the African interior into the Atlantic world. Africa no longer appeared as a simple pie wedge or an appendage of Eurasia on world maps. Extensive surveys of the coast allowed European cartographers to etch a new profile for Africa, one that has remained mostly unchanged to the present. Twenty-first-century students have no trouble identifying Africa on a sixteenth-century map, its iconic form in place by the 1530s.

Yet the discovery of Africa's coast only intensified the mystery of its interior. Europeans continued to wonder about the sources of Nile and the existence of Ptolemy's fabled Mountains of the Moon. Now they added Africa's other great rivers to this list: the Niger, the Zambezi, and the Congo, a river so massive that one explorer marveled, "Twenty leagues from the coast, its waters are sweet." They had known about the goldfields of Mali since antiquity; the gold trade observed by the Portuguese in Southeast Africa meant that other goldfields existed in the south too, near Sofala or Mutapa, or perhaps the lands of the legendary Ophir of the Bible.[26]

In this way, the African interior retained its secrets well into the late nineteenth century, long after its coasts had been explored. These secrets attached not only to river sources, mountains, and mines, but also to Africa's people. From the mouth of the Nile to the Cape of Good Hope lay thirty million square miles of inhabited territory. Despite its contact with West Africans, North Africans, and Ethiopians, the West remained ignorant about the peoples of the interior. This is one reason why Stanley's journey to the Lakes Region of East Africa captured the world's attention.

It also explains why the mystery of Gambaragara took such hold of Stanley, even as he left the mountain behind. His first impression of the sighting, recorded in his field journal in January 1876, simply listed Mount Gambaragara as one discovery among many made on his journey from Lake Victoria. It made no mention of white tribes. Later, in his dispatch to the *New York Herald*, Stanley described Gambaragara in detail, connecting it with the story of the light-skinned men in Colonel Sekajugu's command. By the time he published his full narrative of the expedition two years later, the "white people of Gambaragara" headlined his account, followed by his sighting of the mountain. Over time, in other words, Stanley focused increasingly on his discovery of the people of Gambaragara rather than the mountain itself, despite the fact that it was the third-tallest peak on the continent and the crown of Africa's tallest range. Gambaragara gradually became the scene of marvels, rather than a marvel in its own right.

Why it happened gradually may be due to the demands of travel, which prevented Stanley from telling the full story in his initial account. After all, he first wrote about Gambaragara when his expedition party was being pursued by the hostile forces of Kabba Rega. He may have also been aware, as a good newspaperman would, that the strangeness of a white tribe living in Africa was bound to intrigue readers. Finally, it may have been the case that Stanley's thinking about the European-looking Gambaragarans took time to develop. In the weeks between his diary entry and his dispatch, a period when Stanley said his curiosity was "aroused to the highest pitch," he had time to reflect on earlier experiences in Africa, to reassess encounters that had seemed odd and, at the time, unconnected. Gambaragara triggered insights about things he had witnessed before his discovery but had not initially recognized. Stanley came to believe that East Africa was home to a white race, a race cut off from the rest of the world. He knew this because he had seen it.

3

EARLY ENCOUNTERS

Four years before his encounter with the Gambaragarans, Stanley had been in Africa on his expedition to find the British missionary David Livingstone. Livingstone, for his part, had been exploring Central Africa for thirty years, establishing Christian missions and mapping the lake and river systems of the interior. He was a difficult, mercurial man, poorly suited to the tasks of leading men or evangelizing Africans. During his three decades as a missionary, he made one convert to Christianity and quarreled continuously with the members of his expeditions, dismissing their ideas and opinions. Nor did he express much sympathy for those who fell ill or died under his command. When expedition naturalist Richard Thornton expired from fever and dysentery after seeking food for the party, Livingstone wrote, "Thornton was a fool and went off to Tete to buy goats.... Folly killed him." Serious and solitary as a young man, Livingstone became even more so in Africa, isolating himself from his companions, just as he had from British society. The physician of Livingstone's Zambezi expedition, John Kirk, wrote that Livingstone was "about as ungrateful and slippery a mortal as I ever came into contact with."[1]

Despite his faults, Livingstone was a zealous and intrepid explorer. By the time Stanley arrived in Africa to look for him, Livingstone had

David Livingstone. Credit: *Stanley in Africa* 1890.

traveled to South Africa, from Cape Town to the Kalahari Desert, crossed Africa from west to east along the Zambezi River, and surveyed parts of the extensive lake system from Lake Nyassa to Lake Tanganyika. In the process he had endured malaria, dysentery, and chronic ulcers. He had been pierced by poisoned arrows and mauled by a lion. These adventures and misfortunes took a toll on his health, but they impressed the British public, who marveled over his 1857 book, *Missionary Travels and Researches in South Africa*.

If there was a positive side to Livingstone's temperament, it was that his imperviousness to the opinions of others allowed him to pursue his goals tenaciously and single-mindedly. By the 1860s, Livingstone had mostly abandoned his missionary work to devote himself full time to geographical discovery, in particular the source of the Nile. The rancorous debate that had broken out a few years earlier between Richard Burton and John Speke about the Nile's source provoked Livingstone's interest, not incidentally because he disliked both men, especially Burton. Livingstone had come to believe that the true source of the Nile lay to the south of Lake Victoria and perhaps even south of Lake Tanganyika. Traveling 8° south of the equator in 1867, he had seen a massive river, the Lualaba, coursing north in the general direction of Lake Tanganyika. He believed that this river, which found its source in Lake Bangweulu, five hundred miles south of Lake Victoria, represented the true fountain of the Nile. As Livingstone set off to prove his hypothesis, his health declined and his communication with the outside world became infrequent. In 1869, the British Counsel in Zanzibar stopped receiving his reports from the interior. As concern about the missionary grew, James Gordon Bennett, the publisher of the *New York Herald*, began planning a mission to find him.[2]

Bennett understood—better than anyone—the intensity of the public's fascination with exploration. He had come of age in the 1850s, a time when Europe and North America were in the grip of exploration fever. Scores of expeditions roamed the uncharted regions of the American West, Africa, and the Arctic, sending back reports that became front-page stories in the major dailies of New York, Boston, and London. The biggest story of them all concerned the last Arctic voyage of Sir John Franklin, who had gone missing in the late 1840s along with 128 men while searching for the Northwest Passage. When Franklin did not return from his voyage in 1847 or 1848, British and American expeditions went looking for him on the shores of the high Arctic. Over the next decade, dozens of expeditions searched the bays and icy capes of the polar regions and slowly pieced together the disaster from the discovery of artifacts: a winter campsite on Devon Island; forks, spoons, and relics collected from the Inuit of Pelly Bay; weathered bones, a lifeboat, and a tattered document left by Franklin's officers on King William Island. The mystery of Franklin's disappearance—and the extraordinary efforts to find him—riveted the attention of readers on both sides of the Atlantic. Expeditions to find Franklin and theories about his fate were continually in the news between 1848 and 1860. The lesson for Bennett and other publishers was clear: stories about explorers sold well; stories about missing explorers sold even better.[3]

When news from Livingstone stopped arriving in 1869, therefore, Bennett was ready to act. He dispatched Stanley, the *New York Herald*'s war correspondent, to Zanzibar, the bustling island entrepôt of slave and ivory traders and the major gateway to East Africa. There, amid the cinnamon trees and whitewashed houses of the island, Stanley organized his expedition. He would lead a party due west from the coast toward Lake Tanganyika, where Livingstone was believed to be stationed, in or near the trading town of Ujiji. When his party assembled two months later on the East African coast, it consisted of one hundred African and Zanzibari porters, two British men, and twenty-two donkeys carrying supplies. Stanley led the party into the African interior in high spirits, riding his stallion, Bana Mkuba. "Loveliness glowed around me. I saw fertile fields, riant vegetation, strange trees— I heard the cry of cricket and pee-wit, and sibilant sound of many insects, all of which seemed to tell me, 'At last you are started.'" After months of organizing and tedious negotiation in Zanzibar, Stanley was finally searching for Livingstone. "My pulses bounded with the full glow of staple health; behind me were the troubles which had harassed me for over two months."[4]

Had he known what lay ahead, Stanley would have thought better of his months in Zanzibar. The expedition marched into swamplands swarming with tsetse flies and other stinging insects. As the insects descended upon the party, Stanley's horse was bitten "so sorely in the legs that they appeared as if bathed in blood." Within a week, both of the expedition horses were dead and the donkeys were falling ill. The men did not escape the pestilence. By May 1871, they were falling prey to a menagerie of diseases including malaria and dysentery. As malarial fever took hold of Stanley, he was wracked by chills and delirious visions. "Figures of created and uncreated reptiles…metamorphosed every instant into stranger shapes and designs, growing every moment more confused, more complicated, more hideous and terrible." His weight dropped from 170 to 130 pounds. By September, both British men had to be left behind, too weak to march on. They died soon afterward.[5]

By September, death and desertion had reduced the number of Stanley's party from one hundred to thirty-four. Adding to these trials, the expedition became embroiled in a war between Swahili-Arab traders from the coast and African Nyamwezi traders from the interior over control of the slave and ivory trade. Allying himself with the Swahili-Arabs, Stanley narrowly escaped the massacre of his party by the Nyamwezi. As Stanley's expedition unraveled, the figure of Livingstone seemed to recede into the distance. His party was making progress toward

Lake Tanganyika, but was also edging closer to disintegration. It remained unclear which would happen first. "It requires more nerve than I possess to dispel all the dark presentiments that come upon the mind."[6]

In early November 1871, Stanley's caravan finally entered the town of Ujiji on Lake Tanganyika. Musket fire announced the arrival of the party, and people turned out to greet it. Stanley made his way through the crowds toward a bearded, pale-skinned man wearing a blue cap and gray tweed trousers. It was Livingstone. Stanley maintained his composure, aware of the momentousness of the event. Inwardly, he recalled later in his narrative, he had wanted to "vent my joy in some mad freak." The meeting was emotional for Livingstone, too. He had been living destitute in Ujiji, robbed of his supplies and hobbled by bleeding ulcers on his feet. His efforts to find the source of the Nile had stalled. Whether Stanley uttered the famous words "Dr. Livingstone, I presume?" is unclear. Livingstone made no mention of the greeting in his journals, and Stanley, significantly, tore the pages describing the encounter out of his journal. Nevertheless, the meeting made a spectacular

Stanley and Livingstone on Lake Tanganyika near the mouth of the Rusizi River, 1871. Credit: Henry Morton Stanley, *How I Found Livingstone* 1878.

impact when the *New York Herald* reported it on July 2, 1872. The news spread through Europe and North America. It would become one of the most famous moments in the history of exploration, one that brought Stanley instant fame as an explorer.[7]

Yet it would not be the meeting, but what happened immediately after it, that Stanley remembered as he wrote about the white race of Gambaragara four years later. After their emotional meeting in Ujiji, Stanley and Livingstone agreed to explore the northern shores of Lake Tanganyika together. When Burton and Speke first reached the lake in 1858, they learned of a river, the Rusizi, that attached to the lake at its northern end. The men were unable to visit this region of the lake, and so it remained unclear whether the Rusizi carried water into the lake or out of it. If it flowed out of Lake Tanganyika to the north, as Burton believed, it presumably fed Lake Albert and the Nile. If the Rusizi flowed into the lake, as Speke believed, it was unlikely that Tanganyika was connected to the Nile watershed. Understanding the flow of water at the lake's northern shores, then, promised to reveal whether Lake Tanganyika was the true source of the Nile. Burton and Speke had been unable to do this in 1858, hence Stanley and Livingstone saw this as a chance to resolve the dispute. Reaching Tanganyika without doing this, Stanley feared, would "be greeted by everybody at home with a universal giggling and cackling."[8]

In November 1871, Stanley and Livingstone set off in a long canoe with sixteen rowers and two guides, headed toward the northern shores of the lake. The two men made an unlikely pair. Despite their common interest in African exploration, they approached it with different aims. For Livingstone the missionary, exploration served as a prelude to evangelization. His poor record converting Africans did not lessen his commitment to the spread of Christianity, the ending of the slave trade, or the opening of the continent to contact with the West. For Stanley the newspaperman, exploration offered a bounty of riveting stories. It functioned as a way to sell newspapers and boost his own reputation. Both men could be, at turns, shy or domineering, oversensitive to criticism, and unpracticed at working with others. Yet their meeting in Ujiji had bound them together in a fellowship of danger and social isolation. As they traveled north up the lake, an unlikely friendship grew up between them.[9]

As Stanley and Livingstone moved through the northern reaches of the lake, the hills gave way to grassy plains, fed by a network of river deltas. Sheep and cows grazed near the shore, tended by Uzige villagers who lived on the northeastern edge of the lake. When Stanley lapsed into a malarial fever, the expedition put ashore in Uzige territory. A group of warriors armed with spears met the boat, agreeing to provide the explorers with a hut. The following morning, as Stanley began to recover, the ruler of the Uzige, Mukamba, visited the two men and exchanged gifts with them. When they asked him about the direction of the Rusizi River, ten miles north of their position, Mukamba told them that it flowed into the lake. When the explorers reached the river two days later, they found it exactly as the chief had described.[10]

Mukamba had other news. North of Lake Tanganyika, in the lands west of Lake Victoria, he told the explorers, lived a white race. Stanley and Livingstone were skeptical. They didn't think that Mukamba was lying, but rather that he was describing the brown-skinned peoples of Burundi. "Livingstone and myself smiled at the absurdity of a white people living in the heart of Africa." As a result, Stanley made no mention of Mukamba's claim in his press dispatches, nor did he include it in his published narrative *How I Found Livingstone*. Despite Mukamba's having accurately described the geography of Lake Tanganyika to him, Stanley found the idea of a white race both implausible and unverifiable.[11]

More importantly, the object of the Tanganyika expedition—indeed, most African exploration in this period—did not concern people but places. Interest in Africa continued to be geographical rather than anthropological in nature. No one expected to find the Cyclopes, dog-faced humans, or all the other monstrous races that had been promised by medieval maps and manuscripts. The real mystery of Africa was the source of the Nile, the Mountains of the Moon, and the gold mines of the south, all of which had also been debated since antiquity. In revealing (and sometimes exploding) such mythic places, explorers were not only extending knowledge but connecting themselves to a geographical tradition that extended thousands of years. Hence the search for the Nile's source—much like the search for the Northwest Passage, El Dorado, and ancient Troy—took on a life of its own in the nineteenth century. No one illustrated this impulse better than

Livingstone, who knew more about Central Africa than any other living Westerner, having explored its lake and river systems for so many years. Yet even Livingstone still looked to Herodotus, the ancient geographer, for clues. The ancients still spoke to the modern world, and its explorers still listened, embroidering their stories of discovery with the ideas and accounts of an earlier age as they forged ahead.

The discovery of Africa's human geography, however, lagged behind. Outside of Africa, the peoples living south of the Sahara were understood in the simplest and broadest of terms. From antiquity through the 1600s, Mediterraneans employed the term "Ethiopian," from *Aithiops*, which means "burnt-face," to describe the peoples of the south, a region that extended across Africa, sometimes including the Indian subcontinent as well. "Cushite" also found use, derived from the name of Noah's grandson Cush in the Hebrew Bible; he was thought to have settled his family south of the Nile River. For Muslim writers, the people of the interior were Sudanese, from the expression *Bilad al-Sudan*, "Land of the Blacks." By the eighteenth century, these terms were gradually replaced by "Negro" and "black." For most Europeans, Africans remained a single people, defined by a monochromatic color.[12]

Despite this, some Westerners did come to appreciate the differences between Africans, especially those who came into close contact with them in the course of the slave trade. Portuguese merchants made careful note of the different peoples they encountered on the Guinea Coast and regions farther south, including the Wolofs of Senegambia and the Kongo people of the south. Though unable to reach the interior directly, Europeans also made note of differences in peoples—principally slave traders and the peoples they kidnapped—though it was inspired more by economics than curiosity. For the French clergyman and plantation owner Jean-Baptist Labat, Africans could be divided into types by temperament and behavior: those who were gentle and obedient (Bambaras), those who were clean (Senegambians), and those who were suited for heavy labor (Guineas). With the decline of the Atlantic slave trade in the 1800s, even these hopelessly superficial distinctions were forgotten. Geography became again the preeminent concern of explorers, apart from the rescue expeditions sent in search of Europeans like Franklin or Livingstone.

Their task completed, Stanley and his lost white man, Livingstone, returned south to Ujiji. Within eighteen months, Stanley would be famous and Livingstone would be dead, succumbing at last to malaria and dysentery. The source of the Nile remained the Holy Grail of Africa exploration, a quest that would draw Stanley back to the east coast of Africa in 1874. He would remember Mukamba's words. There were mysteries in Africa beyond rivers and watersheds.[13]

In the months before his contact with the Gambaragarans, he had other encounters as well. Stanley had seen light-skinned Africans in the court of Mutesa, king of Buganda. Mutesa had befriended Stanley in 1875 and pledged to help him in his quest to explore Lake Victoria. Stanley had begun to notice that certain individuals in the Ganda nobility seemed racially distinct. Prince Namionju, brother of the king of Gambaragara, was so "white complexioned" that he seemed Arab rather than African, reminding Stanley of the Egyptians of Cairo. So, too, did the Queen of the Sesc Islands of Lake Victoria. In most cases, these light-skinned Africans appeared to be royalty, possessing a lineage that was separate from the Africans they ruled. His encounters with these Africans persuaded Stanley that a white tribe might exist somewhere in Africa. "It was not until I had seen several specimens of the same pale color that I could believe that there existed a large and numerous tribe of people of such a singular color in the heart of Africa, remote from the track of all travelers and trading caravans."[14]

Stanley had already showed a willingness to stretch the truth when it served his interests, and it would have served his interests here: earlier sightings of light-complexioned Africans would make his discovery of the white tribe of Gambaragarans seem more plausible. There were, he maintained, African witnesses for these events, sometimes even thousands of them, such as for his encounter with the Gambaragarans. Yet none of them could be interrogated directly. They move in and out of Stanley's narrative like figures from a faded diorama: indistinct and two-dimensional. When they speak, they do so through Stanley's pen, leaving no independent records of contact, no confirmation of explorers' claims, no alternate interpretation of events.

Nevertheless, Stanley's reports cannot be dismissed out of hand. He was not the first person to report the existence of white Africans in the regions south of the Sahara. These reports date back to the fifteenth century. Although Prince Henry's African expeditions had not found Prester John in the 1400s, stories about the legendary Christian king of Africa continued to circulate, driven by those hopes that he would ally himself with European Christians and drive Muslim occupiers out of the Holy Land. It seems likely this hope influenced the German scholar Johannes Boemus's description of Prester John as an exceptionally powerful ruler, master of sixty-two lords and commander of an army of one million. The desire of Europeans to see King John as both friend and fellow Christian also likely influenced the way they described him—as light-skinned and European in appearance. "He is not as the moste of the Ethiopians are, blacke," wrote Boemus, "but white." Sixteenth-century illustrations of Prester John supported this view. The cover of a 1540 account of a Portuguese expedition to Ethiopia titled *Verdadeira Informação das Terras do Preste João das Indias* shows a light-skinned Prester John, in European military dress, mounted on a horse. World maps of Africa, published by the Mercators in 1569 and 1628, also show a fair Prester John sitting on his throne in East Africa, near the sources of the Nile (indeed, not far from where Stanley encountered the Gambaragarans 250 years later). By the seventeenth century, however, artists began to darken the appearance of the Christian king. By the eighteenth century, having found no sign of him in Ethiopia or on the Swahili Coast, cartographers and chroniclers followed suit, removing him from their maps and texts of discovery.[15]

Yet accounts of white African tribes did not end in the eighteenth century, even as standards of reporting and mapping became more rigorous. Some came from West Africa, the region best understood by European geographers. In the 1700s, West Africa was no longer the gauzy periphery of empire, but the heart of the thriving Atlantic slave trade. Though not all of these reports survived, they were authoritative enough to be codified by mapmakers. Herman Moll's 1710 map of Africa, for example, labels the lands surrounding the so-called Gold Coast: "Ye Country about hundred Leagues North of the Coast of Guinea, is inhabited by white Men, or at least a different kind of People from the Blacks."[16]

Admittedly, Moll's record of the "white men" of Guinea takes place at some distance—2500 miles—from Stanley's encounter with the white men of Gambaragara 165 years later. Yet there were other reports, nearer in time and space, that corroborated Stanley's account. In 1844, a young American merchant, Michael Shepard, visited Zanzibar and recorded what he heard from Arab ivory traders returning from the African interior. "Those who return to Z[anzibar] give a description of a race of whites similar to Europeans, and having vessels which are represented as being very fine and sailing on large and very beautiful lakes." Shepard's account is secondhand, but it is intriguing because it contains information that would later prove to be accurate. When Shepard recorded it in 1844, no Europeans had yet set foot in the vast Lakes Region of East Africa. Thirteen years later, Burton and Speke would stand on the shores of vast Lake Tanganyika (and later, for Speke, Lake Victoria) and give witness to these "large and beautiful lakes." Some newspapers reported that the explorers had also found evidence of white tribes, making Shepard's account of an African "race of whites" not only plausible but credible.[17]

4

THE STORY BREAKS

Twenty months after seeing the blue silhouette of Mount Gambaragara from a hill in Bunyoro, Stanley and the survivors of the trans-African expedition straggled into Nsanda, a small town near the Atlantic mouth of the Congo River. It had been almost three years since Stanley left Zanzibar with three European men and a party of 228 men, women, and children. In that time, the expedition had crossed an 1800-mile girdle of Africa, from east to west, a trek that translated into 7000 miles of walking, climbing, and paddling. His party was now reduced to 115, many of whom were near death. In other words, nearly half of his expedition had perished along the route. All three of his European men were dead. Forty people were ill with dysentery, ulcers, and scurvy. Commonly, scurvy was the disease of long sea voyages and Arctic expeditions, where it was difficult to find fresh fruits and vegetables. It seemed out of place in the lush valleys of the lower Congo, one of the most verdant regions of the world. Yet there was little food to gather here except for ground nuts. Local villagers were reluctant to trade with the party. They wanted rum, not the beads and bolts of cloth that Stanley offered them. As a result, the expedition was growing weaker as it approached the outlet of the Congo. Stanley and his party were starving to death.[1]

In desperation, he sent a messenger ahead to the port town of Boma, where a small number of European traders lived, to beg for their assistance. "We are now in a state of imminent starvation…," he wrote. "The supplies must arrive within two days or I may have a fearful time of it among the dying." Officers at the Liverpool trading firm Hatton & Cookson received Stanley's letter in Boma and immediately organized a relief party. Two days later, the party arrived at Stanley's camp with rice, fish, sweet potatoes, and other provisions. The party erupted into song. Many ate the rice and fish raw, unable to wait for it to be cooked. Stanley was overcome. "I had to rush to my tent to hide the tears that would issue, despite all my attempts at composure."[2]

Stanley and his party's arrival in Boma a few days later represented the end of his extraordinary journey. He could not see the blue horizon of the Atlantic from the port; the ocean lay just west of his position, but signs of it were all around him. The waters of the Congo widened and its current slackened. The "hateful, murderous river" that had drowned his men and battered his boat, the *Lady Alice*, was calm. The upriver gorges and cataracts that had slowed the expedition for months had been transformed into a gentle alluvial plain that swelled slightly with the tide and smelled of the sea. Boma was an in-between place, not quite river, not yet ocean.[3]

It was an in-between place in other ways, too. The town was the major entrepôt to the vast watershed of the Congo River, a place of exchange between the West and Africa. Until the early 1800s, it had been a base of operations for the Atlantic slave trade and a point of contact between Europeans and Bakongo villagers. When Stanley arrived in 1877, ocean steamer ships arrived at the docks to transfer goods from the half-dozen European trading houses overlooking the river.

Eighteen European traders lived among the town's several thousand residents, overseeing the stores that bartered rum, guns, and fabric for ivory and palm oil. The Europeans of Boma had adapted to their new equatorial home, living in wooden-frame houses set on pilings to protect them from the flood of the great river. Here, among African baobab trees, they wore linen suits and tended their gardens of apples, pineapples, and guava.

Stanley felt elated to be in Boma, "the glowing warm life of Western civilization," and grateful for the welcome offered by its European residents. He was also exhilarated to have completed his mission, tracing the Congo River from its tributaries near Lake Tanganyika to the shores of the Atlantic, a journey that had carried him on a vast counterclockwise arc across Central Africa. Yet he also felt disoriented, unable to find his place in the collision of cultures within the port town. This became clear when he met Boma's European residents:

> *As I looked into their faces, I blushed to find that I was wondering at their paleness.... The pale colour, after so long gazing on rich black and richer bronze, had something of an unaccountable ghastliness.... I did not dare to place myself upon an equality with them as yet; the calm blue and grey eyes rather awed me, and the immaculate purity of their clothes dazzled me. I was content to suppose myself a kind of connecting link between the white and the African.*[4]

Exactly where Stanley stood on the spectrum between "the white and the African" was no longer clear to him. The ghostly color of the Europeans in Boma shocked him, but it also symbolized his growing sense of alienation from the Western world he had left behind. He had lived for so long among Africans that he felt closer kinship to them, especially his Zanzibari porters, than to his social equals in England and America. To underscore the point, Stanley learned that his fiancée, Alice Pike, had broken off their engagement while he was in Africa. By the time Stanley arrived in Boma, in fact, she had already married another man and had a child.

Stanley's return to London did little to help him feel reconnected to European life. Awkward, insecure, and now single, Stanley poured himself into writing his expedition narrative, a 1088-page tome that he completed in eighty days.[5] *Through the Dark Continent* chronicled the extraordinary accomplishments of the trans-African expedition. In two and a half years, the party had mapped the Congo River, crossed the continent from east to west and surveyed the entirety of Lake Tanganyika, the longest lake in the world. It had also circumnavigated Lake Victoria, confirming it as the source of the Nile, finally putting to rest a two-thousand-year mystery that had become an obsession for Victorian explorers. It was, even to Stanley's critics, who condemned the violence and death that seemed to follow the explorer wherever he traveled in Africa, an impressive story of geographical discovery.

Stanley devoted only four pages to the people and geography of Gambaragara in *Through the Dark Continent* (though it included a full-page illustration of his expedition marching in the shadow of the great mountain). Four pages in a book that runs more than a thousand may not seem especially noteworthy, yet by the time *Through the Dark Continent* came to press in 1878, Gambaragara had been discussed by newspapers and scientific journals for almost two years. The light-skinned Africans had become famous in the West before Stanley's expedition had even ended.

Stanley had effectively scooped himself. Seven months after he had encountered the Gambaragarans in East Africa, he sent the *New York Herald* five dispatches, carried by couriers to Zanzibar. These dispatches, which totaled fourteen thousand words, detailed the highlights of the first year of the trans-African expedition, including the discovery of Gambaragara. Despite the volume of other material, the *Herald* had seized on Gambaragara and featured it prominently. The paper's first report, published on July 26, 1876, ran under the heading "Gambaragara and Its Pale-Faced Inhabitants." Over the following weeks, the *Herald* repeated the story six times, published the complete five-hundred-word excerpt of the encounter, and printed a map showing the mountain's location west of Lake Victoria.[6]

Obviously the *Herald* editors selected stories that they hoped would hook their subscribers, but in this they were also being pushed by the *Herald*'s publisher. As the patron and promoter of the trans-African expedition, Bennett had a vested interest in covering Stanley's story intensively, which the *Herald* did throughout the fall and winter of 1876. Stanley's expedition was not simply a story the paper reported but one it had created, in the hopes of selling more newspapers.

Gambaragara soon took on a life of its own. Dozens of American newspapers picked up the story from the pages of the *Herald*. Some told the story of "white Africans" in passing, as but one episode among many in Stanley's series of African adventures. Yet the large metropolitan *Chicago Inter Ocean* and the rural *Maine Farmer* told the story of Gambaragara exclusively as did other papers under such titles as "A Remarkable Mountain and a Race of Pale-Face Africans" (*Washington Evening Star*) and "White People in Africa" (*Hartford Courant*).[7]

In London, the *Times* and *Daily Telegraph* discussed Gambaragara, spreading the story across the British Empire. By August 1876, Gambaragara was appearing in anglophone papers around the world, from the *Madras Mail* in India to the *Auckland Star* in New Zealand. In Mexico City, *El Siglo Diez y Nueve* reported on Stanley's "*tribu de gente de faz palida*" (pale-faced tribe), while Panama City's *Daily Star and Herald* discussed Stanley's "discovery of a race of white negroes."[8]

The scientific community took interest as well. *Nature*, *Popular Science*, and the *American Naturalist* reported on Stanley's African "white race," the last noting that Stanley's discovery was of "very great interest from an ethnological point of view." Geographical societies in America, Britain, France, Italy, and Germany informed their members in journals as well as in lectures. James Grant, who had traveled with John Speke in his expedition to Lake Victoria, discussed "the white people with wooly hair" before the Royal Geographical Society, while American explorer Charles Chaillé-Long lectured members of the American Geographical Society about the subject. These lectures were also covered by the popular press, bringing the story to a wider audience.[9]

By the winter of 1876, the news of Stanley's white tribe had become so ubiquitous worldwide that it was no longer news. It had entered the cultural vernacular and become a touchstone for other subjects. When convicted Tammany Hall politician William Tweed of New York escaped (temporarily) from prison in December 1875, the news prompted papers in Chicago and Washington, D.C., to run a spoof in the form of a dispatch from Stanley:

> *I have previously mentioned in my letters that . . . Gambaragara was occupied by a race of white negroes. Having this in mind, I watched intently during the battle for some of these strange people. Discerning a tall, fleshy, white-faced man, who seemed a leader of his fellows, mingling in the thick of the fray, I captured him. . . . It was Boss Tweed.*[10]

So entrenched was the story of Gambaragara that it was the butt of jokes. The following appeared in the *London Journal*'s humor column "Facetiae": "Mrs. Squills don't [*sic*] believe there ever has been 'a white race in Africa' because from what she has heard of the climate, it's altogether too warm there for such sports."[11]

Other treatments were more respectful. In Ireland, the *Dublin University Magazine* published a poem, "The Pale-Faces of Mount Gambaragara," that waxed melodramatically about the mysterious people of the mountain: "O ye that dwell therein, whence have ye flown / With your brows' pallid splendours, else unknown?" In Portugal, the explorer Manuel Iradier presented his geographical association, La Exploradora, with plans to cross the African continent from the west in hopes of reaching the mysterious mountains and visiting "la raza de hombres blancos" who inhabited them.[12]

Back in England, his expedition book completed, Stanley pondered the significance of his discovery as well. He wrote a lively essay about the landscapes of Bunyoro, as if viewed from a train approaching the great mountains from the east. The essay concludes with Stanley gazing up at "that King of Mountains, 'Gambaragara' who towers sheer up to the azure heavens with a white veil on his crown." The elegiac language of the essay reveals Stanley's inclination to see Gambaragara as something more than the "blue mass" he had viewed in silhouette two years before. Here, Gambaragara is so imposing that it overwhelms the viewer and becomes a catalyst of the sublime. In the presence of such "undisputable sublimity and majesty, his soul seems to recoil and confirm its littleness."[13]

Stanley never published this essay. And when in 1878 he wrote a lecture describing the "King of Mountains" as "a blue-black truncated cone, towering to the height of 13,000 feet," he crossed out that section of his lecture. Stanley stopped discussing the story in the late 1870s, though it remained popular in the press. Perhaps he lost faith in Sekajugu's account of white villagers living at Gambaragara's summit. Or perhaps he had come to feel that there were other explanations for the appearance of these light-skinned Africans, ones that fell short of categorizing them as a "white race." Whether the omission of Gambaragara represented an effort by Stanley to be scrupulous, however, remains unclear.[14]

Stanley rarely felt compelled to fetter himself to the truth. He exaggerated liberally, even enthusiastically, in his autobiography and exploration narratives. Yet he was also highly attuned to matters of reputation and took great efforts to appear truthful and credible. Hence he returns again and again to the issues of accuracy and veracity in his writings. "I must, for conscience' sake, report all things literally as they occurred," he writes in *How I Found Livingstone*, "and to the best of my ability record the incidents and accidents which befell the

Expedition." The story of Gambaragara did not yet reach this bar of proof. It had captured the imagination of reporters, scientists, and explorers, but it remained an expeditionary oddity, opaque in its details. He had seen Gambaragara with his own eyes, yes, but only from a distance. He had met Africans "of European complexion" but had not traced them to their place of origin. The story of Gambaragara came to occupy a place somewhere between the observed and the reported. It remained a discovery half-born.[15]

In the history of exploration, half-discoveries are common—indeed, the rule rather than the exception. For all of the clarity of exploration's best-known moments—Columbus's first sighting of land, Lewis and Clark's arrival at the Pacific, or Apollo's touchdown on the moon—most discovery projects do not yield answers quickly or definitively. That is because such experiences are indeterminate; they do not paint a complete picture of the region explored. Even when explorers are able later to paint a fuller picture, memory can undermine accuracy, and it is not always obvious to them which features in the picture deserve greatest attention; they focus on particularities. The Europeans who first discovered the Galapagos Islands, for example, marveled at the islands' giant tortoises, a ready source of food for ships sailing west into the Pacific. Charles Darwin focused on less obvious subjects when he arrived with HMS *Beagle* in 1835: a world of lizards, finches, and mockingbirds, which showed subtle variations between species. The impact of these observations came to Darwin only later when he was back in England. In short, discovery does not happen immediately or comprehensively. Only in the writing and recollecting of events in more tranquil settings do explorers find their eureka moments and fashion them to the needs of the moment, filling gaps and trimming away loose ends.[16]

However limited or biased, explorers' descriptions of places grew out of what they saw and experienced firsthand: a composite of information about weather, wildlife, sea and landforms. People, however, were not so easily rendered because their mere existence raised questions of history and heritage that could not be resolved from available information. Did natives share a common ancestry with Europeans? If so, when and why had they become separated? And how did they come to look so different in the process? The existence of previously unknown peoples, in other words, could not be explained from the reading of a barometer or a sketch of the harbor. It required a reconstruction of past events impossible to observe directly and, as a result, steered observers into a world of imagined events—wars, famines, marriages, and migrations—that could be used to explain the dispersion of the human family from its original homeland to the long branches of its diaspora, whether the islands of the Caribbean or the summit of Gambaragara. More than the discovery of river sources or mountain ranges, this was becoming the obsession of voyagers and ethnographers: a complete reconstruction of human history and genealogy.

Europeans worked hard to fit native peoples into a genealogy of the human family even as they worked to sell, enslave, and coerce them for economic gain. The irony speaks to differences of opinion about the status of native peoples within European consciousness, as well as to the centrality of inheritance within Christian European society. In kingdoms still governed by hereditary castes, bloodline determined one's place within the social order. For most Europeans, life was structured by genealogy. And the ultimate source of genealogy was the Bible.

5

THE CURSE OF HAM

It may seem strange that scholars who by the late nineteenth century had fashioned telescopes to see into the infinite and microscopes to peer into the infinitesimal, and whose tenacious commitment to natural explanations yielded laws of heat, pressure, and motion would turn to holy writ for answers about the ancient human past. Yet well into the 1800s the Bible remained a key source for information about the origins of humankind because the subject was as much a theological as a scientific issue. There was no talk in the Hebrew Bible of white tribes, or the geographical distribution of races, or even the concept of race itself. But scholars interested in these questions often began their investigations with the Bible because it offered a history of not only creation, but of human origin, migration, and settlement over broad swaths of history, recorded and unrecorded—in short, a complete genealogy of the world. Many Victorian scientists had little difficulty reconciling the stories of the Scriptures with the mechanistic, clockwork universe that they were building around themselves. Even scientists who saw the Bible as incommensurable with the workings of the universe often believed that the book carried the kernel of historical truth. In this way, the Bible still exerted its authority within the increasingly disenchanted world of Victorian science.

Most authoritative was Genesis, the first book of the Hebrew Bible, which detailed the creation of the world as well as the beginnings of humankind. Although Christianity and Islam would later establish their own holy texts in the New Testament and the Koran, the stories of Genesis remained sacred to all three monotheistic religions, which deferred to them for their vision of human origins. Thus, despite the doctrinal differences that often put monotheists at each other's throats—transforming history into a parade of crusades, pogroms, reformations, and inquisitions that periodically seized Europe and the Middle East for a thousand years—all of them agreed, more or less, on basic facts: that a single, providential, all-powerful God had created the world and the life forms upon it; that the first humans, Adam and Eve, had once enjoyed a special relationship with God; and that all humans who walked the face of the earth afterward were descendants of this original pair. Of course it all raised questions, ones that would be debated by religious scholars of all three faiths for centuries. The most fundamental of them all was, if all humans—Asians, Africans, and Europeans—were the descendants of Adam and Eve, why did they look so different from one another?

The Bible had little to offer in answer. The concept of "race," which became so important to later generations of Europeans as they organized their new hierarchy of the world in the 1500s, did not exist in the ancient world. The most important distinctions to the writers of Genesis were tribal and religious. The Hebrews set themselves apart from the other peoples of the Levant by kinship and by faith, not by skin color, head shape, or other physical features. Yet by the Crusades, the extraordinary diversity of the world's peoples, especially as could be witnessed on the eastern shores of the Mediterranean, where the Levant had become a bustling international trade hub connecting Europe, Asia, and Africa, demanded explanation. In addition to burgeoning trade, the Crusades had brought Arabs, Africans, and Indians to the attention of the most remote portions of Christian Europe while the *Hajj* had brought a similar awareness to the peoples of the Muslim world. Arab pilgrims traced the circuit of Mecca with Muslims who arrived there from Central Asia and sub-Saharan Africa. In short, contact with the far-flung peoples of the world brought this question of human diversity into sharper relief.[1]

Theologians looked for explanations in Chapters 6–9 of Genesis, which chronicled the story of the Flood, a story echoed by many cultures of the ancient Middle East (probably because the experience of catastrophic deluges was common to many river cultures in Mesopotamia and beyond). Its universality was partly due to its central drama—the destruction and rebirth of the world—which seemed to lend itself to so many moral and symbolic conclusions. In Genesis, the Flood completed the creation story. As God created the world out of a watery void in Genesis 1, it seemed only fitting—poetic, even—that He would choose to destroy it with water in Genesis 7, erasing all of His handiwork with the exception of Noah, Noah's family, and the great menagerie of animals in the Ark. The story of Noah recapitulates the original Eden story insofar as the Ark's landfall on Mount Ararat represents a new creation. If the Flood represented God's displeasure with humanity's sinfulness and depravity, it also showed His willingness to save the best parts of it, establishing a new covenant with the survivors: a promise to never again to destroy the earth. Catastrophe reaffirmed God's special relationship with His chosen people.[2]

Yet for the ancient peoples of the Mediterranean and the Middle East, the Flood was only half of the story. The Flood offered not merely a new covenant, but also a new genealogy, a fresh start. For this reason, medieval theologians looked to it for answers about the relationships among the world's peoples. The seeds of humanity may have sprouted in the Garden of Eden thousands of years before, but they took root on the summit of Mount Ararat. For scholars attempting to piece together the relationship between the peoples of the world, the story did not begin in a garden but on a mountain, and more specifically with Noah's three sons—Japheth, Shem, and Ham—who accompanied their father on the Ark with their families. Genesis 10 offers the genealogical legacy of the three sons after the Deluge, a complete list of male descendants that extends to Noah's great-grandchildren—the patriarchs of the new post-diluvian world order. Genesis 10 ends: "These are the families of the sons of Noah, after their generations, in their nations; and of these were the nations divided in the earth after the flood."

Although Genesis 10 is quite specific about genealogy, it is vague on geography, offering little information about the regions in which these descendants settled and formed tribes. Early commentators on the Bible did not concern themselves much with regional geography. The shapes of mountains and coastlines, the location of towns and cities, and the position of political boundaries all remained murky until the late Middle Ages. Early attempts to associate these Noachian tribes, as they were called, with geography, such as the commentaries of Flavius Josephus in the first century CE, were largely ignored. Later works of Jewish exegesis on Genesis 9–10, the *Genesis Rabbah*, compiled from the third to seventh centuries CE made little mention of specific migrations. Even when biblical descendants could be linked to specific tribes in known geographical locations, it was hard to identify precise patterns of migration. Ham's son Canaan, for example, settled in the Levant. Ham's other sons—Cush, Put, and Mizraim—became associated with regions in Africa. Cush's son Nimrod became associated with

Fifteenth-century French map manuscript showing Noah's sons standing on the three continents of the world. Ham occupies Africa, bottom right (top of map faces east). Credit: *La Fleur des Histoires* by Jean Mansel.

Mesopotamia. Not surprisingly, those commentators who did stake out geographical regions for each of Noah's sons often disagreed about them.[3]

Despite these ambiguities, scholars began to settle on certain assumptions, and to associate each of Noah's three sons with three different continents. In the eighth century CE, a scholar and teacher named Alcuin of York, a Briton who joined Charlemagne's court in 782 CE, put forward this idea, possibly in hopes of simplifying the tangled genealogy of Noachian descendants for his Frankish students. Whatever the motive, it caught on. Medieval illustrators soon placed Noah's sons on their world maps—called T-O maps because of their shape—with each son taking dominion over a different, pie-wedged continent. The correlation of each son with a continent not only offered a simple and elegant solution to the question of the origin of the earth's different peoples, it fit with the spirit of medieval scholasticism—an approach to learning that sought correspondences between the human world and the cosmic universe, between the microcosm and the macrocosm. The T-O map, useless for purposes of navigation, offered an excellent way of demonstrating these symbolic correspondences. In addition to the T-O maps that correlated each continent with one of Noah's sons, there were T-O maps that superimposed the body of Christ over the world—a way to show the Messiah's dominion over the earth—with his heart over the city of Jerusalem, the *omphalos*, or center of the world. Medieval scholars thus found ways of stitching together the physical and metaphysical realms—of earth and flesh and spirit—into a single cosmic tapestry.[4]

Yet precisely because the settlement of the world became attached to specific members of the Noachian family, questions of race became more pressing. Despite the detailed genealogical information provided by Genesis 10, the chapter provided no explanation for how the descendants of Noah became distinct races over the course of a few thousand years (the age of the post-Flood world if calculated by biblical genealogies). Given that none of the chapters of Genesis discuss the question of race explicitly, medieval theologians had to read between the lines of the scripture—interpreting passages that might offer clues about the physical changes that grew up among the various Noachian lineages.

Of all the passages, Genesis 9 seemed to be most fruitful, for it offered the dark side to this story of the earth's re-creation after the Flood, one that also paralleled the fall of Adam and Eve in Genesis 3 insofar as it told a story of human disobedience and its terrible consequences. The story begins innocuously enough, before taking a disastrous turn:

> *The sons of Noah who went forth from the ark were Shem, Ham, and Japheth. Ham was the father of Canaan. These three were the sons of Noah; and from these the whole earth was peopled. Noah was the first tiller of the soil. He planted a vineyard; and he drank of the wine, and became drunk, and lay uncovered in his tent. And Ham, the father of Canaan, saw the nakedness of his father, and told his two brothers outside. Then Shem and Japheth took a garment, laid it upon both their shoulders, and walked backward and covered the nakedness of their father; their faces were turned away, and they did not see their father's nakedness. When Noah awoke from his wine and knew what his youngest son had done to him, he said, "Cursed be Canaan; a slave of slaves shall he be to his brothers." He also said, "Blessed by the LORD my God be Shem; and let Canaan be his slave. God enlarge Japheth, and let him dwell in the tents of Shem; and let Canaan be his slave." (Gen. 9:18–27, RSV)*

What Ham had done to provoke such anger in Noah Genesis does not explain. It may have been that in seeing his father's nakedness, Ham gained power over him and according to an ancient code of parental respect was guilty of dishonoring him. Some have speculated Ham may have committed an act so heinous against his father (such as castration or sodomy) that the verses of Genesis could not utter its name. Or the crime itself could have simply been lost to history.[5] We know that Genesis 9 represents the filaments of an older story, only parts of which became woven into the Hebrew Bible. Ancient tablets of the Ugarit civilization, for example, tell of a similar Noah-like story in which the god El descends into drunkenness and, rendered insensible, depends on his two sons to look after him. The motives and tacit meanings of these first authors were lost from the story as it traveled across the centuries, adapted by other tribes along the way. Original meanings were sheared away as the story passed further and further from its literary cradle. What remained was the act and its outcome: Ham's crime and the curse of slavery against his son Canaan.[6]

Unsurprisingly, the story of Ham raised more questions than it could answer. No reason is given in Genesis as to why Canaan was cursed, but it almost certainly reflected the contemporary concerns of its authors. The Hebrews became the rivals of the Canaanites in the Near East, and their condemnation served to justify the domination of Canaanite lands and the usurpation of Canaanite labor. This would explain why Canaan appears suddenly in Genesis 9 without introduction, an ad hoc addition by Hebrew writers who target Canaan specifically, ignoring the other sons of Ham. Within the story of Genesis 9, then, Hebrews could find a justification for their treatment of their Canaanite neighbors.[7]

Later theologians would interpret Noah's curse differently. By the fourth century, biblical commentators began associating the curse of Canaan with a curse of blackness. At a time when the Mediterranean world was coming into closer contact with Africans and the African slave trade, this soon evolved into the double curse of blackness and slavery. Some scholars identified the Hebrew word for "Ham" in Hebrew with "black" (an etymological *faux ami*, as it turns out). By the eighth century CE, this interpretation had become more prominent in the Islamic world, too, probably for the same reasons: closer contact with the African slave trade after the Muslim conquests of North Africa. Thus, in graphic representations as well as biblical exegesis, the story of Noachian origins had now been connected to an explanation for the divergence of races.

Still, interpretations of Noah's resettlement of the earth as well as his curse in Genesis 9 remained broad-ranging in the Middle Ages. Discussion of the story now spanned three religious traditions, and it was common to find diverse and competing opinions about the ancestry of the world's peoples. Indeed, the most popular travel book of the Middle Ages, *The Travels of Sir John Mandeville*, written in Anglo-Norman French and circulated in the late fourteenth century, made Ham the father of Asia rather than Africa. Mandeville's story of Ham is interesting, not only because it associates him with the settlement of Asia rather than Africa, but also because Mandeville interprets Ham's curse not as a descent into slavery but as an ascent into despotism. The curse of Ham, in other words, is to acquire power as he loses virtue. "Ham was the mightiest and the most powerful....And because he was the most powerful and none would dare oppose him, he was called the son of God and sovereign of all the world." If some saw Ham as the pitiable progenitor of African slaves, others saw him as a cunning and ruthless tyrant.[8]

Mandeville's interpretation could not eclipse the curse theory, however, and Genesis 9 became more closely associated with blackness and slavery in the late 1400s, when European encounters with new peoples were increasing in the Americas, sub-Saharan Africa, and the East Indies. The reports of Columbus and later explorers to the New World, in particular, introduced the Indians as a race of humanity that needed to be integrated into the Noachian genealogy. As a result, Genesis 9–10 became used intensively as a means of placing newly discovered peoples within the ever-expanding human family tree. Yet it also reflected economic interests in this period, as expeditions into the Atlantic—including the Portuguese conquest of Ceuta and the expeditions down the west coast of Africa—had brought Europeans into closer contact with Africans and their systems of slavery.

By the late 1400s, Europeans were shipping Africans to work on agricultural plantations on Atlantic islands such as Madeiras and São Tomé. The swirl of diverse interpretations about the nature of Noah's curse began to settle on Genesis 9 as a curse of black slavery. For example, the English cleric Samuel Purchas revised his account of Ham in his popular travel series *Purchas His Pilgrimage*, first published in 1613, to reflect the new acceptance of Genesis 9 as a justification for the exploitation of African labor. Whereas his first edition had emphasized the common humanity of God's children "without any more distinction of colour, Nation, language, sexe, condition," his later editions singled out African slaves as "the Sonne of cursed Cham, as are all of that complexion, [are]…from the Curse of Noe upon Cham." Slavery, now most agreed, was the fate of Ham's African progeny, forever cursed by Noah.[9]

The curse of Ham provided biblical justifications of slavery (in general) and black slavery (in particular) for three hundred years. Describing a cargo of African slaves that had arrived in Portugal, the Portuguese official Gomes Eannes de Azurara wrote that "the curse which after the Deluge, Noah laid upon his son Caim [Ham] cursing him in this way: that his race should be subject to all the other races of the world." The curse found particularly extensive expression in the early and mid-1800s in the United States, where white Christian ministers and political leaders found both a biblical precedent and a moral argument

The Curse of Ham

to counter the increasingly vocal efforts of Northern abolitionists. Brigham Young, governor of the Mormon state of Utah, gave a speech in defense of slavery on January 23, 1852, in which he acknowledged the "severe curses suffered by the colored race" but argued they had brought them upon themselves and until "removed by Him who placed it upon them, they must suffer under its consequences." Such was the power of the Hamitic hypothesis in defending a particular vision of race that it remained well after it had been eclipsed by more rational explanations. Biblical authority, if challenged, remained persuasive.[10]

The Atlantic slave trade strengthened the idea that Ham was the forefather of black Africans. Yet by the 1800s, the biblical interpretations that for a thousand years had provided understanding about the cradle of humanity, the origin of nations, and the origin of races were on the decline. White Southerners had embraced the story of Ham as a justification for slavery in the decades before the Civil War, yet fundamental questions about the nature of racial difference were being taken up by antiquarians, philologists, and ethnographers who believed that biblical history was insufficient to answer them.

These scholars began to modify the Hamitic hypothesis, extending it and eventually unmooring it from the Bible, placing it within the realm of the sciences. At the same time, they would flip the hypothesis on its head, changing it from a story about the origins of black Africans to one explaining the existence of *white* Africans. The transformation of the Hamitic hypothesis from a theory about black slaves to one of white tribes did not occur all at once. It was a process that occurred in stages, built upon studies of artifacts and bones, as well as the direct observation of physical traits, as begun by Stanley and other explorers. The new hypothesis would transform the view of Africans throughout the course of the nineteenth century. Ironically, the first step in this movement toward a secular, scientific theory of the Hamites began with another set of scriptures, not skulls or artifacts, written not in Aramaic or Greek but in Sanskrit.

6

ORIENTAL JONES

IN THE 1780s, A BRITISH polymath named William Jones uncovered a new tool in the study of ancient history: language. Comparing words and grammars from ancient languages, Jones believed he could trace the migrations of the world's first tribes independently of the book of Genesis. As a devout Christian, Jones had no interest in overthrowing the authority of the Bible. Nevertheless he believed that language would fill in the gaps left by Genesis, completing the story of humankind's dispersal across the globe. Indeed, Jones's scholarly commitment to philology—what later would come to be called historical linguistics—coexisted with his reverence for Scripture. Thus to him the story of Ham was not some ancient myth, but a fact that buttressed a new theory of human migration—one that later scholars would call the "Indo-European" or "Aryan" theory. Jones would not have known how profoundly these linguistic theories would shape nineteenth-century ideas about racial origins. The tracing of history through language would become a key approach to the study of human populations, in general, and so-called white tribes in particular. In the 1770s, however, his passion attached to language, not race, and his route to discovery took him to India, rather than Africa, where he took up a job as judge in the East India Company.

As HMS *Crocodile* sailed him down the coast of Africa en route to India in 1783, Jones kept the habits of an English gentleman.

He read legal texts. He played chess. He walked the deck for exercise. As the journey advanced, he also studied Persian, the courtly language of Calcutta. He knew it would be useful to him as he took a post as a Supreme Court judge there. Yet Persian was of more than professional interest. "The Persian language is rich, melodious, and elegant," he wrote in *A Grammar of the Persian Language* in 1771. He admired other languages, too. He could speak and write in a dozen tongues, including Latin, Arabic, and Hebrew. "Elegance" was only part of their attraction, however. Languages were portals to different worlds. He felt this particularly true of classical languages, such as Latin, and non-European languages such as Arabic, Hebrew, and Persian. Those who did not appreciate them, he wrote, were "like the savages who thought that the sun rose and set for them alone, and could not imagine the waves, which surrounded their island, left coral and pearls upon any other shore." The judgeship promised stable work and financial security, but it was mostly a way for him to get to India. He was leaving his island in search of pearls.[1]

As the *Crocodile* rounded the Cape of Good Hope and sailed west across the Indian Ocean, Jones drew up a list of projects that would occupy his time, titled "Objects of Enquiry During My Residence in Asia," which gave a glimpse of his wide-ranging interests:

> Hindu and Moslem laws
> history of the ancient world
> Scriptural proofs and illustrations
> traditions about the Flood etc.
> Indian geography and politics
> best mode of governing Bengal
> Asian mathematics and 'mixed sciences'
> Indian medicine, chemistry, and anatomy
> Indian products
> Asiatic music, poetry, rhetoric, and morality
> Shih Ching
> accounts of Tibet and Kashmir
> Indian trade, manufacturing, and agriculture
> Mogul Constitution in Fatawa 'Alamgiryat and
>   Ain-i-Akbari
> Maratha Constitution

The list is revealing not only because it shows the ambitiousness of Jones's intellectual agenda but his plan for working through it. It's understandable that he would place "Hindu and Moslem laws" first. These would be critical to his work on the Kolkata Supreme Court. Yet the next three items—history of the ancient world, Scriptural proofs and illustrations, and traditions about the Flood—had no seeming professional or practical application. Yet Jones listed them as "objects of inquiry."[2]

The reason why lies in Jones's interest in Eastern cultures. He was an Orientalist, but not a cultural relativist. He was committed to a Judeo-Christian view of history and believed that the story of Genesis was generally accurate, that the Flood was global in its devastation, and that Noah was the father of all peoples—the root of the tree from which had sprung the different branches of the human family. Where he differed from most previous scholars was in believing that the Hebrew Bible was but one of many sources for the ancient history of the globe. The ancient Hebrews had chronicled only one branch of the Noachian family. What about the cousins of the Hebrews—the Egyptians, Persians, Indians, and Chinese—who also populated the world after the Deluge and wrote their own accounts of Creation? Integrating these stories into the history of the world was Jones's ultimate goal, one made possible by his knowledge of Persian and other languages and by India's treasures of ancient manuscripts. Before the *Crocodile* reached the shores of India, then, Jones knew what pearls he was looking for and how he planned to string them together.[3]

In September 1783, after five months at sea, the *Crocodile* rounded the tip of Indian subcontinent, entered the Bay of Bengal, and made its way up the Hooghly River. The Hooghly is one of the distributaries of the Ganges River, and as the frigate approached Kolkata it moved through waters that had traveled there from Nepal and China, fed by the glacier fields of the Himalayas hundreds miles to the north. From these sources five miles above the sea, the Ganges descended from the edge of the sky itself, emptying its waters into the vast alluvial plains of the Ganges delta. For Hindus, it was a sacred river, connecting the earthly world to the vault of Heaven and enabling humans to make the passage between worlds. For Jones, who was met on the docks of Kolkata by a large landing ceremony, it also marked a transformation.

He had left England as a barrister; he arrived in India as an explorer of the ancient past.[4]

Before Jones could explore the past, however, he had to contend with the present. In 1783, Kolkata (known as Calcutta to the British) was the capital of the British East India Company, a colonial enterprise that had gradually grown into an empire. The company paid revenue to the Crown but operated largely on its own, outside of the codes of British law. Without oversight, the company had exploited its dominion. General Robert Clive, who led military campaigns to advance the company's fortunes in the 1750s, had been astonished by the lawlessness he found in the region. "I shall only say that such a scene of anarchy, confusion, bribery, corruption, and extortion was never seen or heard of in any country but Bengal." The company extracted the wealth of India in the form of spices, tea, and opium even as Hindus and Muslims were dying of famine. When in 1773 the company couldn't meet its revenue payments, the British government intervened, establishing an independent Supreme Court, one with broad powers of oversight. Bengal's governing council bristled at this, seeing the court's powers as a threat to its authority. When Jones arrived, then, he took his post in a colonial government that didn't want him there.[5]

This wasn't his only challenge. The growing power of the company as a de facto Indian kingdom meant that the Supreme Court had to administer the law to Indians as well as Britons. At issue was this: to which code of laws—Indian or British—should natives be subject? In 1772, the governor-general of Bengal, Warren Hastings, had directed the courts to judge Indians according to native legal codes. This was not as straightforward as it sounded. Indian laws, written in ancient Sanskrit texts, were understood by only a small number of Brahmin scholars, called "pandits," who had studied the sacred Hindu Vedas. Under Hastings's direction, the Orientalist Nathaniel Halhed, whom Jones had known at Oxford, had taken up the project, putting together a team of eleven pandits to select Sanskrit texts that were then translated into Persian by Zayn al-Dīn ʿAlī Rasaʿi. Halhed had then translated the Persian text into English. He would have preferred to learn Sanskrit directly, but the pandits had refused to instruct him. They were, "to a man resolute in rejecting all of [my] solicitations for instruction in this dialect," he had complained, "the persuasion and influence of the Governor-General were in vain exerted to the same purpose." Halhed's *Code of Gentoo Laws* (1776), an English translation of a Persian translation of an ancient Sanskrit text, became an important legal source for British judges writing opinions according to Hindu laws. Given the errors and ambiguities of *Gentoo Laws*, however, the original meaning of the Sanskrit texts remained imprecise, and judges still had to rely on the knowledge of pandits to render their judgments.[6]

Jones was not content with this. He was versed in a dozen languages and the author of a book on Persian grammar, yet his ignorance of Sanskrit forced him to rely on poor translations; and in his role as judge, he had to rely on the opinions of people who had no official training in English jurisprudence. He came to distrust Pandit opinions regarding Hindu laws. "I am almost tempted to learn [Sanskrit]," he wrote to the British prime minister William Pitt, "that I may be a check on the Pandits of the court." By the summer of 1785, he had had enough. He left Kolkata for the ancient university town of Krishingar, sixty miles north. There he searched for an instructor willing to teach him India's sacred language.[7]

Other motives also pushed Jones toward learning Sanskrit. He had become enchanted by Sanskrit hymns and poetry—or rather Persian translations of them—and came to believe that they were the key to understanding the history of the ancient world, a way of understanding the people of the Noachian age.

To be fair, this was a project that inspired many scholars during the European Enlightenment. Jones was not simply indulging in some small scholarly obsession. Nor was he the embodiment of the stuffy Orientalist—a man who stood in isolation from the rest of the world. For Jones and scholars like him, Asia was the gateway to a new Enlightenment—a new history of the world. This work was too important to keep to himself. Jones founded an "Asiatick Society" in 1784 as a forum for scholars interested in Eastern language and culture. "The bounds of investigations will be the geographical limits of Asia," announced Jones at the first meeting of the society, "and within these limits its enquiries will be extended to whatever is performed by man or produced by nature."[8]

Jones's visit to Krishingar did not start well. Many of the university's pandits were on vacation or traveling to Hindu shrines. Those who remained refused to teach him Sanskrit, despite his generous offers. Eventually he turned to Pandit Ramlochan, a sixty-five-year-old medical practitioner of the Vaidya caste who taught Sanskrit at the university. "I have found a pleasant old man of the medical cast," he wrote to the Orientalist Charles Wilkins in 1785, "who teaches me all he knows of the Grammar." Over the course of six weeks, he worked with Ramlochan. The work went well. Jones enjoyed learning the new language and also appreciated the escape from the heat and humidity of Kolkata where he and his wife, Anna, had suffered debilitating fevers. In Krishingar Jones could return to the life of a gentleman scholar, balancing his study of Sanskrit with letter writing, Bible reading, and chess playing. When Jones returned to Kolkata, Ramlochan came with him, agreeing to continue tutoring him on Sanskrit texts.[9]

As he gained proficiency in Sanskrit, Jones decided that the ancient texts confirmed what he already suspected: that the Ancient East held the key for understanding the world as it existed after the Deluge, when the links between Noah's descendants were fresh and humankind had not yet spread to the other continents of the world. Within these writings, Jones saw—or thought he saw—the common heritage of ancient civilizations, the filaments of a culture that had once connected the people of India, Greece, and Egypt.

This common heritage appeared in many forms. In his address before the Asiatick Society on February 2, 1786, Jones laid everything out for the other British members of the society. In philosophy, Jones observed, the ideas of Plato and Pythagoras so closely matched those of ancient Sanskrit writers that the former must have sprung from the "same fountain with the sages of India." A comparison of ancient architecture, he declared, also confirmed a common source. Most importantly, the common heritage of ancient cultures was conveyed not only through the ideas contained within Sanskrit texts but through the medium of the language itself:

> *The* Sanscrit *language, whatever be its antiquity, is of a wonderful structure; more perfect than the* Greek, *more copious than the* Latin, *and more exquisitely refined than either; yet*

> *bearing to both of them a stronger affinity, both in the roots of verbs and in the forms of grammar, than could possibly have been produced by accident; so strong indeed, that no philologer could examine them all three without believing them to have sprung from some common source, which, perhaps, no longer exists.*[10]

These languages, which he thought might also include Persian and Celtic (Gaelic), shared similar structures because they were kin: the children of the same mother tongue. For Jones, "kinship" was not simply a metaphor. The relationships among these different tongues mirrored human genealogy, pointing to connections between peoples that were, to someone looking at geography or human appearance, impossible to see and difficult to imagine; the people of India, Europe, Persia, and Egypt were close cousins, Jones argued, the descendants of one branch of the Noachian family that had dispersed after the Flood to repopulate the world. This lineage had spread across the world at breathtaking speed, spawning complex and powerful societies across Eurasia as it moved: Hindustan, Thebes, Athens and Sparta, the Roman Empire, and now, at the end of the eighteenth century, the British Empire.[11]

Of the three branches of the Noachian family, this Eurasian one represented "the most ingenious and enterprising of the three, but arrogant, cruel, and idolatrous." Jones's language is revealing. He believed that he was treating the Old Testament as one ancient text among others. Yet this reference to an "arrogant, cruel" son of Noah revealed his acceptance of a Judeo-Christian vision of history, one that could not be corroborated in the sacred Vedas, or Persian hymns, or the structures of Sanskrit. It was an allusion to Genesis 9, or, more accurately, the Hamitic interpretation of Genesis 9 as expressed by the *Travels of Sir John Mandeville* in the Middle Ages. In a later discourse to the Asiatick Society, Jones stated his meaning more plainly. The Indians, Europeans, and their brethren were "the children of HAM who…invented letters, observed and named the luminaries of the firmament." According to Jones's research, the tribes of Ham had left their homeland in Persia, spreading east into India and west into the Middle East and Egypt, from which they created settlements around the Mediterranean basin and slowly moved into Europe. "Having improved the art of sailing," he told the society in 1792, "[they] passed from *Egypt*, *Phenice*, and *Phrygia*, into *Italy* and *Greece*, which they found thinly peopled by former emigrants, of whom they supplanted some tribes, and united themselves with others; whilst a swarm from the same hive moved by a northerly course into *Scandinavia*."[12]

This was as we've seen not the typical genealogy associated with Ham's descendants who since the late Middle Ages had mostly been identified with the peoples of Africa, particularly Egypt and Abyssinia. Jones believed that one branch of Ham's family had indeed entered Africa. The ancient monuments of India and Egypt—the Pyramids, the Sphinx, Indian Idols, and Buddhas—"indicate[d] the style and mythology of the same indefatigable workmen." The lettering of such monuments, which appeared to Jones to reveal a mixture of Indian and Abyssinian influence, suggested that the links between India and Europe extended into sub-Saharan Africa as well. It seemed evident, Jones claimed, "that *Ethiopia* and *Hindustàn* were peopled or colonized by the same extraordinary race." Jones thus created a new union of ethnicities under the title of "Hamites." While his study of languages and antiquities affirmed the descendants of Ham as the colonizers of Egypt and Africa, as biblical commentators had suggested, it also vastly expanded the range of this ancient family. "Hamites" were a group that now included Africans, Europeans, and Indians.[13]

Word of his discoveries spread quickly. When the Asiatick Society published its first volume of work, *Asiatick Researches*, in 1789, it included eleven essays by Jones, including his 1786 discourse on Sanskrit. Seven hundred copies of the volume were bundled into British ships and sent to England. They traced, in reverse, the route traveled by Jones on board the *Crocodile* a few years earlier. *Asiatick Researches* proved to be popular, and was excerpted and reviewed in journals such as *Gentlemen's Magazine* and the *Monthly Review*. It was even more popular in the rest of Europe. By the 1790s, reprints and pirated versions of *Asiatick Researches* had become available on the Continent, including German and French translations. A complete collection of Jones's works came out in 1799 and was followed by another edition in 1807. Jones had not discovered India, but he had carved out a place for it in the European imagination. After 1800, "Orientalism" became an accepted subject for scholarship in part because Jones had persuaded everyone of its relevance to history, language, and the Christian Bible. The West, Jones argued, could be understood only in connection with the East.[14]

Jones would not live to see this great synthesis. He promised to follow Anna back to England (she left India in 1793) after he had finished an important Sanskrit legal text and prepared it for publication. He never completed it. He died in April 1794, while preparing to depart for home, and was buried the next day in Kolkata's South Park Street burial ground.

At a time when Enlightenment science had begun to challenge Mosaic ethnography, Jones's discourses on Eastern languages—both about their content and their linguistic structure—confirmed key aspects of the three-pronged lineage of the Genesis story. Each of these lineages could be identified by grammatical and vocabulary forms common to each language group. Patterns of language could even be used to link modern societies to specific progenitors within Noah's family. Those who came to Jones's work committed to a literal reading of Genesis 9 and the dispersion of peoples through Noah's sons could take comfort in these points.[15]

This comfort was temporary. No one, not even Jones while he was alive, knew it yet, but his discourses undermined Noachian history. Over the course of the nineteenth century, the scriptural account of the ancient past would gradually disappear from works of serious scholarship. Jones was not the only one poking holes in it. By the 1800s, a number of naturalists such as Charles Lyell and Jean Lamarck were challenging biblical chronologies. Yet Jones had created not simply a new historical account of racial dispersion, but a new historical method: comparative analysis of language, the foundation for the new discipline of linguistics. Key to this method was recognizing that languages changed over time. They branched out from one another, borrowed from and sometimes killed off each other; they lived, died, and were reborn in daughter languages. The descendants of Noah spread across the world, even as each tribe forgot "by degrees the language of their common progenitor."[16]

Languages seemed to behave like organisms, and indeed by the middle of the nineteenth century, scientists recognized that the branching tree model used to chart the evolution of languages could also be used to describe the evolution of species. When Charles

Darwin introduced the subject of classification in his 1859 monograph, *Origin of Species*, he was careful to acknowledge the debt it owed to linguistics: "It may be worthwhile to illustrate this view of classification, by taking the case of languages." One reason Darwin's model was persuasive was that it was adaptable as well as scalable. It could be used to map both the evolution of language over thousands of years and the evolution of species over millions of years. (Darwin had sketched his own branching speciation tree in a private notebook as early as 1843.) And since language was uniquely tied to one species in particular, human beings, it seemed to follow that changes in one could be used to chart changes in the other. This was, indeed, what Jones had articulated it in his discourses: shifts in language told a story about the human family, about its ancient homelands, its travels, and its new settlements in lands far away.[17]

While Jones proved that a comparative analysis of languages could contribute to knowledge of human history, nineteenth-century scholars went further, arguing that language provided a glimpse of human evolution. Linguistics could be a tool that, beyond the investigation of homelands and migrations, could seek the origin of races itself. As Darwin described it, "If we possessed a perfect pedigree of mankind, a genealogical arrangement of the races of man would afford the best classification of the various languages now spoken throughout the world." This was a legacy of his work that Jones did not foresee. In his vision of the world, the golden age of human society had passed, degenerating from the early days when the Noachian family had spoken the same language and worshiped the same, all-powerful god. His love for Sanskrit—and how it reflected the glory of ancient India—made the contrast to modern India only starker. Jones dismissed Hindu culture—at least based on what he saw walking Kolkata's streets—as "degenerate and abased." By contrast, the evolutionists of the nineteenth century would see human history as progressive: ascending up rather than climbing down the scale of civilization. Despite all of these incongruities between the origin of languages and the origin of species, Jones's work was quickly put to use for understanding the history of the human world. The English jurist and historian Henry Summer Maine, lecturing about India's impact on European thought in 1875, put the issue even more plainly: "The new theory of language has unquestionably produced a new theory of race."[18]

While the family-tree models of language and human evolution looked similar, they were, in fact, distinct. Human evolution operated in the realm of biology, whereas language evolution operated in the realm of culture. A person could learn to speak more than one language, switch to a new language after migrating, and mingle languages in pidgins or creoles, all without affecting his or her biology. Thus, despite the interconnections between languages and humans, they were evolutionary *faux amis*: operating by different means over different scales of time.

Through his study of languages, Jones affirmed key elements of the biblical story of origins, even while he detached it from the Bible itself. Jones and future generations of linguists would continue to maintain that Asia was the cradle of humankind, that the three lineages migrated from Central Asia to populate the other nations of the world, and that the system of languages that connected Europe with India, which later generations would call "Indo-European," could be attributed to the descendants of Ham.

Across the centuries, the West had come to associate Ham with blackness, backwardness, and slavery—a vision that aligned with and justified its exploitation of African peoples. But Jones viewed the Hamitic family as the ur-family of cultural progress, not degradation, the origin of the mighty empires of East, West, and Africa. The idea of the Hamitic line as aggressive, intelligent, and linked increasingly to the light-skinned peoples of the North had been forged, first by Jones and then by those influenced by his notions of language. The linguistic link between Ancient Egyptian languages and Indo-European would eventually erode. However, other forms of evidence were being marshaled to reconnect the people of Africa with the other races of the world—not words but bones.

7

THE BEAUTIFUL SKULL

AT THE SAME MOMENT THAT William Jones was comparing texts, Johann Friedrich Blumenbach was comparing bones, specifically human skulls. Blumenbach, like many eighteenth-century naturalists, believed that skulls held the key to the study of race. Here, in the shape of the facial bones and cranial vaults he saw the key features of human difference. Moreover, because skulls preserved well, new skulls could be compared with old ones, revealing—Blumenbach believed—the story of human racial origins. Thus, as the concept of race became more important in the 1700s, so did the value of skulls, as well as Blumenbach's desire to obtain them.

There were thousands of skulls to be found in Europe in the 1700s if one knew where to look for them. Blumenbach did. As a professor of medicine at Göttingen in Lower Saxony, Blumenbach had the credentials and connections to gain access to these skulls, housed in museum cases and medical cabinets, buried in the holds of expedition ships, and arrayed in the cabinets of aristocratic collectors. By the 1790s, he had begun a collection of his own—"my Golgotha," he told friends. It would eventually include 250 skulls from all over the world. Some had been collected by explorers and men of science like the British naturalist Joseph Banks. Some were collected from former students. Others were the gifts of German lords and barons, taken from

"Wunderkammern," rooms of marvelous objects—shells, rocks, relics, tribal artifacts, and human parts—that had become a fashion of aristocratic life since the Renaissance.

Blumenbach did not like to travel. "To live out of Göttingen is not to live at all," he declared. Yet he was willing to travel to estates in search of skulls. Meanwhile, Banks and others continued to send him crania from the remote corners of the world. Blumenbach was aware of the irony of a network of adventurous explorers collecting skulls for a professor who preferred to stay at home. He referred to his days in the countryside, wryly, as his "Voyages of Discovery."[1]

According to his friends, Blumenbach's first encounter with a human skeleton occurred in a doctor's office when he was ten. Enthralled, he spent hours studying it, and found reasons to return again and again until he had memorized the organization of skeleton and all of its parts. Then he fashioned a replica out of animal bones and hung it in his bedroom. After the creation was discovered by a horrified servant, he moved it to the attic. Whether true or not, the story reflected Blumenbach's single-minded and obsessive scientific interests. Conducting animal vivisections in the medical theater, surrounded by his skulls and instruments, his stout voice bellowing beneath a wig "frizzled and powdered," Blumenbach both inspired and intimidated his students and colleagues at Göttingen. One colleague, Samuel von Sömmerring, himself a well-known physician and anatomist, gushed about him as "a distinguished patron who deigned to treat me as a friend." King George IV, for one, felt unnerved by the great scholar, admitting that he had "never seen so imposing a man as Blumenbach."[2]

To Blumenbach, bones were not just curiosities but records of the past. He had come to this conclusion through the study of natural history, particularly classification. He had read and admired the Swede Carolus Linnaeus's great taxonomic work *System of Nature*, first published in 1735, which organized the known species of the world—about ten thousand in all—into hierarchical categories. In keeping with Scripture, Linnaeus presumed that all species had been formed in a single act of creation. The goal of *System of Nature* was to find the order in this creation, revealing the blueprint of the Creator; it assumed that God operated both as divine architect and master craftsman, that He was the designer and fabricator of all living things. It was therefore not surprising that God would arrange the species of the world like

Russian dolls, nesting creatures within increasingly larger categorical boxes—genera, orders, classes, and kingdoms—as this expressed the more general form of the divine plan, or at least Linnaeus's interpretation of it. It would have surprised him to know that Darwin and other evolutionists would later look at this colossal cabinet of creatures and see something different: trees instead of dolls, branching dendrograms of life with species splitting off from each other from a trunk of common ancestry. The categorical boxes that Linnaeus viewed as divine abstractions—ideas in the mind of God—were for Darwin the shadows of real creatures, the forbearers of living species.[3]

Working eighty years before the publication of *On the Origin of Species*, Blumenbach could not have appreciated this. In the 1770s, no one was advancing the idea that *all* living things shared a common ancestor. This was not because naturalists were unimaginative or closed-minded but because the idea seemed so implausible; it did not fit what was known of world history. In 1650, the Irish archbishop James Ussher had calculated Earth's age from Scriptures to be six thousand years old. It seemed absurd to think—even for freethinkers who dismissed Scriptures and doubled, or even tripled, the age of Earth—that some ancestral form of life could, in merely a few hundred generations, beget all of the world's creatures, from mushrooms to monkeys. Such development required more time. This was the hidden cost of evolutionary thinking: common descent meant accepting that the earth, and by extension the universe itself, were older than had ever been imagined.[4]

Yet, there were other evolutionary ideas circulating in the 1700s that shaped Blumenbach's thinking about the origin of human types. These ideas attempted to answer growing questions about the nature of species, such as whether they were fixed or could change over time. The French naturalist La Comte de Buffon put forward the idea that species could "degenerate" from an ancestral form due to the effects of the environment. Original life forms, in Buffon's view, were the genera themselves. Not all species had been present at Creation but developed over time, slowing changing from a common ancestral form represented by the original genus. These changes were not open-ended. Dogs would not become cats. Yet in Buffon's opinion the environment was powerful enough to produce different but stable varieties of the original species. This would explain why American species of certain animals were different from their European counterparts:

they had degenerated as they migrated away from the ideal conditions of their homeland in the Old World. This assumption drew the ire of Thomas Jefferson, who rejected such notions in impassioned terms.[5]

Nonetheless the idea of evolution through degeneration of an ideal type became more popular. Blumenbach applied the idea of degeneration to humans. In his doctoral dissertation, "On the Natural Variety of Mankind," he created a classification system of five human types—European, African, Mongolian, American, and Malay—all of which, he argued, had degenerated from a single ancestral form. This process was driven by differences in environment: as human tribes migrated farther from their ancestral home, they were forced to adapt to new conditions. In keeping with Buffon, Blumenbach believed that this represented a limited evolutionary scheme. Humans were not related to apes or other creatures in the animal kingdom.

Yet they were, he believed, originally of one kind: European. In later editions of his work, Blumenbach gave this European type a new name, Caucasian, derived from Caucasus, the name of a mountainous region near the Black Sea. It seemed an odd choice—naming a European type after a region located in Asia—but Blumenbach explained why he believed "Caucasians" represented the original form of the human species:

> *I have taken the name of this variety from Mount Caucasus, both because its neighborhood, and especially its southern slope, produces the most beautiful race of men, I mean the Georgian; and because all physiological reasons converge to this, that in that region, if anywhere, it seems we ought with the greatest probability to place the autochthones of mankind. For in the first place, that stock displays, as we have seen the most beautiful form of the skull, from which, as from a mean and primeval type, the others diverge by most easy gradations on both sides to the two ultimate extremes (that is, on the one side the Mongolian, on the other the Ethiopian).*[6]

For Blumenbach, the mystery of humankind's ancestral race—he had started to use the term "race" in 1795—could be settled on the basis of aesthetics. Of all the people of the world, those of the Caucasus,

The Beautiful Skull

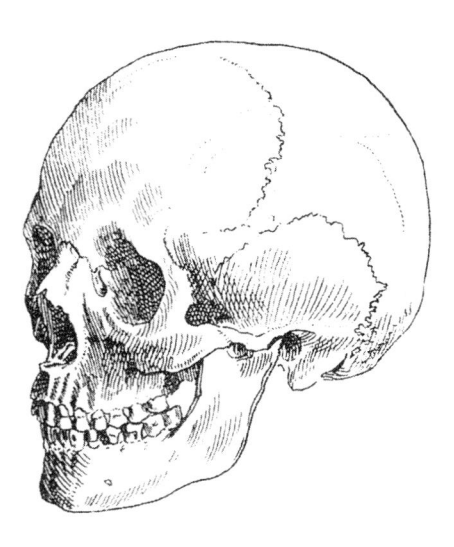

Skull of Georgian woman from Blumenbach's *Natural Varieties of Mankind*, 1795.

specifically of Georgia, formed the "the most beautiful race of men." His conception of beauty involved bones, not flesh. Loveliness was osteological, born of "the most beautiful form of skull" possessed by the Georgians.

Or, rather, one Georgian. Blumenbach procured the skull of a young Georgian woman from his friend Baron Georg Thomas von Asch, a Russian military doctor working in St. Petersburg. Von Asch had received the skull from a pathologist who had performed the woman's autopsy. Of all of the skulls in his collection, Blumenbach cherished the small, round skull "for the extreme elegance of its shape." He included an engraving of the skull in "On the Natural Varieties of Mankind," a drawing that captured the attention of other naturalists as well. "My beautiful typical head of a young Georgian female," he gushed, "always of itself attracts every eye." Using beauty as a taxonomical standard for skulls might seem capricious and subjective, if not a bit creepy, but in the eighteenth century aesthetics was an acceptable tool of analysis. Even in the late Enlightenment, science still carried with it the theological impulses of the Middle Ages, namely that science served to reveal the divine blueprint through natural means.

Aesthetics was an objective mode of analysis, as real as mathematics, offering a way of detecting the architectural style of the Creator. As such, the beauty of a skull not only existed in the judgment of the anatomist, but also represented an attribute as real and precise as the value of pi.[7]

Blumenbach's selection of Caucasians as the original human type relied not only on aesthetics but also geography. When Blumenbach urged his colleagues to select the Caucasus as "the autochthones of mankind," he was acknowledging the powerful hold that the region had on the Western imagination. It was in the Caucasus Mountains that according to Greek myth Prometheus had been chained to a rock as punishment for giving humans the divine power of fire. Christian scholars—including Blumenbach's colleague at Göttingen, Johann David Michaelis—believed that it might also be the location of the earthly paradise described in Genesis. The foothills of the Caucasus range were close—about two hundred miles—from Mount Ararat, believed to be the place where Noah's Ark came to rest. The Caucasus was also close to Persia, the region that William Jones had identified as the cradle of humanity based on the comparative study of languages. Jones had even referred to the Caucasus Mountains in his ninth discourse as the northern border of this primeval homeland of humanity. Blumenbach was a rigorous scholar, but he was not immune to these religious and philological associations, any more than he was free of cultural norms concerning beauty. He shared the view expressed by German scholar C. Rommel that the Caucasus was "the motherland of the world, the watershed of the Earth."[8]

Yet, if the Caucasus was the watershed of humankind, to where did its waters flow? Blumenbach believed that the original Caucasian tribes had traveled out of their homeland in the mountains, migrating west toward Europe, east toward the Ganges River, and south toward the Nile delta and North Africa. As they moved into environments increasingly different from the Caucasus, however, they began to degenerate into other human types: African, Mongolian, American, and Malay. Blumenbach had constructed a set of discrete racial types but viewed these as practical and approximate categories, not fixed ones. Because the climate's effects were subtle and incremental, humankind likewise consisted of a racial spectrum rather than self-contained groups. "As all the differences in mankind, however surprising they may be at the first glance, seem, upon a nearer inspection, to run into one another by unnoticed passages and intermediate shades."[9]

The idea of a racial spectrum fit not only Blumenbach's research but his ethics. After publishing his dissertation in 1775, Blumenbach watched as the Atlantic world erupted into bloody revolution. Although these uprisings had been sparked by many practical issues such as debt and taxation, they had quickly become referendums over the social hierarchy of colonists, serfs, and aristocrats. Revolutionaries in America and France had declared in their new constitutions "All men are created equal" and "Men are born and remain free and equal in rights." Once these ideas had been expressed, they were difficult to contain. Constitutions designed to reorganize the rights of kings and peasants soon became the inspiration for other groups—women, Amerindians, and African slaves—that were even more disenfranchised. In the French colony of St. Domingue (modern Haiti), where five hundred thousand Africans worked in servitude on sugar plantations, the declaration that "men are born and remain free" seemed to have been drafted by men living on another planet. Yet it took root. In August 1792, one hundred thousand Africans in St. Domingue rose up against plantation owners unwilling to apply the ideas of the French Revolution to the governance of their colonies. Blumenbach watched the flames of revolution from his study in Göttingen. He was an insular, almost monastic, man in his pursuits. Yet he understood that racial types were not just labels used in organizing skulls; they were ideas that had been used to yoke entire continents into subjugation.

His explanation for human varieties expressed this understanding. Despite the elevated status he conferred on Caucasians as the most beautiful and original human type, he believed that all humans were more similar than different. In keeping with Scripture, he upheld the idea that all human beings shared a common ancestor. Yet he broke with religious scholars who attributed blackness with Noah's curse. Climate was the real force shaping the differences between Africans and Europeans rather than any "curse of Cain, or Ham, or their posterity." Moreover, he argued, these racial differences wrought by the environment affected physiology rather than behavior or intellect. The human capacity to love, to cooperate, and to reason were universal, unlimited by distinctions of race. The powerful rays of the African sun might darken the skin, but they did not diminish the mind or tarnish the soul.[10]

This was a lot to infer from a single collection of skulls. Yet Blumenbach had other sources of evidence—human remains that to investigate had required he travel outside of Göttingen, out of Germany even. In 1792, four months after the slave uprising in St. Domingue, Blumenbach set sail for England where he had been invited to examine a number of mummies in private collections and at the British Museum. Mummies offered Blumenbach not only new skulls to examine, but skulls that were exceptionally old and well-preserved. Because mummies were known to be thousands of years old, it was believed that Egyptians represented humanity not long after its creation, one of the first wave of migrants to leave the cradle of humankind in Asia. Here, then, was a means of assessing the accuracy of Blumenbach's theory of racial origins. Ancient Egyptians—who lived on what Blumenbach conceived to be the climactic frontier of the Caucasian world—would reveal the secret of their race, and with it, reveal the history of the human species.

Blumenbach performed six mummy dissections in Britain, first in the private libraries of fellows of the Royal Society, Dr. Maxwell Garthshore and Dr. John Lettsome, and later among the collections of British Museum. Three of these mummies were very small: two contained incomplete collections of human bones, while another enclosed the remains of an ibis. Three others, however, were discovered to contain full sets of human remains. The most significant examination took place at the British Museum on February 18. Selecting a large mummy from the collection, Blumenbach uncoiled the painted integuments and rosin-soaked bandages to reveal the desiccated remains of an adolescent boy, still in possession of some of his baby teeth. The body was skeletal and "there were no remains whatever of the soft, fleshy parts." This did not impede Blumenbach, of course, who believed he could deduce all manner of details—race, sex, and beauty—from the smooth calciferous plates of the human skull. What he believed he found, in terms of racial types, was decidedly intermediate. The maxillae bones of the upper jaw were "prominent, but by no means so much as in a *true Guinea face*; and not more so than is often seen on handsome negroes, and not seldom on European countenances."[11]

To Blumenbach, the mummified Egyptian looked like someone he would expect to find in North Africa during antiquity: a boy who had begun to lose his Caucasian features as he entered the climactic border zone of the Sahara. Blumenbach admitted that he also saw evidence of "Negro" and "Hindoo" racial types in ancient Egypt, especially in the figures of Egyptian artwork and statuary, yet these were the product of racial mixing from outside. As for the original indigenous Egyptians, the early migrants from the Caucasus, their features were decidedly intermediate, "which must have been owing to the modifications produced by local circumstances in a foreign climate."[12]

Blumenbach's theory of human types was only one of many racial theories swirling around at the beginning of the nineteenth century. Yet it gained attention in scientific circles, becoming part of a spirited debate that began over the nature of racial differences. In the United States, Samuel Stanhope Smith agreed with Blumenbach's idea of degeneration, but felt that the process could be partially reversed: black slaves would change appearance with freedom and changes in climate. In Britain, Blumenbach's theories were adopted by anatomy professor William Lawrence, who discussed them in his lectures before the Royal College of Surgeons. The great Prussian explorer Alexander von Humboldt adopted Blumenbach's theory of race through climactic change as well as the use of the term "Caucasian." In France, perhaps Europe's most famous scientist, Georges Cuvier, adopted both Blumenbach's term as well as the proposition that the Caucasian type represented the original human. While the term "Caucasian" continued to be used to refer to a person living in the Caucasus, its use was gradually changing. By the 1850s, it had become a signifier of race, rather than place.[13]

Blumenbach's racial theory gained support because it did not depart radically from the work of other naturalists in the eighteenth century, and indeed was successful in integrating ideas often taken to oppose each other: Linnaeus's fixed taxonomy of species and Buffon's evolutionary ideas of degeneration. Nor did his work stray too far from accepted religious history. The idea of a Caucasian tribe originating and then populating other regions of the world was easily reconciled with the story of origins described in Genesis 9. For all of the exuberance for empirical methods among Enlightenment naturalists, most had no interest in casting God out of nature. They embraced scientific methods in hopes of augmenting, not overthrowing, Scripture. Indeed, they were celebrating the faculties of reason given to them by God.

Scripture might illuminate the story of the early humans, the great Noachian repopulation of the world, but it was not enough to follow the stories of Genesis like sheep. Even devout scholars like Thomas Malthus believed that a diet too rich in Bible study would lead to mental indolence, "repress future exertion and damp[en] the soaring wings of intellect."[14]

Blumenbach's theory also gained support because it told a story of human origins similar to one that was emerging from comparative linguistics in the years after Jones. Nineteenth-century linguists such as August Schleicher attempted to reconstruct the language that would become known as "proto Indo-European" (PIE). Scholars believed that the Indo-Europeans who spoke this language found their homeland somewhere in Central Asia. Indeed, it seemed plausible that Jones's Hamites might have descended from Blumenbach's Caucasians, connected by lineage to the primeval cradle of humankind in the Caucasus Mountains. As this original family spread to other regions, its language and culture started to degenerate much in the same manner as Blumenbach believed human physiology degenerated due to these migrations. Both systems, despite reflecting Christian European prejudices, supported the notion of the unity of humankind. The differences among the human tribes—physical, cultural, and linguistic—were superficial and incremental. In this way, both systems anchored secular theories of the modern age consistent with the key ideas of Genesis 9.

Within educated circles, the supernatural curse of Ham was gradually losing its power as an explanation of race, replaced by naturalistic explanations such as the effects of climate on tribes making the long migration into Africa. In the early decades of the nineteenth century, the Hamitic theory appeared to be on the decline, no longer able to justify blackness and bondage as a divine pronouncement. The rise of linguistics and physical anthropology seemed to offer something better: not only a new, scientific method of history making that operated independently of Scripture, but—in the work of Jones and Blumenbach—a vision of the human family that was inclusive, one that accepted racial types as real, but ultimately superficial when compared to the deeper threads connecting humanity by lineage and language in a great global fraternity. It was an inspiring, if naïve, idea.

8

THE HYPOTHESIS REVISED

IN THE MIDDLE DECADES OF the nineteenth century, support for the Hamitic hypothesis began to wane. The idea that blackness originated from a biblical curse was out of step with Western societies that increasingly put their faith in science. While the hypothesis retained pockets of support in the United States, particularly among conservative ministers and white Southerners, serious scholars avoided it. Thus, it is surprising that this idea was rescued, transformed, and eventually championed by scientists themselves. It is even more surprising that these scholars used it to explain the existence of white, rather than black, African tribes, linking them to the ancient settlement of the world.

Ultimately, the theory found new life in the hands of polygenists: scholars who believed that human races were not related to each other. For them, Europeans, Africans, Asians, and Indians all descended from separate stock that originated independently in the distant past. In taking this position, polygenists—a loose network of naturalists in America and Europe—faced resistance. Denying the unity of humankind, they put themselves at odds with other scholars who, like William Jones and Johann Blumenbach in the eighteenth century, believed that racial commonalities outweighed differences.

Polygenists also put themselves at odds with a basic axiom of scriptural history that all human beings descended from Noah, an idea that had anchored Western thought about non-European peoples for more than a thousand years. In the process, they were also challenging long-held interpretations of Genesis, including the notion that the curse of Ham was an explanation of black skin. This did not bother some polygenists, like Josiah Nott, who dismissed the Bible altogether, engaging in this debate about racial origins precisely in order to "cut loose the natural history of mankind from the Bible."[1]

Other polygenists, however, tried to reconcile their idea of separate creations with Judeo-Christian beliefs, and it was in this way they salvaged the idea of an ancient migration of people into Africa, the cornerstone of the Hamitic hypothesis. Polygenist ideas could be made compatible with the origin stories of Genesis, they argued, and with a bit of tweaking, even the story of Noah and Ham. In this creative reformulation of racial origins and history, a new hypothesis emerged, one that would hold sway in scientific circles for a hundred years, long after the idea of polygenism itself had been discarded. It would become the key to explanations of Africa's mysterious white tribes and, more significantly, a foundation stone of colonial policy in Africa in the twentieth century.[2]

Much of the evidence for this new Hamitic hypothesis grew out of the study of ancient skulls. When the naturalist Augustus Granville unveiled an Egyptian mummy in his London home in 1821, he seemed to be reenacting the Blumenbach dissections of three decades earlier. Yet Granville's examination would lead him to conclusions different from those of the German anatomist, conclusions that would grow in importance over the following two decades.

Surrounded by friends and members of the Royal Society, Granville began work on the mummy, carefully prying back the boards of the sycamore case, etched with long columns of hieroglyphics. The ancient body was wrapped in yards of bandages, long strips of linen three inches wide in precise horizontal and diagonal patterns. Uncoiling these wrappings, Granville found more layers underneath. As a physician and former soldier in the British Navy, he was familiar with bandages of many forms—dressings, strappings, and compresses—but he had never seen any as intricate as these. He marveled at the skill of the embalmers who tailored sheets of linen for every limb, toe, and joint, who had mastered the art of bandaging at its highest forms, including "the *couvrechef*, the capularium, the 18-tailed bandage, the T-bandage, as well as the linteum scissum, and capistrum." The mummy was in far better condition than those opened by Blumenbach twenty-nine years earlier.[3]

Granville proceeded carefully. Once removed from their cocoons of wood and cloth, mummies were fragile things. Their embalmers had prepared them for a journey forward into the afterlife, not one back to the world they left behind. The unwrapping took time, but it also reassured him, for he knew that each layer of bandage had protected the remains from centuries of air, light, and moisture. Finally he took off the last coils of cloth. The heap of linen at his feet weighed twenty-eight pounds. Before him lay the body of a middle-aged woman, roughly five feet in height. Naked, hair shorn, her arms crossed over her chest, she looked vulnerable yet also astonishingly well preserved. For Granville and his peers, she was not merely a relic from the ancient past—very ancient, Granville believed, "before the building of the pyramids of Memphis"—but a representative of people as they existed when the world was new, when the human family had just begun its great migration across the earth. She was an example of the first human type.[4]

Granville also concluded that the mummy was Caucasian. His judgment, mirroring Blumenbach's, was aesthetic. The proportion of the mummy's bones perfectly matched those of the Venus de Medicis, which he considered the ultimate female archetype. "The celebrated Medicean statue, which stands as the representative of a perfect beauty, is five feet in height, like our mummy, and the relative admeasurements of the arm, fore-arm, and hand in each are precisely similar." Measurements of the mummy's pelvis approached that of the "the *beau idéal* of the Caucasian structure," as he put it, more so than did those of European women. Finally, the mummy's skull in Granville's view closely resembled the female Georgian skull made famous by Blumenbach in 1791, one that by now had become, if only unofficially, the template of the Caucasian race. Separated by thousands of years, dwelling on separate continents, the remains of these two women—one from Georgia and the other from Egypt—shared a resemblance born of kinship, Granville thought.[5]

Granville's intellectual debt to Blumenbach is apparent; his discussion of the Georgian skull and his use of "Caucasian" are only the most obvious signs. Granville's Blumenbachian focus on bones for racial evidence shows the depth to which it had percolated into scientific discussions of race. Yet whereas Blumenbach believed that environmental factors were the engine of racial difference, Granville believed that racial types were considerably more stable. Both men had concluded from their mummy investigations that ancient Egyptians were Caucasian, but Blumenbach believed that the environment of Egypt had transformed them, "differ[ing] very much by their singular physiognomy from the rest." By contrast, Granville concluded that ancient Egyptians upheld—undiminished and unchanged—the Caucasian ideal.[6]

The differences between the two men may seem minor, but they had big implications. At issue was whether race was fixed, as polygenists believed, or could change over time. The differences between Blumenbach and Granville reflected a larger debate about race, and one that would have important implications for the Hamitic hypothesis in the nineteenth century. If Egyptians living thousands of years ago in the sun-baked valley of the Nile retained the same fair skin and facial features as modern-day Georgians, it would be unlikely that racial differences resulted from changes in climate. Variation in racial types, then, must have been due to different causes, or else those types must be less mutable than Blumenbach believed. Granville was not the only naturalist to arrive at this conclusion. In the early 1800s, Georges Cuvier, France's celebrated comparative anatomist, adopted many aspects of Blumenbach's work—particularly the existence of a Caucasian type and its status as the original human form—yet believed that the differences among the races had existed since antiquity.[7]

To support their arguments, polygenists turned to the work of the American Samuel George Morton. Morton had begun collecting skulls in the 1830s in order to teach anatomy to medical students at the University of Pennsylvania. Inspired by Blumenbach, he took measurements of each skull in order to measure racial differences. Morton's collection was comprised of skulls from Europe, Africa, and the Western frontier and included eclectic subjects: a German dwarf, a Finnish criminal, and a Celtic warrior. By 1850, his collection exceeded in size Blumenbach's, containing more than a thousand skulls. In his 1839 treatise *Crania Americana*, Morton wrote that the differences among the races were too dramatic to have allowed for common descent from a single ancestor: "Each race was adapted from the beginning to its particular local destination. In other words, it is assumed, that the physical characteristics which distinguish the different Races, are independent of external causes." Race was in his view impervious to climate—impervious even to the effects of racial mixing—because the essential type of race transcended any one individual. It was constant, like the chemical properties of iron, fixed and elemental.[8]

But proving that races remained constant over time required more than an abundance of skulls. Morton needed *ancient* skulls, like those studied by Blumenbach and Granville. In this he received help from an eccentric diplomat and amateur Egyptologist, George Gliddon, who collected skulls for him in the Valley of the Nile, pilfering them from ancient tombs, mausoleums, and Cairo's vast necropolis. Beginning in the late 1830s, Gliddon began sending Morton dozens of skulls. Some of them got pulverized by their long journey to the United States, but a significant number—137 in all—made it to Philadelphia intact. He described and carefully measured each skull, concluding in his 1844 book *Crania Aegyptiaca* that Granville had been right and that ancient Egyptians were racially European. Morton's conclusions gave credibility to the polygenist argument. It became the basis of the "American School" of anthropology, and persuaded Louis Agassiz, then one of America's most esteemed naturalists, to become a proponent.[9]

Like Blumenbach, Morton assumed that skulls would reveal racial differences. Yet despite the immensity of his collection and his precise skull measurements, there were flaws in his methods and analysis. He did not procure skulls on his own, so relied on secondhand descriptions of bodies and gravesites. His methods for measuring of skull volume changed over time and did not account for such factors as age and gender. Not surprisingly, he sometimes found it difficult to place skulls in one racial category or another. Those reproduced in *Crania Aegyptiaca* are often tagged with murky descriptions such as "Egyptian, blended with the Negro form?" Morton used the terms "blended," "mixed," and "amalgamated" liberally in his manuscripts, because he had no other way to account for intermediate racial characteristics. Examining five "Negro" skulls unearthed at Thebes, for example, he noted "evident mixture of Caucasian characters." Unable to see other possible causes and unwilling to interrogate his own assumptions, Morton's conclusion was simple. "I therefore regard them as mulattoes." Where Blumenbach saw these ambiguities of racial form as evidence that races could change over time, Morton—convinced that racial types were fixed—saw them as hybrids. His conclusions in *Crania Aegyptiaca*, however, reflect none of the fuzziness of his data. Egypt had been populated by the Caucasian race, he asserted. "These primeval people, since called Egyptians, were the Mizraimites of Scripture, the posterity of Ham, and directly affiliated with the Libyan family of nations.... The physical or organic characters which distinguish the several races of men, are as old as the oldest record of our species."[10]

Morton's findings became an important pillar in the polygenist argument for separate origins, and ancient Egyptians were key figures in debates about racial history: important because of their appearance—and what could be inferred from it—rather than how they lived or what they accomplished. They provided data gathered in defense of polygenism's theory of fixed racial types and took their place alongside other peoples—American Indians, Fiji islanders, Nubians, and Ethiopians—details of whose remains were being amassed by Morton and others.

Yet if polygenism could be reconciled with physical measurements, it could also be reconciled with Scriptures by interpreting them more narrowly. Genesis became the story of Caucasian origins rather than a history of all races. Adam and Eve represented the first Caucasians while other races, sometimes called "pre-Adamites" on the assumption that they were created before Adam and Eve on the sixth day of Creation, were assigned to live in regions of the world to which they were best suited: dark-skinned Africans and Malays in the equatorial regions; Asians and native Americans in more temperate climates. The story of Noah became a story of the near extinction of the European racial type and its repopulation of the world. Noah's sons, who had represented the different divisions of humankind for a thousand years, now became the progenitors of a single race, the white race.[11]

With such big matters at stake, few noted that Morton had identified "the posterity of Ham" as a Caucasian people rather than a black one, breaking with centuries of biblical exegesis. The civilization of Egypt had been built by Hamitic invaders, uncursed descendants of

The Hypothesis Revised
91

Ham who had migrated from their homeland in the Caucasus to the northern shores of Africa. There they ruled over the indigenous "pre-Adamic" African race, and over time, mixed with them to produce the hybrid Caucasian forms Morton described in *Crania Aegyptiaca*. "The valley of the Nile was inhabited by an indigenous race," he wrote, "before the invasion of the Hamitic and other Asiatic nations." As George Gliddon pointed out, it was time to view Ham, Shem, and Japheth as the "three grand divisions of the Caucasian race."[12]

This idea of the Hamite as a Caucasian invader in Africa took hold within the scientific community even as polygenism started to wane in the late nineteenth century. It was adopted by ethnologists who disagreed with the principles of polygenism, such as the English ethnologist James Cowles Prichard (in the 1840s) and later used by others to identify Africans living outside of Egypt. On his expedition to Ethiopia, the Prussian Egyptologist Karl Richard Lepsius described Ethiopians as Hamitic in its new, Caucasian, incarnation. The new view of the Hamite as "Caucasian invader" spread beyond labs and lecture halls of the West, influencing African explorers, too.[13]

In the 1800s only a small percentage of explorers were scientists. Yet many of them studied the scientific literature of their field, poring over the work of naturalists, mapmakers, and other explorers as they prepared for their journeys. These explorers were quick to notice the new conception of Hamite. Still they did not adopt the new terminology all at once. Morton may have written about Hamites as Caucasian, but the French race theorist Arthur de Gobineau adhered to its old usage: "By black men I mean the Hamites." Richard Burton, returned from his East African journey with John Hanning Speke, complained about the new racial terminology: "These are poor words for ethnologists." He declared his intention to use the traditional terms "Hamitic for pure African or negro, Semitic for Arab, and Japhetic for the Aryan, or Indo-European race." Speke also continued to use Hamitic according to its traditional interpretation as a curse. For example, when Speke's East African assistant, Sidi Mabarak Bombay, asked him about the causes of slavery, Speke replied that he had "related the history of Noah and the dispersion of his sons on the face of the globe; and showed him that he was of the black or Hamitic stock, and by the common order of nature, they, being the weakest, had to succumb to their superiors, the Japhetic and Semitic branches of the family."[14]

For Speke, the biblical meaning of Ham was useful not only because it gave historical context to black slavery but also because it explained the general backwardness of African society. "The curse of Noah sticks to these his grandchildren by Ham," he wrote in *Journal of the Discovery of the Source of the Nile* in 1862, "and no remedy that has yet been found will relieve them." So ironclad were the links between Genesis 9 and black Africa, Speke believed, that one could use the backwardness of Africans to confirm the truth of the Bible. "Ham was cursed by his father, and condemned to be the slave of both Shem and Japheth; for as they were then, so they appear to be now—a strikingly existing proof of the Holy Scriptures."[15]

Speke's commitment to this earlier interpretation of Ham did not prevent him from also adopting Morton's idea of the Caucasian Hamite as well. Evidence of an outside invasion appeared most clearly in Abyssinia, where the Blue Nile found its source, and where many Westerners had noted that the native people, the Oromo, appeared distinct in religion, culture, and physical appearance from sub-Saharan Africans. In 1813, James Cowles Prichard wrote, "I think [it is] evident that the Egyptians and Ethiopians were the same race of people, and probably formed originally one nation inhabiting all the fertile country on the banks of the Nile." Speke saw these racial links too, interpreting Abyssinians' "Caucasoid" features as evidence of an ancient invasion from the Near East.[16]

While polygenists confined themselves to the Hamitic invasion of ancient Egypt, Speke believed that this invasion extended to regions south of the Sahara, particularly East Africa. As Speke explored regions farther south, he saw signs of this invasion everywhere, in the physiognomy of the people he encountered. In 1862, trekking through the regions south of Lake Victoria, Speke perceived Caucasian blood in the royal line of the Wahuma: "Uzinza, which we now entered, is ruled by two Wahuma chieftains of foreign blood, descended from the Abyssinian stock, of whom we saw specimens scattered all over Unyamuezi, and who extended even down south as far as Fipa." He offered a similar explanation when he reached the country west of Lake Victoria. Of one of the men there, he wrote, "I admired his race, and believed them to have sprung from our old friends the Abyssinians, whose king, Sahela Selassie, had received rich presents from our queen. They were Christians like ourselves, and had the

Wahuma not lost their knowledge of God, they would be also." By the time Speke reached Lake Victoria, these theories of external descent had become a genealogical certainty: "Ever proud of his history since I had traced his descent from Abyssinia and King David, whose hair was as straight as my own, Rumanika [king of Karague on Victoria's western shore] dwelt on my theological disclosures with the greatest delight."[17]

Speke's belief that the Abyssinians had conquered areas of East Africa became a central tenet of the new Hamitic hypothesis—a migration theory shorn of its biblical curse—for the next hundred years. In his hands, this hypothesis was based on believing that "the physical appearance of the Wahuma...can be of any other race then the Shem-Hamitic of Ethiopia." Still Speke had not entirely abandoned his earlier vision of the Hamites. Some of his writings continued to discuss Ham in his traditional role as cursed father of black Africa, while others adopted Morton's new vision of Hamites as Caucasian invaders.[18]

How he reconciled such disparities is impossible to know exactly. Perhaps Speke—who died at the age of thirty-seven—came to believe in the Caucasian Hamite theory of Morton even as he used the curse of Ham as a symbol of African backwardness. Or perhaps he accepted both incompatible ideas without interrogating them further. Whatever the reason, he was representative of his age: both versions of the Hamitic hypothesis coexisted in the Victorian age. It was a confusing arrangement. The ancient explanation for why Africans were black became, in the hands of polygenists, the explanation for why some of them were white.

By the time Stanley set off into the East African interior in 1874, he would have known something about the new Hamitic hypothesis as well, if only from his reading of Speke's work. His precise beliefs about the origin of human races, however, came into focus only later, after his return from Gambaragara, when he began reading the scientific literature more intensely. Arriving in Buganda in 1875, gliding along the waters of Lake Victoria in *Lady Alice*, Stanley had other things to think about. The people of the Lakes Region, seven hundred miles from the Swahili coast of East Africa, knew nothing about the philology of William Jones, the skull collecting of Johann Blumenbach and Samuel Morton, or the exegeses of priests, rabbis, and imams.

The story of Ham was the product of another world: generated from Hebrew sources, modified by theories about the monotheistic cultures of the Middle East, and adapted by scientists and explorers to explain the peopling of the East Africa.

So it must have surprised Stanley when King Mutesa raised no objections to his biblical meditations. The great Kabaka did not contest the idea of an ancient invasion from the north, nor the idea that African kings—maybe even whole tribes—descended from foreign progenitors on a distant continent. He even appeared comfortable with the story of Ham. In fact, Noah's son—the subject of so much debate in the West across the centuries—was a figure already known to Mutesa. As he later told another visitor to his court, Ham was buried in Uganda. "I will show you his grave."[19]

9

KING MUTESA

MUCH OF KING MUTESA'S KNOWLEDGE and enthusiasm for Ham came from John Speke, who had become the Johnny Appleseed of the Hamitic hypothesis in East Africa: convincing all the African royals he encountered that they were the offspring of a proto-white Abyssinian invasion centuries before. Yet it seems unlikely that Speke, despite his enthusiasm, would have convinced Mutesa to abandon the centuries-old origin stories that anchored his own claim as king. Mutesa's power as Kabaka was based on his hereditary succession, a succession that dated back at least to the 1700s, with royal claims extending even further. To cast off the Kabaka kingship stories would have been to undermine his own legitimacy as leader of the Ganda people. In truth, Mutesa's acceptance of Ham and the Hamitic hypothesis was based on the convergences between the kingship stories of Buganda and the story of Ham. With Henry Stanley's help, he developed a new synthesis of African and Judeo-Christian beliefs that would, in less than a decade, form the foundation for a Christian church in Buganda. Yet this convergence of origin stories had equally important implications for Western science too, convincing anthropologists that the traces of a Hamitic invasion lay not only in the sacred texts of the West but in the oral traditions of African societies.

Mutesa I, King of Buganda. Credit: *Stanley in Africa: The Paladin of the Nineteenth Century*, 1890.

Knowledge of the ancient story of Ham, like all information about the outside world, had come slowly to the Lakes Region, but it had arrived before the Victorian explorers—Burton, Speke, Baker, and Livingstone—entered East Africa in the 1850s, seeking the source of the Nile. It had been brought by Arab and Swahili traders searching the African interior for slaves and ivory in the 1840s. Because they were seeking fortune rather than geographical knowledge, these Arab traders left no paper trail, moving inland without the pomp and ceremony of European expeditions. European explorers were public figures, engaged in the business of discovery. By contrast, Arab traders were men of commerce, anxious to guard information about their routes and contacts. As a result, their expeditions into the interior took place in the shadows of British efforts. While Stanley, Livingstone, and a handful of Europeans searched for African lakes and became celebrities, Arab traders and their African allies were quietly reshaping the continent around them—profoundly, violently, and indelibly—forever changing the peoples and cultures of the interior.[1]

The traders had come from the Swahili Coast, an East African empire that stretched for more than a thousand miles, from Mogadishu to Lindi. Under the dominion of Sultan Seyyid Said of Zanzibar, these traders exploited an opportunity presented by the European ban of slave trade (England banned the slave trade in 1807; France banned slavery from its colonies in 1848). The transfer of slaves across the Atlantic declined, but the ban did not eliminate the demand for slaves, particularly in the Middle East and Asia. As a result, the African trade did not disappear but changed direction—toward the slave markets of the East African coast. Arab caravans pressed inland from Zanzibar and Bagamoyo, trading cloth, firearms, and other goods for slaves and ivory. As they extended their range, they forged alliances with East African communities, such as the Nyamwezi in the lands south of Lake Victoria, who became their native agents in the interior: using firearms supplied by traders, they killed elephants and kidnapped East Africans from nearby villages.

In the 1830s, Arab traders reached the Lakes Region, establishing posts at Ujiji on Lake Tanganyika, and Tabora, south of Lake Victoria. By 1844, the caravans had arrived in Buganda on the northwestern shores of Lake Victoria. As the most powerful kingdom in the Lakes Region, Buganda offered Swahili merchants an important trading partner in the East African interior. For Ganda rulers, particularly Kabaka Suna II and the members of the royal court, traders offered a glimpse of life beyond the Lakes Region and the shores of Africa. They provided a different vision of the world as well. Through his conversations with Arab trader Medi Abraham, Suna II became interested in the ideas of Islam, and under Abraham's tutelage, learned the first four chapters of the Koran.[2]

His first contact with Swahili traders made an impression on Mutesa. When the traders arrived at the Ganda court, he was a boy, still known by his childhood name of Mukabya, and a son of Suna II. In the 1840s, Mukabya was not a powerful prince and did not appear to be a likely successor to the throne, given that Suna II had many wives and older, more eligible sons. He grew up on a rural estate in Singo seventy miles from the Kabaka's court. There, among the grass-thatched huts and banana groves, he lived with his mother, a palace cook, far away from the intrigues of the capital. Even at these distances, however, Mukabya learned something of the Arab travelers who were entering his father's kingdom. News of the Arabs' firearms would have traveled quickly, as would talk of the Arab sultan who was so powerful that he could direct his traders from a coastal fortress hundreds of miles away. Years later, after he had assumed the throne, Mutesa would ask one of these traders, Katukula, what he had talked about with his father, Suna II. "We used to tell him about God," Katukula replied, "and the King of Kings, and that He will raise people from the dead."[3]

In 1857 or 1858, after the death of Suna II, Mukabya became the new Kabaka. He had emerged as a consensus candidate, someone acceptable both to the Kabaka's prime minister, the Katikiro, as well as the chiefs of Buganda's major clans. Having accomplished the transition of power without bloodshed, Mukabya took the name Mutesa, which means "statesman." The title proved ironic. Mutesa inaugurated his rule by executing clan chiefs who had opposed his kingship and imprisoning the Katikiro who engineered his rise to power. Once secure, he established a new capital on the shores of Lake Victoria. There, in his residence in the royal court, he came into contact with Swahili traders and other foreigners who entered the realm, interrogating them about the marvels that lay beyond his kingdom.

Through his conversations with Arab traders, Mutesa learned of Islam, and the doctrines and origin stories of the Koran: the creation of Adam and Eve, the Flood, and the repopulation of the world by Noah and his offspring. The Koran is silent on the figure of Ham, but for centuries, mullahs and imams had debated the story of Ham and the nature of the curse Noah placed on him. Hence as Zanzibari traders entered Mutesa's court in the late 1800s, they related the story of Ham as well. It may seem odd that Arab traders would be eager to voice their beliefs about Ham with Africans since it meant telling their hosts that they were cursed among God's people. Yet, as we've seen, the story of Ham had many valences, not all of them negative. As much as the story described a fall from grace, it also expressed a belief in common origins at a time when some believed that human races constituted separate species. The biblical story of Ham affirmed the common descent of all peoples—Arabs, Africans, Asians, and Europeans—from a single family, chosen and beloved by God.[4]

By whichever channels Mutesa learned the story of Ham, it captivated him. He spoke of it when he met with Stanley in 1874 and also when he met with other Westerners during the same period. When the French explorer Ernest Linant de Bellefonds arrived in Buganda to meet with Mutesa in 1875, a few months before Stanley's arrival, he marveled at Mutesa's appetite for studying the Scriptures. "I left the King at two o'clock after we had arranged to meet again at four," wrote de Bellefonds. "[The] talk was of Genesis. Mutesa had the story of Genesis from the Creation to the Flood taken down on a writing-tablet. We parted at nightfall. Mutesa is spellbound."[5]

It's perhaps understandable why Mutesa would embrace the story of Genesis in general and the story of Ham in particular. At a time when he was learning about powerful peoples who lived beyond the Lakes Region, the stories connected the Ganda people to the broader human family, including the Arabs and Europeans whom he so admired. By establishing kinship between the peoples of Lake Victoria and the West, the story of Ham also brought Buganda into history, at least the Judeo-Christian vision of it, aligning Mutesa more closely with his foreign guests.

Mutesa also found much to like in Speke's version of the Hamitic hypothesis, given that it argued that some East Africans, particularly those in royal clans, were the descendants of Abyssinian or Caucasian invaders from long ago. In Speke's opinion, Mutesa and other rulers were more closely related to Westerners than his Ganda subjects, a flattering claim that only confirmed Mutesa's right to rule. It was blood that tied the king to his father, Suna II, and to the Sesekabaka before him: a long line of hereditary rulers whose trail went back into the mists of prehistory, a chain that—if Speke were correct—eventually led to the figure of Ham, son of Noah and first king of Buganda, father of all future Kabakas including Mutesa. In a kingdom that understood both history and political power as the expression of a sacred bloodline unfolding over time, the seeds of the Hamitic hypothesis found fertile soil.[6]

Moreover, the story of Ham was congruent with Ganda origin stories, particularly the legend of Kintu. Among the people of Buganda, Kintu was the original man, who arrived in the Lakes Region from the north. Kintu traveled with his cow in this empty country until he met Nambi, daughter of the sky god Ggulu. When Nambi sought to marry

Kintu, her father demanded that Kintu first perform a series of difficult tasks. After he succeeded, Ggulu allowed Kintu to marry Nambi and settle in the Lakes Region, where they had children and populated the earth. In another version of the story, Kintu defeated a cruel ruler of the Lakes Region, Bemba the Snake, to become the first king of Buganda. Taken together, the stories established Kintu not only as the first man but also the first Kabaka, ruler of Buganda from which all future Kabakas, including Mutesa, would descend.[7]

Stanley saw superficial parallels between the story of Kintu and Genesis, specifically the story of Adam and Eve. Mutesa saw them as well, particularly after Stanley produced a Kiswahili translation of the Bible that Mutesa could read. Working with his young Zanzibari assistant, a freed slave named Dallington Scorpion Maftaa, Stanley produced "an abridged Protestant Bible in Kiswahili," he explained in *Through the Dark Continent*, "embracing all the principal events from the Creation to the Crucifixion of Christ." By late 1875, Stanley and Mutesa were discussing the creation stories of both traditions in detail, identifying congruencies between them. "It is impossible, while reading the tale of Kintu," continued Stanley, "not to be reminded at one time of Adam, at another of Noah—for both Adam and Noah found the earth void and uninhabited, as Kintu is said to have found Uganda and the neighboring lands."[8]

Yet these biblical congruencies did not persuade Stanley that Kintu was Ham. His view of history—like that of Speke, Livingstone, and other explorers—was informed by a scriptural chronicle of events, and he adhered to an almost literal interpretation of the Bible. This may have been a personal expression of faith, or what Stanley took to be his readers' expression of faith. Yet, it also reflected a view common to scholars of the late Victorian era: that ancient texts, sacred and otherwise, might distort historical events, but at their core they still offered a kernel of truth. The Iliad had inspired Heinrich Schliemann's search for Troy in the 1870s. The role of science was to reconcile the ancient and modern by separating them from the chaff of myth. Both the explorer and the anthropologist could still discuss Noah, Ham, and the population of the world, even if that required secular detachment and a measure of impartiality. Thus, it is not surprising that Stanley would accept Kintu as a historical figure, perhaps not as the original Adam or the patriarch Noah. More likely, Kintu was an early Christian priest, a man who migrated to the Lakes Region from Abyssinia or the Middle East. As Stanley describes him, Kintu was a kind of saint, "a mild, human, and blameless man, and from his character was probably a priest of some old and long-forgotten order."[9]

Mutesa came away from their conversations with a different interpretation. He believed that Kintu and Ham were one and the same—a man who entered the Lakes Region after the Flood to repopulate the country and establish the first dynasty of Bugandan kings. This was the view he maintained even after Stanley had left his court in the fall of 1875, heading west toward Gambaragara. When the British missionary G. S. Smith arrived in Mutesa's royal court in 1877, the king brought up the subject of Ham with him as well. It was to Smith that Mutesa indicated that he knew where Ham was buried.[10]

To the Christian missionaries who arrived in Buganda in the late 1870s, the theory linking Kintu to Ham was an appealing story principally because it supported the idea that East Africans were part of the Noachian heritage, linked with Europeans and other races by kinship to Adam. If the Ganda people were truly the direct descendants of Ham, this meant that they had once been part of the Judeo-Christian family. In the course of their migration and settlement of Africa, they must have forgotten the stories and traditions that tied them to Scripture. For missionaries, this provided added incentive for their work in Buganda: they not merely evangelized, but also returned a biblical people back to their scriptural heritage. One had to look no further than Mutesa, now enthralled by Christianity, to see this recovery at work. Observed British colonel C. E. Gordon in 1878, "My belief is that M[u]tesa has the germs of Christianity...from his Abyssinian ancestors." Missionaries extended this idea to other groups of East Africans originally described by Speke—Wahuma, Watusi, and East African royals—who they believed shared a lineage with other Judeo-Christian peoples through Ham.[11]

For missionaries as well as explorers, the links to Ham were racial as well as spiritual, creating a line of kinship that tied Mutesa and others to non-African ancestors. Traveling north of Buganda, the Irish missionary A. B. Fisher heard stories of Kintu that indicated he was Caucasoid in appearance:

> *The oldest inhabitants of the country related to me how a white man and woman many years ago landed on the right bank of*

Lake Albert, and settled in Bunyoro. On being questioned as to whether they referred to Sir Samuel and Lady Baker, they replied that they remembered them well, and described them to me. But, said they, these other white people arrived a long, long time ago, and founded their first dynasty. The story is that this man and his wife came down from the Nile, and caused a great sensation, the people all flocking round them, exclaiming, "Kintu ke?" (What is it?) So they named the man Kintu.[12]

The legend of a white Kintu was not limited to scholarly texts. When Stanley's assistant, A. J. Mounteney Jephson, wrote a children's book about African stories in 1893, it included the story of Kintu, identified by Jephson as the "personification of the influential immigrants from Galla [Abyssinian] countries." If this was a rather veiled way to describe Kintu's racial heritage, the illustration in Jephson's book, in which Kintu and his wife appear as white-skinned Europeans, made matters clearer.[13]

One problem with portraying Kintu as white was that it did not correspond with the color of his descendents, particularly Mutesa, who was dark-skinned and unlikely to be confused with Europeans,

Kintu and Nambi as they appear in A. J. Mounteney Jephson, *Stories Told in An African Forest*, 1893.

Arabs, or Abyssinians. He had been described by many explorers, from Speke to Stanley, and photographed as well. Yet defenders of the Hamitic hypothesis had an explanation. Traits that could not be reconciled with this Abyssinian, Arab, or Caucasian heritage, such as wooly hair or dark skin, could be explained as the product of intermarriage with "negroid" Africans. Writing in 1882, the British missionaries C. T. Wilson and Robert Felkin explained that Mutesa, "through the admixture of Negro blood," had lost his "pure Mhuma features," but was still distinct from his subjects. "He professes to trace back his descent through an unbroken line of between thirty and forty kings, to Kintu or Ham, the founder of his dynasty."[14]

As Christianity gained a foothold in Buganda in the 1870s and 1880s, so, too, did support for the connection between Kintu and Ham. With the support of European church fathers, Ganda converts began looking for more evidence of the historical connection that went beyond Scripture and oral tradition. In 1887, newly converted clan chiefs arrived at the Kintu shrine in Magonga in search of a bark-cloth-covered Bible that had been rumored to exist at the site. (They found a jawbone but no Bible.) In 1894, another group of Christian converts organized an archaeological expedition to discover evidence of Kintu's origins.[15]

In their enthusiasm for finding a Kintu-Ham connection, missionaries and their African converts ignored troubling discrepancies between these two myths of origin. One problem lay within the evolution in the Hamitic hypothesis itself. As we've seen, the story of Ham had been used by biblical scholars to explain the darkness of Africans and justify their enslavement by European powers, but also, ironically, to reaffirm their common heritage with the other peoples of the world. According to this worldview Ham was the father of all of Africa's peoples. Yet the secular theory of Ham emerging in the late nineteenth century identified Hamites more narrowly as a special lineage of Africans, racially distinct from the so-called primitive "Negroid" or "Bantu" peoples who made up the general population of Central and East Africa.

In addition to sowing confusion about the identity of Hamites themselves—were they black or white?—the hypothesis in this form posed a practical problem in interpreting the story of Kintu as the figure of Ham. Whether Kintu was the first human to arrive in East Africa or simply the first Caucasian invader was an issue that had consequences for the hereditary kings of Buganda and other kingdoms in East Africa. For example, Mutesa ruled on the basis of his direct descent from Kintu, the original Hamite. Did he represent a special Caucasoid lineage of Africans, as Speke seemed to think, or was he merely a "son of Ham" in the same manner as all Africans, as literal readers of the Bible maintained? There was also a problem of chronology. According to Biblical chronology, Ham lived more than three thousand years before Kintu. For those who treated Holy Scriptures and African kingship lists as a chronicle of history rather than collections of legends, this was difficult to reconcile.[16]

Enticed by the idea of reconnecting Western and African history, missionaries, anthropologists, and Ganda converts seemed willing to overlook such matters, however. Many saw or suspected some of these problems of interpretation, because they remained flexible to how they attached the theory of a Caucasoid invasion to the oral traditions of African history. If Adam, Noah, and Ham were too ancient to be Kintu, the founder of Buganda might have indeed been an early Christian priest, as Stanley had suggested, or an Abyssinian king of non-African descent. It was becoming clear that there were many figures who could represent Kintu within the Holy Scriptures or within the broader canon of historical texts.[17]

By the late nineteenth century, it was dawning on the supporters of the Hamitic hypothesis that they didn't really need the Bible, Kintu, or Ham. The idea of a Caucasoid invasion of East Africa had become so widely accepted by scholars and missionaries that it became a framework for interpreting other kingship legends, legends that, not surprisingly, also seemed to indicate a Caucasoid invasion from the north. In the mountainous kingdom of Toro (Western Uganda), wrote one missionary, "The Batoro tell of how a white man came down from the north and settled among them and reigned over them." To the south, in the kingdom of Rwanda, missionaries thought that the legendary figures of Kigwa and his companion Bimanuka were the first Hamites, bringing civilization to the savage and indigenous Bazigaba. North of Buganda, in the kingdom of Bunyoro, missionaries recorded kingship legends of the Bachwezi, a dynasty of light-skinned kings that arrived from the north and ruled over a vast empire called "Kitara," which encompassed Bunyoro, Buganda, and lands south of Lake Victoria. Like the story of Kintu, these stories went back and forth across the borders of history and myth, the natural and supernatural. Yet it was unclear to missionaries and ethnologists exactly where these borders were, which elements to classify as historical and which as apocryphal. The Bachwezi, for example, represented not only a dynasty of enlightened kings, but also a family of demigods that inhabited the spirit world. In the words of Harry Johnston, a British colonial administrator in East Africa, the Bachwezi "really seems to mean two things, or the same thing with two meanings. It indicated originally both the ghost of an ancestor or chief and the individuals of the superior, light-coloured Gala [Oromo] race of almost Caucasian stock, which entered these lands at different periods in remote and relatively recent times."[18]

The "two meanings" of African stories—one mythical and the other historical—did not trouble Johnson or other Victorian scholars who had come to view the Hebrew Bible in exactly the same way: a mixture of fact and fantasy. The careful scholar did not discard African legends, but worked to disentangle the threads of truth them from the embroideries of myth. In the end, the African origin stories recorded by Stanley and others provide a rich trove of material that could be used to buttress the new Hamitic hypothesis, adding to the evidence that had already been collected in linguistics and physical anthropology.

Origin stories had their own unique properties. Unlike skulls, stories were not fixed as objects but subject to change over time and from person to person. No written record of these stories existed before the 1860s, nor could they be easily confirmed by archaeological methods. An investigation of the Kintu shrine by Christian converts in 1887 yielded little. Moreover, most legends claimed that Kintu had disappeared rather than died, fleeing Buganda after accidentally killing his deputy, a man named Kisolo. The legend of the light-skinned Bachewzi kings ended in similar fashion, with the disappearance of the dynasty after a series of bad omens pointed to the decline of their rule. Some said that Kintu headed south toward Lake Victoria. Many said the Bachwezi headed west, into the misty mountains of Gambaragara. In both cases, it was doubtful whether graves, relics, or artifacts could be used to tie these kings to Caucasoid ancestors. Ultimately, the stories were evocative, rather than conclusive, suggestive without being testable.[19]

Was it a coincidence that oral traditions spoke of light-skinned kings disappearing into the Western mountains exactly at the moment

Stanley was investigating a "white race of Gambaragara" in the same location? Were the soldiers of his African escort sharing kingship legends when he thought they were describing living tribes? This remains unclear. The categories that nineteenth-century Europeans created to demarcate history from myth, past from present, natural from supernatural, did not apply so neatly to the peoples of the Lakes Region who understood the world and its operations in very different terms. Yet they did confirm one thing: the idea that a light-skinned people lived in the Mountains of the Moon was not something Stanley invented. The mountains already occupied a storied place within the African imagination, a world of divine spirits, lost kings, and missing peoples.

In the fall of 1875, Stanley did not know of the myth and history that bound Gambaragara to the people of the Lakes Region. Yet the looming peaks, cloaked in bamboo and heather trees, capped by glaciers, did provoke Stanley to wonder about the threads linking this world to the past. "I have never been able to cross any high ridge of the country lying between the two great lake feeders of the Nile," he asks in his book, "without asking myself the question, 'What was this country long ago? Is this an old or a new country?' Also I have sat hours on the summit of a smooth grassy hill trying to resolve those problems satisfactorily to myself."[20]

Stanley tended to imagine this history in geological rather than anthropological terms. This wasn't from lack of interest, but because he thought the peopling of East Africa had been so recent as to make the study of tribal prehistory unfruitful. As he gazed over the massive lakes, volcanoes, rift valleys, and mountains of the Lakes Region, Stanley concluded that they had been formed in a violent, cataclysmic uplift. All human settlement of East Africa would have to have occurred after these geological events. This would explain why African culture, to Stanley's mind, was not as advanced as European or Asian cultures. It was not a matter of racial inferiority but of the limited time African cultures had been given to germinate and develop. As evidence of this, Stanley pointed to the fact that sub-Saharan Africa did not possess the ruins of older cultures in Europe or Asia.

Stanley didn't know it, but he was already being proved wrong. Hundreds of miles to the south, a young German explorer had found ruins larger than any other in sub-Saharan Africa. It was a discovery that would demonstrate the existence of an African prehistory. It would also anchor the Hamitic hypothesis more firmly in the past, a past that, in the Lakes Region, had relied on Scripture and African origin stories. These mighty ruins would carry the story of the Hamitic invasion back in time, and spread it over the vastness of the continent, to the very tip of Africa itself.

10

GREAT ZIMBABWE

On September 5, 1871, the German explorer Carl Mauch saw a great labyrinth rising out of the mist of Mashonaland in Southern Africa. Long granite walls wound among the trees and the rock domes of the plain in every direction. They were even perched on a cliff that rose three hundred feet above the valley. Few of the walls were straight; they traced convoluted routes that curved into loops, ovals, and ellipses, each made from granite blocks held in place without mortar. Punctuating these walls were other intricate structures—bastions, ramparts, and walkways—that indicated the sophistication of those who had constructed them. Within the whole complex of buildings, one enclosure alone stretched eight hundred feet along its circumference, tracing out a great ellipse. Its walls reached thirty-two feet high and seventeen feet across; the enclosure proved to be the largest prehistoric structure in sub-Saharan Africa. To Mauch, the city appeared a "mighty fortress." Perhaps it was more than this, too. The ramparts of the Great Enclosure—as it would come to be called—were massive and intimidating, but they were also elegant, with the top of the walls adorned with blocks in a double-chevron pattern, like the filigree of a crown. As the sun descended over the ruined city, an enraptured Mauch ended his investigation. The local Karanga called it "Zimbaoë," or "Zimbabwe." In his journal, Mauch noted, "No further information about the 'when' and 'how' could be obtained."[1]

Conical Tower at at Great Zimbabwe. Credit: Theodore Bent, *The Ruined Cities of Mashonaland*, 1892.

Mauch already knew—or thought he knew—the answers to the "when and how" of Zimbabwe: it had been built in antiquity by white conquerors from outside of Africa. "All are absolutely convinced that white people once inhabited the region, for even now there are signs of habitations and iron tools to be found which could not have been produced by the blacks. What became of this white population, whether it was chased away or killed, nobody can tell." This idea would become the basis of research on Great Zimbabwe for the next thirty years and would, simultaneously, anchor it to the new Hamitic hypothesis—one that now extended the Caucasian invasion of Egypt, Ethiopia, and East Africa to the velds of southern Africa. It would also tie together eclectic forms of data—biblical texts, sacred Vedas, African myths, comparative grammars, skull measurements, and eyewitness accounts—with ancient artifacts.[2]

Mauch's ideas about Great Zimbabwe, however, were formed long before he walked among the walls of the ruined city. For three hundred years, Europeans had written of a mysterious city in the African interior, one made wealthy by its gold mines. When Portuguese ships sailed around the Cape of Good Hope in the early 1500s, making their way toward the riches of India, they heard rumors of a wealthy kingdom called Mutapa. The Portuguese established the port of Sofala on the southeastern coast of Africa in 1505 in hopes of participating in (or at least intercepting) the kingdom's trade with the coast. In Sofala, Portuguese merchants learned about the African interior from Swahili Arabs who had traded the length of the long East African coast. From these reports, Diogo de Alcacova wrote in 1506 about the city of Zunbanhy, capital of the powerful Mwene Mutapa, where stone houses appeared "very large and on one level." Another Portuguese writer, Antonio Fernandes, wrote of interior fortresses made of stone without mortar. The most detailed description came thirty years later, from Joao de Barros, who identified a mysterious city named Symbaoe, located due west of Sofala, between twenty and twenty-one degrees south latitude (a position that corresponds accurately to Great Zimbabwe).[3] In his history of the Portuguese conquest, *Da Asia*, de Barros gives a detailed description:

> *These mines are the most ancient known in the country, and they are all in the plain, in the midst of which there is a square fortress, masonry within and without, built of stones of marvelous size, and there appears to be no mortar joining them. The wall is more than twenty-five spans in width, and the height is not so great considering the width.... The natives of the country call all these edifices Symbaoe, which according to their language signifies court, for every place where the Benomotapa may be is so called; and they say that being royal property all the king's other dwellings have this name.*[4]

As for the builders of the city, de Barros believed that they came from a northern homeland, above the equator or perhaps even out of Africa, since buildings appeared similar "to some which are found in the land of Prester John at a place called Acaxumo, which was a municipal city of the queen of Sheba, which Ptolemy calls Axuma." As described in the Hebrew Book of Kings, the Queen of Sheba was a rich sovereign living during the time of King Solomon. Her kingdom, many believed, was located on the Horn of Africa, near Abyssinia. In 1609, the Portuguese missionary Joao dos Santos, developed the link between

Symbaoe—a city still unseen by Europeans—and biblical figures in his book *Ethiopia Oriental*. He wrote that some believed that these houses were "a factory of the queen of Sheba, and that from this place a great quantity of gold was brought to her, it being conveyed down the rivers of Cuama to the Indian Ocean." Still, others, continued dos Santos, "say that these are the ruins of the factory of Solomon, where he had his factors who procured a great quantity of gold from these lands."[5]

These reports would link Solomon's gold mines to the African city of Symbaoe for the next three hundred years. The great atlas of Abraham Ortelius (1570) located Symbaoe inland of Sofala and also identified it as "the Ophir," the name of Solomon's mines in the Hebrew Bible. The name was adopted by mapmakers and geographers from England to Italy. Even John Milton's *Paradise Lost* (1667) referred to the Ophir of southern Africa. The idea of a gold mine founded by an ancient people from outside of Africa continued to be popular in the nineteenth century, particularly among the Boers of South Africa, who remained attached to the idea of African lands as connected to biblical history, in part because it justified their hold over large portions of it. It was from these European migrants to South Africa, particularly the German missionary Alexander Merensky, that Mauch learned of the fabled city of the "Far Interior," and with it, the theory of its construction by King Solomon or the Queen of Sheba. Already, in the months before he arrived at the ruins, Mauch was speaking about them in biblical terms. He excitedly confided to his diary that he was entering "the most mysterious part of Africa...the old Monomotapa or Ophir!"[6]

Mauch's enthusiasm would be tempered by the difficulties of reaching these fabled lands. After traveling from Germany to England, and then by ship from England to Natal, South Africa, he embarked on a number of expeditions in the late 1860s to the interior from the Transvaal, always pushing closer to the region described by the Portuguese as the "land of Symbaoe." In the end, he only just made it to the ruins.

As he had entered Mashonaland, he was set upon by robbers who took nearly everything he had, except for "a few beads and copper rings." Traveling alone, unable to speak the Shona language, and with nothing to trade, he found himself at the mercy of those he encountered. Happily, a local chief, Mapansule, took pity on him, giving him food and shelter. He also expected Mauch to stay with him, indeed insisted upon it. Mauch had no choice but to comply. Even had he been able to travel, his expedition was likely finished for the season; the monsoon rains would have begun in a matter of weeks and made travel across muddy trails and swollen rivers impossible.[7]

In the end he was liberated, somewhat improbably, by a fellow German. Adam Render had been living in the lands north of the Limpopo River, trading, hunting elephants, and residing with a Shona woman named Pika, the daughter of a neighboring chief. Seeing Mauch's plight, he offered his service as a translator, arranged his release, and helped him rebuild his supplies. Mauch was elated. This was the kind of reversal of fortune usually reserved for the heroes of Victorian novels. "The good Lord has guided me in a wonderful way," he wrote. Render also did his part. The elephant hunter had guided him to the prize, the object of his quest: the great ruined city that lay between the banks of the Limpopo and Zambesi Rivers.

Convinced that Great Zimbabwe had been built by Mediterranean invaders, Mauch found artifacts that seemed to confirm his theory. Burning a piece of wood from one of the fallen lintels, Mauch found that it smelled surprisingly like cedar. In this, it confirmed the account of Solomon's temple in the *Book of Kings*, which spoke of cedar wood being transported from the Ophir to help build it. (It turned out to be the local sandalwood, *Spirostachys Africana*.) He also found small iron triangles, connected by a short, curved iron stem. Mauch had no idea about its function—"its use was a complete riddle to me"—but the object seemed too advanced to have been manufactured by the Karanga. He wrote in his journal, "It proves that a civilized nation must once have lived here."[8]

Mauch sent his reports to the German geographer Augustus Petermann, who published them in his geography journal, *Geographischen Mittheilungen*, including Mauch's theory of Zimbabwe's "white inhabitants." One would have expected Mauch's discovery of a lost city in Africa, with claims that it represented a colony of King Solomon or the Queen of Sheba, to have caused a stir in the popular press. Instead, news of the discovery spread slowly in the late 1870s, limited to small-circulation journals focused on geography, antiquities, or biblical history, or in such publications as the *American Education Monthly* (New York), the *Sunday School Teacher* (London), and the *Ecclesiastical Observer* (London).[9]

The problem did not lie with Mauch's story—which possessed both drama and historical significance—but with Mauch himself. He lacked the social connections and scientific authority to promote his discovery, despite the fact that he had been preparing for the life of an explorer since the age of fifteen: reading about Africa, schooling himself in botany and geology, forcing himself to march six miles each day over rugged terrain without food or water. Through these trials, he wrote to Petermann, "I have tried to steel my body." Steeling the body served him well in Mashonaland, where he had to endure both bandits and malarial swamps. Yet, as it turned out, this was only half the journey, the easier half. The harder part was bringing the story of Zimbabwe to the world's attention. For this, he was ill prepared. All of Mauch's expeditions had been low-budget, go-it-alone affairs, relying on little public or private support. He possessed none of the institutional connections of military or scientific explorers—the massive expeditions to the Arctic, the Pacific, and the American West—that had become newsworthy for their size and expense even before they left port. For all of his physical vigor, then, Mauch lacked the most important skill of the nineteenth-century explorer: self-promotion.[10]

The significance of this becomes clear when one compares Stanley's activities during the same year. As Mauch arrived in Great Zimbabwe in September 1871, Stanley was a thousand miles to the north, slowly making his way across central Africa toward David Livingstone. While Mauch traveled alone, Stanley led a 100-strong party bankrolled by Bennett's *New York Herald*. When the stories of Mauch's discovery of Great Zimbabwe arrived in Europe and North American in 1872, they were eclipsed by Stanley's finding Livingstone. By the end of that year, Stanley had become the most famous explorer in the world. Mauch, sick with malaria and out of money, returned to Germany and obscurity. Unable to find work in academia or in a museum, he became the foreman in a cement factory in Blaubeuren. In April 1875, he fell out of his apartment window—possibly due to cerebral malaria that he had contracted in Africa—and fractured his skull. He died in a hospital shortly thereafter of his injuries. Following Mauch's death, his great discovery languished. As books celebrating Stanley and Livingstone arrived in bookstores, Great Zimbabwe remained unknown to all but a small community of scholars, geographers, missionaries, and Sunday school teachers.[11]

Zimbabwe's eventual rediscovery arrived through the actions not of an explorer or missionary but a British entrepreneur. In 1890, Cecil Rhodes—inspired by Mauch and others' reports of gold—essentially invaded Mashonaland with a "Pioneer Column," a force of five hundred soldiers and settlers traveling in wagons and on horseback. Ostensibly, Rhodes's force arrived with the permission of Lobengula, king of the Matabele. The king had signed a treaty with Rhodes's British South African Company, giving it "exclusive charge over all metals and minerals situated and contained within [his] kingdom." In practice, Rhodes's treaty served as a pretext for British rule. While Lobengula probably believed he had agreed to allow only a small number of prospectors into Mashonaland, Rhodes saw it differently. Miners required factories, settlements, infrastructure, and police. In the process, Mashonaland would become a colony, part of a chain of British colonies from Egypt to the southern tip of Africa, from Cairo to Cape Town. "All that shall be English," Rhodes declared to the press, "That is my dream." As the Pioneer Column passed by Great Zimbabwe, it established Fort Victoria and, later Fort Salisbury, where it raised the British flag. Mashonaland was now under British control, and Great Zimbabwe became accessible to European scientists.[12]

Archaeologists who followed in Mauch's footsteps also adopted his theory of foreign origin. When the British antiquarian and explorer James Theodore Bent set off across the Kalahari Desert with his wife and a team of assistants, he professed a healthy skepticism about the identity of Great Zimbabwe's founders. Bent had been invited to investigate the ruins by the Royal Geographical Society, the British Association for the Advancement of Science, and the British Chartered Company of South Africa. Once there, he expressed frustration with the number of European travelers arriving at the site—a steady stream of visitors who came up from the Transvaal to see the Ophir described in the Bible. "The names of King Solomon and the Queen of Sheba were on everybody's lips [and] have become so distasteful to use that we never expect to hear them again without an involuntary shudder."[13]

Still, if Bent expressed skepticism about the Solomon/Sheba theory, he had little doubt that Zimbabwe's founders were foreign to Africa. He had no experience with African ruins, and his training in archaeology came from working on sites in the Middle East and the Persian Gulf. Like Mauch, he found it difficult to believe that native Africans could have produced such complex architectural structures. His inclination to see evidence of outside influence was clear even before he saw Great Zimbabwe for the first time. On arriving in Mashonaland, he wrote that many of the inhabitants had "a distinctly Arab cast of countenance, and with their peculiar tufts on the top of their heads looked in profile like the figures one sees on Egyptian tombs." There was, he was convinced "a Semite drop of blood in their veins," though he acknowledged that its source would remain a mystery.[14]

Bent tried to make sense of this new world by comparing it to the one he knew, framing Mashonaland through the ancient cultures of the Middle East. From the sands of the Kalahari to the verdure of the veld, African landscapes were extensions of Arabian ones. "The dreams of the old Arabian story-tellers," Bent marveled, "here seem to have a reality." When his excavations at Great Zimbabwe turned up African rather than Arabian artifacts, then, he was disappointed. Digs at the Elliptical Building yielded nothing but evidence of longstanding "Kaffir occupation." He changed sites, moving up the ridge above the Elliptical Building to the "Hill Ruin," a long complex of buildings that he hoped "might possibly be free of Kaffir desecration." Yet here, too, he found artifacts that seemed consistent with local Karanga manufacture: pottery, spearheads, axes, and adzes.[15]

Eventually, and perhaps unsurprisingly, Bent found was he was looking for. At the top of columns he saw massive birds carved in soapstone that, he believed, resembled figures found at Assyrian, Phoenician, and Egyptian ruins. He found other traces that seemed to indicate non-African influence: monoliths with geometric pattering, a tall conical tower, and the floor plan of the Elliptical Building. Bent believed that the artifacts of Great Zimbabwe pointed to ancient founders outside of Africa. Yet exactly *who* they were wasn't clear.[16]

He began to see resemblances everywhere, and his theory of origin spiraled outward, embracing an ever-widening list of ancient cultures, beginning with Egyptian gold:

> *Where did [Ancient Egyptians] get the large supply of gold from, which they poured into Egypt and the then known world? In Mashonaland we seem to have a direct answer to this question. It would seem to be evident that a prehistoric race built the ruins in this country, a race like the mythical Pelasgi who inhabited the*

> shores of Greece and Asia Minor, a race like the mythical inhabitants of Great Britain and France who built Stonehenge and Carnac, a race which continued in possession down to the earliest dawnings of history, which provided gold for the merchants of Phoenicia and Arabia, and which eventually became influenced by and perhaps absorbed in the more powerful and wealthier organizations of the Semite.[17]

However far-fetched, Bent's attempt to link Great Zimbabwe with ancient cultures from Britain to Saudi Arabia grew out of an earnest attempt to explain how cultures change over time, and why some societies advanced more quickly than others. Any attempt at an answer revealed certain assumptions. First, it assumed that societies advanced rather than merely changed, that progress was a natural attribute of human societies over time. Second, it assumed that advancement could be measured, namely in fields of science, agriculture, and technology. Not surprisingly, these were fields where European culture excelled, particularly in the eighteenth and nineteenth centuries.

Scholars offered various answers. Auguste Comte, Edward Burnett Tylor, and Lewis Morgan embraced an "evolutionary" model of societal change. All societies, they argued, passed through similar stages of development—savagery, barbarism, and civilization—but independently and at different rates of speed. Evolution, as they imagined it here, was a cultural phenomenon rather than biological one, applying to societies rather than species. Human societies were like human children growing toward adulthood at their own individual pace. Europeans had hit their growth spurt early, according to their views, whereas other societies of the world lingered in a kind of protracted prepubescence. This was a chauvinistic vision of the world, to be sure, yet one that was also oddly affirming of human potential. If the civilizations of the world corresponded to rungs on a ladder according to their figurative developmental ages, no single one was stuck to a particular rung for eternity. Primitive societies would eventually ascend to the same height as European ones. They shared what the German ethnographer Adolf Bastian called a "psychic unity" (an idea that would later influence Carl Jung's "collective unconscious") with the other societies of the world and would mature, one day, into their cultural adulthood. It was an idea simultaneously both inclusive and exclusive, a psychic version of the curse of Ham, since it both embraced the principle of the commonality of humankind even as it ranked particular human groups higher or lower on a scale of civilization.[18]

Doubts about this model of social progress began to grow in the late nineteenth century, at least among some social commentators. While technological progress—from skyscrapers and steam-powered trains to electric lights—seemed undeniable, that progress had also opened Pandora's box of social ills: urban slums, pollution, contagious disease, and social unrest. They began to look wistfully at the pre-industrial past, a time when they imagined people lived pastoral lives in harmony with nature. At the same time, anthropologists such as Friedrich Ratzel and Fritz Graebner began to wonder whether all human societies were moving toward the same goal. As we've seen, the rise of polygenism—as pushed forward by Morton, Agassiz, and others—raised questions about the commonality of all human peoples. Did all racial groups really share the same "psychic unity"? If this were not the case, progress in most cultures was due not to some internal process of cultural evolution but to the transfer of culture from outside sources. Advanced societies spread art, science, and technology to less advanced ones through migration and conquest. Progress, in short, was not something that evolved but diffused.[19]

When James Bent noted similarity after similarity between Great Zimbabwe and the relics of other cultures, he was expressing his support for this "diffusionist" view of social progress. Indeed, his work at Great Zimbabwe, wrapped in this cocoon of diffusionist ideas, lent credibility to Mauch's theory that non-Africans had established an outpost in southern Africa in the distant past. European and North American newspapers covered Bent's expedition extensively, including his 1892 account of the expedition, *The Ruined Cities of Mashonaland*, in which he expressed his strong convictions about the foreign origins of Great Zimbabwe's builders. There were few skeptics in the press or scientific community. "[Bent] has proved beyond a doubt," wrote the *Sun* of New York, "that at a very early day this region was inhabited by a people who did not originate in Africa."[20]

The theory appealed to Cecil Rhodes. He had purchased artifacts from Mauch's 1871 expedition, and in 1889 obtained a soapstone bird from the South African hunter and trader Willi Posselt. Rhodes also obtained new artifacts, including a spear discovered during Bent's excavations. To investigate further, he traveled to Great Zimbabwe in September and October of 1891, shortly after Bent had completed his work. Walking through an enclosure that Bent had described as a temple, Rhodes's traveling companion, D. C. De Waal declared that "there can be left no doubt that the building had been erected by a white nation." Rhodes agreed. In a letter to the English newspaper editor William Thomas Stead during this period, Rhodes declared, "Zimbabye [*sic*] is an old Phoenician residence." His interest in the subject inspired him to sponsor more investigations into the Portuguese history of southern Africa. He underwrote Alexander Wilmot's *Monomotapa* (1896) and George McCall Theal's nine-volume *Records of South-Eastern Africa*.[21]

Theal's extensive work would make him South Africa's leading historian, and throughout his career he defended the foreign builder theory of Great Zimbabwe. When he wrote *Yellow and Dark-Skinned People of Africa South of the Zambesi* (1910), he devoted an entire chapter, "The Mystery of South Africa," to Great Zimbabwe, in which he argued that the city was founded by an ancient people from the Middle East. It seemed implausible to Theal that native Bantu tribes could have built such majestic structures. They were the products of a more sophisticated culture, one that constructed and then deserted them centuries later, leaving them to the childlike Bantu, who "learned nothing from the strangers, but remained as wild and savage as they were before."[22]

Rhodes's own interest in all this was of course never purely academic. He had made his fortune in South Africa from gold and diamond mining. He now extended these interests to Matabeleland and Mashonaland, granting the Rhodesia Ancient Ruins Ltd. rights to explore for treasure there in 1895. Over the next decade, a legion of do-it-yourself archaeologists inspired by Rhodes—including Henry Schlichter, John Willoughby, and Richard Hall—descended on the enclosures of Great Zimbabwe to dig for evidence about its ancient inhabitants. All of them adopted Bent and Mauch's theory of foreign origin. Because of this, they treated the archaeological deposits left by local Africans as recent "desecrations" of the original Arabian or Semitic site, digging and discarding layers of strata in the process. Richard Hall, whose position as curator of Great Zimbabwe charged him with protecting the ruins, dug up trees, vines, stones, and spoil heaps, removing deposits—up to twelve feet deep in some places—from the

Elliptical Building, Hill Ruins, and Valley Ruins, all in hopes of reaching the artifacts of the original founders. So extensive and casual were these removals of deposits that the British South Africa Company was eventually forced to intervene, removing Hall from his position in 1904.[23]

The damage was already done, however. Few deposits within the ruins lay unspoiled for later archaeologists. Those who questioned the foreign builder theory would have to work very hard to find new clues in the rubble heaps left by Hall and others. The amateurism of the archeology at Great Zimbabwe and the destruction of so many deposits would become a blot on archaeology. That this destruction was carried out to defend the thesis of a foreign invasion of Africa would also be remembered. Rhodesia represented the Wild West of southern Africa, the new frontier in the scramble for Africa.

Here, the new Hamitic hypothesis took root, as it had in Egypt and East Africa. Yet by the late nineteenth century, even supporters of the hypothesis acknowledged that it was grounded in flimsy soil. Evidence from shoddy archaeology and half-baked anthropometry did not seem sufficient to transform the idea from scripture to scientific theory. Not, at least, until Stanley's return to Gambaragara.

11

AT THE SUMMIT

TWELVE YEARS AFTER LEAVING EAST Africa, Henry Stanley saw Gambaragara again. As he stood on the grasslands at the edge of the Congo forest in May 1888, the mountain floated above the edge of horizon, "a peculiar shaped cloud of the most beautiful silver color." Stanley's final expedition to Africa would lead him to alter his story of "the white race of Gambaragara." He would see the mountain differently in 1888 than he had in 1875, viewing it from the Congo side rather than from East Africa. His change in perspective was not simply a matter of new coordinates. His ideas about Africans, race, and history were shifting as well. As a result, Gambaragara would come to represent something entirely new.[1]

Stanley had come back to Africa in 1887 not to visit Gambaragara but to rescue Emin Pasha, the embattled colonial governor of Equatoria, appointed in 1878 by the Khedive of Egypt as a replacement for the (assassinated) British general Charles George Gordon. In part due to his opposition to slavery, Emin had been threatened by a Muslim rebellion in central Sudan. Stanley's party steamed up the Congo River and then branched off to follow one of its tributaries, the Aruwimi River, which coiled its way west toward Lake Albert. As it did so, it traveled through the Ituri Forest, an almost impenetrably dense region of the eastern Congo. Leaving a force of men on the

At the Summit

Ruwezori Mountains as seen from by Stanley from the Congo, 1888.
Credit: Henry Morton Stanley, *In Darkest Africa*, 1891.

lower river at a settlement in Yambuya, Stanley took an advance column of 389 men into the forest. They groped their way along the Aruwimi, where vegetation rose fifty feet over the banks, kept in check only by the dense canopy of trees nearly two hundred feet above. Unable to hunt for game in the crowded brush and vines, prey to malarial fevers, attacked with poison arrows and stakes by fearful tribes, the party dwindled. Of the 389 who left Yambuya, only 147 remained with Stanley at the journey's end.[2]

It was on the Aruwimi River that Stanley found the darkest Africa that would become the title of his book and the image of the continent that would imprint itself into the minds of Europeans and Americans for generations to come: a twilight world cut off from the rest of the planet, a region where everything seemed to be fighting for its life. "Self, for the self; the devil take the weakest." For Stanley, the jungle was a Darwinian theater in which the feeble were culled: plants, animals, and explorers alike, "removing the unfit, the weakly, the unadaptable, as among humanity." Stanley and his men had been doing their part in this merciless process, shooting villagers to preempt attack, or to force passage through defended territory, or simply because Aruwimi villagers resisted the party's attempts to steal their food. The men of his rear column had acted even more brutally, killing local villagers and abusing their African porters. Ill-managed, underprovisioned, and beset by disease, the base camp of the rear column had become "a charnel house," as Stanley put it.[3]

It was with relief that Stanley's party emerged from the eastern edge of the forest. On the grasslands west of Lake Albert, the curtains of cloud and vapor finally broke to reveal the ice peaks—an inspiring sight after so many deadly months of travel. "Lo! a stupendous snowy mountain appeared, bearing 215 magnetic." Yet Stanley's search for Emin Pasha put him on a different bearing, in the direction of Lake Albert rather than southeast toward this snowy summit.

Meanwhile, Emin's situation was desperate. For three years, he had been fighting a losing battle against the Mahadiyya, an Islamic resistance movement that had spread like a brushfire through central Sudan. Led by the Mahdi, a devout Sudani cleric named Muhammad Ahmad, the Mahdists were wresting control of Sudan from its Egyptian and British occupiers. They began evicting Egyptian forces from the Upper Nile in the early 1880s. In 1883, they had defeated a force of four thousand soldiers at Al-Ubayyid as well as an eight-thousand-man relief force led by British commander William Hicks. In January 1885, Ahmad stunned the world by capturing Khartoum and killing Gordon, the British governor-general of Sudan. In seizing Khartoum, which lay at the convergence of the Blue and White Niles, the Mahdists had cut off British access to the Lakes Region from the north and stranded Emin in the southern outpost of Equatoria. Gambaragara would have to wait.

The economic consequences of the Mahdist rebellion as far as the English were concerned were minor. The Sudan offered neither significant commerce nor strategic position. Indeed, Gordon had intended to evacuate the British from Sudan shortly after arriving in 1885. Yet the symbolism of Gordon's defeat and death was more distressing: a native African movement had driven the British and its allies from the field. While the scramble for Africa had resulted in a massive colonial expansion among the European powers, it had also begun to foster native resistance, something that Britain, at least, had already encountered in India and China. Even in Buganda, where

Mutesa had accepted the presence of British missionaries, his successor, Mwanga, had killed British bishop Hannigan and dozens of Christian missionaries in a religious purge. Gordon's murder, therefore, was seen as an ominous harbinger: pointing out the vulnerability of Britain's colonial position.

Emin was now the lone symbol of British power in Equatoria. His letters, which trickled out of East Africa to Zanzibar, were reprinted in the daily papers and painted an increasingly dire picture. The Mahdist advance had forced him to retreat southward toward Lake Albert. "Help us quickly," he pleaded, "or we perish." As calls to save Emin grew in the House of Commons and the British press, William Mackinnon, a wealthy British philanthropist, organized the Emin Pasha Relief Fund and approached Stanley. Given that Stanley had found Livingstone, it followed that he could find Emin, particularly in a region that was smaller in size as well as closer to regions he had already explored. With funds from the Royal Geographical Society, the Egyptian government, and wealthy patrons like Mackinnon, Stanley headed off for Africa in 1887.[4]

Eventually Stanley reached Emin, but the meeting did not go as expected. It was hard to see how Stanley's now meager force, a shadow of its former size and strength, could rescue the Pasha from the Mahdists. More importantly, as it turned out, the governor was in no hurry to be rescued. Emin wanted weapons and ammunition to defend Equatoria, something that Stanley, his stores and munitions depleted, could not provide. Still, gradually recognizing that he had few options available to him if he stayed on Lake Albert, Emin finally agreed to continue with Stanley to the Zanzibar coast, and then on to Europe. Adding five hundred soldiers, servants, and officers to the party, Emin set off with Stanley south of Lake Albert, along the Semliki River, and into the heart of the mountains Stanley had seen from afar.[5]

From the valley of the Semliki, Stanley could finally study the great mountains that he had first glimpsed in 1875. Gambaragara was not a solitary peak, he now realized, but a long range of snow-capped mountains that stretched from Lake Albert to Lake Edward. The Bakonjo people who lived on the mountain's lower slopes called them "Ruwenzori" rather than "Gambaragara," the name that Ganda soldiers used for it on the eastern side of the mountains. As for the white-capped peak that Stanley saw in 1875, the one he had subsequently named Mount Gordon Bennett in honor of his employer, he believed that it lay on the far side of the mountains to the east, a lone sentinel to Africa's most massive range.[6]

Stanley did not have the time or the equipment to attempt a thorough exploration. Moreover, many of the men in his party, including Stanley himself, were still recovering from fever and in no condition to scale mountains. Still, he was not about to pass up the opportunity of reaching the mountains for a second time. Within the rainy, hothouse environment of the Semliki, Stanley moved through groves of thirty-foot tree ferns, wild banana plants, and carpets of lichen and moss. "I sounded the note to prepare to win immortal renown by scaling the heights of the famous Mountains of the Moon." On June 6, 1889, Emin and one of Stanley's men, William Stairs, gathered forty Zanzibaris to attempt an ascent of the range. The men left camp with two aneroid barometers and one thermometer. They used native paths for the first part of the ascent, where they saw circular huts constructed of bamboo. The lower slopes of the Ruwenzoris proved as fertile as the Semliki Valley: there were plantations of bananas, maize, and taro cultivated by the local Bakonjo. As the expedition moved beyond the highest Bakonjo settlements, the vegetation changed, the crops giving way to tall dracaenas, tree ferns, lichens, and the long tufts of lichen hanging from the trees called "old man's beard." By the end of day, the party had reached 8500 feet. The exertion of the ascent proved too much for Emin who headed back to Stanley's camp. The following day, Stairs reached an altitude of 10,677 feet. In the mist and dampness of the lower range, his porters had begun to suffer from cold. Realizing that he was not equipped to summit the peaks that were at least two miles distant, and which he estimated (accurately) to be about 16,600 feet, he turned back to Stanley's camp.[7]

When Stanley sailed to Europe from Zanzibar six months later, it was without Emin Pasha. Having survived the Mahdist insurgency, a coup attempt by his men, an ascent of the Ruwenzoris, and the long trek through East Africa, the Pasha had arrived in Bagamoyo on the African coast only to be seriously injured at a banquet held in his honor. At the port city of Bagamoyo, Emin toppled over the veranda wall, falling two stories to the street. While he recovered in a nearby hospital, Stanley headed home. His return to London created a sensation. He gave a lecture at Albert Hall before the largest crowd ever gathered for a Royal Geographical Society event: more than six thousand people, including the Prince and Princess of Wales and the Duke of Edinburgh. Stanley stood in front of a sixty-foot map of the Congo, illuminated by newly installed electric lights.[8]

Although Stanley did not summit Gambaragara, his survey of the Ruwenzoris helped him salvage something from his ill-fated expedition. He made the attempted ascent of the mountains a centerpiece of his Albert Hall lecture, connecting them to that particular obsession of Victorian explorers and geographers: the source of the Nile. In surveying the Ruwenzoris, Stanley declared, he had not only described the complete watershed of the White Nile, but finally confirmed the source to reside in the foothills of the Mountains of the Moon, the mythic peaks prophesied by ancient geographers. "What good has been derived from our late expedition?" Stanley asked rhetorically—a reasonable question that was being posed by the press as well, given the death toll of the expedition and the failure to rescue Emin Pasha. The answer was geographical. The expedition had explored the Aruwimi River and the Ituri Forest. Most importantly, it had revealed Gambaragara to be part of an ancient range of mountains that separated East Africa from the Congo. "You now know to its very fountain head those lofty Mountains of the Moon, which have been so anxiously sought for since Homer's time, have now been surveyed and located."[9] Stanley expanded this theme in his book *In Darkest Africa*. He devoted one chapter to the historical debates about the Mountains of the Moon, in which he lingered over their flora and fauna and speculated on their geologic formation in the ancient past. While the subject of the Ruwenzoris was never featured in any plans for the Emin Pasha rescue expedition, it now comprised three chapters of his book. Most telling were his impressions of the Ruwenzoris, which he describes as summits of

> *cold brightness and perfect peace, so high above mortal reach, so holily tranquil and restful, of such immaculate and stainless purity, that thought and desire of expression were altogether too deep for utterance. What stranger contrast could there be than our own nether world of torrid temperature, eternally green sappy plants, and never-fading luxuriance and verdure, with its*

savagery and war-alarms, and deep stains of blood-red sin, to that lofty mountain king, clad in its pure white raiment of snow, surrounded by myriads of dark mountains, low as bending worshippers before the throne of a monarch, on whose cold white face were inscribed "Infinity and Everlasting!"[10]

Stanley's description of the Ruwenzoris sounds melodramatic to our ears, but it fit within the conventions of nineteenth-century writing. For a century, romantic painters and poets had sought to capture the emotional power of nature, and mountains in particular had become the ultimate catalysts for the sublime, a portal to intense experiences not found in quotidian life. To Stanley, who endured a bloody phantasmagoria of violence and desperation, the mountains offered something else: quiet, solitude, simplicity. Contemplating the empty, shining peaks only a few miles distant, he could briefly forget the pall of "blood-red sin" that had descended over his expedition like a shroud.

Neither his RGS lecture nor *In Darkest Africa* makes any mention of the pale-faced inhabitants, the people who had so provoked his interest in the late 1870s, and whom he had discussed only four years before with the journalist David Ker. Absent were the stories of the white tribe who tended cattle and ate bananas, living on the shores of a crater lake at the summit of the mist-shrouded mountain. One reason for this omission could be that he now had more precise information about the mountains. Stairs had reported that African settlements ended below ten thousand feet. The upper reaches, with their jagged rock and fields of ice, appeared too frigid to be inhabited.

Yet Stanley had not banished white Africans from his discussion of Africa; he had merely relocated them to lower altitudes. Only a few weeks after Stairs's survey of the Ruwenzoris, Stanley wrote of a Bakonjo chief named Bevwa who mistook Stanley and his men for members of the Wanyavingi, a Rwandan tribe that shared the same features as the European explorers. "What, are they white people like us?" Stanley had asked. Bevwa replied that they were "Tall big men, with long noses and a pale colour, who came, as I heard from our old men, from somewhere beyond Ruwenzori, and you came from that direction; therefore you must be of the Wanyavingi."[11]

Bevwa's story of the Wanyavingi echoed other reports that Stanley had heard, particularly those from Mukamba, chief of the Uzige, who had told Stanley and Livingstone that a race of white Africans lived in Rwanda north of Lake Tanganyika, which corresponded to Stanley's own encounters farther north with light-skinned Africans of Mutesa's court on Lake Victoria. He had written at length about these encounters, as noted earlier, in his press reports in 1876 and his book *Through the Dark Continent.*

Despite the disappearance of the white Gambaragarans from Stanley's account of the Ruwenzoris, he was rapidly expanding the range of Hamitic Africa, placing other clans within this demographic umbrella. Along with the Bachwezi and the Batutsi of East Africa, he now added members of the Balegga and Bavira clans of Congo. Together, these peoples comprised the "Wahuma" who, despite their broad dispersal across the forests and mountains of Equatorial Africa, shared similarities of foreign origin: Caucasian features and a complexion that approximated "the colour of yellow ivory."[12]

Stanley's account of the Ruwenzoris inspired others. Between 1889 and 1906, seventeen more expeditions set off to the climb the mountains, extending the mark of 10,677 feet set by Stairs and Emin, and edging ever closer to the summit. They extended beyond the Stairs survey in other ways, too, collecting detailed information about the mountains' spectacular flora and fauna—its towering lobelias, roaming elephants, yowling rock hyraxes—as well as its sloping ice fields and stark geology that characterized the range above 14,000 feet. And they confirmed, implicitly, what Stanley had surmised in 1889 when he had gazed up at the peaks from the Semliki Valley a few miles distant: the peaks of the Ruwenzoris were uninhabited, a world of rocks, ice, and mist.

Even so, these expeditions confirmed Stanley's anthropological findings, too, particularly about the existence of Hamitic Africans. As they made their way toward the mountains through the kingdoms of East Africa and Congo, they tended to rely on the racial theory of Hamitic invaders. As Harry Johnston, high commissioner of the Uganda Protectorate, trekked toward the mountains on his own attempt in 1900, he described the Bankole people as a combination of "sturdy negro" farmers and an aristocracy of "Hamitic stock." "I have seen some men and women so light in complexion that I actually thought they were of Emin Pasha's refugee Egyptians," he wrote in a 1902 essay in the *Geographical Journal*, "until it was proved to me that they had been born and bred in Ankole. These people, no doubt, are the

The Ruwenzoris. Photographed by Vittorio Sella of the Duke of Abruzzi's 1906 Expedition. Credit: *Ruwenzori: An Account of the Expedition of H. R. H. Prince Luigi Amedeo of Savoy*, 1909.

origin of many of the legends of a white race dwelling in Equatorial Africa.[13]

Moreover, there were other reports of white tribes in the 1880s and 1890s. Serpa Pinto, a Portuguese explorer of Southern Africa, returned with his own account of a Central African race that was "whiter than Caucasians." Zebehr Pasha, who served with Gordon in the 1880s, reported a variety of "white races" living in the slave country of Central Africa. In West Africa, Captain Larrymore, adjutant of the Gold Coast Constabulary, described the existence of white tribes in the interior. All of these stories were reported widely in the press, with some newspapers weighing in with their own analysis of Africa's racial geography. "South of Timbuctoo and north of Kong mountains, in the western part of Africa, live the Foolahs, the white tribe of the Dark Continent," reported the *Juniata Sentinel and Republican* of Pennsylvania. "This tribe has good features, a skull modeled like that of a white man, and a complexion about as dark as that of the Italians."[14]

As this race to summit the Ruwenzoris heated up, Stanley was slowing down. He turned fifty-nine in 1900. White-haired and portly, he no longer resembled the "Bula Mutari" who by sheer force of will had driven his men through the interior of Congo. Thousands of miles of travel, and along the way malarial fevers and intestinal maladies, had taken their toll. Bouts of gastritis left him bedridden for months at a time. So excruciating were these attacks that his wife, Dorothy, gave him morphine injections.

There were other kinds of pain that couldn't be so treated. By 1900 Stanley had come under attack for the bloody toll of his expeditions through Africa. Even his work in Congo, undertaken as a humanitarian effort for King Leopold of Belgium, now appeared to have assisted the king in Africa's most brutal European occupation. No wonder then that Stanley seemed ready to leave Africa behind and embrace domestic life. He bought and renovated a new home in Surry, forty minutes outside of London and a world apart from the rolling hills of East Africa.[15]

Nonetheless, Africa was never far from his mind. He never again wrote about Gambaragara or the Ruwenzoris, but there is ample evidence that the mystery of racial origins in Africa continued to occupy his thoughts. One of the last articles he ever wrote was an essay in the *North American Review*, "The Origin of the Negro Race," which drew on many of the ideas he had developed since the 1870s, when he first encountered light-skinned Africans and began thinking in earnest about the subject. The article offered in a more detailed fashion the elements of the Hamitic hypothesis that he had described in 1890 in his lecture before the Royal Geographical Society. Central Asia represented the cradle of humankind, and a wave of Caucasian invaders had occupied Africa in the past, moving through Egypt and Ethiopia en route to the highlands of the Lakes Region. These light-skinned foreigners still occupied parts of Africa, such as seen on the high slopes of Gambaragara or among the ruling classes of the East African highlands, including the Wahuma, Watutsi, and the Nyamwezi. Indigenous Africans had fled south and west before the white invaders, occupying regions of Congo and southern Africa, or becoming the peasant classes within the Caucasian Hamite kingdoms of the Lakes Region.

Yet Stanley's thinking had shifted in important ways by 1900. The story of Africa's settlement, he realized, required a longer period of time than he had once thought in 1875. When he first encountered Mutesa and the people of the Lakes Region, he had perceived them through the framework of scriptural history, not only the Bible's description of the curse of Ham but its short chronology for human origins and settlement. To view history this way was to accept that all of the world's civilizations, historical migrations, and technological advancements had taken place within a six-thousand-year window from Creation to the present.

The biblical time frame was even shorter. As calculated by the genealogies of Genesis 5, at least one thousand years separated Creation from the repopulation of the world after the Flood. The story of Africa—its pygmies, Bushmen, Bantus, and Hamites; its thousands of languages; its prehistoric architecture of pyramids and granite-coursed cities—would have had to unfold within a four-thousand-year span. And for some regions the time frame was tighter even still. The jagged, twisted scarps and smoldering volcanoes of the rift valley suggested a recent history of cataclysms, convincing Stanley that this region of East Africa supported human life only recently. During his 1871 trip, on his way west toward Gambaragara, he had looked out at these fantastic landscapes from a grassy hill in Bunyoro and imagined their creation in a moment of terrestrial violence. From this he concluded, "The earliest traditions of its inhabitants do not date more than a few centuries back." As a younger man, Stanley had accepted this. (In the 1870s, angry at Europeans who belittled Africans for their backwardness, Stanley retorted, "It has taken 60 centuries for the boasted European descendant of Adam to invent the sewing machine!")

The more mature "Origin of the Negro Race" shows that Stanley's thinking about scale of history had changed, and with it, the authority of the Bible in explaining the origins of African peoples. His change of mind did not occur spontaneously; it recapitulated a broader shift in thinking among Victorian scientists who sought naturalistic explanations for events. Neither Stanley nor indeed most scientists went so far as to renounce God. The labor of the Divine Creator was invoked at the outset of creation, assembling the great clockworks of the universe and setting them in motion. Mountain ranges, canyons, long-necked giraffes, hummingbirds, and even the marvels of human difference—hues of skin, ranges of height, shapes of skull—might be explained naturally, if only the scale of history was made long enough. Stanley no longer believed that the Ruwenzoris had been produced in some geological apocalypse of recent date. "A hoary old mountain like this of Ruwenzori," he wrote, "we know to be countless thousands of years old."[16]

"The Origin of the Negro Race" cites not biblical events, but instead the work of Victorian naturalists, ethnographers, and linguists. It describes the Aryan conquest of Egypt in the ancient past, and then the gradual expansion of their dominion over East Africa. Citing the work of Egyptologist Flinders Petrie, Stanley claimed, "When the Aryans finally extended their conquests to Egypt, we may reasonably suppose that, however few or many of the primitive people had already started on their wanderings into unknown Africa, the shock of the Aryan advent must have then given those remaining a stronger impulse to scatter inland."[17]

The survey of the African interior began in earnest in the mid-1800s and was almost complete by 1900, approximately the same time that Americans finished their surveys of the American West. With the closing of the African frontier, the continent had few remaining regions in which white tribes might dwell undisturbed and undiscovered. Stanley himself had abandoned the idea of a light-skinned race on Gambaragara, and so too did the explorers and missionaries who followed him into East Africa. When Prince Luigi Amedeo, the duke of Abruzzi, summited Gambaragara in 1906, only two years after Stanley's death, he honored the explorer by renaming the mountain Mount Stanley. Standing on its glacial summit, the Italian prince confirmed Stanley's vision of the mountain as uninhabited, yet flanked by people of Hamitic origin. "There are many natives here of the Bahima tribe. These are handsome people, alleged to be of Ethiopian origin, tall of stature, slender of figure, with finely proportioned limbs, a somewhat lighter colour than the Baganda, and regular features similar to those of the white races."[18]

Abruzzi's ascent of the Ruwenzoris symbolically signaled the closing of the African frontier, yet the idea that white Africans existed continued to thrive. The difference was that they could be found in plain sight. A century of race science and African ethnography had given Europeans a number of names for describing these Africans who were supposedly of foreign descent: Caucasian, Aryan, Hamitic, Abyssinian, Galla, and Wahuma. Each term carried its own, special connotations. Yet regardless of the terminology used, the story followed the same broad outlines proposed by Samuel Morton, George Gliddon, and John Speke decades earlier: all were the progeny of ancient invaders from the Middle East who had conquered Abyssinia and then moved into East Africa, sometimes intermarrying with black Africans, sometimes driving them out, and sometimes ruling over them as a racially separate royal class.

Stanley arrived in Africa during a time when European explorers looked to solve the world's most compelling geographical mystery—the ultimate source of the Nile. In the process Stanley had discovered a riddle that continued to stir scientists and lecture goers until late in the century. Yet, in the process of solving the mystery of the white tribe of Gambaragara, it had become bigger. It has grown from a search to identify a tribe living on a mountain to a mission to identify a lost race. After Stanley it would become greater still: a search for the essence of whiteness itself.

PART II

A WORLD GONE WHITE

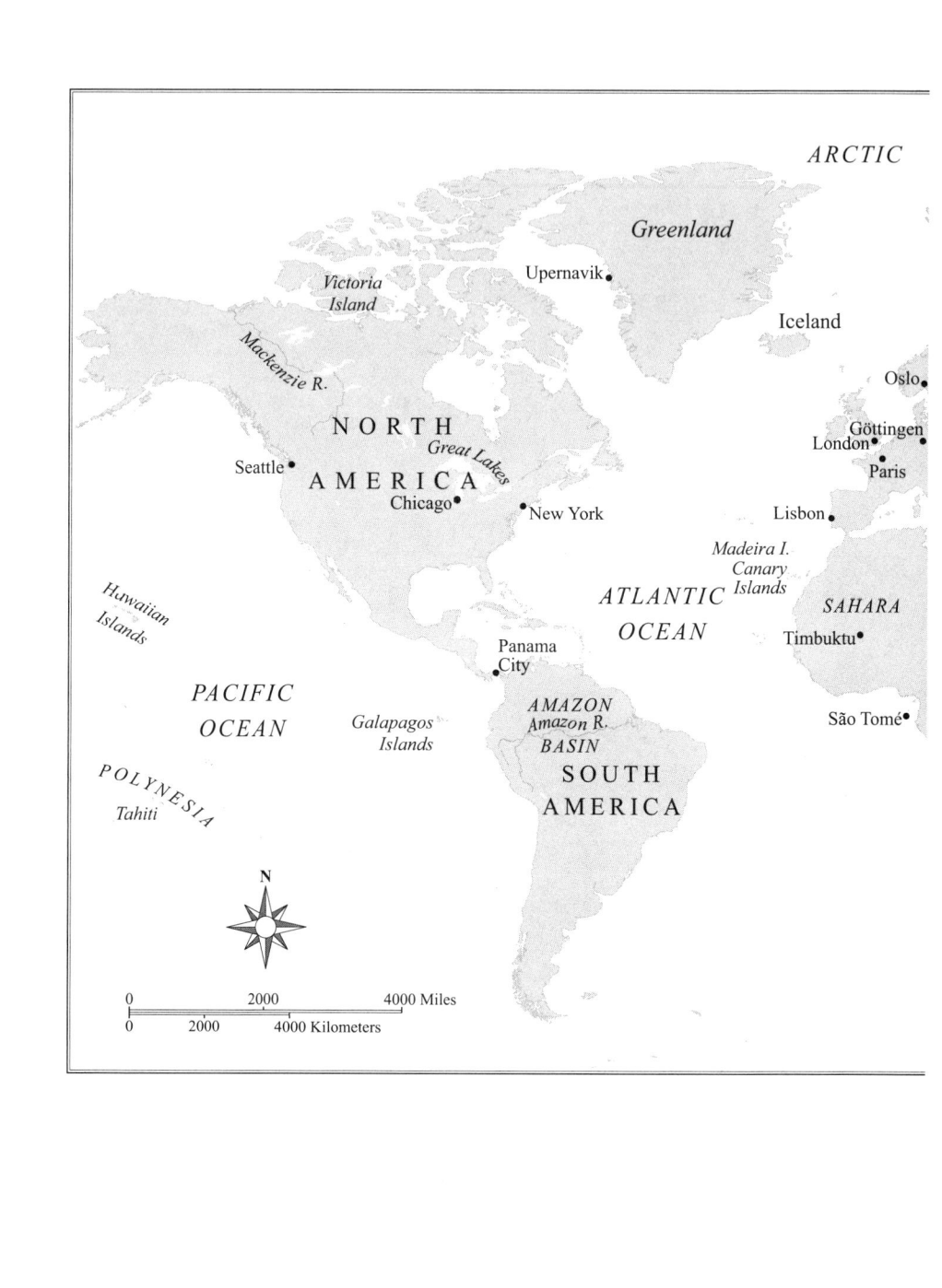

Map

OCEAN

Lapland

ASIA

• Moscow

• Berlin
EUROPE
Aral Sea
Tarim Basin

• Rome
Caucasus
Mt. ▲ Ararat
• Baghdad
Tibetan Plateau
Japan

• Cairo
New Delhi •
INDIA • Krishnangar
PACIFIC OCEAN

DESERT
• Mecca
Indus Delta
Kolkata
Ganges Delta

• Khartoum
Philippines

AFRICA

• Kampala
• Nairobi
• Boma • Ujiji • Zanzibar
INDIAN OCEAN

Malay Archapelago

Zambezi River
✧ **Great Zimbabwe**

AUSTRALIA

• Maputo

• Cape Town

New Zealand

12

THE DYNASTIC RACE

OVER THE COURSE OF HIS expeditions to Egypt, British archaeologist Flinders Petrie developed his own "invasion theory" about Egyptian civilization. In a 1906 book titled *Migrations*, Petrie posited that prehistoric Egypt was a region populated by an indigenous race of Africans. Seven thousand years ago, a new race entered the Nile Valley from outside of Africa, taking control of the region and developing the sophisticated culture that produced hieroglyphics and pyramids. Faced with this invasion of a more advanced race, much of the indigenous population took flight southward. Those who remained behind eventually intermarried with the foreign invaders, giving rise to a new "amalgamated" race. Petrie's "dynastic race" theory closely resembled the new version of the Hamitic hypothesis put forward by Samuel Morton, George Gliddon, and others: "It may not be unreasonable to see in this the last remains of the paleolithic man of Egypt, whom we can thus restore to view as a steatopygous and hairy Bushman....An entirely different people succeeded these, of European type, tall, slender, pale, with long brown wavy hair."[1]

What made Petrie's dynastic race theory different from earlier incarnations, however, was the methods he used to prove it. When he dated this invasion to a "predynastic period" seven thousand years ago, he did so by careful examination of burial sites in the Nile valley south of Cairo. Within the physical environment of each grave, Petrie posited, were clues about the identity of the deceased as well as how and when they lived. "Very few Europeans in Egypt, and still fewer natives," he wrote, "would think of spending the needful time to secure details before they are lost in working." In this way, Petrie advanced the new Hamitic hypothesis by attaching it more closely to current methods of scientific analysis.[2]

When Petrie first came to Egypt as a young man the early 1880s, it was because of an interest in architecture rather than race. He was particularly fascinated in the construction of the great pyramids in Giza. His early work on them eventually led him to a smaller and lesser known pyramid at Meidum, located forty miles from Cairo. Unlike the solid, imperturbable Giza pyramids, the Meidum pyramid bore the marks of an ancient catastrophe. Its blocky core rose up out of a massive pile of casing stones and debris. Petrie postulated that Meidum might represent the first attempt to produce a smooth pyramid—as opposed to older ziggurat-like step pyramids—an early version of the great pyramids at Giza. If so, the site might offer a window into Egypt civilization at this moment of early transition from boxlike

The broken pyramid of Meidum.

mastabas to more sophisticated forms. Maybe it would reveal, too, something about the evolution of ancient Egyptian society toward its cultural zenith. For Petrie, the structural failure of the pyramid was also its promise, the allure of Meidum. From Meidum, he wondered, "Could we learn how conventional forms and ideas had arisen? Could we find Egypt not yet full grown, still in its childhood?" At stake in this question was more than an esoteric chronology of Egyptian civilization. Understanding Egypt's early period promised to reveal its parentage—whether indigenous to Africa or imported from some other source. In this sense, Petrie pursued a question that would have been of interest to Blumenbach, Morton, and Gliddon as well.[3]

For weeks in 1891, Petrie's team of Egyptian laborers removed casement stones and rubble from the massive debris field of the Meidum pyramid. When the outlines of the funerary temple were revealed, Petrie was elated. The rubble had protected the temple from the corrosive effects of wind and weather as well as the predations of tomb robbers and Egyptian quarrymen. "Nothing seemed to have been disturbed or injured throughout the whole length of recorded history. Here stands the oldest known building in the world as perfect, except for slight weathering, as it was when even Egypt was bare of monuments."[4]

The structures of the temple—roof, stelae, and altar—were in excellent condition. Working for months at this massive twenty-acre excavation site, carefully measuring the structures of the pyramid and temple, Petrie pieced together the methods of its construction. Meidum seemed to have been built before the great pyramids, during the reign of the Pharoah Seneferu, first king of the Fourth Dynasty (2613–2589 BCE). It did appear to be a transitional form, a tomb of stacked mastabas that workers had attempted to convert into a smooth, angled surface before it had collapsed. Later, those who constructed the pyramids at Giza would abandon this middle step of stacking mastabas, building the smooth, angled pyramids without this transitional stage.

Yet Petrie's most important discovery, in his view, came not from the pyramid itself, but from the older mastabas that surrounded the site. Here lay dozens of tombs of varying age. Older tombs, those dating from before the dynastic period, contained square boxes inside of which were skeletons curled in the fetal position, often wrapped in a small kilt or girdle of plain linen. The graves contained no food vessels or other objects. By contrast, the graves of the dynastic period contained bodies that were mummified, laid out straight within their coffins and surrounded by objects and adornments. Petrie also thought he detected physical differences between the predynastic and dynastic skeletons. "Here is clearly a total difference in beliefs, and probably in race. We know that two races, the aquiline-nosed and the snouty, can be distinguished in early times; and it seems that the aborigines used the contracted burial, and the dynastic race the extended burial."[5]

Petrie's idea of a foreign "dynastic race" pushed back the settlement of ancient Egypt to at least seven thousand years. His dating troubled those scholars who had hoped to keep the settlement of Egypt within timeframe allowed by the Hebrew Bible. Nonetheless, the idea of the dynastic race itself, the result of a Caucasian invasion of Africa during prehistoric times, would have been accepted by Hamitic hypothesis believers, including Blumenbach, Augustus Granville, or Morton, all of whom put forward similar ideas. Like Petrie, these scholars had supported their ideas by combining evidence from ancient artwork, hieroglyphics, and human remains.

However much his race conclusions buttressed an old idea, Petrie's attention to the details represented a new kind of archaeology—one that valued the context of the site as much as the quest for the artifact. In his decade of excavation work, between 1881 and 1891, Petrie had constantly been confronted with the blundering, careless work of earlier archaeologists, who ruined sites in their pursuit of precious objects. Petrie's careful work at Meidum represented an entirely different approach to the archaeology pursued at Great Zimbabwe, where Theodore Bent (and soon Richard Hall) was digging pell-mell through archaeological deposits, tossing out objects of "Kaffir desecration." While Petrie shared Bent's belief that Africa's great civilizations were the product of Caucasoid invaders from the Middle East, he intended to prove it through more careful methods than ones used in Egypt and sites farther south in Africa. "A beginner is vastly disappointed that some great prize does not turn up after a week or two of work; while all the time he is probably not noticing or thinking about material for historical results that is lying before him all the time."[6]

None of the early proponents of a Caucasian invasion of Egypt made much use of evidence from excavation sites. Blumenbach and Granville had done their mummy investigations in London. Morton and Gliddon had done theirs in Philadelphia. Because these remains were often purchased from antiquity dealers and grave robbers, their provenance could not be verified, making them questionable as sources of evidence. Petrie, on the other hand, was able to connect human remains to other materials found at the grave site, such as pottery, ornaments, and hieroglyphics, which helped locate the deceased in culture and time.

Petrie's dynastic race theory was taken seriously also because it seemed to be built on an impressive collection of data. Blumenbach and Granville's ideas about the race of ancient Egyptians had relied on the examination of a handful of mummies. Morton's and Gliddon's relied on the measurement of 137 Egyptian skulls. By comparison, Petrie drew upon the measurements of thousands of skulls, skeletons, and mummified remains. In 1887, he excavated so many mummies from one site, the Hawara Pyramid, that he could only preserve the skulls for anthropometric measurement. As the headless corpses began piling up around the campsite, they were used as benches for local boys. Soon Petrie's tent was completely surrounded. His workspace, like his theories of race, had become a landscape of bodies.[7]

Petrie put to these remains an increasingly sophisticated battery of anthropometric measurements. While Morton and his colleagues had based their conclusions on a number of craniometrical measurements, such as skull volume and facial angle, they had also believed that the differences among the races, particularly in skull shape and size, would simply reveal themselves. Yet, as we've seen, Morton's confident conclusions contrasted with his rather tentative typology of individual skulls, with labels such as "Egypto-Pelasgic form," "Austral-Egyptian," "Egyptian blended with Negroid?" Those skulls that did not fit the ideal racial forms he explained away as the result of interbreeding between races.[8]

Ambiguities of racial classification could be eliminated, Petrie believed, by narrowing the focus of measurements. The shape of the head and the volume of a skull depended on a number of different bones, each of which could vary independently of the others. He thought it "better to study single bones where there is only one factor of change." Understanding Egypt's history of invasions required an analysis of specific skull features and individual bone measurements—nasi-alveolar height, skull curvature, bizygomatic and biauracular widths—and then tracking how these measurements changed in populations over time.

From these more narrowly focused measurements, he believed, the true origin of the dynastic race would be revealed.⁹

Petrie's push to find progressively more precise anthropometric measurements reflected rising support for the field of race science at the beginning of the twentieth century. This new appreciation of the field represented the view that race was not only measurable, but meaningful: a biological category that was key to understanding humanity's past. Optimism in race as a scientific concept grew after Charles Darwin's publication of *On the Origin of Species* in 1859. *Origin* carefully avoided the subject of human evolution because Darwin feared the controversy that it would raise. His allies, however, eagerly applied his arguments to the question of human evolution; the next decade saw a number of books on the subject by Charles Lyell, Alfred Russell Wallace, and Thomas Huxley. Eventually Darwin, too, decided to weigh in, presenting the evidence for human evolution in *The Descent of Man* (1871).

Darwin's work gave inspiration to race scientists, largely because he confirmed the importance of heredity in explaining human difference. Races were not produced by the environment acting directly on the individual. Migrating to the desert might cause one's skin to darken, but would not, by itself, make one's offspring darker. It was this notion of "soft heredity," also known as the inheritance of acquired characteristics, that Buffon and Blumenbach believed could explain the emergence of different races over a few dozen generations. By contrast, Darwin introduced the idea of "hard heredity." Climate and living conditions were important within the Darwinian system, too, but only because they created selective pressures upon heritable traits. By affirming the importance of heredity, Darwin inspired a growing number of scientists and policymakers who believed that nature (which included racial inheritance)—not nurture—was the most important factor in an individual's life.

Moreover, Darwinian theory gave Petrie and other scientists interested in race a new way of explaining the progress of civilization. Darwin's vision of the natural world, as depicted in *Origin*, was no Garden of Eden. It was a global coliseum, where violent contests for existence played out over and over again. Some of these contests involved competition between species, pitting predator against prey. Most, though, took place within species, as individuals battled with one another for limited natural resources. While death sometimes arrived

The Dynastic Race
143

from the embrace of predators, greater numbers came from combat with one's friends and neighbors. As certain individuals gained the upper hand, outliving and out-reproducing others of their kind, they expanded in number and geographical range. In short, evolutionary change arrived in the form of conquest, in which the fit were continually annexing the habitats and resources of the less fit.

In a nineteenth-century world where pale-skinned Europeans and their colonial kin were rapidly annexing the lands and resources of darker-skinned peopled, the idea that conquest represented a form of progress, an inexorable process of nature in which superior forms overtook inferior ones, took hold. It would come to be called social Darwinism, though it was, in fairness to Darwin, an idea that existed long before he penned *Origin*. Thomas Hobbes, Edward Gibbon, and Thomas Malthus had all written about competition and conquest as features of social progress. In truth, Darwin resisted a simplistic application of natural selection to human society. Just because competition ruled nature did not mean that it also ruled—or should rule—human ethics. To the contrary, advanced civilizations were those in which "sympathies becom[e] more tender and more widely diffused," Darwin argued, "until they are extended to all sentient beings."[10] Still, the practical effect of *Origin* was to give greater currency to race science and the idea of race conquest. When Petrie and others found evidence of new patterns of artwork, tools, or other novelties in their digs, they were inclined to see it as proof of outside influences, the extension of stronger races and their superior capacities.

Yet, for all of the inspiration (and misapplication) of Darwin's ideas to race science, his theories also raised problems for scholars like Petrie because they effectively eroded the very concept of race. For Morton and other polygenists, races were fixed types, the blueprints of the human varieties ordained by God (or in Ham's case, by a curse). In a Darwinian world, however, race was not a fixed thing but a fluid category, one defined by populations of heterogeneous individuals. Natural selection, after all, worked only when individuals were different enough to allow nature to select winners and losers. There was no original pair of organisms for each species in the Darwinian world, no Adam and Eve progenitors who would serve as representatives of the ideal type. Instead, species existed as populations of organisms with varying traits among whose members nature selected those that were most "fit." By extension, varieties within a species—or, as they were known within the human species, "races"—also revealed a heterogeneous collection of traits. Within any racial type, one found a range of hair textures, skin colors, and skull shapes. These traits were not anomalies, superfluous elements that strayed from some ancestral ideal. In Darwin's universe, they were the raw material of evolution, the heritable differences upon which nature acted to select its winners and losers. Darwin's work had suggested that race was a moving target, one that could not be uncovered by comparing individuals to a description of "Hamite," "Negro," or "Caucasian." These terms were abstractions rather than timeless categories, ones that could not be gleaned from measuring facial indexes or pouring lead shot into skulls.

Race scientists found support, however, in the work of Francis Galton. Galton spent much of his adult life in the 1860s and 1870s thinking about the issue of human heredity, having been deeply moved by his cousin Charles's publication of *Origin of Species* in 1859: "[It] made a marked epoch in my own mental development," he wrote in 1908. "Its effect was to demolish a multitude of dogmatic barriers by a single stroke." Galton shared Darwin's shyness of groups, love of the outdoors, and wide-ranging interests in science, yet he took a greater interest in mathematics, particularly statistics. Sometimes this interest bordered on the obsessive. A nervous breakdown while a student at Cambridge prevented him from achieving honors in his mathematics degree. A more severe breakdown followed in 1866. Even in quieter moments, when he appeared fine to others, his thoughts looped. "I frequently suffered from giddiness and other maladies prejudicial to mental effort.... Those who have not suffered from mental breakdown can hardly realize the incapacity it causes...small problems...obsessed me day and night, as I tried in vain to think them out."[11]

In spite, or perhaps because, of these "maladies," Galton worked out new methods that he believed salvaged some concept of race as a scientific certainty, placing it on the foundation of statistics rather than types, a field that came to be known as "biometry." Analyzed in large numbers, anthropometric measurements could be used to establish race based on the frequency with which traits appeared in a particular population. In the opening issue of the journal he founded titled *Biometrika*, Galton explained that "in order that any process of Natural Selection may begin among a race, or species, is the existence of differences among its members; and the first step in an enquiry into the possible effect of a selective process upon any character of a race must be an estimate of the frequency with which individuals, exhibiting any degree of abnormality with respect to that character, occur."[12]

As Petrie was working through his dynastic race theory a decade or so later, he found inspiration in Galtonian thinking about race. Petrie applied statistics to the anthropometric measurements of mummies and skeletons from different dynasties. His proof that the dynastic race represented an invasion of non-Africans into the Nile valley is shown not by illustrations of a particular skull or series of skulls, as Morton would have done, but by a series of graphs demonstrating the bell-curve distribution of particular traits, and how those traits changed over time.

The association between Petrie and Galton was more than intellectual. In 1886, Petrie began to collaborate with Galton on a historical study of race, taking photographs of ancient Egyptian artwork, hoping to "type" original racial populations before they had intermixed. Petrie learned statistical techniques from Galton, and Galton in turn benefited from Petrie's access to ancient human remains. Galton's eugenic laboratory at University College London received thousands of human remains from Petrie, a collection that would become vital to the work of race scientists in the twentieth century.[13]

Galton's interest in Petrie's work was not based solely upon the Egyptologist's work on dynastic race theory or his documentation of early racial types. Galton himself had traveled to Egypt and Sudan as a young man, and with the assistance of the Royal Geographical Society, made an expedition into South West Africa. His interests in exploration were so strong that he published a book for would-be explorers called *The Art of Travel*. Becoming a member of the RGS Council, Galton had communicated with Richard Burton and John Speke and had written up the instructions for Burton, to assist in his expedition in search of the Mountains of the Moon. Indeed, Galton at one point had been asked by the RGS to lead his own expedition in search of the mysterious mountains of the interior—perhaps he could have seen the Wahuma and the Gambaragarans with his own eyes. This never happened. As it stood, he recognized the power of Petrie's work to the history of civilization, one based on the power of race. And he also must have recognized—as a key player in East African exploration—that such efforts might lead to a broader theory of racial conquest in Africa.

This broader theory was already being pieced together. By 1900, the Hamitic invasion of Africa was becoming part of a larger story of prehistoric racial conquest, one in which Gambaragara, Great Zimbabwe, and Meidum represented a single branch of a massive, prehistoric "Aryan invasion" out of Asia. The grand narrative of this invasion, its scope and central storyline, was being established not by archaeology or anthropology but by linguistics.

13

THE ARYAN TIDAL WAVE

FIFTY YEARS BEFORE "ARYANISM" BECAME a fixation for Nazi leaders in Germany, it was already being used as a racial category all over the world. Europeans applied it frequently to native peoples from the mountains of Persia to the shores of Peru, populations not commonly associated with the fair-haired, blue-eyed Nordic who came to define the Aryan ideal in the 1930s. The rise of the Aryan "type"—as well as its association with peoples far from Europe—grew mainly from the work of Friedrich Max Müller, a German Orientalist who spent most of his career as a professor at Oxford.

Max Müller was an unlikely father for such a theory. He was interested in language, not race, and his studies focused on India rather than Europe. Born from his linguistic study of Sanskrit, the Aryan invasion theory would be adapted by other scholars seeking explanations for the existence of white or proto-white tribes from Central Asia and the Pacific Region. Once Aryanism became combined with the Hamitic hypothesis, new theories of race promised something more than a way of classifying anomalous-looking tribes. They offered way of explaining racial origins for all of the people on the planet.

Max Müller's fascination with India took hold of him at an early age. As he recalled in his 1899 memoir, *Auld Lang Syne*, it had begun in grade school in the 1830s in the German city of Dessau and at a particular

Friedrich Max Müller. Credit: Friedrich Max Müller, *My Autobiography; A Fragment* (New York: Charles Scribner's Sons, 1901).

moment. He noticed a picture on the cover of his copy book: the Ganges River coursing through the city of Benares (Varanasi), India's holiest city. The picture was rough, but he could still make out people descending the banks of the Ganges, stepping down the long ghats to the water's edge. These Indians were tall and beautiful, "not like niggers," as he put it in his memoir. Until then he had thought India was a barbaric place where "the people were black [and] they burnt their widows" (referring to the practice of Sati). Yet this picture of Benares revealed something else to Max Müller—a place of sophistication and loveliness, with mosques and temples crowding the riverbanks that certainly outshined the churches and palaces of Dessau. As he was daydreaming of India, his master swooped down. Taking him by the ear, he ordered Max Müller to copy out the names of the places—Benares, Ganges, India—that had carried him away from the day's lesson. Writing out the names over and over again on sheets of paper, the city and its people became "a kind of vision" engraved in his mind.[1]

Max Müller's "first and somewhat painful acquaintance with India" appears to have been a chance event. "Boys will dream dreams," he admitted, and it seems plausible that, had the young Max Müller seen Tenochtitlàn or Baghdad or Timbuktu on the cover of his copybook, we would now remember him for his work on other languages. Yet it was no accident that he found Benares there, or that, of all the languages of the ancient world, Max Müller would find and fall in love with Sanskrit. Nor was it a coincidence that the celebrity that he achieved as a scholar grew from his knowledge of India and East. Max Müller's awakening to India was part of a larger love affair with Eastern culture taking place in Europe, an "Oriental renaissance" that caught on in the 1700s and was still burning brightly in the mid-nineteenth century. This renaissance had been fueled by the work of William Jones and other British philologists who had learned Sanskrit and demonstrated its close relationship to other languages such as Greek, Latin, and Persian. By the time Max Müller came upon his copybook picture of Benares, "Indomania" had crossed the Channel and swept the Continent, first in France, and then in Germany, where the study of Oriental languages had become a vibrant discipline within the university.[2]

German intellectuals were quick to realize the artistic and philosophical power of ancient Sanskrit texts. Goethe delighted in the beauty of *The Sign of Śakuntalā*, a piece of the epic *Mahabharata*. When Arthur Schopenhauer came upon the newly translated *Upanishads* in 1814, he called them "the solace of my life." They influenced his seminal treatise, *The World as Will and Representation* (1818). Following Jones, German scholars believed that Sanskrit was part of an extensive family of languages encompassing Latin, Greek, and Persian, among others. In 1813, the English polymath Thomas Young—who had done his dissertation on the subject at Göttingen—described this family as "Indo-European," a term that gained popularity after Franz Bopp published his *Comparative Grammar* (1833–52), which included the first systematic study of Indo-European languages and represented the first modern methods of comparative philology. That such languages might reveal something about the original Indo-Europeans—or as Germans were inclined to call them, "Indo-Germans"—generated excitement among scholars, particularly those who sought to uncover the history of ethnic origins. The hunt for those origins was especially spirited in Germany, spurred by the fact that "Germanness" itself was such a puzzle—desperately sought, yet difficult to define. In the 1830s, Germany existed as a loose confederation of kingdoms, principalities, and duchies—divided by culture as well as by religion (predominantly Protestant in the northeast; Catholic in the southwest). Within the idea of an Indo-European language, then, lay the idea of a German identity rooted in language, a heritage that brought different groups—from Austrians to Prussians—together.[3]

Encountering India again as a university student in Leipzig in 1841, Max Müller perceived something latent and powerful within the language of Sanskrit. It gave him "that feeling which the digger who prospects for minerals is said to have, that there must be gold beneath the surface, if people would only dig," as he put it in his autobiography. He began digging. After studying Sanskrit in Leipzig, Max Müller continued his studies in Berlin, then Paris, and finally, England, where he undertook the project that would establish his career: a translation and commentary of the *Rg Veda*, the most sacred of the ancient Hindu texts. Within the passages of the *Rg Veda*, Max Müller discovered stories about the origins of the Hindu Brahmins, stories that he believed revealed the early history of the Indo-Europeans and their migration into India. Within this text, he saw evidence of the ancient conquest of dark-skinned natives by Indo-European invaders. The Sanskrit-speaking people called themselves the "Arya," a term that meant "noble" or "respectable." Max Müller—and soon many others—began to describe the ancient Indo-European family by this term as well: the Aryans.[4]

Max Müller's idea of an ancient conquest did not rest solely on the stories of the *Rg Veda*. The research on Sanskrit had moved beyond the discoveries Jones had made in the 1780s. While Jones's key idea, that Sanskrit was connected genetically to other ancient languages such as Greek and Latin, had been widely accepted, the question of how Sanskrit connected to the modern languages of India remained a matter of debate. At the beginning of the nineteenth century, British philologist Henry Thomas Colebrooke had argued that all of India's major languages shared an "aboriginal unity" with Sanskrit. Soon, however, scholars began to challenge this, arguing that certain Indian languages—Tamil, Telugu, Kannada, and Gujarati—were so dissimilar from Sanskrit that they must have had separate origins. It was these non-Sanskritic or "Dravidian" languages that scholar Francis Whyte Ellis believed represented the "pure native language of the land."[5] By the 1840s, this became the consensus view among philologists.

The Aryan Tidal Wave

And with it came the belief that the ancient Indo-European settlement of India had begun with an invasion. As Aryans entered India from the cradle of humankind—somewhere in Central or Western Asia—they dominated and scattered the indigenous Dravidian peoples before them. As imagined by John Stevenson, a missionary with the Scottish Missionary Society in Bombay in 1849, the more advanced Aryans "found a rude aboriginal population, speaking a different language, having a different religion, and different customs and manners; that by arms and policy the aboriginal inhabitants were all subdued and in great numbers expelled from the Northern regions, those that remained mixing with the new populations, and being first their slaves, and then forming the Sudra caste."[6]

Influenced by the work of Stevenson and others, Max Müller became even more convinced that the passages of the *Rg Veda*, though mythopoetic in form, contained kernels of historical truth. In these stories of ancient conquest, he saw the origin stories of the Brahmins, India's highest caste, ones that "put it beyond all doubt that the Brahminical people was of an Arian [*sic*] origin." In the decades to come, Max Müller became the most prominent defender of the "Aryan invasion" theory, an idea that soon found application beyond the shores of India.[7]

Max Müller saw the outlines of a larger story in the history of Indian origins. The occurrence of an advanced, light-skinned people who seized territory by "vanquishing, destroying, and subjecting the savage and despised inhabitants of these countries" was one that he saw repeating itself in the modern world as fair-skinned Europeans colonized peoples at the farthest edges of the earth. "We generally find that it is the fate of the Negro race when brought into hostile contact with the Japhetic race, to be either destroyed or annihilated," as he wrote in 1848. That he identified Indo-Europeans tribes as Japhetic—in other words, the descendants of Noah's son Japheth, rather than Ham—as had Jones, would once have been a matter of serious theological debate in the 1700s. Yet the difference in biblical genealogy had become less important in the nineteenth century, as Japhetic, Hamitic, and Semitic evolved into terms that specified linguistic or racial identities no longer tethered to Scripture. As we've seen, polygenists such as Samuel Morton and George Gliddon were happy to modify, even discard, biblical interpretation as they saw fit to match the tenets of the new Hamitic hypothesis. Their reinterpretation of the Flood story, put forward as Max Müller worked on the *Rg Veda*, argued that all three Noachian sons—Japheth, Ham, and Shem—were simply different branches of the same Caucasian race. As a result, these separate projects—African anthropology and Asian linguistics—became increasingly connected. Scholars from a variety of fields began to interpret the Aryan conquest of India as one front in a larger prehistoric contest, one that pitted Brahmins against Dravidians in India, the dynastic race against indigenes in Egypt, and Bahima against Negroes in East Africa.[8]

And it did not stop there. In 1885, the New Zealand polymath Edward Tregear argued that an "Aryan tidal-wave" had washed over India and continued to push south, through the islands of the East Indian archipelago, reaching the distant shores of New Zealand. Tregear's book *The Aryan Maori* argued that the linguistic, mythological, and cultural features of New Zealand's native peoples tied them to the Indo-European conquerors of ancient India. Tregear was not formally trained as an ethnologist, and his work provoked controversy in the New Zealand press. Yet, it had its supporters, too, especially outside of New Zealand, where politicians and scholars (including, not surprisingly, Max Müller) spoke in its defense. Tregear's *Aryan Maori* was built upon a body of scholarship on the origins of Pacific islanders that had already emerged, done mostly by Christian missionaries. Understandably, given their religious training and inclinations, these missionaries initially tied the arrival of Pacific islanders with biblical events, not only to the resettlement of the world under Japheth, Ham, and Shem, but also to the lost tribes of Israel in the *Book of Kings*. Later, as Max Müller and other scholars brought new methods to the question of origins, scholars began tying the Maori to the Indo-European invasion of India.[9]

A similar process was occurring in Japan. When European traders and missionaries arrived on the islands in the 1600s, they observed physical differences between the Japanese of Honshu and the southern islands compared with the Ainu, a population of roughly fifteen thousand villagers on the northern island of Hokkaido. As the Italian Jesuit missionary Hieronymus de Angelis wrote in 1622 from Japan, these northerners were "more inclining in colour to white than brown." The Ainu, with their light complexion, high cheekbones, and prominent brow ridges were easy to distinguish from the Japanese. Ainu men grew thick, shaggy beards and spoke a language very different from Japanese. After Japan was compelled to open its ports to foreign trade in the 1850s, foreigners came into closer contact with the mysterious Ainu just as the Aryan invasion theory was coming into wide circulation. As a result, to many, the Ainu came to represent an Aryan offshoot of the Indo-European tidal wave, one that reached the eastern edges of the Asian continent. The English missionary John Batchelor became the West's primary source of information about the Ainu, writing books about Ainu language, folklore, and culture. In 1904, he helped organize transport of nine Ainu villagers to the Louisiana Purchase Exposition—also known as the St. Louis World's Fair—in the United States, an event that generated considerable interest. Batchelor believed that the structure of the Ainu language was essentially Aryan, a view that became popular with other European scholars as well. When University of Chicago anthropologist Frederick Starr arrived back in the United States with nine hundred feet of motion picture film and 350 negatives of Ainu culture, he was hailed for his work chronicling the "aboriginal Caucasian inhabitants of Japan."[10]

By the early 1900s, the Aryan invasion theory was being applied to peoples across the Pacific and Pacific Rim. French anthropologist Armand de Quatrefages used the theory to explain the racial spectrum of Indonesian peoples, arguing that Aryan migrants had arrived there from the Indian subcontinent, driving dark-skinned Papuan natives away. The American ethnologist and archaeologist Daniel Brinton, albeit with a bit more ambivalence, discussed the same theory in regard to the ancient conquest of the Philippines where Aryan settlers drove native Negrito populations into the bush. "The small blacks were either killed or had to take refuge in the interior of the islands," he wrote in *American Anthropologist* in 1898, "where the mountains and the jungles offered them protection." In Australia, anthropologist Griffith Taylor wrote of "fair-haired aborigines" who had arrived on the continent in ancient times, "who marched down the east centre of the continent, driving the earlier hordes to the north-west and south east." The Swedish ethnologist Abraham Fornander used linguistic comparisons to argue for an Aryan settlement of the Polynesian islands in his three-volume *Account of the Polynesian Race* (London, 1885). Herbert

Gowen, who established the Department of Oriental History at the University of Washington in 1909, advanced a similar idea to explain the Aryan heritage of native Hawaiians, a population of "long lost brethren of the same stock and blood" as Europeans. "They are therefore kin to the Anglo-Saxon."[11]

Having tracked Aryans far into the Pacific Ocean, supporters began to see them coming ashore on the other side. Prehistoric America, they imagined, was the beachhead of Indo-European colonies. This idea fired the imagination of Miles Poindexter, U.S. senator from Washington State whom President Warren Harding appointed ambassador to Peru. He began compiling evidence in the 1920s to prove that Incan rulers were the descendants of ancient Aryan seafarers who had come across the Pacific Ocean. In his book *The Ayar-Incas*, Poindexter argued that Pacific Aryans had eventually come to dominate the darker-skinned inhabitants in the same manner as they had throughout the islands of Oceania. In prehistoric America, the struggle of this white race of rulers, to preserve the purity of its blood in the midst of a mass of "darker peoples," carried on just as it had in Asia, especially in India, and also in Polynesia, by a system of caste. It was a losing struggle, one in which the appeal of sex overcame the priestly and kingly caste's attempts to preserve the purity of their race. It ended with the absorption of the smaller white element into the larger pool of dark-skinned peoples.[12]

From the chronological distance of the present, the Aryan invasion (and its extension to all regions of the Pacific, even to the edges of the American continent), seems an implausible theory. It was a controversial idea even in the early twentieth century. Some scholars found it hard to believe that so many peoples—Ainu, Malay, Maori, Filipino, Hawaiian, and Inca—were the descendants of a single light-skinned, Indo-European-speaking people driving southeastward from their homeland in Central Asia. Yet, while it's tempting to see this Aryan invasion idea as racial quackery—the product of amateur ethnologists so driven by the pursuit of an idea that they blinded themselves to other data and interpretations—to dismiss it out of hand is to ignore the reasons for its broad appeal, not only among the self-trained ethnologists-missionaries of the Pacific Basin, but also among elite European and North American scientists. The theory gained traction because it proved so useful in updating earlier theories of human migration and

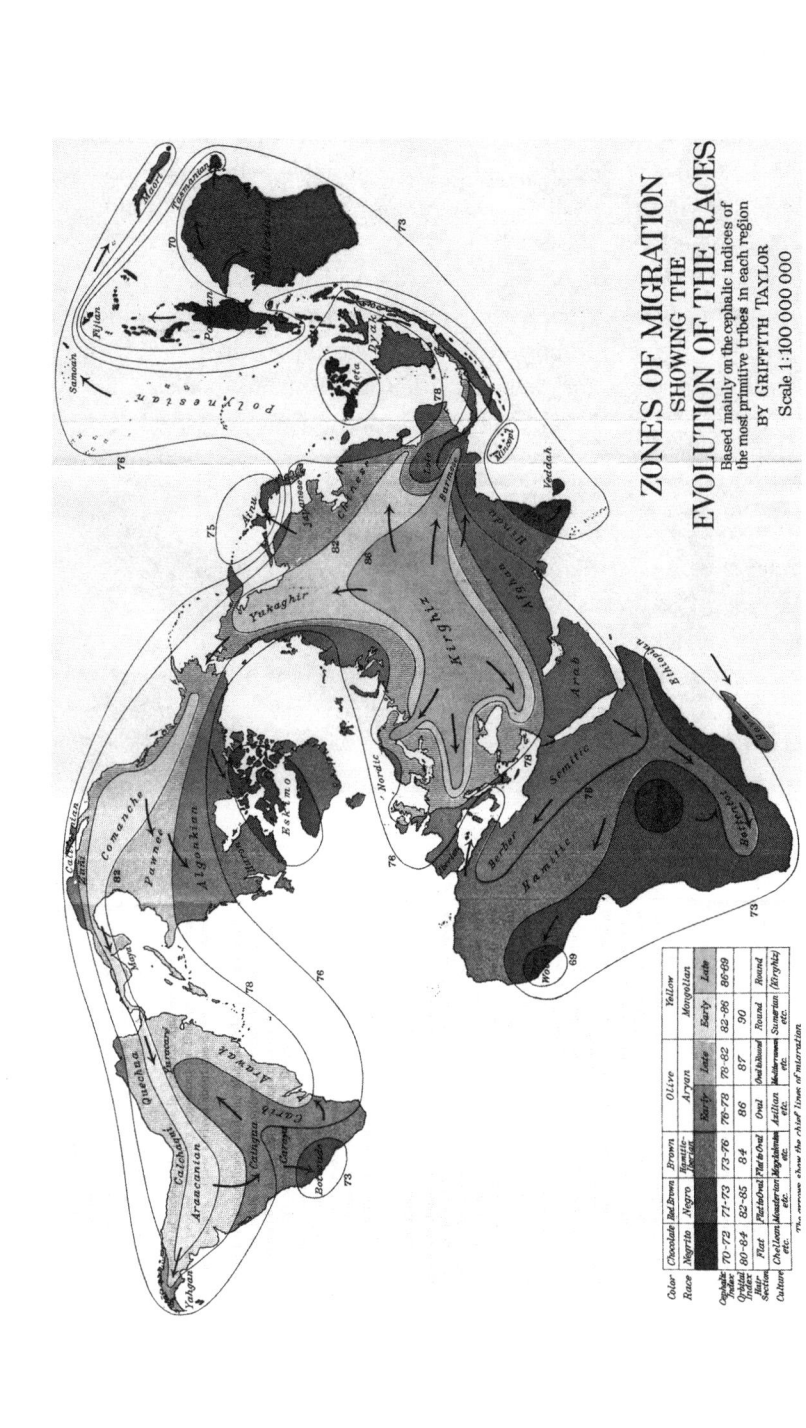

Griffith Taylor's world map showing waves of racial migration out of Asia. Credit: Griffith Taylor, "The Evolution and Distribution of Race, Culture, and Language," *Geographical Review* 11 (1921): 119.

integrating them into a new scientific framework, especially at a time when the scriptural explanations of human races and their origins were coming to be seen as insufficient. As a result, the invasion theory rolled through the field of anthropological ideas, gathering up other theories—the Hamitic hypothesis, the Caucasian migration theory, and the dynastic race theory—like a snowball.

Indeed, the main reason the Aryan invasion idea was successful was because it wove together so many threads of earlier, seemingly incongruous, migration theories. It was consistent with the view of monogenist scientists and ministers that the human species originated in Central Asia, then branched outward to Europe, Africa, Asia, and the Pacific. Yet it also appealed to the polygenists, who believed that the human races originated separately around the globe, because it confirmed that migrations involved the conquest of dark-skinned, aboriginal peoples by light-skinned intellectually superior peoples. Where did these dark-skinned, aboriginal inhabitants come from? Supporters of the Aryan invasion theory generally believed, of course, that they had originated in Asia, then migrated to other parts of the world in the ancient past, representing the first wave of human settlement. As more advanced races developed in Asia, they migrated outward from their homelands, driving the more primitive races to the periphery.

By 1920s, Edward Tregear's notion of an Aryan "tidal wave" that washed over India and the south Pacific had become a global tsunami, rolling out from its epicenter in Central Asia in a series of waves that reached the farthest peripheries of the planet. Each wave represented a more evolved race, migrating from its Asian homeland to conquer the lesser-developed peoples who had migrated in earlier periods. No one visualized this epic history of conquest more elaborately than anthropologist Griffith Taylor, who used a slightly different metaphor—that of a volcanic eruption—to express the current distribution of races around the globe.[13]

Despite certain similarities with earlier theories, however, the Aryan invasion theory represented a radical shift in thinking about race and the origins of humanity. Enlightenment theorists had imagined the original human family to be the acme of perfection. For Johann Blumenbach, this perfection had been embodied by the lustrous-skinned, finely skulled Georgians leaving their homelands in the Caucasus to

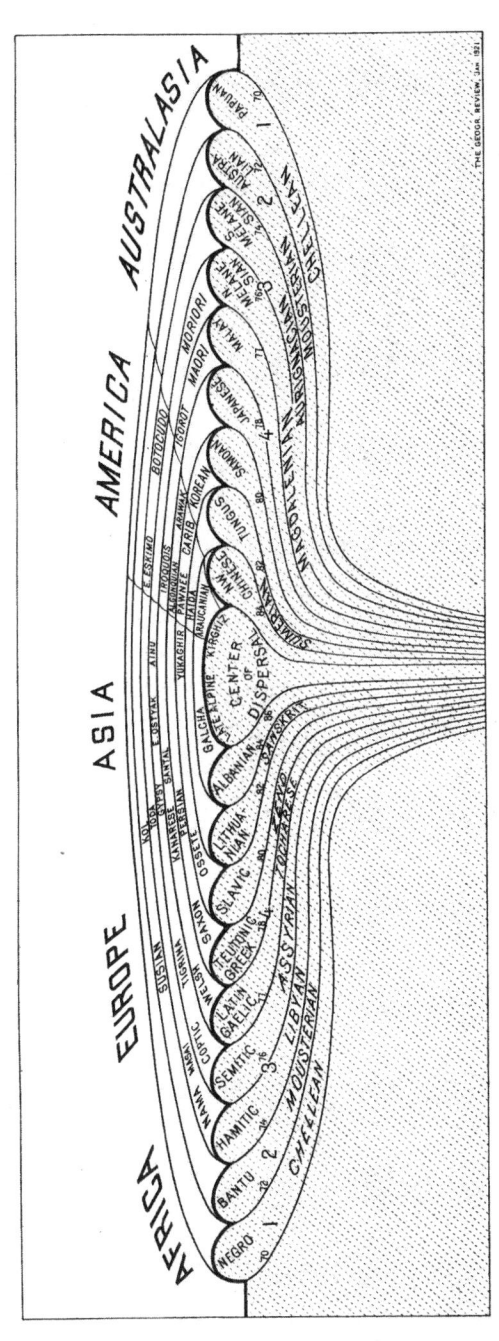

THE LAVA-FLOW ANALOGY

FIG. 9—The lava-flow analogy applied to studies of evolution and linguistics. The center of dispersal in Central Asia is pictured as a sort of "fissure eruption" sending forth streams of lava in all directions. Each new eruption arises from the center and, while covering some portion of the previous flow, pushes most of the previous lavas out to the periphery. Other analogies are represented in Figure 8. Fossil languages, buried under existing tongues, are seen in section. On the surface are shown existing languages typical of the several migration zones.

In Griffith Taylor's "Lava-Flow Analogy" waves of advanced races migrated outward from Asia, conquering less advanced races in their path. Credit: Griffith Taylor, "The Evolution and Distribution of Race, Culture, and Language," *Geographical Review* 11 (1921): 104.

populate the earth. For William Jones, decoding Sanskrit texts in India, the first humans represented the cultured, monotheistic, linguistically advanced offspring of Noah's sons. Only as these racially and religiously advanced tribes migrated to other regions of the world, encountering different climates, did they begin to "degenerate," producing an array of racial types, low cultures, and polytheistic beliefs. Despite their belief in the shared humanity of the human races, then, Blumenbach, Jones, and others such as the Comte de Buffon imagined the history of humankind as a history of decline, a transition from white to brown to black, from civilized to barbarous to savage, with only its European, light-skinned, monotheists representing the original human type.

The Aryan invasion theory reversed the history of race formation from a story of degeneration to one of advancement. Built on Darwin's theory of evolution, it told of racial progress in which primitive, dark-skinned peoples settled the globe first, only to be gradually displaced by successive waves of more advanced races. Aryans represented the newest racial type, with its gradual and inevitable conquest of the globe representing the brutal interspecies competition predicted by Darwin in *Origin of Species*.

Yet there was a problem with this evolutionary hierarchy of races. If dark-skinned races represented the ancestors of the Aryan race, how was it that they survived into the present? Put differently, if Pygmies and Negritos represented the great-grandparents of the human species, how did it happen that they were still living alongside their fair-skinned, cephalically endowed great-grandchildren? After all, the living varieties of any species were connected laterally rather than serially, cousins on the branching evolutionary tree of life. Only with considerable effort, then, did race theorists shoehorn Darwin's ideas to fit their ideas of the Aryan invasion. Pygmies and Negritos became living ancestors of the human race, a branch of the evolutionary tree that, while living, remained static and stunted. According to this view, ancestral forms continued to live into the present but remained unchanged from how they existed in the prehistoric past. They were, within popular literature, described as "missing links" and Stone Age peoples, retaining the physique and behavior of the human species as it existed in its evolutionary childhood. Light and dark races were technically cousins, but in fact the latter were relics of a former age, living as if frozen in time. And this is how they were represented

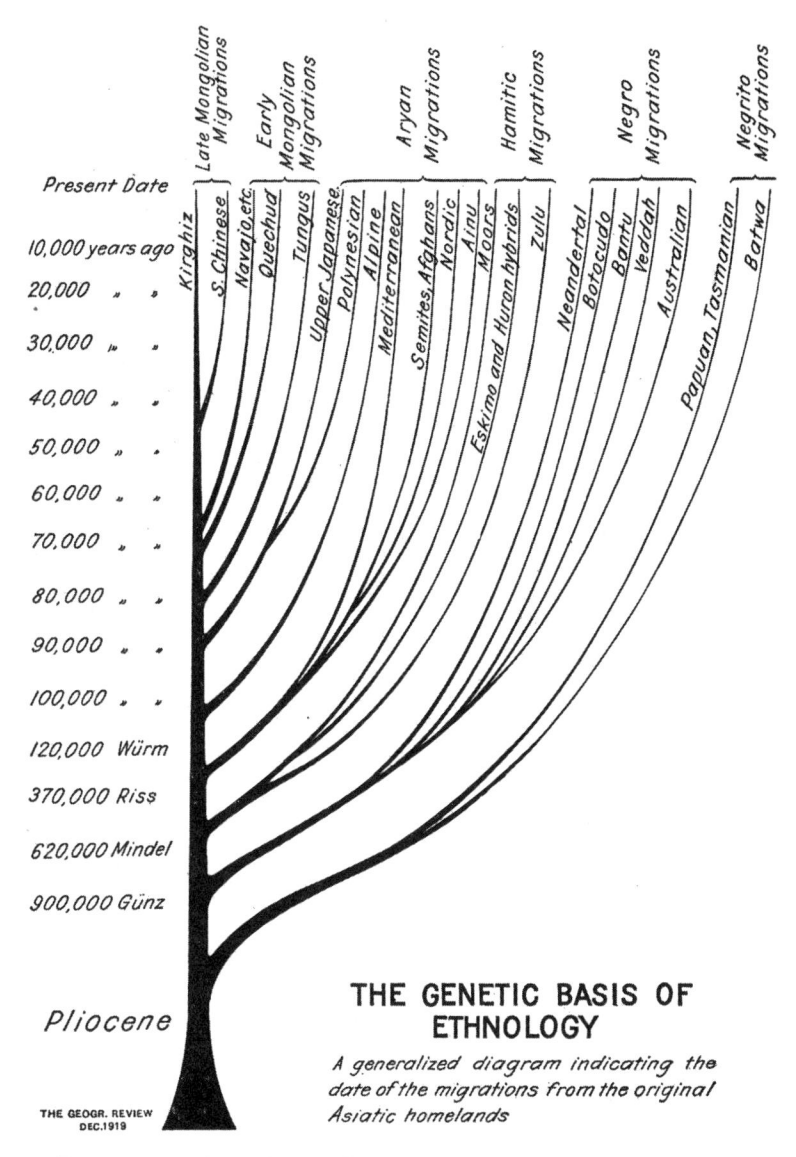

Fig. 10—Generalized diagram indicating the period in the geological time scale of man's migrations from the original Asiatic homelands.

In Griffith Taylor's tree of human evolution, "Negrito" and "Negro" branches of the human species appeared before "Hamitic" and "Aryan" ones, even though all branches continue into the present. Credit: Griffith Taylor, "Climatic Cycles of Evolution," *Geographical Review* 8 (1919): 312.

in the scientific diagrams of Darwinian evolution, which pictured the tree of humankind throwing off its ancient African branches close to the ground while its newer Aryan and Hamitic shoots budded more recently, high in the canopy of human evolution.[14]

When Max Müller began working on the *Rg Veda* in the 1840s, he believed that the speakers of Aryan languages—from Great Britain to the Indus Valley—might feel themselves part of a great brotherhood, connected across the boundaries of nation and culture by language and possibly by blood. Perhaps this also inspired missionaries like Batchelor and Gowen to see Aryans among the people they spent their lives with, people who seemed so different and yet, in some ways, so like them. Aryanism—much in the same way Stanley used Hamitism in Africa—could express a kind of empathy and admiration for peoples who had been cut off from the march of global modernity. An Ohio newspaper described the Ainu as "white savages" in 1913, not to disparage them but to marvel at their survival. "Their faces, features, eyes, beards, and mental processes are exactly like our own." At a time when race science divided the world into types, the Aryan invasion allowed missionaries, linguists, explorers, and scientists to sort peoples within the same broad categories as they placed themselves.[15]

As Aryans, native peoples gained claim to another kind of relationship with Europeans. By the first quarter of the twentieth century, ministers, scientists, and colonial administrators were—for reasons both empathetic as well as self-serving—dividing up the native peoples of the world into categories of "us" and "them." Or, more accurately, into categories of "more like us" and "less like us." Max Müller saw some of this at the end of his career—the dangers in using language to define race—and the use of race to create barriers. Increasingly Max Müller worried about the use of "Aryan" as a racial rather than linguistic category: "I have declared again and again that if I say Aryas I mean neither blood nor bones nor hair nor skull: I mean simply those who speak an Aryan language."[16]

But it was too late. "Aryan" had over the course of a few decades evolved from a linguistic category to a racial one, taking its place alongside "Caucasian" to represent the world's light-skinned races. Moreover, the Aryan invasion, originally used to describe the origin of a dominant population in India, had now become an explanatory device to explain the haves and have-nots of racial demography around the globe. The world was full of racial diversity, and here was a theory to explain it: a way of making sense of the light- and dark-skinned, the high- and low-cheekboned, the aquiline-nosed, and the long- and round-skulled. As much as Europeans viewed the peripheries of the world as places of darkness, they had become places of whiteness too, where the descendants of ancient Aryans lived, cut off from their European cousins by thousands of years of migration, but connected, nevertheless, an ancient bloodline rediscovered. In this way, the Aryan invasion theory explained the discovery of white tribes around the globe in the late 1800s.

Perhaps it even brought them into existence. Did these diverse peoples—Stanley's Gambaragarans, Petrie's dynastic Egyptians, Tregear's Maori, and Batchelor's Ainu—become Aryan because scholars found a scientific theory by which to connect them? It seems hard to believe that such communities—living at great distances from one another, exhibiting different physical traits, and speaking radically different languages—could be combined into a single racial group on the basis of pure observation. Theories are powerful things. They do not merely grow out of or organize observations, but actively shape observations as they are being made. As the story of the Hamitic hypothesis makes clear, they can even shape the process of seeing itself.

Yet, if there were cultural reasons for the appearance of white tribes all over the world in the late 1800s, it would require more than scholars' attachment to the Aryan invasion theory to explain it. The pace of discovery of white tribes increased in the early 1900s, even when many of these discoveries could not be connected to the ideas of Max Müller, Taylor, or others. From high Arctic islands to dense equatorial jungles, explorers were finding white tribes that did not seem fit any of the global racial models scientists had yet devised.

14

BLOND ESKIMOS

In may 1910, the canadian anthropologist Vilhjalmur Stefansson sledged over the ice of the Canadian Arctic with two Inuit men, driving dogs toward a group of snow houses on the shores of Victoria Island. One of the Inuit men ran ahead to announce their arrival. A few minutes later, a group of men and boys emerged from the huts and walked toward Stefansson and Natkusiak, his guide. The Victoria Islanders raised their hands above their heads as they greeted the strangers. "We are friendly. We are as we seem. Your arrival makes us glad." Stefansson raised his hands too. He approached each man in the group, gave his name, and received theirs in kind. As he looked at the faces of each man, Stefansson knew he had found something that would change his life. "I was standing face to face with an important scientific discovery."[1]

The Victoria Islanders looked "like sunburned, but naturally fair Scandinavians." Some of them had brown or red beards and blue eyes. While they spoke the language of the Inuit, wore furs, and lived in snow houses, they seemed Europeans in appearance. As the women of the village prepared food for the party—boiled seal meat and blood soup—Stefansson noted that one of the women "had the delicate features one sees in some Scandinavian girls." The islanders began building a snow house for Stefansson and his men. In the months that followed, he made detailed observations of the Victoria Islanders and the native peoples of the surrounding regions. The physical traits of the group varied considerably, in hair and eye color, height, appearance, and facial index (a ratio of facial length to facial width multiplied by 100). At the time, the last measurement was often used by anthropologists—along with the cephalic index—as a key marker of race. Whereas Inuit generally measured above 100 on the facial index, Stefansson observed that the Victoria Islanders scored in the 90s, the same range as Europeans or peoples of mixed European-Inuit ancestry.[2]

Yet if they weren't Eskimo, who were they? It was hard to imagine that these natives could be the descendants of some Aryan invasion of Asia. Victoria Island was 250 miles above the Arctic Circle and over a thousand miles from the Pacific Ocean. It was not an obvious destination on the path of human migration, even within the more imaginative island-hopping scenarios being proposed by Pacific missionaries and ethnologists. On Griffith Taylor's map of racial migration, the Canadian Arctic archipelago was a racial backwater, a stagnant pool of low-cephalic "Negroid" natives cut off from the swift currents of racial progress. One would also expect, if the Victoria Islanders were part of an Aryan invasion emerging from Asia and the Pacific, to find native peoples who shared similar physical traits to the west of the island, as one approached the routes of migration near the ocean. Yet this was not the case. West of Victoria Island lay "a barren strip 300 miles wide," declared Stefansson, separating the light-complexioned tribe from the Inuit of the Mackenzie River. This in turn led Stefansson to believe that the people of Victoria Island had come not from the west but from the east, that they were the direct descendants of a European colony in more recent times. This would explain why the islanders did not look Ainu or Maori but, to Stefansson at least, like Northern Europeans.

If Victoria Islanders were descended from European colonists, there was a very small list of possible explanations. They may have been descendants of the survivors of the lost Franklin expedition. This expedition, under the command of Sir John Franklin, had sailed into the Arctic in 1845 seeking to uncover the Northwest Passage. Under Franklin's command, two naval ships, *Erebus* and *Terror*, sailed into the Canadian archipelago with 128 men, none of them ever to be seen again. A massive search for the expedition yielded artifacts, human remains, and a document left in a cairn on King William Island. The document, dated April 25, 1848, reported the deaths of Franklin and 24 officers and crew. The bones scattered along the coast of King William Island pointed to death of many more. Yet some of the remaining 105 men may have survived with the assistance of the Inuit, assimilated to Inuit life, and raised families in the high Arctic. Perhaps the Victoria Islanders were the descendants of these survivors, the mixed-race offspring of a band of Britons who had gone native sixty-five years earlier.

A number of reasons made this theory unlikely. The survivors who ultimately "went native" would likely number less than one hundred men, and yet the presence of European physical traits—brown and red hair, round eyes, light complexion, blue eyes—appeared not only among the communities of Victoria Island, but also among settlements south of island: the two hundred miles of coastline of Coronation Gulf. A small group of Englishmen could not have made such a big demographic impact. Moreover, because Franklin had entered these waters in 1845, only sixty-five before Stefansson, Inuit communities would presumably still remember—and be able to recount through oral tradition—the arrival and integration of their European forefathers. Yet none of the Inuit interviewed by Stefansson spoke of having European kin. "Neither they nor their ancestors have come into contact with any of the middle-century explorers," he wrote. As another explorer, Knud Rasmussen, would later write, "It would be unthinkable that such a blood mixture could have taken place a few generations ago without there being many fresh stories about this among the group."[3]

More likely, Stefansson believed, was that the Copper Inuit (as they became known for their use of copper tools) traced their heritage to more distant European ancestry, namely Leif Erickson's fourteenth-century Greenland colony, a community of Scandinavians who prospered in Greenland in the 1300s and then vanished without a trace. As the Icelandic sagas tell the story, the Norseman Erickson was exiled from Iceland in 982 CE for three years for committing murder. He spent this time in Greenland. When he returned to Iceland, he convinced a number of Icelanders to follow him back to the ice-capped island. There, in 985 CE, he set up a colony on the southern coast, one that flourished through the 1300s. Greenland was then cut off from

Iceland and the rest of Europe for two hundred years. When Europeans returned—British mariner John Davis arrived on the shores of the island in 1585—they found no trace of the former colony. For centuries, Europeans had pondered the mystery of the Greenland colony's disappearance.[4]

Stefansson's theory assumed that members of the Norse colony traveled west across Baffin Bay, settling in the archipelago of Arctic islands crowning the Canadian north. Given the colony's larger numbers, and the presence of European men as well as women, the presence of Scandinavian traits could have been preserved over the five-hundred-year period of their disappearance. To Stefansson, a Scandinavian ancestry for the Copper Inuit seemed more likely than a British one, even if the Norsemen had been a more distant line.

However scientifically he approached the question of the origin of these people, and however much he later declared it to be a speculative theory, Stefansson had personal reasons for finding Scandinavian origins of the blond Eskimo. This would have made Stefansson, who was of Icelandic heritage, a countryman of sorts with the Copper Inuit. It also appealed to him as an ethnologist, someone who, as much as possible, sought to adapt to the life and culture of the people he studied. Despite their dependence upon the Inuit, Western Arctic explorers had been minimizing and misrepresenting northern peoples for three hundred years. Here was an opportunity for Stefansson to bridge the gap between these people and the outside world. "I wanted, if I lived with the Eskimo at all, to live exactly as one of them, in their houses, dressing like them, and eating only such food as they did," he wrote in *My Life with the Eskimo*. It gave him some satisfaction that one of the native men near Victoria Island mistook *him* for a Victoria Islander. Moreover, Stefansson may have had personal reasons for identifying and promoting Victoria Islanders as the descendants of Scandinavian or Scandinavian-Eskimo parentage. He had fathered a son in the Artic with Fannie Pannigabluk, an Inuit woman from the Mackenzie River delta.[5]

Arriving in Seattle by steamer in September 1912, Stefansson granted an interview with *Seattle Times* reporter John J. Underwood in which he described his encounter with the "Blond Eskimo." The *Seattle Times* ran the story on its front page on September 9 under the headline "American Explorer Discovers Lost Tribe of Whites,

Descendants of Leif Erickson." While Stefansson had been careful to chart the broad spectrum of traits among the Coronation Gulf Inuit, few of these subtleties made it into Underwood's article. As the reporter explained it, Stefansson had discovered "a lost tribe of 1,000 white people, who are believed to be direct descendants from the followers of Leif Erickson," a people "purely of Norwegian origin." The story took off. By the following morning, it was the front-page story from San Francisco to Richmond, Virginia. The *New York Sun* declared "Lost White Tribe on Arctic Coast," while the *Daily Missoulian* claimed "New Eskimo Race Is Discovered in Arctic." As the story grew, so did the claims. The *Princeton Union* announced, "Lost Tribe of 2,000 Whites Found on the Arctic Coast," an assertion that was also made in many other newspapers. In the coming months, Stefansson's blond Eskimo story appeared in newspapers from Switzerland to Argentina.[6]

For good reason. The story enthralled audiences, particularly in Europe and North America, who approached it with equal measures of fascination and disbelief. Theories of alternate origins—the islanders were the lost tribe of Israel, a colony of Russians, a shipwrecked crew of Irish monks—appeared in newspaper accounts, while others lampooned the story. Stefansson's expedition partner, biologist Rudolph Anderson, confirmed aspects of his report—"There features bore the characteristics of the Caucasian race"—even as he also declared that the idea of a "blond Eskimo" was exaggerated. The Royal Mounted Police found no people of this description on their patrol of the Coronation Gulf region, while others not only confirmed the story but claimed priority of discovery: three Canadian trappers declared that they were with the Victoria Islanders, a people "whiter than the white man," when Stefansson had arrived. Meanwhile, others looked for earlier sightings of light-skinned Inuit in the historical record. American polar explorer and U.S. Army officer Adolphus Greely compiled accounts of light-complexioned Eskimos from old expedition reports for the *National Geographic Magazine* in 1912 establishing a precedent for Stefansson's account. On the other hand, Norwegian explorer Roald Amundsen, who had sailed near Victoria Island on his bid to complete the Northwest Passage in 1906, dismissed Stefansson's claim as "the most palpable nonsense that ever has come from the North."[7]

The most significant criticism of Stefansson's theory came from the anthropologist Diamond Jenness who, after spending two years

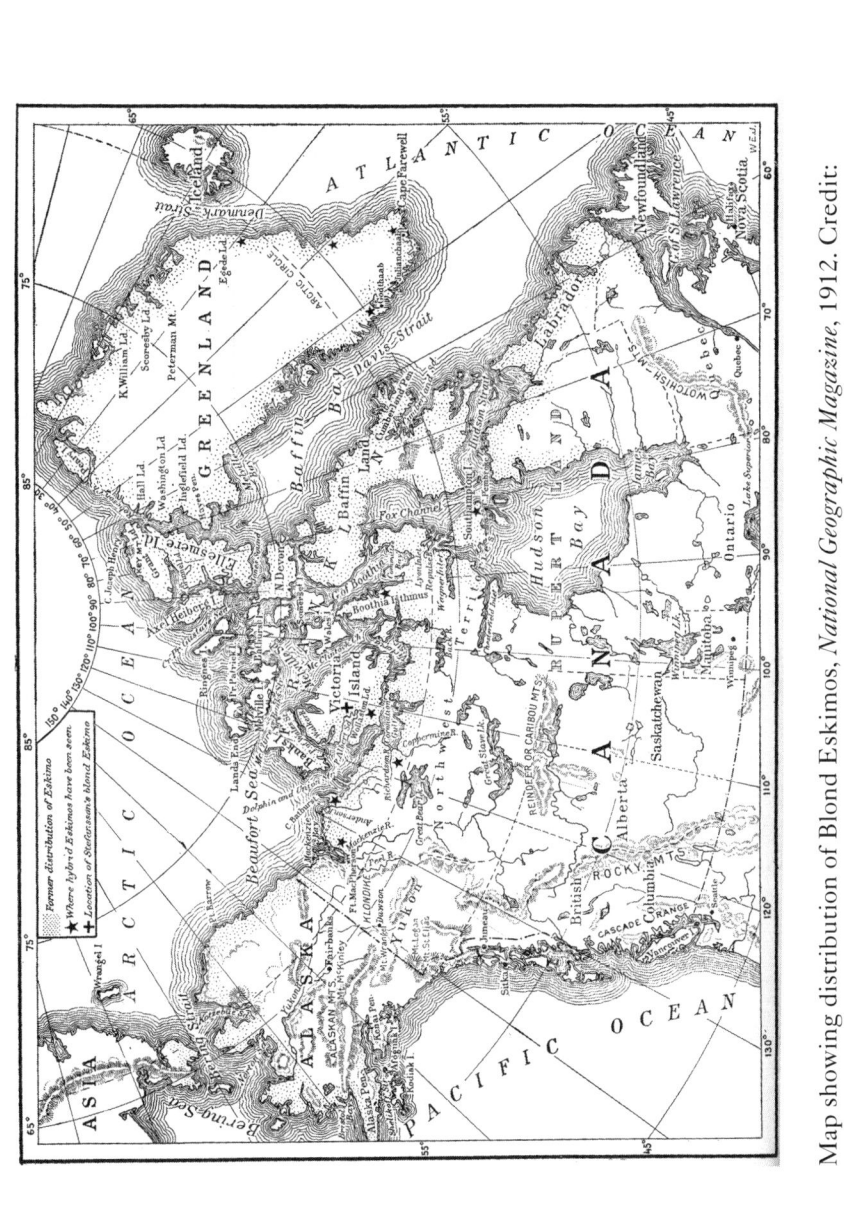

Map showing distribution of Blond Eskimos, *National Geographic Magazine*, 1912. Credit: Adolphus Greely, "The Origin of Stefansson's Blond Eskimo," *National Geographic Magazine*, December 12, 1912.

with the people of Victoria Island and Coronation Gulf, disputed Stefansson's lost Greenland colony hypothesis. In his 1921 paper "The 'Blond' Eskimo," Jenness laid out his arguments. He began by confirming a number of Stefansson's earlier observations: eye color among the natives of the region ranged from brown to gray to milky blue; eye shape varied too, from "straight" eyes to "Mongolian" eyes; while skin color ranged from "the olive color of the Italian" to the fairness of "the average Englishman." Jenness then critiqued Stefansson's use of physical measurements. If the facial index of Victoria Islanders was different from that of other Inuit populations, it was because Stefansson had been measuring the heads of living people and comparing the numbers to those collected from Inuit skulls. Moreover, there were other measurements that should have been different but weren't. If these natives were fully or partially Scandinavian, they should show differences in average height compared with other Inuit groups but they didn't.[8]

Most importantly, Jenness challenged Stefansson's assumptions about *other* Inuit groups. The heterogeneity of the Victoria Islanders became significant only in contrast to Inuit populations that were expected to be homogeneous. This homogeneity was widely assumed. In 1876, French anthropologist Paul Topinard had declared that "there is not a more homogenous [race] that than of the Esquimaux." Jenness's observations, combined with reports he had collected from other researchers, told a different story. In Point Barrow, Alaska, the army sergeant and naturalist John Murdoch observed that the Inuit community expressed significant "natural variation in the complexion."[9]

Jenness's critique of Stefansson on this point had implications for the broader scientific study of race. For nearly a century, race scientists had used hybridity—mixed-race offspring that they attributed to the intermarriage of an invading population with an indigenous one—as a way of dealing with troublesome anthropometric data, those measurements of height, hair color, or cephalic index that did not conform to expected racial types. As this thinking went, indigenous crania that were too big, complexions that were too light, noses that were too aquiline could all be explained away as the result of racial mixing due to the invasions of outside peoples. Jenness did not contest the idea of a "pure" racial type in principle, but he didn't believe it existed in practice, at least not within communities of the Eskimo, no matter how isolated they appeared in the sere, wintry lands of the Canadian Arctic. "We should hardly expect on a priori grounds that the Eskimos would be an absolutely pure race, meaning by pure that from those early times when first they separated from the rest of the human family and developed peculiar characteristics of their own they have preserved themselves rigidly free from all intermixture with other races."[10]

None of these problems with Stefansson's hypothesis, however, dampened interest in the blond Eskimos. Nor did they induce any greater caution among explorer-scientists who entered the remaining wild places of the world in search of "lost tribes." Jenness's careful, thoughtful critique was largely ignored in a world under the spell of new anthropological discoveries from all over the globe. For centuries, the heart of anthropology's terra incognita had been Africa—bound up with tales of monstrous races since antiquity. In the early 1900s, however, South and Central America became a region of special interest to anthropologists. In part this was a consequence of the region's difficult, tropical terrain, much of it cut off from coastal cities, as well as the region's new commercial importance in the West—with the development of the Panama Canal and the development of Western fruit and rubber companies. It was here, fifty years after Stanley's journeys through Africa, that explorers found an American version of the Gambaragara story.

Travel writer Alpheus Hyatt Verrill did not have Stefansson's extensive background in anthropology, but he had explored many regions in Latin America while writing guide books for the new ranks of tourists, merchants, and diplomats making their way south toward the American tropics. These travels had brought him into contact with many people who believed in the story of lost tribes. By 1924, he admitted that the idea of white tribes existing within the Americas had become a commonplace, not only of European explorers, but of Indian communities. "From Brazil to Mexico—in Guiana, Venezuela, Colombia, Panama, and Central America—one hears from natives and Indians, innumerable tales of 'white Indians'—strange, savage, retiring denizens of the vast jungles or interminable mountains of the interior," he wrote in 1924. Verrill himself had had his own encounters in Guiana on the Demerara River. At a dancing festival above a place called Great Falls, Verrill watched as an old man entered the dancing circle. In "Hunting the White Indians," Verrill wrote that his "hair was gray, upon his good natured grinning face was a straggling gray beard and mustache, and—his skin was white.... There was no hint of brown, copper, or yellow in his skin. Rather, it was that of a sunburned European and the old man's cheeks were as rosily pink as any Englishman's."[11] Upon questioning him, Verrill learned that he came from a village between the Demerara and Berbice Rivers. Ascending the Demerara River to its source, he found the village of the Akurias, where the people looked similar to the dancing man. "I was more than ever convinced that the Akurias were the descendants of some forgotten European expedition—Dutch or British or perhaps Spanish or French—that had been lost or cut off in the bush and had mixed with some Indian tribe."[12]

Another American writer, Arthur Olney Friel, returned from Venezuela with a similar story. After working as editor for the Associated Press for many years, Friel traveled to Guiana in 1922 to chart the unknown upper reaches of Orinoco River. He was also driven by "the enticement of mystery and legend—the tradition, long extant, but never proved true or false, that in the unknown region near the Alto Orinoco existed a 'lost white race.'" Here on the Ventuari, a tributary of the Orinoco, Friel found the "blond Maquiritares." "Pure whites. Yellow haired. Blue eyed." And yet this tribe consisted of exactly two people. They were light-complexioned people born to other Indians of darker coloring. To account for such a phenomenon Friel relied on the idea of biological atavism. The new science of genetics had showed that not all inherited traits are expressed. Some remain dormant or "recessive" to more dominant traits. In Friel's view, the white Indians represented a distant generation of white Europeans. They were, he said, "'throwbacks' to some forgotten generation and some long-dead blond man or men," probably the offspring of the men of Spanish garrisons from two hundred years before. With this, Friel believed, "it may be a pity to abolish so romantic a legend, it must be done." In 1924 he published an account of his expedition voyage: *The River of the Seven Stars: Searching for the White Indians on the Orinoco*.[13]

If these sightings of white tribes were the fanciful discoveries of writers eager to generate copy for home audiences, their credibility was enhanced by the explorer-geographer Alexander Hamilton Rice in 1925. After earning a medical degree at Harvard in 1904, Rice had pursued geographical discovery, focusing primarily on uncharted rivers. While charting the Parima River in northern Brazil, Hamilton and his pilot Walter Hinton reported sighting "white Indians." Speaking to the *New York Times* upon his return, Rice told the paper "They move in and out between the trees like jaguars without making a sound or causing a rustle of the leaves."[14]

Discoveries of white Indians weren't limited to the American tropics. In 1930, an academic named Ralph Glidden, curator of the Catalina Museum of the Channel Island Indians, reported finding evidence of a "prehistoric race of white Indians of gigantic stature believed to have inhabited Catalina Island." Glidden speculated that these Indians might have migrated from Panama during the ancient past.[15]

The most significant encounter, however, took place on the Isthmus of Panama in 1923—a decade after Stefansson's discovery of the blond Eskimos—where the American entrepreneur Richard Marsh claimed to have discovered "white Indians." Marsh's encounter took place after he had arrived on the isthmus to survey sites for American rubber plantations. While his observations of native peoples lacked Stefansson's precision and depth of knowledge, Marsh's account echoed Stefansson's in a number of ways. As he made his way through the isolated village of Yaviza, he viewed three native girls, naked except for loincloths, walking through a narrow clearing. "Their almost bare bodies were as white as any Scandinavian's. Their long hair, falling loosely over their shoulders, was bright gold!" The people of Yaviza told Marsh that the home of the White Indians lay at the headwaters of the Chucunaque River. Like Stefansson, Marsh had a nose for a good story and shared the same instinct for self-promotion. He began planning a second Panamanian expedition to continue plantation surveys, conduct science, and discover the home of the "White Indians."[16]

When Marsh's second expedition arrived in Panama later in 1923, it included a newspaper reporter and cameraman, as well as some experts—Smithsonian Institution ethnologist John L. Baer; University of Rochester geologist Herman L. Fairchild; and the New York Aquarium naturalist Charles Breder. Marsh's ability to secure men of science had less to do with his story than his ability to offer access to this difficult and remote region. The chief of anthropology at the Smithsonian, Walter Hough, didn't put much stock in Marsh's fantastic tale of White Indians, nor did he harbor illusions about Marsh, whom he described as "a soldier of fortune." Nonetheless, Hough supported the expedition because he wanted access to the rainforests of Panama, a world "from which the Museum has almost no specimens." It was on this basis that the assorted members of the Marsh expedition gathered in New York City in December 1923, setting sail for Colón.

For two months, the expedition party conducted work in regions near Yaviza—shooting monkeys, collecting frogs, measuring skulls—before ascending the Chucunaque River. Most of the peoples encountered by the expedition until this point had been (disappointingly) brown in complexion. In March they headed upriver with local guides in a party numbering twenty-four in six canoes. The Chucunaque was barely navigable, even in the small canoes. Massive trees toppled across the breadth of the river, requiring the men to blow up the trunks with dynamite. Flash floods threatened to carry away the canoes. Soon typhoid, malaria, and a case of appendicitis weakened the American and Panamanian crew. Baer died of a combination of infections—due to insect bites—complicated by a chronic kidney ailment.

Just as the expedition was falling apart, it finally found the "white Indians" whom Marsh had observed fleetingly a year earlier. Arriving in the town of Ailigandi, Marsh wrote, "We saw many more white Indians in the street—whole families of them." Back in the United States, the drama of the Marsh expedition—from the death of Baer and the dissolution of the expedition to the discovery of villages of white Indians—began to resemble an adventure novel rather than a scientific expedition. Regretting the loss of his ethnologist and revolted by the sideshow atmosphere that swirled around reports from Panama, Aleš Hrdlička, head of the Smithsonian's anthropology division, threw up his hands: "I am disgusted with the whole affair."[17]

Marsh had one more card to play. As he gathered his collections before leaving Panama, he arranged to bring a party of Kuna Indians with him: two boys—Olo and Cheepu—with light hair, blue eyes, and "white tender skin," and a teenage girl named Margarita. Along with them, a number of darker-skinned Kuna joined the party, including Margarita's parents, Inez and James Berry. The fact that fair-haired, light-complexioned Margarita had dark-skinned parents raised the question of whether her fair traits—and those of all the "white Indians"—were a product of racial heritage or albinism. The fact that Marsh's "White Indians" appeared sporadically throughout native populations in Panama, not simply the Kuna, also seemed to indicate albinism. This was the position staked out by the Panamanian paper

Star and Herald, which declared Marsh's party to be a group of albinos and therefore of little scientific value. Marsh defended his claim. "I am confident that they are offshoots of the ancient paleolithic type, from which the first Nordic differentiation occurred perhaps fifteen-thousand years ago."[18]

When Marsh's ship *Calamares* pulled into the docks of New York City on July 6, 1924, the Kuna Indians disembarked into a sea of reporters and photographers. Over the next few days, the reporters covered the travels of the white Indians to the zoo and the American Museum of Natural History, where they were examined by anthropologist Clark Wissler. The museum staff concluded that the white Indians did not constitute a separate race, but showed traits consistent with albinism. Undeterred, Marsh brought the Kuna with him to the British Association for the Advancement of Science meeting in Toronto and presented them to a number of other anthropologists and geneticists who also came to a similar conclusion—the traits of the white Indians were consistent with albinism. Having somehow managed to patch up his disagreements with Hrdlička, Marsh then brought his retinue to Washington, for further examination by members of the Smithsonian Institution. Here, finally, Marsh met with success. Linguists J. P. Harrington and Paul Vogenitz concluded that the Kuna language showed links to Norse vocabulary. Although the similarities were superficial, it was enough for Marsh to report to the newspapers that "it is pure Aryan, and most closely resembles Sanskrit in its syntax." When Marsh and the Kuna visitors returned to Panama, Hrdlička, for one, breathed a sigh of relief.[19]

In the 1920s, the central mystery surrounding all of these discoveries focused on questions of physiology and origin, such as whether indigenous whiteness was a product of direct European heritage or that result of a "throwback" connected to distant European ancestors. Another question was whether these white Indians were more simply understood as the product of genetic albinism or environmental effects. Yet by the time these events unfolded, reports of white Eskimos and Indians had been circulating—as the explorers in the 1920s themselves pointed out—for hundreds of years. Yet what strikes us a century later is why their rediscovery—told in a deluge of expedition reports from the Arctic to the tropics—happened all at once.

The reports of Stefansson, Marsh, and others mostly avoided larger theories of racial migration. These reports show that the proliferation of white tribe discoveries could not be wholly explained by the rise in race theory or the expansion of anthropological expeditions. The vision of the white native—divorced from the rest of the civilized world—seemed to touch a chord in Western culture. It raised a more fundamental question: was the existence of white tribes really a mystery of racial biology or a mystery of the Western mind? Evidence suggests that it reflected a shift in thinking that reached beyond the popularity of a particular theory or expeditionary encounter. And the evidence for this comes not from science or exploration but from literature.

15

TRIBES OF THE IMAGINATION

WHEN H. RIDER HAGGARD PUBLISHED *King Solomon's Mines* in 1885, the novel was immediately a huge hit. It sold five thousand copies in its first month of sales and thirty-one thousand copies in its first year, eventually—through eighteen printings—selling hundreds of thousands more. Haggard followed up by producing two sequel novels, *Allan Quatermain* and *She*, which also sold well. All of them involved the discovery of lost civilizations in the African interior. In fact, together, they established a new genre of adventure fiction "lost race literature," which would dominate the popular market for decades to come. Central to this new genre was the discovery of lost tribes who, more often than not, were of white ancestry.[1]

In effect, novelists like Haggard filled in the gaps of the story left by explorers, linguists, and archaeologists. The debates about Hamitic migrations and Aryan invasions that had unfolded in scholarly journals for half a century give the impression that white tribes were merely objects of scientific scrutiny. The popularity of *King Solomon's Mines* and others gives the lie to this idea. Haggard and other adventure novelists succeeded because they found a topic that resonated with their readers: a thought experiment that examined, apart from the contaminating influence of civilization, the essential qualities of whiteness.

H. Rider Haggard. Credit: 1915 sketch by M. Strang.

Haggard was nineteen when he disembarked in Cape Town, South Africa, from England, a tall man with blue eyes and pale complexion. He had accepted a job in Natal Colony—adjutant to the new colonial governor—not out of a love of adventure but out of a lack of options. School had proven disastrous; he admitted he was "a dunderhead at lessons." His examinations in London were so dismal that his father had lost his temper, telling him he was "only fit to be a greengrocer." After failing his Royal Army entrance exam, he began looking for other paths. Discovering that a family friend had become the new governor of Natal Colony, his father had made appeals, and in 1875—after six weeks at sea—he had arrived, a youth fumbling through the scramble for Africa, flotsam on the great wave of empire. His letters home were upbeat about the new setting, though colonial officials were less upbeat about his prospects. The outgoing governor described the new adjutant as "the picture of weakness and dullness."[2]

Yet Africa awakened something in Haggard. Natal was a place of wonders, a world of sparkling rivers, violent thunderstorms, and grass fires "creeping over the velt at night like snakes of living flame." Like most Europeans when they first encountered Africans, he was struck by the contrasts. The Zulu were weird and marvelous. He watched witch doctors' rituals and war dances, "the most strange and savage sights I ever saw." All of this he found "splendidly barbaric" even though native mores made him begin to wonder about his own. Why was it so immoral, he wrote, "to marry several wives than to marry one"? He noted that most of the European men had black mistresses in the shantytowns of Natal. He defended the superiority of British civilization and its value to the goal of "civilizing" Africa, even when it was administered at the end of a Gatling gun. Yet he also appreciated Zulu culture. Most of all he admired those Britons who "went native" without losing themselves, such as Theophilus Shepstone, secretary for native affairs, who became a Zulu king in order to avoid war. Although he wasn't able to articulate it yet, Africa had become a psychological frontier as much as a geographical one.[3]

Haggard married, and when war broke out in the Transvaal in the early 1880s, he returned to England, took up the study of law, and began a new life as a barrister. He also began to write. His first work, *Cetywayo and His White Neighbors* (1882), was a defense of British colonial policy. After that, changing tack, he wrote a novel, *Dawn*, and then a second one, *The Witch's Head*. Having read and admired Robert Louis Stevenson's *Treasure Island*, he decided to try his hand at writing adventure stories, known as "romances." Now the father of two girls, working in chambers and studying for the bar, he could write only in spare moments, mostly at night, at the pedestal writing desk in his dining room. In spite of these hurdles, he finished his first adventure story in six weeks. It was published in serial form as *King Solomon's Mines*.[4]

The story follows three Britons—an aristocrat, a naval officer, and an ivory hunter—as they trek across the deserts of southern Africa in search of the aristocrat's missing brother. The party comes into possession of an old map "drawn by a dying and half distraught man on a fragment of linen three centuries ago," which leads them to the villages of the light-skinned Kukuanas, spread within a fortress of mountains, the tallest of which are two ice-covered massifs fifteen-thousand-feet high, wrapped in "strange mists and clouds." The Kukuanas live in villages dotted by ancient ruins, ruled over by a despotic king, Twala, and his ancient, shriveled witch, Gagool. After the three men lead a rebellion against king, engaging in a Homeric display of bloodletting,

Image from *King Solomon's Mines* (1905). Credit: Watkinson Library, Trinity College, Hartford, Connecticut.

Twala and Gagool are defeated. Gathering up a bounty of diamonds in the mines, they soon discover the aristocrat's lost brother on their way out of the mountains.[5]

When asked about the inspiration for this novel, Haggard downplayed the importance of recent discoveries in Africa. "I heard faint rumors of these things during my sojourn in Africa, having made it my habit through life to keep my ears open; but at the best they were very faint." It was true that he had never visited Great Zimbabwe, never seen the intricate granite courses that Carl Mauch had described so exuberantly as the works of King Solomon. Yet, it would have been hard to avoid talk of Mauch and Great Zimbabwe in Natal Colony. Haggard had almost crossed paths with the German explorer when he arrived there in 1875. Illustrations of the ruins were appearing on the latest maps of the Transvaal. Still, in his novels, Haggard was careful to keep these allusions indirect. *King Solomon's Mines*, despite its name, remains agnostic on the identity of the foreigners who first settled Kukuanaland. The British adventurers discover Egyptian inscriptions on the roadways, and yet they find Hebrew characters etched on boxes of treasure. The stone colossi that guard the entrance appear to be "designed by some Phoenician official who managed the mines." When the three British adventurers arrive in the mountain fastness, the ancient colonists are gone. Nevertheless, it is clear in the words of the evil king Twala, "It was a white people who were before ye were."[6]

King Solomon's Mines also built on the discoveries of Henry Stanley. While the position of fictional Kukuanaland was close to Great Zimbabwe, its landscapes more closely represent Gambaragara: a civilization built within a fortress of ice-covered mountains fifteen-thousand-feet high. Mountains like this do not exist near Great Zimbabwe, where the tallest peaks reach 8500 feet. One has to travel farther north, to the Ruwenzoris of East Africa, where Stanley first reported the existence of a lost white race. There were other indications of Stanley's influence as well. *King Solomon's Mines* was written as the account of Allan Quatermain, who, like Stanley in his narrative *Through the Dark Continent*, tells his story by alternating firsthand observations with excerpts from his journal entries. The blood-soaked battles with the Twala also recall Stanley's gory battles on Lake Victoria against the Burimbeh.[7]

The idea of lost white tribes, a background feature of *King Solomon's Mines*, became a central element of Haggard's next two romances, *Allan Quatermain* (1887) and *She* (1887). *Allan Quatermain* assembles the trio of British adventures of *King Solomon's Mines* and traces their journey beneath the surface of Africa, into the subterranean world of Zu-Vendis, where they find a white feudalistic society structured on a combination of agriculture, chivalric traditions, and free love. In *She*, the trio discovers a lost African civilization governed by the cruel, beautiful Persian princess named Ayesha, who has reigned over her people for two thousand years using a combination of magic and terror. The three romances, which he wrote "in a white heat" between January 1885 and March 1886, sold far better than Haggard had imagined. He had set out to "try to write a book for boys" in 1885 with *King Solomon's Mines*, but early evidence showed that it reached broader audiences.[8]

The novels' popularity owed something to Haggard's skills. He wove together stock elements of the Victorian romance—adventure, fantastic peoples and places, a love interest with sexual tension—with contrived plot devices (the discovery of an old map came directly from Robert Louis Stevenson's 1883 *Treasure Island*). To these, he added details from his own experiences of Africa. Out of this fusion came remarkable characters. The ruthless, beautiful Ayesha, who mocks democracy and preaches survival of the fittest, broke with the conventions of female characters. "Those who are weak must perish; the earth is to the strong.... [W]e win the food we eat from out of the mouths of starving babes. It is the scheme of things." Sir Edmund Gosse wrote to Haggard, telling him, "It does not appear to me that I have ever been thrilled and terrified by any literature as I have by pp. 271–306 of 'She.' It is simply unsurpassable." Stevenson wrote to praise him for his "fine weird imagination."[9]

Yet fine weird imagination, by itself, could not hide the weaknesses of his novels. His relentless pace in producing his first works—followed by their spectacular success—had convinced him that speed was a virtue. His writing became sloppy and, at times, formulaic. He mostly avoided revising drafts. Even Stevenson warned him, "You should be more careful; you do quite well enough to take more trouble." He remained unconvinced. British critics were even harsher, broadly panning his work in the London papers. Yet his novels prospered because Haggard connected his stories to subjects that were in the spotlight of public attention: the colonial conquest of Africa, the search for gold, diamonds, and ivory, and—most important—the recent discoveries of missing links and lost civilizations.[10]

Lost societies had become a fascination of Western culture. The lost tribe of Israel described in the Hebrew Bible had long been invoked as an explanation for the existence of native peoples. The quickening pace of exploration in the eighteenth and nineteenth centuries, combined with new secular theories of human origin, resulted in a steady stream of "lost civilization" discoveries. In addition to the discovery of living peoples—by Stanley, Stefansson, and others—archaeologists were unearthing the great cities of the ancient world. As Mauch and Petrie brought back relics of ancient African civilizations, from Great Zimbabwe to Giza, other explorers were doing the same in Mayan cities (1839), Angkor Wat (1858), and Troy (1871). Not that interest in lost civilizations required the discovery of actual ruins or relics. Ignatius Donnelly's 1882 book, *Atlantis: The Antediluvian World*, sparked a revival of interest in the legendary civilization first described by Plato.

To these discoveries of civilizations were added others of more ancient provenance, bones and artifacts from the murky depths of prehistory. The discovery of thick-boned, heavily browed skeletons in Germany's Neander Valley in 1856 gave rise to the mystery of the Neanderthals, a hominid species whose relationship to modern humans remained mysterious. Adding to the mystery was the discovery of more recent remains at the Cro-Magnon rock shelter in 1868 by French railway workers. Excavation of the Cro-Magnon site by paleontologist Louis Lartet a few years later revealed five human skeletons, anatomically similar to modern humans, with red ochre, seashell necklaces, and the bones of prehistoric fauna. These discoveries gave heart to explorers and the geographical societies who looked at the dwindling blank spots on the global map with dismay. The realms of terra incognita were melting away like snows on a spring pasture, but other forms of discovery—in archaeology and paleontology—were blossoming in their place. If geographical exploration was reaching its zenith, explorers still continued to strike out into the wild places of the world, no longer to chart rivers and mountains, but to discover peoples, dig for artifacts, and disinter graves. They were no longer searching for new lands, but for the traces of the human past.[11]

Increasingly, these anthropological and archaeological discoveries were framed by evolutionary theory. Although *On the Origin of Species* had, as already noted, studiously avoided mention of *homo sapiens*, it was clear to everyone that it could be used to explain the human past. Discoveries of ancient cities and even more ancient human fossils, therefore, were quickly arranged into evolutionary sequences, lineages of progress and extinction driven by the engines of the Darwinian world: competition and conquest. These explanations were not limited to the past. Natural selection was invoked to explain the processes of the industrial age, the triumph of the strong over the weak, the smart over the feeble-minded, the industrious over the indolent. "Social Darwinism" became a pet theory of captains of industry such as Andrew Carnegie, while others, as already noted, applied it to the European conquest of Africa and Asia. They increasingly saw past, present, and future unfolding because of evolution, extinction, and conquest.

It was not the pronouncements of Ayesha, then, that horrified and titillated readers. These things were already being said—in quite different ways, of course—by Friedrich Nietzsche and Herbert Spencer.

It was that the one playing the role of Nietzsche's *Übermensch* was a lithe, leopard-skin-wearing princess. Ayesha was not, however, the only vehicle for expressing these ideas about human and racial evolution. They were widespread in Haggard's work and in the thousands of lost race stories that grew up in the shadow of *King Solomon's Mines*. Anglo-American writers dominated this new genre, but they were followed by French writers such as Jules Verne (who had already established himself as a writer of scientific romances), Russian novelists Vladimir Obruchev, author of *Plutonia* (1913) and *Sanikov Land* (1924), and German writers of pulp fiction in magazines such as *Horst Kraft der Pfadfinder*, which published dozens of lost race stories in the years before World War I.[12]

These fictional works took many forms and had many messages. European adventurers discovered tribes of Neanderthals, Egyptians, Roman legions, medieval crusaders, and the members of lost expeditions. In some novels, isolation has preserved traditional traits—chivalry, piety, and other virtues—that seemed to be disappearing in the modern world. In still others, isolation initiated a process of cultural and biological degeneration. Under the tyrannical rule of Ayesha, for example, followers practice all manner of taboo practices—cannibalism, homosexuality, necrophilia—that were abhorrent to most readers and fell outside of the realm of traditional novels. Even those stories at the edge of lost race literature—such as H. G. Wells's *The Time Machine* (1895), considered one of the urtexts of modern science fiction—took up this theme of human evolution and cultural degeneration, describing the future branching of the species into different varieties.[13]

Stories about the virtues and vices of non-European peoples had long been used to put forward arguments about European culture. Michel de Montaigne and, later, Jean-Jacques Rousseau had developed the literary tradition of the noble savage, developed from the discovery of new peoples, such as American Indians and Pacific Islanders, whose social mores compared well against what critics viewed as the decadence of European society. In their works it is clear that Europeans had a lot to learn from native peoples. Here were human populations that shared Europeans' faculties for reason and virtue but had been shaped differently by their environments. The noble savage stories bore out the philosophy of John Locke, who argued that humans are born into the world as empty vessels or "blank slates" (tabula rasa). His thesis, put forward in *An Essay on Human Understanding* (1690), imagined human children as—to use an anachronistic example—unformatted hard drives, waiting to receive data and command instructions that would shape them into unique forms. It was a radical view, one at odds with ideas that supported the industries of slavery as well as the institutions of monarchy. Kings, lords, and plantation owners were the groups inclined to press the distinctions of birth: some babies arrived with divine right, others under the curse of Ham. Yet Locke's radical notions had helped to unleash a storm on the Western world, one that can be seen in the revolutionary declarations of France, the United States, and South American countries that ultimately used Locke's idea to break with the idea of special birthrights. Their constitutions declared that all men are born equal, with the same innate abilities, rights, and prerogatives as their swaddled brethren. That such declarations did not apply to sisters, Africans, Indians, mestizos, and other people of mixed race show the limits of these ideas. Such words might break down the Bastille, but it would take more to bring down the plantation.

In short, Haggard and his peers lived in an age of expanded rights and enfranchisements, and yet they remained convinced that human difference, particularly racial difference, was real and significant. As a result, the lost-race literature of the late nineteenth century had a very different feel from the captivity narratives and noble savage literature of the preceding centuries. For Rousseau, Tahitians were more or less the same as Europeans, with fewer clothes and greater beach access. They were, as such, perfect test subjects for examining human society in its natural, "uncivilized" state. For late Victorians convinced that other races were fundamentally different from Europeans, however, the idea that tawny-skinned savages might offer lessons to the great civilizations of Europe seemed less convincing.

Perhaps this is the reason that discoveries of white tribes were always greeted with such popular and scientific enthusiasm. Lost races had always offered opportunities for comparison and self-reflection. Stories of Pacific Islanders living close to nature had enthralled Europeans, making them critical of their own civilization as artificial, unnatural, and decadent. But in this age of race science, when racial groups were perceived to be so different as to sometimes be classified as separate species, it was not enough anymore to find Negrito islanders to draw comparisons. Far more compelling was the discovery of savage peoples descended from the same racial stock, those who were cut off from Western culture, but who shared its ancestry.

This explains why Victorian novelists wrote about lost Europeans and Mediterraneans in such great numbers, far more frequently than they wrote about other groups. *King Solomon's Mines*—built on the premise of a Mediterranean lost colony in Africa—was the central catalyst in this process. The novel was taking London by storm when David Ker arrived at Henry Stanley's London home and began asking him about the "white race of Gambaragara." Within the year Ker had put together his own lost race romance, *Lost Among White Africans*, featuring Stanley on the Aruwimi River in eastern Congo, this time accompanied by two boys, the nephews of a British missionary. While exploring, they discover the Fidaserra, a white tribe descended from the first Portuguese settlers in East Africa. Over the centuries the Fidaserra—which derived from the Filha de Serra—had gradually lost their European customs and dress, adopting many of the ways of other African tribes. Of the hundreds of adventure novels and short stories published in Britain between 1880 and 1920, eighty percent of them concerned the discovery of white or proto-white tribes. In the process, the expeditions not only of Stanley and Mauch, but of other "white tribe" explorers such as Stefansson, Marsh, Batchelor, and others, became the subject of fictional accounts.

Not all of this was new to Haggard and to the legions of lost-race authors who followed him. White tribe stories of late Victorian fiction shared traits with two older traditions in literature: the whites-in-captivity stories of the early 1800s that focused on colonists captured by American Indians, and the whites-going-native literature that dated back to the Wildman stories of the Middle Ages. While these literary traditions dated back hundreds of years, they took on new urgency in the industrial age, which, for many, seemed to be the product of racial superiority, a Darwinian contest in which white races were demonstrating their superiority over the people they conquered and colonized. Yet there were growing legions of critics of the industrial age, people who believed that the processes of "progress" were dehumanizing to the working classes, enervating to the ownership classes, and corrosive to the environment that provided humans a place within the natural order.

By taking white people out of civilization, either as explorers who leave the gaslit cities of Europe behind, or as white colonists who—bounded by mountain ranges, jungles, subterranean caves, and polar glaciers—have lived in perpetual isolation, novelists considered the issue. In an era increasingly dominated by the idea that history was driven by biology (or, in human terms, race) rather than environment, these dime novels took on the great questions of the age. All of these stories wore the garments of adventure literature, but they had serious designs: to explore the frontier between human culture and human nature.

For some authors, like Edgar Rice Burroughs, confrontation with the wilds of nature offered an important corrective to the emasculating influences of the industrial world. Tarzan, the young abandoned Lord of Greystoke, raised by African apes, retains his intelligence, character, and moral center even as he lives in the ruthless world of the African jungle. Moreover, Tarzan gains strength and agility from the savage world that makes him orders of magnitude stronger than his civilized white peers. Burroughs followed up *Tarzan of the Apes* (1912) with a series of sequels that not only followed Tarzan, but also turned him into the vine-swinging explorer of other lost white worlds from the colony of Atlantis (located in the Congo) to the Valley of the Sepulchre, an ancient colony of British crusaders living in Kenya. Beneath these fantastic plot premises lay serious questions. How would the Briton without his tweeds, gun, and Oxford degree size up alongside the African? Was there anything different about a baron or earl once the veneer of polite society had been stripped away?

The answers differed. For Burroughs and other adventure writers, stripping away this civilization revealed the core racial character, as much as their white-gone-native novels demonstrated the benefits of casting off civilization for a life in the wild. While Burroughs offered a positive vision of the white hero—inoculated from the ills of civilization by life in the bush—Joseph Conrad offered a much bleaker vision in *Heart of Darkness* (1902). In his long travel up the African river—largely assumed to be the Congo—the narrator Marlow finds a man, not a colony. Mister Kurtz is, like the other "gone native" protagonists of Victorian fiction, a white man of exceptional intelligence and capacity. It is an intelligence that has allowed him to harness the power of native African clans, ivory hunting, and territorial command. Ivory flows from the high watershed of the river toward the stations below, eliciting both respect and envy from other company officers.

Yet Kurtz is lost, too. He knows where he is but not who he is. He is a man who cannot see the way forward, unmoored from the moral attachments of civilization in the world he left behind. *Heart of Darkness* did not employ any of the fantastic elements of *Tarzan* or *King Solomon's Mines*, but created a world rich in description and yet devoid of real-world particulars. It unfolds somewhere between story and allegory—brooding and ominous—as if the narrator doesn't know if he's recounting an expedition or a nightmare. "It seems to me I am trying to tell you a dream—making a vain attempt, because no relation of a dream can convey the dream-sensation, that commingling of absurdity, surprise, and bewilderment in a tremor of struggling revolt, that notion of being captured by the incredible which is of the very essence of dreams."[14]

In Conrad's story, the sharp distinctions between European and African, savage and civilized, lose clarity. London—with its shops, cafes, and stately homes—is the thinnest veneer covering the dark truths of the human condition, ones that are all too present in the heart of Africa. While *Heart of Darkness* can be read as a political critique of colonization of Africa—an aspect of the story that Conrad surely intended—its more disturbing lines are psychological, offering a grim inverse of the cheerful Tarzan who retains an essential racial differentness—from the apes who reared him to the Africans who battle him—that environment cannot obliterate.

Haggard's novels, choppy and formulaic, nevertheless made readers confront basic questions about human nature and racial heritage, ones that were more accessible than the statistical work of Francis Galton and the archaeological work of Flinders Petrie. If Haggard had used reports from Great Zimbabwe and Gambaragara as the settings of his imaginative romances, the novels themselves soon gained greater recognition than the work of Stanley or Mauch. When the African king Zebehr Pasha reported the existence of white tribes in Central Africa in 1887, "At Sakara and Bengbieh, in the very heart of slave country, there are tribes as white as Europeans, with long and silky hair," it was reported in the press as the "most remarkable confirmation" of Haggard's novel *Allan Quatermain*.[15]

The appeal was not limited to Europe. So popular were Haggard's novels that British South Africans began adopting the Zulu speech found in his novels. By the late 1920s, Longmans was translating *King Solomon's Mines* and its companions *Allan Quatermain* and *She* into Swahili, Zulu, and Sotho, and eventually into the click language Xhosa. Multiple editions of the books came out in Afrikaans in the 1930s. A 1956 survey of African readers in Ghana listed Haggard third among favorite authors (Marie Corelli and Shakespeare were first and second; Dickens came in fourth). In Africa, Haggard's romances also became part of Michael West's "New Method" of English-language training that grew up in the countries of the British Empire in the 1920s and continued into the 1950s. Such was their reach that African novelist Chinua Achebe puts West's editions of Haggard's *She* and *Ayesha: The Return of She* on the bookshelf of his powerful demagogic minister, M. A. Nanga.[16]

Although Haggard's novels have more in common with Burroughs than Conrad, written with an eye to swashbuckling adventure, they are also psychological novels if one looks closely, stories in which white heroes often become carried away by the violence and the pleasure of their adventures. In this, they echo Robert Lewis Stevenson's *Strange Case of Dr. Jekyll and Mr. Hyde*, which came out in 1885, just as Haggard was in the midst of composing his early works—and was "enough to cause the hair to rise." Stevenson articulated the dual nature of the human psyche—of conscious and unconscious longings—one that Haggard also expressed in the form of his racial romances. The lost white colonies of Haggard's fiction—in the mines of Solomon or in the city of She—offered a way of examining the central tension of his life, a feeling of living in two realities or of expressing two natures—civilized and savage—at the same time. In truth Haggard's protagonists were always walking the knife's edge between civilization and their true nature, a nature expressed by the savage white protagonists that they found in the bush. It was the inward-looking aspects of these white tribe novels—the mingling of race and psychology—that gave them additional force among those professionals, working in Vienna, who sought to chart the unknown regions of the mind.[17]

16

THE WHITE PSYCHE

SIGMUND FREUD LOVED H. RIDER HAGGARD's novels. It wasn't the battles, or romances, or discoveries of fabulous treasure that enchanted the Viennese psychologist, but the stories' confessions of deeper urges: cravings too disturbing to express in other forms of fiction. All of Haggard's characters—explorers, witch doctors, and rapacious priestesses—appeared to be the agents of barely repressed longings. In Kukuanaland and Zu-Vendis, they did and said things that could not be uttered within the polite society of London or Vienna. Yet Freud believed it was these unutterable desires that, working in his clinical practice in Austria, he was detecting in his women patients suffering from "hysteria" and other conditions. Freud's treatment for these conditions relied on a new "talking cure" that would come to be called psychoanalysis. Yet he relied on other methods of treatment, too: hypnosis, cocaine, or Haggard, as needed. So when Louise N., a patient who arrived in his office requesting material to read, Freud complied. "I offered her *She* by Rider Haggard. A strange book, but full of hidden meaning."[1]

The "hidden meanings" would appear to Freud in his own dreams, and, never one to take dreams lightly, he set about analyzing them. In *The Interpretation of Dreams* (1900), a book that would become a foundational text in the field of psychoanalysis, he discussed his

Haggard dreams at length. In one, he found himself with Louise N., dissecting his own pelvis ("the self-analysis necessitated in the communication of my dreams") and then, running past a girl, Indians, wooden houses ("from [Haggard's novel] *Heart of the World*") before reaching muddy ground and crossing a chasm ("awakened in me by...Rider Haggard's *She*"). Here was the heart of the dream, "an adventurous journey to the undiscovered country, a place almost untrodden by the foot of man."

Set within the world of *She*, Freud's "undiscovered country" referred to Africa, specifically those regions of the interior newly charted by Stanley and other explorers. Yet, in fact, Stanley never walked upon grounds that hadn't been trodden and settled by Africans for thousands of years. This was equally true of Haggard's fictional characters; Allan Quatermain sets out seeking ivory and other treasures in lands long inhabited by others. Yet Freud was clearly being allegorical. The undiscovered country was psychological terrain, a terra incognita of dangerous thoughts and desires, a place difficult to access from the illuminated regions of the waking mind. He labeled it, for that reason, "the unconscious," a place cut off from the rest of the psyche. If Freud imagined himself as the Stanley of psychoanalysis, the unconscious was his great quest, the key to his metapsychology, the human mind's "darkest Africa."

Here, possibly, was the reason Freud's Africa seemed so empty. It was a place moved by white figures, not black ones, a world that despite its distance from Europe, still conformed to the rules of Viennese society, in which Freud was surrounded by white patients and colleagues, and in which Africans didn't exist—or, to be more accurate, didn't exist as people. They were the dark background that brought foreground objects—explorers, protagonists, or, in Freud's case, Austrian patients—into sharper relief. Not surprisingly, then, Freud's interest in *She* focused wholly on the figure of Ayesha, the Persian priestess who expressed, as he confided to Louise N., "the eternal feminine [and] the immorality of our emotions." Africans were interesting to Freud—in fiction as well as fact—only because he thought they had the power to illuminate the white psyche.[2]

At the heart of Freud's interest was the concept of the primitive. It was an old idea, but one that had gained force as Europeans tried to make sense of their encounters with peoples around the world. In the

Frontispiece of *Theatrum Orbis Terrarum*, 1590. Credit: Watkinson Library, Trinity College, Hartford, Connecticut.

Middle Ages, the European benchmark for civilization—a word that didn't exist yet within the European vernacular—was religion. The world could be divided into Christian, heathen, and pagan. These divisions continued to obtain through the fifteenth and sixteenth centuries when Europeans came into contact with peoples—Africans, South Asians, and Americans—that were separated not only from Christianity but also its monotheistic cousins Judaism and Islam. The hierarchy of the world's peoples into stages of civilization can be seen in the frontispiece of Abraham Ortelius's *Theatrum Orbis Terrarum*, ("The Theater of the World"), Europe's first published world atlas. There the peoples of the world are organized according to relative height on the scale of civilization, with the goddess of Europe on top, fully clothed, the heathen goddesses of Asia and Africa in the middle, and the savage, cannibal goddess of the Americas reclined at the bottom.

Later thinkers maintained this scale of civilization, even as religion began to give way to race as the most important category of human difference. While earlier scholars had thought of heathen and pagan beliefs as the degeneration of humankind's original, Noachian, monotheistic flock late Enlightenment thinkers flipped the process. Humans were originally simple in their social organization and savage in their worship. Only over time did some of them—read, Europeans—progress to become more sophisticated in their culture, habits, and beliefs.

According to this new framework, all human races were moving along the same path of social evolution, from savage to civilized, but at different rates of speed. Europeans were winning this race, followed by Arabs, Asians, and Indians. Pygmies and Negritos lagged furthest, loitering near the starting blocks of human progress. It became common for anthropologists to view so-called primitive peoples as living relics: people moving through the early stages of cultural evolution toward a more civilized—in other words, European—system of customs and beliefs. As they ventured into the interior of Africa, Central Asia, or the Arctic, Europeans felt as if they were traveling back in time. Believing that human cultures followed fixed stages of evolution, Europeans encountering natives in these places viewed them not only as prehistoric, but as the placeholders of a European past—a cultural stage that Europeans had passed through centuries or millennia before. While some Europeans saw virtue in the life of native peoples, mostly they were seen negatively through a prism fashioned by nineteenth-century Europe mores: simplistic in technology, savage in customs, and immature in behaviors. For every essay written in defense of native customs, a dozen more portrayed them as irrational, emotional, and violent. Not surprisingly, in an age that admired progress, Europeans imagined these peoples as backward, and as such, a close representation of European races as they existed during their prehistoric period of barbarism.

The analogy proved adaptable. If nonwhite races corresponded to the white race during its evolutionary childhood, might not these natives also correspond to the developmental stage of white children as well? After all, children expressed many of the behaviors—emotional outbursts, impulsive violence, lack of judgment—that Victorian scientists had used to portray the non-European peoples of the world. These types of descriptions had become common after Columbus's first encounters with Caribbean islanders in 1492. This idea became so fixed in Europeans' descriptions of native peoples—the "children of nature"—that the analogy was taken for granted by the eighteenth century. "Why should one be amazed," wondered the scholar Charles De Brosses in 1760, "to see peoples who constantly pass their life in an eternal infancy and who are never more than four years old reason incorrectly?"[3]

The analogy also proved long-lasting because it was so useful. As Europeans expanded their reach across the continents of the world, the idea of natives as children helped shape and justify colonial policies. How should a British officer govern his African colony? The same way a parent guides his children or a teacher leads her students: firmly, kindly, and autocratically. Democracy had as much utility among native peoples, they argued, as it did among children at the dinner table or pupils in the classroom.

The rise of evolutionary theory in the 1800s complicated this analogy further. Added to the idea of progress as the rise of a civilization was the transformation of a species. Darwin's work catalyzed this intellectual shift, igniting the fires of many disciplines—from botany and archaeology to anthropology. Yet elements of Darwin's theory, particularly natural selection—that blind engine of evolutionary change that drove species from one adaptation to the next—were not popular outside of Britain. Many of those who embraced the idea of evolution did not believe that it could be random and capricious, but that it must be somehow directed, a process that nudged species up the ladder of progress much in the way a seedling transforms into a tree. Humans, too, were gradually climbing the ladder of evolution, passing through a variety of racial stages before arriving at their most advanced form, the white European.

To this, Ernst Haeckel, Germany's most famous supporter of evolution, added another idea. He argued in his 1866 book, *Generelle Morphologie der Organismen* ("General Morphology of Organisms"), that every species' path up the evolutionary ladder could be witnessed in the development of the organism over the course of its life. Before a human embryo arrived at the form of a human child, Haeckel argued that it passed through the evolutionary stages of its ancestors. Thus, the gill-like structures that appeared on human embryos during their fourth week of development represented the passage of the human through the fish stage of its evolutionary development. In all of nature, "ontology recapitulates phylogeny," he declared: the development of the organism repeats the development of the species. It would also become known as the biogenetic law, an expansion of the human progress analogy to its fullest form, one that would exert its influences on social science—from theories of education to those of childhood development—for decades to come.

Some of its most profound effects, however, emerged in psychology. Freud adopted the idea of human evolution as a climbing of the ladder toward more evolved—in other words, more European—forms. He also believed that individuals moved through the stages of their evolutionary history as they matured from child to adult. Then, Freud took these ideas even further, applying them to the evolution of the human psyche. In feelings and behaviors, the white child reenacted the evolutionary history of the human psyche, from its savage beginnings to its civilized present. The child was, in other words, a throwback to an earlier moment in the history of the white race when the psyche was less developed. Within this complicated web of analogies, the white child, the adult savage, and the prehistoric European were now linked as psychic equals.

The savage element of the child psyche never disappeared. It remained at the core of the personality even as the child progressed into adulthood. Like the gills of Haeckel's embryos, the savage mind was soon covered over by other structures, but it remained buried within the architecture of the mind. The maturing mind expressed new traits—empathy, reason, and reflection—ones that equipped it for the challenges of living in the civilized world. Yet these traits were laid across the top of the savage mind like an asphalt tarmac, smoothing its jagged surface, containing from the rest of the world the wants and desires that would otherwise jar the mind off its pursuit of higher goals. Those thoughts and desires that could not be tolerated by the conscious mind—usually rooted in taboo sexual desires—were driven underground into the unconscious. While Freud believed that the unconscious served a function, protecting the conscious mind from unacceptable thoughts, it could also lead to neuroses if it became overburdened. Here, then, lay the root of Freud's interest in the unconscious mind, as well as his admiration of Haggard's novels, and his more general curiosity about primitivism, white tribes, and Europeans who "went native": all expressed the workings of the savage mind, that hidden core of the psyche that cooperated with, and struggled against, the conscious mind. Within this essential tension of mind lay the heart of Freud's psychoanalytic theory.

Once anchored to the concept of the "primitive mind," the unconscious became an idea that could be investigated in different ways. There was the couch, where Freud and others interviewed patients and discussed dream interpretations; and there was the expedition, where the so-called primitive mind could be studied directly in encounters with native peoples. Freud, happy in his life as a bourgeois clinician, had little interest in the latter. Despite his dream adventures, he had no interest in traveling to the Haggardesque landscapes of the world in search of the unconscious. Nor did his disciples, the physicians, neurologists, and psychiatrists who met Wednesdays over coffee and cake, discussing papers as they smoked cigarettes (for Freud, cigars) and developing the ideas that would launch the international psychoanalytic movement in the twentieth century.

Yet one of Freud's disciples did follow the other path. Carl Jung, a Swiss psychologist, took to the field in search of the unconscious. He began corresponding with Freud in 1906, and soon became an important figure in the psychoanalytic movement. Freud considered Jung to be his successor within the movement, but the two men fell out in 1912, largely over disagreements over the nature of the libido and the unconscious. Despite this, Jung continued to embrace the idea of the unconscious as a core structure of the mind, primitive in origin and function. Jung developed this idea even further, arguing that the veiled region of the mind contained a "personal unconscious," which held thoughts and memories unique to the individual, as well as a "collective unconscious," which carried memories and forms carried forward from the ancient history of the tribe and the race. Europeans were born, as Freud believed, not only with the structures of the primitive mind but also with the *content* of this mind, the forms and symbols of ancient memory. Here, then, was added incentive for Jung to travel in search of so-called primitive peoples, not simply because they offered a living model of the unconscious mind unfettered by the higher structures of the civilized mind, but because such encounters might be used to trigger the dormant memories of his own collective unconscious.[4] "The sight of a child or a primitive will arouse certain longings in the adult, civilized persons," he wrote in his autobiography *Memories, Dreams, Reflections*, "longings which relate to the unfulfilled desires and needs of those parts of the personality which have been blotted out."[5]

Certainly, he believed, this work in the field would be more productive than searching for the unconscious in Vienna or Zurich. Jung had come to believe that for all of its wonders, the civilized world was exacting a toll upon the human soul. In this, he expressed the spirit of the age. Paul Gauguin fled Paris in 1891 with his canvases and paints, seeking to escape "everything that is artificial and conventional." In Tahiti, where he spent the rest of his life, he painted scenes of native life, far from the "the disease of civilization." In America, anxious parents tried to inoculate their boys from the disease of civilization by sending them into the Boy Scouts, where they would enter the woods, build fires, and engage in "savage play." The Boston illustrator Joseph Knowles took this approach to the extreme, shedding all of his clothes and entering the Maine woods in 1913 to live like "a primitive man...from the land of civilization to the forest of antiquity." Closer to home, Jung watched the rise of the Völkisch movement in Austria and Germany among men anxious to find a core German identity that had been diluted by the luxuries and racial mixing of European cities. Young men discussed Germany mythology in secret societies and climbed mountains in alpine clubs, hoping to find the primal Aryan heart beating beneath the linen and lederhosen. "The European is, to be sure, convinced that he is no longer what he was ages ago; but he does not know what he has since become." Ascending so high up the ladder of racial progress, Jung believed that Europeans had lost sight of the ground.[6]

In 1925, he made plans to climb down the ladder. He would explore Africa in search of the primitive. The "Bugishu Psychological Expedition" consisted of a small group of analysts and patients who accompanied him on a trip to Kenya, joined him on safaris and train rides into the interior, then cruised north with him on the Nile River. After teaching a final seminar in Zurich—where participants were asked to analyze Haggard's novel *She*—he set off on his quest. Jung's interest in Africa did not have much to do with Africans. Ultimately, they were the means to an end, the catalyst for personal discovery: to understand those aspects of his psyche that still lay in the shadows "to find that part of my personality which had become invisible under the influence and the pressure of being European."[7]

In 1925, Jung and his party sailed for Africa aboard the German steamer *Wangoni*. The ship steamed down the Suez Canal and into the Red Sea. As they advanced further down the coast, Jung and his party grew increasingly sober, thinking about the dangers of the African interior. "The serious undertone was evident." It wasn't so serious, however, that Jung and his party failed to enjoy themselves. Jung's voyage down the Swahili coast was hardly Marlow's steamboat trip in the *Heart of Darkness*. The *Wangoni*, a 7,768-ton steamer, carried more than two hundred passengers in comfort. Jung's party traveled first class, mingling with other European travelers, playing deck games, and lounging in the smoking parlor (where Jung smoked pipes). Arriving in Mombasa, the party boarded the Uganda Railway ("The Lunatic Express"), a narrow-gauge train that set out from Mombasa to Nairobi, a town that had begun as a British rail depot in 1899 but had subsequently become the capital of British East Africa.[8]

These "explorers" followed paths well-trodden by earlier ones. Jung arrived in Mombasa seventy-eight years after the German missionaries Johann Krapf and Johannes Rebmann had arrived in the port city, setting off into the interior to become the first Europeans to see Mount Kilimanjaro and Mount Kenya, Africa's tallest mountains. When Jung boarded the Uganda Railway a few days later, he did so eighteen years after the Duke of Abruzzi took the same train toward Lake Victoria and the successful summit of Gambaragara, which he renamed Mount Stanley. Even when they weren't tracing the paths of earlier explorers, they were living in their shadows. In Nairobi, the Bugishu Psychological Expedition checked into the New Stanley Hotel, a spacious building of arched columns, red-tiled roofs, and high verandas, named in honor of an explorer who had surveyed so much of the Lakes Region—in considerably less comfort—fifty years earlier.

Retracing old ground did not bother Jung and his band of roving analysts, however, since the object of their quest concerned psychological, not geographical, exploration. That they arrived in East Africa's highlands decades after Stanley had traced the source of the Nile was beside the point. They were tracing the watersheds of the human psyche. Because the ultimate goal of this quest was to understand the European's buried primitivity, rather than understand Africans in and of themselves, no one felt compelled to travel far from the New Stanley Hotel, especially when it was in the thrall of one of its free-wheeling European parties. On November 14, 1925, Jung and his group attended an Armistice Day dance at the New Stanley. Here mingled the ranks of big-game hunters, pith-helmeted tourists, debutants, and wealthy landowners, drinking and dancing late into the night, shedding the mores of Europe without any assistance from "primitive" Africa or Africans.

There, Jung met a young English nurse, Ruth Bailey, who would become one of his lifelong intimates, a member of a group of women, the "Jungfrauen," who would attend to his intellectual and emotional needs throughout his life. "I am not sure whether I picked CG up," wrote Bailey, "or he picked me up." Did Jung consider this research? A path back to the child-mind of the savage? In its write-up of the party, the *East African Standard* put it slightly differently: "Colours rioted everywhere, changing, overflowing, intermingling in every corner of the main dancing apartment and the lounge [where] overgrown children danced the night away." Jung's had begun his climb down the ladder.[9]

Riding in his cabin in the Lunatic Express, Jung had another encounter with "the primitive" one morning when he noticed an African man leaning on a spear "looking down on the train." The image was enough, apparently, to trigger memories from Jung's collective unconscious. "I have the feeling that I had already experienced this moment and had always known this world which was separated from me by distance in time. It was as if I were this moment returning to the land of my youth, and as if I known that dark-skinned man who had been waiting for me for five thousand years."[10]

By the time Jung reached the Athi Plains, he had a revelation that would become known to Jungians as his "discovery of self," one of the most discussed episodes of his African expedition:

> *From a low hill in this broad savanna a magnificent prospect opened out to us. To the very brink of the horizon we saw gigantic herds of animals: gazelle, antelope, gnu, zebra, warthog, and so on. Grazing, heads nodding, the herds moved forward like slow rivers. There was scarcely a sound save the melancholy cry of a bird of prey. This was the stillness of the eternal beginning, the world as it had always been, in the state of non-being; for until then no one had been present to know that it was this*

world. I walked away from my companions until I had put them out of sight and savored the feeling of being entirely alone. There I was now, the first human being to recognize that this was the world, but who did not know that in this moment he had first really created it.[11]

Among many contemporary thinkers, this revelation represented Jung's deeper understanding of human consciousness. Yet it is hard not to return to Freud's dream of Africa—the undiscovered country that existed depopulated of Africans. Jung had taken this to the next level. The act of creation was an act of consciousness, and Jung—standing on the Athi Plains—was the only human capable of such consciousness. The rest of Africa did not exist until he witnessed it.

Jung's ascent of Mount Elgon in Western Kenya represented one of the other high points of his journey. Here, among the Elgonyi people, Jung hoped to find the source of true primitivism. It was almost exactly fifty years after Stanley had looked upon Mount Gambaragara, on the other side of Lake Victoria, and wondered about its implications for the nature of human history. "We discovered a new form of a very primitive psychological religion with the tribes on the slopes of Mt. Elgon, where nobody advised us to go. They apparently worship the sun. But it isn't the sun, it is the moment of dawn: that is God. I think it's rather amazing. It is the origin of the Egyptian Horus idea."[12]

When Jung arrived in Egypt, he would see evidence of this religion and came to the conclusion that African beliefs had filtered north to the culture of the Pharaohs in ancient times: an inversion, of sorts, of the Hamitic hypothesis offered by Petrie and others.

Still, it was clear that Jung's interests were primarily in discovering the white psyche in the heart of Africa. His interest in Aryan racial psychology would continue into the 1930s when, disturbed by the rise of National Socialism, he began to distance himself from the work. For the moment, however, Jung could revel in his ascent of Mount Elgon with his new companion Ruth Bailey. He had finally escaped Europe, "the mother of all demons." "There were no telegrams, no telephone calls, no letters, no visitors. My liberated psychic forces poured blissfully back to the primeval expanses." Jung could imagine himself with his band, for a few hours at least, a primitive white tribe on a mountain, much like the one Stanley imagined on Gambaragara.[13]

17

CRACKS IN THE THEORY

FIFTY-EIGHT YEARS AFTER CARL MAUCH first came upon the mist-shrouded enclosures of Great Zimbabwe, the English archaeologist Gertrude Caton-Thompson headed to Rhodesia to try to solve the mystery of the majestic ruins, which even by 1929 remained a cause of much controversy. Mauch had believed that the city had been settled by an ancient people from the Middle East, a theory that grew, as we've seen, from Portuguese legends of a city of gold in the African interior, one that took African reports of the ruins and attached them to the Old Testament story of the Ophir, a city of gold. In the following decades, as archaeologists gave their support to Mauch's theory, they tore through centuries of stratified debris at Great Zimbabwe searching for evidence of the city's non-African founders. They ignored or discarded artifacts of clearly African design, attributing them to a more recent "Kaffir" occupation. In the end, they found enough artifacts to conclude that Great Zimbabwe's builders had come from outside of Africa. Their foreign-builder theory had become the standard interpretation of Great Zimbabwe, in part because careless digging had destroyed much of the evidence that could be used to refute the hypothesis.

In January 1929, Caton-Thompson arrived in Beira on the coast of Portuguese Mozambique aboard a Union-Castle ship. She hadn't

Gertrude Caton-Thompson. Credit: Royal Anthropological Institute.
RAI 36032 Portrait of Gertrude Caton-Thompson. Ramsey
& Muspratt. Cambridge, 1938.

found the passage down Africa's eastern coast as entertaining as Carl Jung had four years earlier. She shared none of the psychologist's delight in passengers who cast off their European mores as they approached Africa. She found her shipmates "noisy and given to too much drink." So she kept to herself, reading *The Records of South East Africa* for hours each day, mailing each of the nine volumes home as she finished them. When the ship had docked in Mombasa, she considered an excursion to Nairobi, not to chase Jung or encounter the primitive, but to find Louis Leakey, who was finishing up his dissertation on the prehistoric peoples of Kenya. She was on a tight schedule, however, so she scrapped the idea. The British Association for the Advancement of Science had directed her "to undertake the examination of the ruins at Zimbabwe...to reveal the character, date, and source of the culture of the builders." Caton-Thompson would report her findings at the British Association meeting in South Africa a few months later.[1]

Walking past the tin shacks lining the main avenue of Beira, she looked for a hotel where she could wait for the twice-a-week train to Rhodesia the following day. In 1929, the town did not offer many amenities. Like most visitors, Caton-Thompson arrived here en route to someplace else. The port was the colonial entrepôt to the lands of southern Africa, popular with European ships because of its good harbor and its railway terminus. Once the train arrived, she would take it to Salisbury, a Rhodesian city four hundred miles in the interior, where she would travel by motor car to Great Zimbabwe, wait for her two assistants, and begin her work.

It didn't work out as planned. As Caton-Thompson retired to her room, a cyclone struck the coast. Wind ripped through the port, tearing off roofs, collapsing walls, and shattering windows. Ships groaned against their moorings as massive waves entered the harbor. When she emerged from the hotel the following morning, the Union-Castle steamer lay piled with other ships on the shore. The waves had wreaked havoc with the railway as well, washing away low sections of track built on the alluvial flats of the river. She idled in Beira for nine days before realizing that she was waiting for a train that wouldn't arrive. Her route to Great Zimbabwe now lay to the south: down the coast of South Africa, overland to the Highveld, then north by train to Rhodesia. She boarded the next ship, an American cargo vessel carrying chrome ore, heading for South Africa. Despite the black ore dust that pervaded food, bed, and clothing, she stayed with the ship until it made port in Lourenco Marques (Maputo), then boarded a train to Johannesburg.[2]

This was not the first time that the British Association tried to bring order to the study of Great Zimbabwe after the chaos left by Theodore Bent and others. Alarmed by the rapid destruction of the ruins by careless archaeologists, the association had commissioned David Randall-MacIver—a student of Flinders Petrie in Egypt—to investigate the site. Two things recommended Randall-MacIver to the task. He appeared to be impartial on the issue of origins, and he was trained in the new techniques of stratigraphy. In contrast to earlier archaeologists, Randall-MacIver found no evidence of foreign builders at Great Zimbabwe. In his 1906 book, *Medieval Rhodesia*, he observed that artifacts and architectural styles at the ruins were all consistent with those of local African design. Moreover, the city itself dated no earlier than the 1400s, a period too recent for it to have been the outpost of King Solomon, the Queen of Sheba, or any other representative of ancient Mediterranean peoples.

Randall-MacIver's findings only inflamed the controversy. By the turn of the twentieth century, the Hamitic hypothesis, as we've seen, benefited from a band of supporters respectable as well as diverse. If the early claims of Stanley and others that white tribes dwelled within the heart of Africa had seemed flimsy, archaeologists had provided a flying buttress of support from digs north and south. In Egypt, Flinders Petrie argued for the invasion of Egypt by a superior "dynastic race" seven thousand years ago on the basis of careful craniological study and dating techniques. In southern Africa, Zimbabwe's investigators all concluded that the site bore the marks of a Mediterranean culture rather than an African one, confirming Old Testament stories of Solomon, Sheba, and the Ophir. How the "ancients" of Great Zimbabwe were connected to the living Bahima and Bachwezi of East Africa or the long-past dynastic race of Egypt remained an open question. Some believed that Great Zimbabwe was a great colony, the vanguard of a Hamitic invasion in southern Africa, while others argued that it operated as a fortified outpost among hostile Africans, its giant walls built to defend its builders from local tribes. Despite these variations in the theory, the Hamitic hypothesis seemed to stand firmly upon many evidentiary pillars from archaeology to anthropology, including old skulls, ancient artifacts, and expeditionary eyewitness accounts.

It did not help Randall-MacIver's cause that white Rhodesians were largely convinced that native Africans were incapable of building such sophisticated structures. Rather, they preferred to imagine the ancient city as a prehistoric colony of white or proto-white foreigners in southern Africa, a story that echoed their own rapid colonization of these lands under the command of Cecil Rhodes. Rhodes was a defender of the "foreign builder" hypothesis and an enthusiastic collector of artifacts from Great Zimbabwe. After visiting the site in 1891, he had purchased one of the large soapstone birds of prey, identified by Bent and others as fabricated by the ancients. (Exactly what these ancient birds represented—Phoenician icons, Egyptian gods, or Arabian totems—remained a matter of debate.) The birds, once perched on the walls of the ruins, were hacked down and set to roost in Rhodes's Cape Town manor. Wooden birds of the same design adorned the banisters of the house, while larger-than-life replicas were placed in Cambridge to watch over the gates of his English home.[3]

It is not surprising, then, that Randall-MacIver's short, technical account of his expedition in *Medieval Rhodesia* provoked a furious response. Hall and other archaeologists quickly wrote a rejoinder, *Prehistoric Rhodesia*, which took aim at Randall-MacIver's inability to conclusively date the strata of the site (dating made more difficult by Hall's own destruction of the strata within the enclosures). As Caton-Thompson later observed, "These objections, and about 400 pages of additional ones, were bundled together, and *Prehistoric Rhodesia* was flung at MacIver's head in 1909." Now, twenty years later, on the eve of another meeting in South Africa of the British Association, the organization was trying again.[4]

It had therefore selected Caton-Thompson—who had trained with Flinders Petrie—to excavate Great Zimbabwe in hopes of clearing up the controversy once and for all. By the 1920s, she had made a name for herself in the male-dominated world of archaeology for her investigations in Egypt, where she learned from Petrie's careful methods, even while she bristled against his "dictatorial and obstinate" manner and his "queer obsession" with Egyptian invasion theories. Caton-Thompson harbored no such obsessions about Hamitic invasions or Aryan conquests. As she prepared for her work at Great Zimbabwe, she tried to construct a plan of work that would avoid such traps, a plan that "contained no germ of preconceived ideas as to the ruins' origin and age, [and remained] unconcerned with speculations, unencumbered by *a priori* hypotheses as to who might have done what." In so doing, she believed she could avoid the pitfalls of earlier archaeologists who had fallen into the "wildernesses of deductive error."[5]

In Johannesburg, she met Raymond Dart, one of a small community of archaeologists who welcomed her en route to her Great Zimbabwe expedition. Dart has become something of a sensation in Southern Africa for his discovery of an early hominid skull, the "Taung child," in 1924. For six years, Dart had been professor of anatomy at the University of Witwatersrand. A native of Australia, he had earned his medical degree at the University of Sydney, and then, after World War I, taught anatomy at University College London under the tutelage of the diffusionist archaeologist Grafton Elliot Smith. Only reluctantly, and with much coaxing from Elliot Smith, did Dart leave London for a teaching position in Johannesburg, a place he viewed as an intellectual backwater. Dart had made the best of it, focusing on physical anthropology and archaeology—making use of the bones and artifacts that were being discovered in large numbers all over southern Africa.[6]

Neither Dart nor Caton-Thompson left an account of their meeting, but it is easy to imagine possible outlines of their conversation. Dart, a man bursting with ideas and opinions, would have discussed his own research on Great Zimbabwe, published a few years earlier in the British journal *Nature*. Caton-Thompson probably said less, not only to preserve her impartiality on the excavation that lay ahead, but also because she was constitutionally adverse to speculation. The two scholars were, despite shared interests, opposites of temperament. Caton-Thompson had made a name for herself in archaeology by her commitment to careful and deliberate methods. Dart proceeded precisely in reverse: using wit, charisma, and bold—sometimes reckless—theorizing to stay relevant in the world of archaeological science, one centered thousands of miles away from his new home in Johannesburg.

Dart's research on Great Zimbabwe was full of this characteristic theorizing. In his study of Bushman cave art, he had observed similarities of design between the African paintings and ancient Babylonian art. He concluded that southern Africa had been colonized by a Mediterranean people, a finding that supported the theories of Bent, Hall, and others. He had criticized Randall MacIver's findings, arguing that African-style artifacts at the ruins were merely signs of "Bantu contamination." Caton-Thompson would hear many similar theories about the ruins' origin on her slow, circuitous trip to Rhodesia.[7]

It would take another month of travel—two weeks traveling through the monsoon and another two weeks recovering from malaria—before she began her work at Great Zimbabwe. She was joined by two assistants, Dorothy Norie and Kathleen Kenyon, as well as a crew of Shona workers from nearby towns. A survey of the site convinced Caton-Thompson to avoid the most spectacular regions of the ruins—the Elliptical Building and the Acropolis—because they had been "extensively ransacked" by earlier excavations. Instead, she focused her work on the curious structures of the Maund Ruins, a landscape of twenty-nine finely coursed, disconnected walls, doorways, platforms, and bastions. These ruins remained largely untouched. As the weeks passed, the three women established a routine. Excavation work began at 8:30 a.m. and, after a break for lunch, continued until 5:30 p.m. In the waning light, they shared a thermos of tea, then walked back to their mud-and-daub huts half a mile away. Here, at her small writing table, Caton-Thompson worked up her daily notes under the light of a kerosene lamp.

The work was going well. In six weeks, the team had completed a detailed plan of the Maund Ruins. They had excavated a series of trenches from the surface to the bedrock of the site, finding hundreds of artifacts—shards of earthenware pots, iron tools and weapons, gold wire bracelets—none of which showed signs of foreign design. Yet, the architecture of the Maund Ruins mystified her because the disconnected walls and doorways-to-nowhere did not match any pattern of building—African, Mediterranean, or other—that she could recognize.

Perplexed, she decided to forgo digging on her final day at the site, taking the day to study the layout of the ruins. The birds-eye view of the site plan looked like a strange experiment in calligraphy, with swooping walls punctuated by gaps, doorways, and platforms. Then she saw it. Grabbing her calipers, she drew a circle that linked one set of walls together like spokes around a hub. The answer wasn't in the walls, but in the gaps between them. The circle, she realized, was the position of a mud hut that had eroded away over the centuries, one that had anchored the walls together. She drew more circles—ten in all—until the design of the settlement became clear. It was a design she had seen before, indeed, one that was ubiquitous through the African interior: mud-thatched huts and circular enclosures, a design that extended from the Central African "boma" to the South African "kraal." In design, the Maund Ruins were clearly African in origin. "This alone seemed to make the whole enterprise and six weeks worthwhile." By June 8, the patterns were becoming clear. She wrote to her mother, "I am quite certain that the ruins are native work and show no outside civilizations. The actual date is still in suspense.... [I]t is most improbable that the buildings are older than 1000 AD and probably 4 or 5 hundred years later." While Caton-Thompson was giving form to the

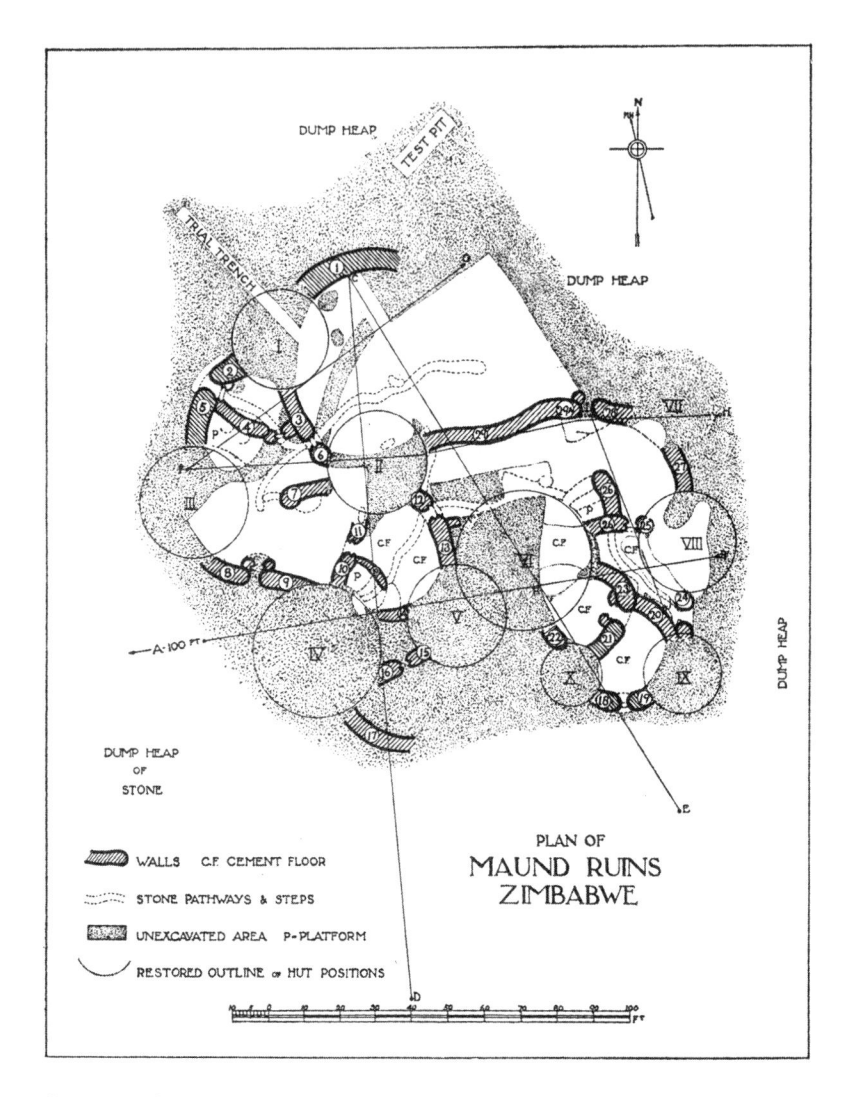

Gertrude Caton-Thompson's illustration of the Maund Ruins at Great Zimbabwe. Circles show location of mud-thatched huts. Credit: Caton-Thompson, *The Zimbabwe Culture; Ruins and Reactions*.

elegant African city, she was knocking loose one of the great foundation stones of the Hamitic hypothesis.[8]

By 1929, the scientific edifice of the Hamitic hypothesis was showing other cracks. As Caton-Thompson chiseled away at the idea in archaeology, others were finding faults in craniology, widely believed since the early 1800s to be the best identifier of race. Samuel Morton and George Gliddon had of course justified their own Egyptian invasion theory, comparing skulls on the basis of volume and facial angle. Others used the cephalic index, a measurement of head shape. By the late 1800s, however, race scientists still disagreed on the best method for measuring skulls. The volume of a human skull varied according to the age and sex of an individual, as well as environmental conditions such as famine. Unless these factors could be identified, the typing of a skull by volume was useless. Even measurements of face and skull shape seemed increasingly suspect. In 1893, Italian anthropologist Giuseppe Sergi came to the conclusion that however important skulls were as a determinant of race, the cephalic index offered "measures [that] only discover some secondary characters of the skull; I have proved that, under the same cephalic index, we have many different forms of skulls, and under various cephalic indices we have the same shape of the skull." Petrie also had voiced his doubts. "The cephalic index is just as likely to depend on place as on parentage," he wrote in 1906. These doubts were confirmed in 1912 when American anthropologist Franz Boas published a craniological study of recent immigrants and their children in America. He found that immigrant children born and raised in America had cephalic indexes different from their immigrant parents. His conclusion was that skulls did not offer a pure measurement of race since they could be affected as much by environment—such as practices of child-rearing—as they were by heredity.[9]

At first, the dynastic race theory, built upon Petrie's fanatical attention to skull measurements and site stratigraphy, seemed to withstand such criticism. In his careful, methodologically sophisticated studies of Egyptian skulls, such biases were difficult to detect. Petrie's papers seemed to be towers of empirical evidence, raised upon a framework of advanced "biometrics": statistical methods for studying racial difference in human populations. For a new generation of archaeologists, including MacIver and Caton-Thompson, Petrie had redefined what it meant to do good archaeology. Yet even Caton-Thompson realized that Petrie's careful work was leading to sometimes dubious conclusions, ones filtered through an ideological fixation on foreign invasion theories. If volumes, facial angles, and cephalic indexes were influenced by the environment, why did Petrie think that specific skull structures were a better measurement of racial identity?

Yet the Hamitic hypothesis, along with the Aryan invasion theory, struggled with an even more existential problem as a scientific theory, one that extended beyond debates about best practices. It had to do with the existence of race itself as a category. Even Francis Galton and Flinders Petrie—while accepting that racial populations expressed a range of traits, typified by their relentless use of bell curves—believed that these variations were the static that masked the sound, the scatter of traits that lay like a fog over the pure type lying just beneath. Although most scientists had not perceived this yet, new concepts in population biology and Mendelian genetics posed a critical threat to the idea of pure racial type. One could isolate a racial type only if one supposed that races were fixed. Darwinian biology declared that they were not. Species—or even races—were not fixed, unchanging entities designed by God but fluid things, changeable, constantly adapting to different environmental conditions. Within the new biology, race made sense only in the aggregate: as the sum total of genetic traits within a given population.

Even as Petrie and others acknowledged the difficulties in fitting individuals into the box of biological race, they still held on to race as an ideal: real and yet maddeningly abstract. French anthropologist Paul Topinard expressed this unshakable faith in races as real entities, despite their evasion of all forms of measurement. "We cannot deny them, our intelligence comprehends them, our mind sees them, our labor separates them out; if in thought we suppress the intermixtures of peoples, their interbreedings, in a flash we see them stand forth—simple, inevitable, a necessary consequence of collective heredity."[10]

Caton-Thompson arrived in Johannesburg on July 29, 1929, to give her report to the British Association for its annual meeting. She spent the evening preparing her notes. When she arrived at the conference the next morning, a large crowd filled the lecture hall. Organizers hastily set up a relay-wireless system to broadcast her report for an additional crowd of three hundred people in the courtyard. The normal thirty-minute time limit for presenters was waived, giving her the entire ninety-minute session for her remarks. She began by discussing the directive given to her by the British Association, then detailed the excavations her team had made at six separate regions of the ruins, including the Acropolis, the Elliptical Building, and the Maund Ruins. At all of these sites, artifacts indicated native African design and manufacture, with the exception of glass beads and a few other items that could be linked to the ocean trade with China and India from the thirteenth to fifteenth centuries. The mysterious design of the Maund Ruins, she argued, was resolvable into the plan of a traditional African kraal, more closely related to the designs of Buganda and Bunyoro in East Africa, than to any foreign architecture from the Middle East or the Mediterranean coast. Through the long journey to Great Zimbabwe, and the six weeks of excavation, she had carefully avoided engaging in debate about the original builders of the ruins. Now, as she brought her remarks to a close, she indulged in one personal reflection: "I will allow myself one subjective observation. It is this. It is inconceivable to me now [that] I have studied the ruins how a theory of Semitic or civilized origin could ever have been foisted on an uncritical world. Every detail in the haphazard building, every detail in the plan, every detail in the contents apart from imports, appears to me to be typical African Bantu."[11]

It was a devastating blow to the Hamitic hypothesis. Against such a careful and comprehensive body of evidence, Great Zimbabwe's foreign settlement hypothesis crumbled as a credible theory. The idea that had launched Haggard's lost-race romances, inspired Cecil Rhodes, and anchored the study of African archaeology for fifty years would never again enjoy the consensus support of the scientific community. In the weeks ahead, many scientists cheered their approval. Despite the inclinations of white Rhodesians and South Africans to support the foreign-settlement theory, a number of English newspapers voiced support for her work as well. "Miss Caton-Thompson's epoch-making researches seem definitely to have put an end to romance," wrote the *Cape Times*. "The work of Caton-Thompson may begin from now on," noted the *Church Times*, "to affect, insensibly but yet surely, all white relations with the Bantu race." Most pleasing of all, from her point of view, was the support of the British Association committee that followed her back to Rhodesia to see her work at Great Zimbabwe for themselves. Leading them through the ruins, the members praised her work and confirmed her findings. Given her disinclination to subjective or emotional descriptions, Caton-Thompson's record of these weeks back in Rhodesia comes across as almost ebullient. "We had lively dinners in the inn after care-free days in the incomparable sunshine and sparkling air. Everyone was happy."[12]

Well, not everyone. Raymond Dart had listened to her lecture with growing anger. In the discussion afterward, he rose and—"in a tone of awe-inspiring violence" reported the *Cape Times*—declared that her work, combined with MacIver's, had "killed interest in the subject for twenty years." He then stormed from the room. It was a telling criticism coming from someone so anxious to bring more attention to the work of South African archaeology. He would remain unmoved by Caton-Thompson's findings, traveling to Great Zimbabwe himself the following year, and publishing more findings that affirmed the foreign invasion theory in Southern Africa. Dart's position would carry support among many white South Africans and Rhodesians as well. Of the eighty articles and letters that Caton-Thompson collected from British, Rhodesian, and South African newspapers in the years between 1929 and 1933, only twenty-four supported her findings. Most were either negative or neutral. Indeed, the weight of her findings had not destroyed the foreign-builder hypothesis, any more than Franz Boas had killed off anthropometry as a measure of race by studying the skull shapes of immigrants. Rather, these ideas were being driven to the margins of scientific and popular discourse. There they remained—in subdisciplines of anthropology, racist pamphlets, popular editorials, in myths of origin, and the unrecorded conversations of village life—waiting to be roused to life again. Yet the search for lost white tribes had one last gasp.[13]

18

THE ROOF OF THE WORLD

ERNST SCHÄFER'S TIMING COULD NOT have been worse. As he arrived in Calcutta in May 1938 with four other members of the German Tibet expedition, the monsoon was almost upon them. With the rains approaching, he would have to work fast to prepare the team for the trek north into the Himalayas. More ominous, however, was the storm descending over Europe. With Adolf Hitler threatening to invade the Sudetenland in Czechoslovakia, British officials were in no mood to allow passage of a German expedition through British India, especially one that was funded and organized by the Nazi Schutzstaffel, or SS. Before leaving Europe, Schäfer had traveled to London, in hopes of securing permission from the India office. This went nowhere. Heinrich Himmler protested to British contacts that the expedition was purely scientific, an endeavor free of political motives. Reluctant to assist, but anxious to avoid a political incident, the British government offered Schäfer a sop: permission to proceed to Sikkim on the Tibetan border. This wasn't far enough, but Schäfer accepted. He was a driven, mercurial man, the veteran of two previous Himalayan expeditions. He was confident he would find a way into Tibet to complete his mission: to discover the origins of the Aryan race.[1]

Although the British and Germans were on the cusp of war in 1938, the SS expedition was an homage, of sorts, to British research on the

German Tibet Expedition. Sitting from left to right: Krause, Wienert, Beger, Geer, and Schäfer. Credit: Ernst Schäfer, *Geheimnis Tibet, erster Bericht der Deutschen Tibet-Expedition*, 1938–1939.

Aryans. It had been 148 years since William Jones addressed the Asiatick Society of Bengal on his investigations of Sanskrit, arguing that it was related to ancient Greek, Latin, and other languages. In the nineteenth century, scholars would point to these linguistic connections as evidence of the existence of an ancient people, the Indo-Europeans, who spoke a "common source" language from which all the others had sprung. The idea of common origins fueled the Oriental Renaissance, particularly in Germany, and demonstrated the usefulness of linguistics in charting the movement of ancient peoples. Through the work of Jones and others, Friedrich Max Müller had found inspiration in the *Rg Veda* and pioneered the Aryan invasion theory in the late 1800s. As Indian laborers carried Schäfer's expedition crates off the ship and up the ghats of the Hoogli River, they retraced the steps made by Jones and his wife, Anna, when they arrived at these docks on the HMS *Rattlesnake* 155 years before. On the eve of world war, the story of the Aryans had come full circle.

Yet, the theory Schäfer sought to confirm in 1938 scarcely resembled the one that Jones expressed to the Asiatick Society in Kolkata in 1786. Schäfer and his party operated on the assumption that the first Aryans had originated in Europe, and then, driven by a mental and physical vigor unequaled by other tribes, conquered southern Europe, the Middle East, and Central Asia. If the far-flung peoples of the East and West spoke languages descended from a common source, it was because blond-haired, long-skulled Aryans of northern Europe had brought their language with them on their long conquest of Eurasia. (Himmler subscribed to a variation of this: that Aryans had descended from heaven to rule over the continent of Atlantis before beginning their conquest of Europe—an idea to which Schäfer, when he heard Himmler explain it, remained silent.) Most of these Aryan tribes had intermarried with local peoples, diluting the racial vigor of the original conquerors, but among the more isolated peoples of Tibet, Schäfer hoped to find something akin to what Mauch, Bent, and Dart had hoped to find at Great Zimbabwe: evidence of an ancient invasion by a superior, light-skinned tribe from another part of the world.[2]

This idea contrasted with Jones's belief that the first tribe of the Aryans, the speakers of the "common source," which later evolved into Sanskrit and its sister languages, first originated in Central Asia and then spread to other parts of the world. It was also a radical departure from the work of Max Müller, though he had given life to the "Aryan invasion" theory in the 1850s. As Max Müller had imagined it, the Aryan invasion represented a prehistoric conquest of India by Aryan speakers from Central Asia. For all of his talk of superior Aryans, Max Müller had remained wary of connecting the idea of the Aryans too closely to race. He knew that the Aryan speaker would never be a perfect marker of racial identity because language did not follow the rules of human inheritance. Words leapt the divides of caste and tribe in ways that heredity did not. Armies, hordes, and invaders may have imposed their languages on the people that they conquered, but language did not require such conquests to move through human societies. On docks and boardwalks, in souks and brothels, language spread as people bargained, argued, and exchanged.

These subtleties of language, however, were lost on Himmler and the *Ahnenerbe*—Himmler's eccentric band of scientists and zealots. They had already found a vein of scholarship suited to their preconceived visions of race and German superiority. They seized upon the work of anthropologists who subscribed to *nordische Gedanke,* or Nordic race theory. The idea had sprung up in the mid-1800s in the work of German scholars who, inspired by ancient works on German history such as Tacitus's *Germania* (98 CE), as well as by a rising spirit of nationalism after the Franco-Prussian War of 1871, had reversed the direction of Jones's Aryan migration. They argued that northern Europe represented the original homeland of the Indo-Europeans. These ideas were at odds with the views of most German anthropologists, most prominently, Rudolf Virchow, whose study of cranial measurements led him to conclude that the search for Nordic supermen was a fantasy. Yet with the death of Virchow in 1902, Germany anthropology found itself in flux. Within an environment of rising nationalism and professional rivalries, many race theories took root.[3]

In Scandinavia, *nordische Gedanke* received a boost from the work of physical anthropologists who were inclined to define Aryans by skull shape rather than by language. Examining skulls disinterred from ancient graves, Norwegian anatomist Justus Barth began to see the outlines of an ancient *vikingtypen* (Viking type). Contributing to this theory was the work of army physician Carl Oscar Eugen Arbo, who by compiling the skull measurement of army recruits believed that he detected two racial types—the brown-eyed, dark-skinned Sami type and a blue-eyed, blond-haired Germanic type. While Arbo and others thought the blond Germanic type had migrated into Norway from points south, the anthropological writer Andreas Hansen argued that this Nordic type was indigenous to Norway. At a moment when Norwegians were trying to find a national identity independent from Sweden, the idea of an indigenous "Viking type" carried popular appeal.[4]

It also gained support among German nationalists, particularly in the years after Germany's defeat in World War I. Hans H. K. Gunther had no training in anthropology, but he had become an ardent German nationalist and defender of "race hygiene." With encouragement from the right-wing publisher Julius Lehmann, he became a leading advocate of the Nordic race theory, popularizing it in books such as *The Racial Lore of the German Volk* and *The Racial Ethnology of the German People* (1922). According to Gunther, Nordic tribes conquered southern Europe and the Mediterranean before heading east, carrying the Indo-European

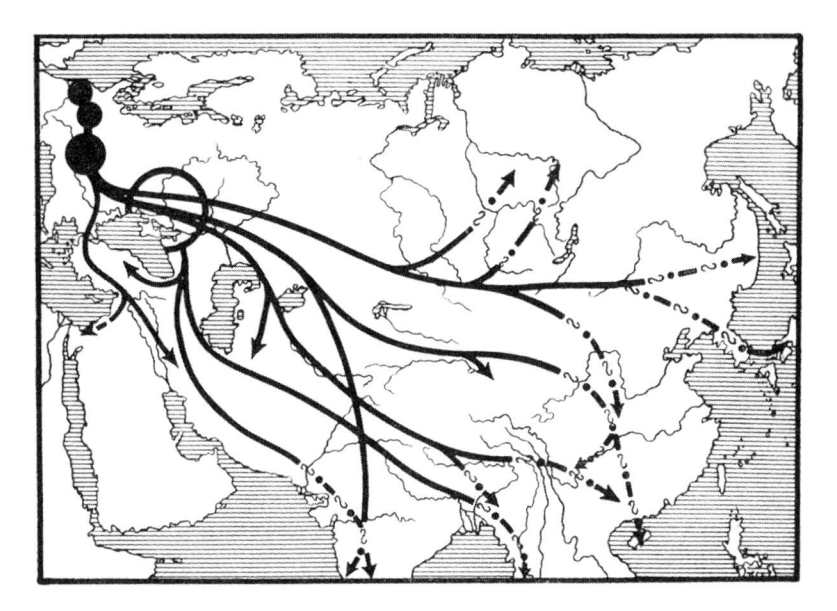

Hans F. K. Gunther's map of ancient Nordic tribes invading the East. Credit: Gunther, *Die nordische Rasse bei den Indogermanen Asiens*, 1933.

language beyond India to the western boundary of China. As they pushed farther east, he argued, the Aryans began to mingle with other races, weakening their bloodline as they produced mixed-race offspring. Only the echoes of this invasion remained in the Indo-European languages spoken by the peoples of India and Central Asia and in the physiognomy of native peoples who maintained some vestiges of their Aryan racial inheritance.[5]

Gunther's views brought him to the attention of Himmler and other Nazi elites. When the National Socialists tripled their vote in the 1930 state elections in Thuringia, they pushed for the creation of a new program at Jena University in *Rassenfragen und Rassenkunde* (Racial Questions and Racial Knowledge). Gunther became its first chair. Securely installed at Jena, buoyed by the rising Nazi tide, he poured himself into an investigation of the ancient Aryans and their conquest of the world. By 1933, he had identified their invasion routes east across Central Asia and the India subcontinent, charting them in his book *Die nordische Rasse bei den Indogermanen Asiens* (The

Nordic Race and Asian Indo-Europeans). He also mapped the locations of remote Asian tribes that retained visible aspects of their Aryan ancestry.[6]

Were there Asian tribes that had retained their Nordic purity? This was the question that Gunther discussed with his tall, fair-haired student Bruno Beger in the early 1930s. Looking at photos of Tibetan nobles, Beger thought he detected traits "long head, thin face, drawn back cheekbones...straight hair and imperious, self-confident behavior" that indicated Aryan ancestry. Perhaps Tibet hid tribes of even purer pedigree, isolated in their mountain fastness from the polluting influence of racial mixing, living relics of the first Nordic invaders. Beger's racial research interests, his connection with Gunther, and his strong Nordic features made him a perfect candidate for the science wing of the SS. By 1937, he had ascended to the head of the SS Race Division (*Abteilungsleiter für Rassenkunde*). It was there that he came to Schäfer's attention, and after an interview with the expedition leader, accepted the job of field anthropologist, pledging to "collect material about the proportion, origins, significance, and development of the Nordic race in this region."[7]

With travel permissions approved, Schäfer, Beger, and the other three members of the German expedition made their way north from Kolkata by train. Under torrents of rain, the party began a long, sodden journey up the mountain paths of Sikkim, trailing a long line of native porters, horses, and pack mules. Despite the vexations of weather and politics, Schäfer was slowly drawn into the magical world of the Himalayan foothills. He was a zoologist by training, and he marveled at the birds and other fauna. At night, luminous glowworms inched over the ferns of the Teesta valley, a sight he found "fantastical and surreal."[8]

Beger found other marvels. Having studied the features of Tibetan nobles only in photographs, he now observed the physiognomy of mountain peoples with his own eyes. He planned on making use of this close access. Within the crates now tottering up the trail on the backs of mules were precision instruments—calipers, sliding compasses, somatometers, tape measures, and eye-color tables—that would help him advance the Nordic race theory espoused by Gunther. Himmler, too, would be pleased to see evidence that confirmed the Aryan invasion he knew to be true.

Yet getting these measurements proved challenging. Many Tibetans and Nepalese were suspicious of outsiders, particularly Europeans. Despite the remoteness of their mountain villages, these lands had long been the stage for the "Great Game," the imperial contest for control of Central Asia that had been playing out between Russia and Britain since the early 1800s. The Europeans who arrived in this high-altitude frontier always wore many hats. Explorers played roles as spies and diplomats. As a result, villagers were wary of the bearded German men huffing through the mountain passes with their swastika flags. Few were inclined to be Beger's test subjects: poked and prodded by calipers or lathered in suffocating latex face casts.

Beger tried a different approach. Proclaiming himself a physician, he offered Nepalis and Tibetans medicine and medical advice. Announcing that he could treat all forms of malady—malaria, skin and eye problems, broken limbs, and venereal disease—Beger soon had lines of people waiting for him in each village. After winning their trust, he found villagers were more inclined to submit to his strange battery of measurements that he used to determine racial ancestry.[9]

In Sikkim, Schäfer managed to win an invitation from Tering Raja to enter Tibet. Crossing the high mountain pass on Tibet's border, he looked out across a "lunar landscape" of peaks and valleys "monotonous, deep, fantastic, and wild." The expedition had arrived at the heart of the Himalayas, the "roof of the world," a 1500-mile crescent of mountains formed by the relentless, slow-motion collision of the Indian subcontinent with the Eurasian continental plate to the north. Here, Beger began collecting measurements in earnest. He measured 376 people, made two thousand photographs and seventeen face casts, and collected 350 sets of handprints. It appeared to Beger and Schäfer that Tibetan nobility showed Aryan traits more visibly than the peasants. This, too, fit the idea of the Nordic race theory as imagined by Gunther and others. If Aryans descended out of northern Europe to conquer the peoples of Central Asia, one would expect the superior race to occupy the highest offices of the societies they conquered.[10]

It was not a new idea. Gunther's speculations that noble classes represented a purer, separate line of ancestry—the last vestiges of a superior racial conquest—had already been expressed by an earlier generation of "Aryan invasion" scholars in the 1800s, starting with Max Müller's association of the Brahmin caste with Aryan invaders and other castes with indigenous Dravidian speakers. Those scholars and missionaries who applied Max Müller's Aryan invasion theory to the peoples of the Pacific imported this idea as well—using it to explain the dominance of some island tribes over others.

This idea of racial differences between nobles and peasants was hardly unique to Aryan studies. As Max Müller had put forward the idea of an Aryan caste in India, John Speke had made similar arguments in East Africa, telling local rulers that they were the descendants of Abyssinians—people from the Horn of Africa who, according to the Hamitic hypothesis, had originated in the Middle East—in contrast to the black Africans that they ruled over. Indeed, the underpinnings of this "different castes equal different races" idea dated all the way back to Medieval Europe, when scholars speculated that nobles and peasants might represent different branches of the Noachian tree. Noble families descended from Japheth, while serfs and other commoners were the offspring of Ham. Beger's instruments and anthropometric methods were modern, but his analysis of culture and caste were not far removed from the Middle Ages.[11]

Not that Beger had time to do much analysis. The Munich Agreement of 1938, which allowed Hitler to dismantle Czechoslovakia, had briefly calmed the tempest roiling Europe. In the summer of 1939, the storm was rising again as the Nazis turned their attention to Poland. War appeared imminent. As the German Tibet expedition made its way back to India, Schäfer and his men worried that they would be arrested and interned by the British government. Alarmed, Himmler hastily arranged for the party to exit Kolkata by flying boat. In Baghdad, they transferred to a Junkers U90 airplane, which flew them to Vienna, and then, made a final transfer to Munich where Chamberlain, Mussolini, and Hitler had met only months before to secure "peace in our time." The leaders were gone from Munich when the party arrived, but they were met on the tarmac by Himmler himself, who escorted them to Berlin for an exuberant reception in their honor.[12]

The SS leader was thrilled at the results of the expedition, confident that the anthropological results confirmed the Nordic race theory that had become a sacred idea for him and the *Ahnenerbe*. Tibet was only the first step. The string of "lost race" discoveries—by Stanley, Stefansson, Marsh, Batchelor, and others—no longer carried the same scientific significance in Western Europe and North America as they had in prior decades. In Germany, however, they were embraced by the SS *Reichsführer* and his cohort of Aryanists, evidence of race wars that had played out in the ancient past. Already, Himmler had plans to extend the search for Aryan prehistory to sites around the world, including Bolivia, Iceland, and the Canary Islands.

In the process, he believed, these expeditions would not only illuminate the Aryan past, but point forward to a new world order. As Himmler fêted the German Tibet expedition in Berlin, he was already putting the final touches on a new project. As Schäfer and Beger received the congratulations of their SS colleagues, details were being finalized for *Fall Weiss* (Case White), the German invasion of Poland. Twenty-seven days after the expedition party landed in Munich, a swarm of Junkers *Stukas* (dive-bombers) descended out of the predawn sky above Poland, releasing their 500 kg bombs above the town of Wieluń. The raid, which killed 1300 Polish civilians, signaled the opening act of World War II. It was a preview of the approach the Nazi regime would take toward peoples they considered non-Aryan.

The German conquest—in Himmler's view, reconquest—of the East did not stop with Poland. It was only the first step in a larger invasion, one laid out in the secret *Generalplan Ost* (General Plan for the East), an SS blueprint for the conquest and colonization of the Eurasian continent. While Germany's invasion of Poland was made possible by a hasty détente with the Soviet Union, Hitler was soon looking ahead to the annihilation of his new ally. This act of betrayal, Operation Barbarossa, came so quickly on the heels of the German-Soviet pact that even Joseph Stalin, a man who had elevated a paranoid personality disorder to a governing philosophy, was taken by surprise. He watched, disbelieving in 1941, as four million Axis troops poured across the borders of the Soviet Union along a 1800-mile front, the largest military invasion in human history.

When the German Army Group A smashed through Rostov-on-Don on July 23, 1942, the Nazi invasion reached the "the Gates of the Caucasus." Hitler's goal was practical: he needed to secure the Caucasian oil fields in order to fuel his war effort in the East. Yet the invasion had symbolic value too. With German Panzers (tanks) idling in the shadow of the Caucasus Mountains, the Nazi empire extended now from the Atlantic Ocean to the eastern boundaries of Europe. In August 1942,

German troops reached the Volga River outside of Stalingrad. At the same time, alpine troops from the Edelweiss division ascended the 18,510-foot Mount Elbrus, the tallest mountain in Russia, planting the Nazi flag on the summit. To the south, beyond the white-capped sea of mountains, lay Georgia, Armenia, and Iran: the gateway to Central Asia.[13]

Hitler's dream of *Lebensraum* (living space) was coming to fruition, realized through the decimation of twenty million Russians, Poles, and Ukrainians, and the occupation of their lands. In so doing, the Führer seemed to be re-creating the great Nordic invasion theory envisioned by Gunther, patronized by Himmler, and pursued by Schäfer. The routes of the ancient Nordic conquest traced out on Gunther's 1933 map now appeared to be an eerie prognostication of the invasion routes Barbarossa would take a decade later. The tribes of long-headed, fur-clad, *viking-typen* marching east had been replaced by Waffen-SS and Wehrmacht troops, wreaking destruction through Russian towns and villages.

Schäfer and Beger, who had benefited from Nazi support in their pursuit of Aryan tribes in Tibet, were now drawn inexorably into the brutality of their patrons during the war. By January 1943, Schäfer had become the director of the Sven Hedin Institute for Inner Asian Research, an organization that retained ties to Himmler's *Ahnenerbe*. If the institute shielded Schäfer from the worse brutalities of Himmler's campaign for "racial hygiene"—that is, the expulsion, enslavement, and extermination of Eastern Europe's Jews, Slavs, and Gypsies—he wasn't entirely in the dark. Ordered to record Sigmund Rascher's human medical experiments at Dachau, Schäfer observed the conditions of the concentration camp firsthand, including a demonstration of a prisoner being subjected to low-pressure altitude tests in a pressure chamber. The experience left him shaken. "It was the worst experience of my life," he later told Allied interrogators at Nuremburg. Still, he was not so shaken that he protested the experiment or resigned from his SS post.[14]

Nor did Beger offer any objections to SS instructions for him to work on human subjects. At the request of the *Ahnenerbe*, Beger set about producing a *Skelletsammlung* (skeletal collection) of non-Aryan racial types. To ensure the accuracy of the collection, the project would begin by the identification of *living* subjects who would be measured and photographed before they were executed. In June 1943, Beger spent more than a week at Auschwitz, selecting 115 male and female inmates: "79 of them were Jews, 2 Poles, 4 Asiatics, and 30 Jewesses." The prisoners were later transported to the Natzweiler camp where, in August 1943, they were gassed and their bodies preserved in ethanol. For the rest of his life, Beger denied knowing that the subjects he selected would be killed, a claim that, given his knowledge of SS research interests and his time spent among the inmates of Auschwitz, seems dubious.[15]

With the Caucasus now under German control, Schäfer began planning a new expedition, one that would replicate the combination of mountain climbing and scientific research that had been the hallmark of the German Tibet expedition and had made him a celebrity in Germany. Schäfer's interests inclined to zoology, but he was happy to include anthropologists—Beger was selected—to study the racial typology of Caucasians, that mixture of people who lived at the crossroads of the alleged Nordic invasion. By 1943, however, the SS was interested in more than learning new details about Aryan migrations. It wanted an accurate typology of the Caucasian peoples so that the expanding project of race hygiene—already under way to murderous effect in Poland, Ukraine, and the Baltic States—could be applied to new Nazi conquests. If descendants of the original Aryans lived in the Caucasus as they did in Tibet, they needed to be distinguished from other groups—Muslims, Slavs, and "Mountain Jews"—who would be targeted with expulsion or elimination. Schäfer may have been happy to imagine himself in the high Caucasus Mountains, 1500 miles from the grim reality of Dachau—but he would be furthering the Nazi project all the same.

In the same way that the Tibet expedition offered twisted Nazi homage to the theories of Jones, the Caucasian expedition was its corollary to the ideas of Johann Blumenbach, Germany's great eighteenth century race theorist. It was on the basis of the shapely skull of a young Georgian woman that the original human tribe was described by Blumenbach as Caucasian, the most beautiful of the human races. Certainly, Beger and the scientists of the *Ahnenerbe* would have agreed with him on this point, even if they believed that Blumenbach had located the cradle of the European race two thousand miles southeast of its location in Scandinavia. Undoubtedly, Blumenbach would have shown great interest in Schäfer's Caucasian expedition, focused as it was on the measurement of human crania in hopes of understanding racial types.

Yet the rest of the SS project would have repelled him. Blumenbach was, despite his love of the Caucasian type, a liberal humanist. He always believed that the physical differences that separated humans into racial types were superficial in comparison to the great unities among the peoples of the world: they shared the same faculties of reason, aptitudes for learning, and moral sentiments.

The Caucasian expedition never left Germany. Operation Barbarossa ground to a halt in the summer of 1943, unable to continue against mounting Soviet counterattacks. The crossing of the Volga and the ascent of Elbrus turned out to be the high-water mark of the German advance. Gradually the German Sixth Army at Stalingrad was encircled and destroyed, its Caucasus force pushed back, and its other army groups forced to retreat. Ethnic Slavs, so derided by the Nazis, had begun a great counteroffensive against Hitler's armies in the East—driving them back toward Europe.

Schäfer and Beger would both spend time in internment after the war, their scientific careers forever blemished by their association with the SS. The horrors of the Nazi campaign, and their justification upon unsupportable theories, would also represent the end of serious race science in Europe and the United States. Aryanism—once a respectable term within the study of linguistics and physical anthropology—would be forever tainted by its association with the Nazi policies of racial extermination. Already in decline elsewhere, Nazi Germany had prolonged, for a time, the commitment to race as a key identifier of human behavior and ability, as well as the notion that race could be found in anthropometry. By the time Hitler became chancellor of Germany in 1933, such ideas were already on the wane among cultural anthropologists, who questioned the legitimacy of race as a category, and geneticists, who questioned whether phenotypes—the expression of traits shaped by a combination of genetic and environmental factors—could ever express something meaningful about racial identity. After the barbaric results of Nazi race theory became known to the world, this brand of anthropology fell into disrepute. The 1950s and 1960s would witness the rise of the social sciences in North America and Europe, the diminishing of race as a meaningful category, and the acceptance of environment as the primary factor shaping human experience. No longer would expeditions seek out white tribes in southern Africa, the jungles of Panama, or the mountains of Tibet.

The Roof of the World

Yet the story of white tribes was not finished. Even as the idea of prehistoric white migrations lost scientific credibility, it had become, among some peoples of the world, part of the myth of human origins—a creation story. Nowhere did these stories gain greater traction than in Africa, in the lands that lay in the shadows of the Ruwenzoris—the place of mythic white tribes that Stanley had described a century before. Here was the final legacy of this century-long search for whiteness—its final expression; its last killing field.

19

COLORED BY WAR

DISCOVERIES OF SO-CALLED WHITE TRIBES ended after World War II. The quest, which had begun with Henry Stanley's trans-African expedition in 1875, ended with Ernst Schäfer's Tibet expedition in 1939. One reason for this was geographical. By 1945, once-remote places were now easily accessible. Most of the inhabited regions of the earth had been surveyed by explorers and anthropologists. The long, malarial journey to Africa's Lakes Region had once taken months of travel and years of planning by Victorian explorers. Now, tourists less rugged than Stanley—less robust even than Carl Jung—could reach Lake Victoria in a few weeks' time by steamer and train. With only a bit more effort, they could charter seaplanes to Victoria Island, realm of the Blond Eskimos, or San Blas, on the Panama Isthmus, home of the white Indians. Apart from the interior of Papua New Guinea and pockets of the South American interior, the surfaces of the globe that were both inhabitable and unexplored had dwindled to almost nothing, brought into the realm of the known by ever-growing fleets of trains, boats, planes, and automobiles.

Yet the ever-shrinking world was only one, and perhaps not even the greatest, reason for the end of the white tribe quest. The Second World War had profoundly changed the West's attitudes toward the search for "lost races" under their many labels: Aryan, Caucasian, and

Hamitic. The war had killed sixty to eighty million people, more than three percent of the world population. At least twelve million of these—Jews, Slavs, Roma, Chinese, and others—were targeted specifically because of their racial identity. The Allied liberation of concentration camps in Poland in 1945 horrified the public in Western Europe and North America, searing into consciousness the reality of Nazi policies of "racial hygiene." More slowly, the world also learned of atrocities in the East, conducted by the Japanese Army in China, Korea, and the Philippines. Race science—which assumed the importance of biological differences among races—became implicated in this great global carnage.

The caliper-wielding explorer had once been a respected figure in the West. Hacking through jungles, scaling mountains, and driving dogsleds, he had pursued ancient Aryans and missing Britons and lost Vikings, feeding the public's fascination about lost races. Now, as the West learned about the full extent of race experiments conducted by the SS *Ahnenerbe* in Poland and by the Japanese Army Unit 731 in Northeast China, race science carried more sinister connotations. It was hard to look at photos of Beger, measuring smiling Tibetan villagers on the Himalayan plateau, without also imagining him in his SS uniform at Auschwitz, making the same measurements on Jews and Slavs before they were gassed and preserved for study. His arsenal of sophisticated instruments—calipers, eye-color charts, tape measures, once a source of pride for race scientists and physical anthropologists—now seemed macabre.

As the full measure of the horror emerged in 1945 and 1946, political elites in the West were forced to act. The world was beginning to fracture upon new lines, communist and capitalist, yet on the issue of race, the United Nations still managed to find consensus between East and West. To protect the peace, to bring stability to the new world order, it argued, racial distinctions needed to be minimized, treated as a kind of pathogen, a point made repeatedly in the UN's declarations, including the United Nations Charter (1945), the UNESCO Constitution (1945), and the Universal Declaration of Human Rights (1948). In its first report on "The Race Question" in 1950, a UNESCO committee concluded that "all men belong to the same species," and "the likenesses among men are far greater than their differences." While race might have scientific validity in distinguishing among human populations with different gene frequencies, such distinctions were mostly ignored by the public. "To most people," it observed, "a race is any group of people whom they choose to describe as a race." The *New York Times* heralded the news under the headline, "No Scientific Basis for Race Bias Found by World Panel of Experts." Politicians began approaching race largely as a problem of society rather than biology.[1]

The war also affected scientific attitudes toward race. After a century in which scholars frequently explained differences in human behavior and aptitude as the product of biological inheritance, the pendulum began to swing toward environmental causes: education, upbringing, and general culture. Haltingly, unevenly, the cultures of the West lurched away from explanations based on nature toward ones of nurture. Anthropologists, psychologists, and sociologists increasingly looked to human experience, not genetics, for their answers. Within this new view of the world, the search for lost white tribes seemed anachronistic and unscientific; Aryans and Hamites became the fantastic obsessions of an earlier, racially obsessed age.[2]

Yet UN declarations and scientific treatises could not purge racial thinking from the populations of the postwar world. Even in Eastern Europe, heartland of the Nazi genocide, old ideas were slow to die. The German Army had barely been driven out of Poland when a mob in Rzeszów began a pogrom against Jews on June 12, 1945. More anti-Jewish riots followed in Kraków and Kielce. In the United States, 110,000 Japanese-American citizens had been forcibly interned during the war because of their ancestry, losing farms, homes, and other property in the process. Black American soldiers, arriving in the South, confronted a society still divided by Jim Crow. The fight to liberate Europe from fascism and Nazism could not reweave the fabric of human culture, hued and patterned as it was by the colors of race. These were the unwritten codes that existed beneath the noble constitutions and declarations of the West: humans were born unequal, incompatible, and incommensurable. The war had not changed this.[3]

Not surprisingly, then, the conclusion of expeditions searching for white tribes did not end talk of Aryans and Hamites, but only drove these discussions underground or, in the case of the sciences, back to more specialized forums. While the Nordic race theory, once espoused by Gunther and embraced by Himmler, was now dismissed as a Nazi fantasy, the idea of Aryan invasions did not go away, but returned to where it had begun: India. Sir Mortimer Wheeler, director-general of the Archeological Survey of India from 1944 to 1948, accepted Max Müller's idea that the subcontinent was settled by a dark-skinned, indigenous Dravidian-speaking people, who were conquered by a more advanced, light-skinned, Indo-European-speaking people who emerged from Central Asia in the ancient past. When the ruins of an ancient civilization in the Indus River valley were unearthed in the early 1900s, Wheeler concluded that this Indus valley civilization (IVC) had been the original inhabitants, conquered and decimated by the invading Aryans. Gradually, this Aryan invasion theory (AIT) gave way to the "Aryan migration theory" (AMT), one that proposed a spread not by racial conquest, but by waves of migration, and the dissemination of Indo-European culture and language. The AMT returned the discussion of the Aryan from race back to language—a shift more compatible with the postwar focus on culture over genetics.[4]

By 1945, however, debate about Aryans in India had spread beyond Western drawing rooms and scientific societies to become a matter of debate among Indians themselves. Before the mid-1800s, most Hindus believed that they were the original inhabitants of India. With the rise of Max Müller's Aryan invasion theory, however, these views began to change. By the early twentieth century, Brahmin scholars and statesmen like Jawaharlal Nehru and B. G. Tilak had accepted the foreign origins of Hindu culture, a theory that had also been used to explain the caste system as the reign of the original invaders (Brahmins) over indigenous peoples (Dysus) and the efforts to protect their ancestral lineage by prohibiting intermarriage.

In the years after World War II, Indians began to challenge the Aryan migration theory. The first salvo came from lawyer and activist B. R. Ambedkar in 1946. Ambedkar believed that the theory of foreign Aryan founders lacked evidence, either linguistic or archaeological. "The Aryan race theory is so absurd that it ought to have been dead long ago. But far from being dead, the theory has a considerable hold upon the people." The reason, he believed, was that it was useful for Europeans, giving legitimacy to the idea of advanced invaders ruling India, bringing higher civilization to its primitive cultures. In short, the Aryan invasion theory served as a scientific apologia for the British occupation of India. At the same time, Ambedkar argued, the story also appealed to Brahmin elites, who saw it as a justification of the caste system that placed them at the pinnacle of Indian society. "[The Brahmin] claims to be the representative of the Aryan race and he regards the rest of the Hindus as descendants of the non-Aryans. The theory helps him to establish his kinship with the European races and share their arrogance and their superiority."[5]

Ambedkar was not without his own ideological commitments. Born into the "untouchable" Mahar caste, he endured years of discrimination at school before being admitted to Elphinstone College—the first of his Mahar community to do so. Eventually receiving a law degree and PhD in economics, Ambedkar represented non-Brahmin clients and became a leader in the movement to eliminate caste from Indian society, eventually converting to Buddhism as well. In the growing ferment against British rule, the "indigenist theory" of Aryan origins soon began to take hold among Indian scholars and political elites. The idea of Aryans as an indigenous race of India, which spread Indo-European culture to other parts of the world, was also in keeping with the rise of Indian nationalism after World War II, a movement that would lead to independence from Britain in 1948. Ironically, the indigenist theory of Aryan origins soon became popular with the groups that Ambedkar would have objected to: fundamentalist Hindu parties who sought to protect "Hindutva," the purity of Hindu culture. Working to erase the categories that so divided Indians, Ambedkar had developed a theory that helped Hindu nationalists exclude Muslims, Christians, and other groups.

In Africa, the Hamitic hypothesis was going through its own complicated transformation. Long gone were the days when Europeans dreamed about discovering light-skinned tribes living in the mountain fastness of the Ruwenzori. Not since Stanley's encounter with the Gambaragarans in 1876 had explorers returned with tales of white tribes in Africa. Only in the works of H. Rider Haggard, and the thousands of lost-race novels that he inspired, did explorers still stumble upon fair-complexioned peoples in the Africa interior. Yet even as this idea of the lost tribe became relegated to pulp fiction, the Hamitic hypothesis continued to live on in the social sciences, particularly in the fields of linguistics, archaeology, and anthropology.

Until the end of World War II, African linguistics generally supported the Hamitic hypothesis. In this, it followed in the footsteps of

Indo-European scholarship. Where Friedrich Max Müller had seen signs of Aryan invasion in the language trees of Asia and Europe, Carl Meinhof had found Hamitic invasions in the languages of Africa. In his book *Die Sprachen Der Hamiten* (The Language of the Hamites), he articulated that an advanced language class connected the descendent peoples of the great ancient invasion of Africa. Shortly after Meinhof's death in 1944, however, the linguist Joseph Greenberg began publishing a series of papers on African languages that challenged Meinhof's classification of so-called Hamitic languages. In particular, Greenberg criticized Meinhof's methods for defining "Hamitic language" as entirely capricious. Meinhof studied African languages that attracted his attention, Greenberg argued, rather than approaching them systematically. He ignored obvious connections with neighboring languages in favor of isolated comparisons with standard Hamitic languages. Studied in this way, Meinhof found superficial similarities among the languages of allegedly Hamitic peoples even while he overlooked deeper structural differences separating them.[6]

In archaeology, the idea of a Hamitic invasion was also under fire. In Egypt, Flinders Petrie's dynastic race theory, which proposed that the great civilization of ancient Egypt had been the product of invaders from the Middle East, remained controversial. Major excavations farther south in Nubia (northern Sudan) added more skulls, but little clarity, to the debate over the racial identity of ancient Egyptians. In southern Africa, Gertrude Caton-Thompson's careful excavation of Great Zimbabwe, combined with her forceful refutation of the "foreign builder" hypothesis in 1929, had made a powerful impression on British archaeologists. Meanwhile, cultural anthropologists and population geneticists became increasingly critical of physical anthropology: for some, because of its obsession with cranial measurements as a measure of race, and for others, because race, by itself, was gradually losing its usefulness as a biological category.[7]

Even from within the physical anthropology community, the dynastic race theory came under attack. In 1946, Ahmed Mahmoud el Batrawi—an Egyptian anatomist who worked with Europeans on the digs in Egypt and Nubia—published an exhaustive report on the human remains excavated in Egypt and Nubia, concluding that while there might have been two closely related races living in ancient Egypt, there was no evidence to support that they were foreign to the

Nile valley. Such racial differences were "not due to the incursion of any non-Egyptian people in to the Nile valley in Neolithic times, as has been suggested by numerous investigators."[8]

Yet even these powerful critiques could not drive the Hamitic hypothesis out of scientific scholarship. British Egyptologist Reginald Engelbach declared in the early 1940s, "That the Dynastic race came from outside Egypt cannot as yet be definitely proved...but the probability that they did is so strong as to make it practically a certainty." Archaeologist Frank Addison, working for the Wellcome excavations in Sudan, concurred. In his 1949 report on the ancient cemetery site Jebel Moya, he ascribed the differences in burial practices at the site to a difference in race: "Crouched and contracted burials are, in general, earlier than the more sophisticated extended form, and the introduction of this latter into the southern areas was no doubt due to Hamitic influence radiating from the north." Even Batrawi's mentor, the London University archaeologist D. E. Derry, was not persuaded by his student's work to think outside of the Hamitic box. A decade after Batrawi's publication, he was still writing that the exhumation of ancient remains had confirmed "the presence of a dominant race, perhaps relatively few in numbers but greatly exceeding the original inhabitants in intelligence." It did not help that anthropology books such as C. G. Seligman's *The Races of Africa*, which went through many editions between 1930 and 1966, continued to use the Hamitic hypothesis as an explanation for African civilization. Nor had Caton-Thompson's conclusive findings eliminated the publication of various invasion theories to explain prehistoric cultures in southern Africa. Raymond Dart, who had been so exasperated by Caton-Thompson's lecture in 1929, continued to use invading Hamites as explanations for southern African ethnic groups, which, he argued, represented various admixtures of African and invader stock. The tribes of the upper Zambezi, for example, represented a Bushman people "strongly impregnated with Semitic and other Caucasian as well as Mongolian blood."[9]

Astonishingly, the use of the Hamitic hypothesis seemed to expand in the twentieth century, even as it found itself under fire in Egypt, Sudan, and Great Zimbabwe. In West Africa, Sir H. H. Johnston wrote "The pure-bred Fulas were at least semi-Caucasian in physique and brain; and this race was all unconsciously carrying on the Caucasian invasion and penetration of Africa." In Uganda, discovery of giant earthworks at Biggo in 1909 quickly drew comparisons with Great Zimbabwe, along with its theories of foreign builders. In the highlands of Kenya, British archaeologist G. W. B. Huntingford spent his time surveying stone mounds and enclosures that he believed were from an "Azanian Civilization," that had invaded Kenya from the north. On Mount Kenya, the English guide and naturalist Raymond Hook reported Stonehenge-like structures that echoed prehistoric ruins in Europe. In Tanganyika, the district surveyor G. E. H. Wilson believed that terraced farming was evidence of a Hamitic invasion. Even Louis Leakey, the white Kenyan anthropologist who had visited Caton-Thompson at Great Zimbabwe in 1929 and departed Rhodesia convinced that the city had been built by Africans, did not eliminate the Hamitic hypothesis from his own work. For decades, he insisted on singling out certain African skulls for their "non-Negroid" appearance.[10]

Eventually, combined weight of criticism—questionable methods of racial typing in physical anthropology, speculative theorizing in archaeology, and the cherry-picking of Hamitic languages in linguistics—would take their toll on the Hamitic hypothesis. Yet, the most devastating blow came from the collapse of the theory that undergirded the Hamitic hypothesis: the "out-of-Asia" theory of human evolution. For hundreds of years, a consensus of Western scholars had located the cradle of humankind in Asia. Asia Minor, the Caucasus Mountains, Persia, and India had all been offered as the human species' place of origin, relying on biblical sources, as well as linguistic, archaeological, and anthropological evidence. Yet the succession of ancient hominid discoveries in Africa—the most important of which, ironically were made by Raymond Dart (Taung child) and the Leakeys (*Zinjanthropus*)—had eventually nudged archaeologists and anthropologists to reconsider Africa and not Asia as the site of origin. The advent of radiocarbon dating in the 1970s confirmed the antiquity of African hominid remains, and they were further supported, in the 1990s, by the use of mitochondrial DNA comparisons of modern populations. Both of these new techniques corroborated an "out-of-Africa" hypothesis for human evolution. In the light of these discoveries, Hamitic invaders from Asia now required a convoluted itinerary that defied common sense: migrating out of Africa, evolving into a new race in Asia, and then returning to Africa to dominate the cultures of Egypt, East Africa, and southern Africa.

Even as the Hamitic hypothesis persisted in science beyond its usefulness as a theory, it also survived among African communities unwilling to let it go, even with all of these arguments arrayed against it. In the late 1800s, the hypothesis found favor in the explorers' clubs and universities of Europe. A century later, its support drew mostly from African communities, both colonial and indigenous. The remaining, white-dominated colonial governments of South Africa and Rhodesia promoted scholarship defending the Hamitic origins of African tribes. When Southern Rhodesia declared unilateral independence from Britain in 1965, largely to impede efforts to bring about majority rule, the white-controlled government took efforts to resurrect the foreign builder hypothesis of Great Zimbabwe. By 1969, scholarly works that defended the idea of indigenous builders were banned. Eventually, the foremost scholar on the ruins, Peter Garlake, was forced into exiled from the country. In this increasingly polarized environment, black nationalists in Rhodesia began adopting Zimbabwe in the names of their political organizations.

Even among the African countries that gained their independence from Europe in the 1950s and 1960s, shadows of the Hamitic hypothesis lived on. In many countries such as Uganda, Rwanda, and Nigeria, the theory had become the basis of colonial organization. European explorers—and, later, colonizers—viewed the ruling families of East Africa much like they did the Brahmin caste in India: the descendants of a racially superior stock that had imposed their civilization and language on the more primitive clans of the region in the ancient past. For the ruling families of Uganda and Tanzania, the Hamitic theory of Speke, Stanley, and others only augmented their legitimacy as special rulers with special powers—conveyed through the power of their bloodline. In some cases, entire ethnic groups, such as the Bahima and the Batutsi, gained prestige as Hamitic peoples. In Tanzania, the Iraqw clan described a migration out of Mesopotamia in the ancient past. In West Africa, colonial administrators tagged some groups—the Aro, Ishan, Igbo, Urhobo, and Efik—as Hamitic, giving them a social advantage over others. For clans labeled as Hamitic, the myth conveyed a connection to the history of the world outside of Africa. As Mutesa understood in the 1870s, being "a people of Ham" promised social progress and religious redemption within a white-dominated world. Africans, in other words, had the potential for great things despite their racial background because they were, in fact, partially or wholly white.

As Africans countries gained their independence in the 1960s, the Hamitic legend took on different meanings. In the post-independence world of Africa, identification with Hamites was a double-edged sword, identifying clans with the colonial oppressor. Groups who were thought of as Hamitic like the Iraqw and the Maasi were chastised for seeming tribal rather than national. The image of the Maasi was removed from the Tanzanian 100 banknote. Many ethnic groups concealed identifying dress and piercings in order to hide their ethnic identity.[11]

Nowhere were the effects of this more evident than in Rwanda. Speke had originally identified the Batutsi of Rwanda as a race of superior northerners when he arrived in the region in the 1850s. Stanley had added support to this theory when he reported on his discussions with King Mukamba while he was with Livingstone exploring Lake Tanganyika. Not surprisingly, the colonial missionaries that arrived in Rwanda in the late 1800s used such models for dividing social groups—the Batutsi and Bahutu—into racial lineages. Belgian Father L. Classe, who presided as bishop over the Catholic Church in Rwanda from 1907 to 1945, declared that "the Batutsi are superb men, with straightforward and regular features, with something of the Aryan and Semitic type." In the 1920s and 1930s, the Belgian colonial authority organized a large anthropometric survey of Rwandans in order to understand its racial demographics. As with the story of Kintu in Buganda, the origin stories of the Rwandan clans could be easily grafted to the Hamitic invasion myth. As a result, the designations of Bahutu and Batutsi, which operated as social classes in precolonial times, now emerged as racial categories. Moreover, these categories became important to Belgian authorities in organizing the power hierarchy of the state. The story of Hamitic invaders as Rwandan history was introduced within the missionary schools and became a dominant aspect of clan history. Seen as racially superior by Belgian officials, Batutsi youth were given jobs within colonial administrations at the expense of Bahutu men. The result was not only the creation of racial distinctions, but social resentment between the two divisions within

Rwandan society. With the arrival of independence, the Bahutu populations advocated for the revocation of racial policies in 1957. In 1959, a bloody social revolution brought the Bahutu into political power. Political violence between the Bahutu and Batutsi continued through the 1960s and 1970s. It was the assassination of the Bahutu president in 1994 that led to the wide-scale slaughter of the Batutsi people and their allies.[12]

It would be simplistic to blame the Hamitic hypothesis itself for this genocidal attack. Certainly the presence of divisions based upon dubious Hamitic ethnicity did not lead to the same results in Uganda, Nigeria, or Tanzania. Yet the idea became a catalyst for the explosion of Bahutu anger since it confirmed for those inclined to believe it that the Batutsi were foreign invaders. They were colonizers from outside empowered by the Europeans to repress them. In this way, the Hamitic hypothesis served to facilitate the violence of 1994.[13]

In the aftermath of the great genocide, the theory of an ancient white invasion of Africa came under harsh criticism much in the way that the Nordic race theory was dismissed after the atrocities of World War II. As Rwanda sought to mend the divisions caused by ethnic hatred, it was no longer acceptable to point to theories of foreign invasion. Yet even with the decline of Hamitic and Aryan migration theories, the idea of race conquest had not been put to rest. Sophisticated techniques of genetic testing, forensic identification, and population mapping gave new life to stories of white tribes all over the world.

20

KENNEWICK MAN

ON SUNDAY, JULY 28, 1996, the coroner of Benton County, Washington, Floyd Johnson, arrived at James Chatters's house with a human skull in a five-gallon bucket. Chatters invited him up on the porch. Earlier in the day, two young men had found the skull on the banks of the Columbia River in the town of Kennewick, Washington. They had been on their way to watch hydroplane races. To avoid paying an entrance fee at the ticket booth, they circled down to the river when they came upon the skull, lying in the mud. They reported it to the police, who visited the site and informed Johnson. Uncertain if he was dealing with a murder, accident, or archaeological discovery, Johnson looked to Chatters, a forensic anthropologist, for help. On his porch, Charters lifted the skull out of the plastic container. The bones were in good condition, bronze-colored from age. Fused suture lines on the skull indicated advanced age, probably forty years or more. The teeth were extremely worn, suggesting a diet of nuts, berries, and fibrous foods. To Chatters, this indicated that the skull may have belonged to an Indian, or perhaps even a more ancient "Paleo-Indian"—one of the earliest inhabitants of the America continent. Yet, the skull had puzzling features that didn't fit this picture. The high bridge of the nose, prominent brow ridge, and other dental features indicated to him a person of European ancestry. "This looks like a white person," Chatters told Johnson.[1]

Chatters returned with Johnson to the Columbia River site, where they found more bones that had evidently recently eroded out of the bank—vertebrae, ribs, lower jaw, and pelvis bones—almost a complete skeleton. In the following days, he had the bones X-rayed, CT scanned, and radiocarbon dated. A picture of "Kennewick Man," as he would come to be known, began to emerge. The person who died on the banks of the Columbia River was a middle-aged man about five feet, nine inches tall who had sustained a number of injuries over the course of his life. He had suffered from a serious head injury and fractures to his ribs, shoulder, and elbow. Arthritis affected his neck, knees, and elbows. Imbedded in his pelvis was a spear point, the wound partially healed over, that had continued to drain through an opening in the bone. The most stunning revelation, however, came from radiocarbon dating. Kennewick Man was 9500 years old.

The age of Kennewick Man changed the significance of the discovery. Only two sets of human remains—those discovered at the Marmes Rockshelter in Washington and at another site in Buhl, Idaho—were more ancient in the entire Northwest. Yet while these other remains were partial skeletons, Kennewick Man was almost complete. Indeed, on the entire American continent, only one other complete ancient skeleton had ever been found. The surprising shape of the skull, which seemed more European than Native American, also raised significant questions. The conventional view held that the Americas were peopled by Asian tribes migrating over the Bering land bridge 14,000 years ago, spreading across the North and South American continents. Did Kennewick Man represent a separate migration of people from Asia unrelated to the lineage of Native Americans? Or had his ancestors come from Europe, arriving from some other long transit across the frozen shores of the Atlantic? For anthropologists and archaeologists, the bones threw open a number of exciting possibilities.[2]

By contrast, many American Indians watched the Kennewick discovery with dismay. For a number of Northwest tribes—the Umatilla, Yakama, Wanapum, Colville, and Nez Percé—the location and antiquity of the bones suggested that Kennewick Man was an ancestor and, as such, needed to be given the respect of repatriation and reburial. Many tribal members looked with suspicion on the scientific arguments for the further study of Kennewick Man. Similar arguments had been used for hundreds of years to justify the disinterment of Indian remains and the pillaging of burial sites. Since Thomas Jefferson first excavated a burial mound in Virginia in 1788, white settlers and scientists had engaged in a frenzy of grave robbing and artifact gathering in the name of science. Before Samuel Morton used Egyptian skulls to revise the Hamitic hypothesis in the 1840s, he had focused his energies on American Indian remains. Through the efforts of his collectors in the field, Morton amassed a collection of 147 Indian skulls that he analyzed for his book *Crania Americana* in the 1830s.

Morton was only one of many scholars interested in studying Indian remains. With the opening of American museums in the 1850s and 1860s, demand grew for Indian bones as institutions such as the Smithsonian Institution, the Museum of Comparative Zoology at Harvard, and the Army Medical Museum competed with one another to build up their ethnographic collections. In most cases, these museums relied on amateur collectors who rummaged through graves with little care or discretion. No one could claim ignorance of Indian views of the subject: scholars and collectors both understood how offensive such disinterments were to tribal members. As early as 1809, John Bradbury declared of the Mandans, "They have in a very high degree that veneration for their remains which is a characteristic of the American Indians." Rather than change their ways, however, collectors changed their methods, waiting until dark so they could carry out their grave robbing without detection. Even though similar treatment of their family graves would have horrified European Americans, collectors and scientists kept up the pace of digging in the name of science. The fever for Indian bones did not merely afflict race scientists like Morton. Franz Boas forged his name as a cultural anthropologist by undermining the biological significance of race. Yet, in spite of this, he spent a great deal of time hunting for Indian bones. "It is most unpleasant work to steal bones from a grave," Boas admitted, "but what is the use, someone has to do it."[3]

For this reason, the discovery of Kennewick Man stirred up painful memories for the Northwest tribes. Hoping to make their case before the public, Armand Minthorn, tribal representative of the Umatilla, wrote an editorial urging for the repatriation of "the Ancient One" in the *Tri-City Herald*: "Thousands of native human remains sit on the shelves of museums and institutions, waiting for the day when they can return to the earth, and waiting for the day that scientists and others pay them the respect they are due." Minthorn presented a worldview completely at odds with Chatters and other anthropologists. He rejected the idea that Kennewick Man was Caucasian or that he migrated from another region of the world. History did not emerge from the scientific study of fossils but from the stories of elders: "From our oral histories, we know that our people have been part of this land since the beginning of time. We do not believe that our people migrated here from another continent, as the scientists do."

If this view was at odds with scientists as well as many in the general public, Minthorn and the Umatilla had a stronger card to play. The remains had been discovered on federal lands, and, as such, the Northwest tribes requested the return of the remains under the provisions of the Native American Graves Protection and Repatriation Act (NAGPRA). According to NAGPRA, Indian tribes could request the return of artifacts or remains that could be proven to be linked to their lineal descendants. Based on the tribal request, the Army Corps of Engineers ordered a halt to scientific testing on Kennewick Man and published its intention to return the bones to the tribal claimants for reburial. In late July 1996, Floyd Johnson arrived at Chatters's lab to recover the bones.[4] With repatriation and reburial looming, Chatters quickly began to photograph the skeleton. "In panic, my hands shaking, I began to take black-and-white pictures of the fractured ribs, the spear-point wound, and anything else I could think of that needed to be documented."[5]

While Chatters was locking horns with Pacific Northwest tribes over Kennewick Man, another battle was raging over the ancient—and allegedly Caucasian—remains of "Cherchen Man" in China. The story of Cherchen Man began a few years earlier in 1988. While touring a museum in the Xinjiang province of western China, University of Pennsylvania professor Victor Mair found himself standing before a glass case in the "Mummy Exhibition." Within the glass case lay a well-preserved man, six feet tall, dressed in a red wool tunic. The man had pale skin, high-cheekbones, and ginger-colored hair. Mair was stunned, not only because the man looked Caucasian, but because he resembled someone he knew. "He looked like my brother Dave sleeping there, and that's what really got me. I just kept looking at him, looking at his eyes. I couldn't tear myself away. I went around the glass case again and again. I stayed in there for several hours. I was supposed to be leading our group. I just forgot about them. I sort of got lost for two or three hours."[6]

The man had been discovered by local Chinese archaeologists in the Tarim Basin, an arid, blistering hot region of southern Xinjiang Province. The hostile conditions of the Tarim Basin were perfect for the preservation of human remains. The body in the case, which the Chinese named Cherchen Man from the local county, was in exceptionally good condition. Mair noted that many of the mummies—or to be more accurate, naturally desiccated corpses—were tall, red- or fair-haired, and had craniological measurements similar to Europeans. Although Cherchen Man had been unearthed in the 1970s, discoveries of this kind weren't new. In the early 1900s, Western explorers in Central Asia had commented on the Caucasian features of certain mummies in their reports back home. Yet these mummies were often assumed to be those of European travelers rather than local peoples. After the rise of the Communist Party in China, Western expeditions to the Tarim Basin came to an end. With the easing of Cold War tensions, however, scholars returned to China in the 1970s and 1980s. At the same time, large-scale construction projects in the Tarim Basin uncovered hundreds of bodies with similar, Caucasian features. As Mair began to examine the Tarim mummies, he realized that the features of Cherchen Man (or ur-David, as he named him in honor of his brother), were common within the population. This was confirmed by Chinese archaeologist Dr. Han Kangxin, physical anthropologist at the Institute of Archeology in Beijing, who, while examining the mummies of Loulan, also found features consistent with Caucasoids.[7]

The discovery of these remains, like those of Kennewick Man, fed into a simmering political dispute. Tensions between the Uighurs—the Turkic-speaking Muslim people of Xinjiang—and the Han Chinese had been running high for decades. Uighur separatists claimed that Xinjiang has always been geographically and ethnically separate from China. Under communist control, the Uighurs staged at least nineteen revolts between 1951 and 1981, protesting government actions and policies. While Beijing treated Xinjiang as an integral part of China since antiquity, the Uighurs identified with the cultures to the West—in language as well as religion.[8]

For the restive Uighur community, the discovery of Cherchen Man and other mummies with Caucasian features fit nicely into their argument about origins: the Tarim Basin was originally settled by peoples from the west who arrived with new crops and technologies. Only later were these lands brought under the control of Han Chinese to the east. In this way, the past was used to make a political argument about the present: the Chinese were not the original inhabitants of western China; they were occupiers. The Caucasian nature of the mummies only confirmed that the region was first settled by an Indo-European people from the west, rather than a Mongoloid people from the east. The archaeological data showed that the earliest cultures of Tarim, dating back to the second millennium BCE, relied on animals and crops that derived from the west. Moreover, Buddhist manuscripts discovered in the Tarim Basin region, dating from 800–600 BCE, were written in an Indo-European language, subsequently named "Tocharian." While the linguistic data was speculative—no one could be sure whether Cherchen man and his contemporaries spoke the language found in the Buddhist texts—it added to the circumstantial weight of the findings.[9]

Back in the United States, Chatters and other anthropologists mobilized against the decision by the Corps of Engineers to stop tests on Kennewick Man, filing a petition in US District Court. NAGPRA, they argued, applied only to the repatriation of remains that could be linked by culture or descent to living tribes. Bones that were nine thousand years old couldn't possibly be linked to a specific modern-day Indian tribe. Moreover, the unique physiognomy of Kennewick Man suggested that he was not related to any living Indian tribes. If this was confirmed, NAGPRA would not apply to the remains and the scientific study could continue. Chatters's observation that Kennewick Man looked like "a white person" suddenly carried implications beyond anthropological theory. As the lawsuit unfolded, most American newspapers took the side of scientists.[10]

For Native Americans, this, too, conjured up unsettling memories. It was not the first time that scientists—citing archaeological evidence—had claimed that Indians were not the original Americans. Beginning in the 1700s, white colonists came across massive earthworks, such as flat-topped pyramids, elongated ridges, and conical mounds. Some, such as the one-hundred-foot-tall flat-topped pyramid in Collinsville, Illinois, indicated the existence of large and organized agricultural settlements. Such a civilization, later scientists argued, must have been built by a race that predated the American Indians, who did not possess the sophistication to build such structures. As a result, ethnologists divorced the impressive work of the "mound builders" from the American Indian tribes currently living in these regions. In 1848, Abraham Lincoln wrote, "The eyes of that species of extinct giants, whose bones fill the mounds of America, have gazed on Niagara, as ours do now." Similar arguments would be used by Mauch and others at Great Zimbabwe in the late 1800s: native peoples were too primitive to build such complicated structures.

The Chinese government worried about a similar argument emerging from the study of the Tarim mummies. The influx of an advanced Indo-European culture in western China raised questions about the source of China's sophisticated culture. Mair's argument, as archaeologist Philip Kohl pointed out in 1999, played into a stereotype of Chinese civilization, which was that it was "derivative" of the peoples who settled in the Tarim Basin, who were "racially distinct."[11]

The theory of foreign mound builders was not the only one to divorce Indians from their history and culture. Another was that certain Native American tribes were the descendants of a European race that had gone native. The idea grew out of the legend of the Welsh prince Madoc, son of the real twelfth-century king Owain Gwynedd. As later accounts recorded it, Madoc's brothers and half-brothers quarreled violently over who would succeed Owain when he died in 1170. Tired of the fighting, Madoc sailed into the western ocean with his brother Rhirid and a hundred followers, soon discovering new fertile lands to begin a colony. They returned to Wales to recruit new settlers, then sailed away, never to be heard from again. Over the course of the seventeenth century, British colonists in North America frequently reported evidence of "Welsh Indians," natives who were presumably the descendents of Madoc, now living in the manner of American Indians.

The light complexion and European features of some Indian tribes, such as the Mandan, became the subject of much discussion in the eighteenth century. Such was the power of this story that in 1804 Meriwether Lewis and William Clark had specific orders to research the Mandan tribe in hopes of testing the theory. Thus when the anthropologists filed a claim against repatriating Kennewick Man to the Northwest tribes on the basis of race, it opened an old wound. Writing in the *New Yorker* about the case in July 1997, Douglas Preston noted that "Kennewick Man's bones are part of a growing quantity of evidence that the earliest inhabitants of the New World may have been a Caucasoid people."[12]

Few scientists questioned that these discoveries raised significant questions about the past, challenging traditional accounts of the peopling of North America and Central Asia. Yet, for many, identifying the bones as European brought them uncomfortably close to the race-invasion theories of old. Only a few decades had passed since scientists squeezed data of many types—linguistic, cultural, and craniometrical—into one boilerplate argument: that civilization advanced by means of racial conquest. These theories went beyond ivory tower debates to become well-circulated ideas, ones that gave Western governments legitimacy in pursuing colonization as a form of civilization building. From the scramble for Africa to Operation Barbarossa, European powers justified their conquests in the present according to the imperial legacies of the past.

To say that Kennewick Man did not resemble Native Americans or that Cherchen Man did not look Chinese did not mean that these men represented ancient European tribes. The shortcomings of craniological measurements in determining race—indeed, the squishiness of race itself as a biological category—had made most anthropologists reluctant to tether Kennewick Man too closely to a "racial type." Yet the clay facial reconstruction of Kennewick Man—which bore a striking resemblance to the actor Patrick Stewart—only underscored the racial aspects of the story. In China, the scientific investigation of the mummies intensified political friction between Han Chinese and Uighurs for claim to the original identity of the Tarim Basin.

These debates over Caucasian origins also illuminated fracture lines within the scientific community. Among physical anthropologists, the use of anthropometry for categorizing racial types remained—as it had since the end of the Second World War—very controversial. Western anthropologists, sensitive to the tainted legacy of anthropometry, eugenics, and genocide, were reluctant to make too much of such measurements. Yet, other, non-Western scholars relied on these measurements from skulls, teeth, and bones without the same inhibitions. Kangxin Han went so far as to delineate the mummy skulls of Tarim according to the racial categories common to the beginning of the twentieth century: Nordic, Alpine, Mediterranean, and Mongoloid. Mair, too, seemed at times emotionally invested in the Caucasoid identity of the mummies he was investigating. In addition to his feelings about Cherchen Man—his "ur-David"—Mair also waxed poetic about the 2003 discovery of a fair-haired mummified woman soon called the "Beauty of Xiaohe." "I always refer to her as very alluring—almost seductive," he admitted to the *Pennsylvania Gazette* in 2011. "She has such beautiful features—just lovely. Her lips are great; her teeth are great. She is gorgeous!" Mair seemed to be echoing Blumenbach, marveling over the beauty of a female skull he had obtained in the 1790s from the Caucasus, a skull that confirmed for him the ur-status of the European type, now defined as "Caucasian."[13] This hardly proved that the Beauty of Xiaohe, Cherchen Man, and other ancient mummies were actually Europeans who "migrated thousands of kilometers across two vast mountain ranges and the entire Eurasian Steppe just to settle on the outskirts of one of the most inhospitable deserts in the world." This was not, wrote Philip Kohl, "the only interpretation for these data."[14]

The return of this kind of racial exuberance, of lost fair-skinned peoples bringing their advances to primitive regions of the world as well as the categorizing of world peoples according to racial types, worried many archaeologists who remembered the use to which such categories had been put—as well as the dubious methodology that had been used to justify them. Reviewing Mair's volume of papers on the Tarim mummies, Kohl noted, "Many myths need dispelling, including, sadly, one of the most dangerous and persistent of this century: that of the peculiarly gifted, racially pure proto-Indo-Europeans who spread from their circumscribed, spatially ascertainable homeland, to bestow their technological innovations and spread their genes across most of Eurasia."[15]

Kohl had grounds for concern. The white tribes were back. The discovery of Kennewick Man was soon folded into the a growing literature that argued for an indigenous white race. So, too, was the discovery of Cherchen Man. They were added to the scientific data on the Hamites, the Aryans, and other groups reputed to have European or Caucasian lineage far from Europe. Indeed, as anthropologists filed a suit to prevent repatriation, they were joined by a California pagan group, the Asatru Folk Assembly, who claimed that Kennewick man was a person of Germanic origin. By 1998, the battle for Kennewick Man had been joined by white supremacist groups as well. As much as World War II and critiques of racial science had discredited the stories of Hamitic and Aryan migrations—of white tribes existing in Africa and Asia—they could not extinguish them. As psychologist Graham Richards expressed it, each time the arguments supporting the biology of race have been killed off they rise again. Like vampires, he writes, "the controversy is not so much alive as undead."[16]

Debate over Kennewick Man and Cherchen Man quickly jumped from scientific circles into the public forum. In the Northwest, it became tied to a power struggle between Indian tribes and scientists over the boundary between science and cultural respect. More seemed to be at work in these white tribe discoveries than the recovery of lost racial ancestors. Until the middle of the twentieth century, one of the goals of physical anthropology had been the identification of a pure racial essence among human populations. The discovery of remains had always held out the promise of recovering not only a particular piece of esoteric history, but something more existential. What had been lost, and what scientists had hoped to recover, was not the existence of a particular tribe, but the core identity of whiteness itself. It was an idea that enchanted—indeed, still enchants—people on three continents despite its dubious value as science and its terrible costs as policy. Those still chasing whiteness have found that it—like Stanley's lost tribe—retreats into the mists. Cast out of science, it maintains its power by eluding capture, remaining just out of reach.

EPILOGUE
What Did Stanley See?

IN THE DARK HOURS before dawn, Kampala's Namirembe Road pulses with minibuses and motorcycles, the smell of exhaust mingling with charcoal smoke as street vendors roast ears of corn. I boarded a bus to Kasese, a town at the western edge of Uganda in the foothills of the Ruwenzori Mountains. For five years, I had been chasing white tribes through old books, science journals, and expedition reports in archives from Dartmouth College to the Smithsonian Institution. I had even found Stanley's field notes in Belgium—reading his careful, crimped handwriting in his journals at the Royal Museum of Central Africa in Tervuren. From these materials, the broad arc of this story—the rise and fall of the Hamitic hypothesis—has taken form. Yet nowhere in these materials was the answer to the question that had originally launched this quest: what did Stanley see in the fall of 1875? This was a question that probably did not have an answer, at least one that transcended speculation and conjecture. This is because our knowledge of Stanley's encounter comes exclusively from Stanley himself. No amount of forensic sleuthing in Uganda nearly a century and a half after Stanley's expedition would crack this mystery. I decided to go to Uganda anyway, to do research at Kampala University, but also to visit

Bamwanjara Pass, Ruwenzoris (14,600 feet). Two days from
Mount Stanley (background).

the places where Stanley met with Mutesa, to talk with Ugandans about these stories, and to spend time on the mountain that Stanley had once believed was the sanctuary of Africa's lost white race.

As the bus squeezed through narrow city streets on the way to the highway, I thought about Stanley's journey west across the continent. He had left Mutesa's court near here in the fall of 1875, headed west toward Muta Nzigé (Lake Edward) in hopes of solving the mystery of the Nile's source. There were no buses to transport his Zanzibari porters and Bugandan soldiers then, so his route west took him up the marshy Katonga River, his men loaded with bundles of food and equipment, fabrics and gift beads, as well as the sections of Stanley's boat *Lady Alice*, carried aloft like a giant, disarticulated insect. Under the weight of this load, and under the threat of attack by Buganda's enemies, it had taken Stanley's expedition two months to make the journey that took us eight hours, our bus rocketing through banana groves and tea plantations on Uganda's east-west highway, Afro-reggae blasting from open windows.

Epilogue

I was happy to be in a bus rather than a marsh, careening through lush green countryside rather than hacking my way through swamps and spear grass. Still, Stanley had witnessed things along this journey that I wish I had witnessed, not just the pale-skinned Gambaragarans that would absorb his attention for years to come but the snow-covered Mount Gambaragara from a high bluff near the Katonga, a towering wall capped in white, buttressed against the blue horizon.

These experiences—for which we have only Stanley's testimony—convinced him that a white race lived the interior of Africa, a view he continued to hold for decades. And because Stanley was the world's most famous explorer, news of the "white race of Gambaragara" traveled far and wide. His press reports were copied and excerpted by newspapers around the world, and within a few years percolated into books, atlases, and school primers as anecdotes that could be used for many purposes, explaining the geography of Africa, the history of exploration, and the trials and adventures of Stanley himself. Africa's white race became an object of fascination for poets, adventure novelists, and other explorers. Most important, it became a key discovery for scientists interested in questions of race, particularly in the wake of Darwin's *On the Origin of Species*, published fifteen years before Stanley's journey to Gambaragara. *Origin* said nothing about the evolution of the human species, which Darwin thought too controversial for a work that, he knew, was going to be controversial enough. It didn't matter, however: both Darwin's allies and his critics read between the lines of *Origin*, extending his arguments to human evolution. Then, they took up the subject in their own works on the subject over the following decade.

As Stanley set off across East Africa to find David Livingstone in 1871, Darwin himself was weighing in on the subject in *The Descent of Man*. All human races were varieties of one human species, he claimed, their differences arising from natural selection working upon geographically isolated populations. Not only did this claim challenge the ideas of biblical literalists but also those of many scientists who believed that human races were not merely varieties of the same species, but separate species all together. Within this debate, the story of Stanley's lost white race—and later, other stories of blond Eskimos, white Indians, and Tibetan Aryans—became important because they offered something more powerful than inferences from skulls, bones, and biblical texts: they were living populations, ones whose very existence demanded explanation.

As such, white tribe claims were not merely sensational but profoundly influential. Stanley's claim, in particular, gave new life to an old theory of racial origin rooted in the book of Genesis. The white race of Gambaragara now became a foundation stone for a new Hamitic hypothesis, one that took the Genesis account of racial origins and adapted it for scientific use. Growing from the consensus view that the human species originated in Asia, it postulated that a wave of superior, light-skinned Hamites had invaded Africa in the ancient past, overrunning, enslaving, and sometimes intermarrying with, black Africans. Stanley had not begun this process, of course. Talk of fair-skinned Hamites invading Africa had begun in the 1840s. Stanley's claim, however, ensured that the discussion of the Hamitic hypothesis would move beyond ancient bones and Hebrew texts to explain the world of the present.

Built from fact and fantasy, measure and mismeasure, the Hamitic hypothesis eventually fell apart. In archaeology, all of the Hamitic spin-off theories—the foreign builder theory of Great Zimbabwe, the dynastic race theory of ancient Egypt, and the Azanian civilization theory of East Africa—were eventually put to rest by a combination of new evidence, better methods, and moral outrage. In anthropology, the claim that ancient Egyptians were Caucasians was debunked. So, too, in linguistics, the work that supported the idea of a Hamitic invasion based on the creation of a Hamitic language group was undermined by those who revealed the flaws in the ways linguists selected and compared words. Even Stanley's blockbuster claim never made it out of the nineteenth century. A small party of his men had climbed the western flanks of the Ruwenzoris: the mountains were uninhabited above 10,000 feet.

Yet the Hamitic hypothesis continued to come back to life. It was put down time and time again, only to reappear in a new form. While the theory has now been decisively exiled from the social sciences, it continues to live on among fringe groups who cling to race history as a way of explaining the world and justifying their racist beliefs. More importantly, it continues to live on among Africans themselves. Even after African colonies gained their independence from Europe in the decades after World War II, the idea of a racial divide between different clans continued to shape African societies. While this distant

Epilogue

and distorted echo of the Hamitic hypothesis was not the cause of the 1994 Rwandan genocide, it made it easier for Hutus and Tutsis to see each other as racially different. It became easier to see neighbors—who spoke the same language, attended the same schools, worked in the same businesses—as outsiders.

None of my Ugandan friends in Kampala put any stock in the idea of ancient invasions. Though Christian and religious, they also did not believe in a connection between the son of Noah and African Kintu. Still, the Hamitic idea lingers on in Africa even as evidence against it continues to mount. Since the 1960s, evidence from hominid fossils, prehistoric settlements, and population genetics has indicated that the human species originated in Africa rather than in Asia. More recent analyses—from comparative linguistics as well as population genetics—show that while the people of East Africa do share ancestry with northern peoples from North Africa and Ethiopia, this is only one of many migration events that occurred in prehistoric Africa: the peoples of the Lakes Region are also the descendants of Bantu migrants from West Africa and Khosian migrants out of southern Africa in the ancient past. Moreover, these migrations correlate closely to climactic change. The migrants into East Africa were probably fleeing drought and famine, heading to more climactically stable and fertile lands that could support them.[1]

Yet if the Hamitic hypothesis and all of its variations and distortions have been exploded, my original question remained, and it gnawed at me as my bus dropped me off in Kasese, a dusty mining town near the Congo border, only fifteen miles from Stanley's position in 1875. Whom did Stanley see? One possible explanation is that the Gambaragarans were albinos. A number of African populations—in South Africa, Zimbabwe, and Tanzania—have high rates of albinism, a genetic condition caused by genes that limit or prevent production of pigmentation. Stanley's "white Africans" might parallel Richard Marsh's discovery of the "white Indians" of Panama, a population that was later shown to have a high rate of albinism. Yet even among clans with the highest rates of albinism in Africa, it remains a rare condition. Among the Tonga of Zimbabwe, who have the highest rate of albinism on the continent, only one child in a thousand is born with depigmented skin. By contrast, all of the Gambaragarans identified by Stanley showed the same traits. Nor did Stanley's description of the Gambaragarans fit the classic profile of albinism. In skin color, the Gambaragarans reminded Stanley of southern Europeans, "Greeks in white shirts." Nor did he describe any albinistic traits in eye or hair color. In his interview with David Ker, he depicted the Gambaragarans as having "brown curly hair" and skin "no darker than a light mulatto."[2]

Another possibility is that Gambaragarans evolved light skin as an adaptation to a specific environment. Dark skin results from the presence of melanin, a pigment that protects the skin from damage caused by ultraviolet radiation (UVR). UVR is most intense in equatorial regions, and as a result human populations living in these latitudes produce melanin as a survival mechanism. Yet dark skin loses its survival advantage in environments where UVR is low, and can even be a threat to survival, because while UV exposure can lead to skin cancer, it also allows the human body to synthesize vitamin D, a vital compound for bone growth and the immune system. The importance of vitamin D synthesis can be seen in the rapid depigmentation of populations as they left Africa 60,000 years ago. In the higher latitudes of Eurasia, humans were exposed to less UVR, not only because of the diminished intensity of the sun, but also because colder temperatures required them to cover their skin. As the danger of UVR damage declined, so, too, did the value of melanin.[3]

Could this process of depigmentation have happened to the Gambaragarans? Possibly. While the Ruwenzori Mountains lie almost directly on the equator, a high UVR zone, these mountains are often shrouded by mist. Moreover, the regions west of the Ruwenzori are under the canopy of dense rainforest. As a result, there are many regions in and around the Ruwenzoris that do not receive much sunlight, a point that Stanley observed as he approached the Ruwenzoris from the Ituri Forest in 1887. A study by Jean Hiernaux in 1976 suggested that a single population from West-Central Africa had undergone significant skin color changes as it split into three groups (Sara, Oto, and Twa) and migrated to different UVR environments over a two-thousand-year span, a relatively short period of time in evolutionary terms. Of the three groups, the Twa, who live in the dense undergrowth of the Congo rainforest had the lightest colored skin. Perhaps the Gambaragarans, too, developed lighter skin as an adaptation to darker habitats.[4]

Epilogue

This is speculation. It is impossible to say whether this process was at work among the Gambaragarans, a group that—like the existence of race itself—always seems to elude capture. In truth, white tribes were never identified merely by skin color. The Hamitic theory grew out of other features—aquiline noses, head shapes, cultural behaviors, and dress—which identified these people in the eyes of explorers and colonists as "white."

This raises another possibility for what Stanley saw, one that could also be used to explain other sightings by David Livingstone, Serpa Pinto, John Speke, and others: perhaps these explorers were interpreting natural variation among African populations as racial differences according to their own preconceived categories. With the growing sophistication of genetic research, scientists have demonstrated that African populations show the broadest range of genetic diversity among the earth's peoples. This finding has to be put into context. The human species is, in fact, quite homogenous across different populations. Human beings are about 99.9 percent identical to one another genetically. Other mammalian species, such as chimpanzees, are considerably more diverse. Yet within this small spectrum of human difference, much of it expresses itself within Africa populations, presumably because Africans populations have had about 200,000 years to differentiate from one another whereas non-African populations began to differentiate from one another with their migration from Africa around 60,000 years ago. Interestingly, most of this human variation exists within large population groups; so, for example, about 85 percent of human variation can be found within African populations, whereas only 15 percent of this variation exists between Africans and other groups such as Asians, Europeans, and Native Americans. In other words, the nineteenth-century project to build an ironclad system of race turned out to be pure misadventure. A far greater range of difference existed within regional populations than existed between them. And within these populations, Africans expressed the most diversity of all.

As I walked with my guide, William Kiminywa, through Kilembe village, at the trailhead to the Ruwenzori Mountains, I talked with him about Stanley's encounters with the Gambaragarans. He found it difficult to believe. Kiminywa was Bakonzo and, like most of the Bakonzo who live in Kilembe and the lowlands of the Ruwenzoris, dark-skinned. No one would mistake any of these men and women raking coffee beans, selling phone cards, or driving cows in Kilembe for "Greeks in white shirts." Nor would they say this about the Ugandans living in the other Ruwenzori towns of Fort Portal, Hima, or Kikura. The point was made clear when we passed a Kilembe woman who with her children was working the vertical fields of bananas and cassava on the Ruwenzori trail. As her young daughter, about three years old, saw me approach, she began to cry. I removed my sunglasses, thinking it would help, but it just provoked her to scream, cover her eyes, and leap off the trail. Not everyone is used to such depigmented people in their midst.

Our climb up Mount Stanley took six days—a series of ascents through farms and bamboo forest to the glacier at the top of the range. This was a landscape that Stanley himself never saw close up: bamboo forests, giant lobelias, rock hyrax, and blue monkeys. In Kampala, I had become close with the Ugandans who were helping me. But here, I felt the isolation of the mountains as we pushed higher. Kiminywa was a fantastic guide; along with the porters, he made my trip possible. Yet as polite, knowledgeable, and professional as they were, it was clear that I was a client, not a friend. Every afternoon at four, the porters served me tea, even if we were in rainstorms on windy cliffs. In the evening, they brought me my meals, checked my supplies, and resupplied me with water (river water for the porters, boiled water for the clients) before retreating to their own tents. Unaware of the rules of the system, I went down to the porters' tent as they prepared their own tea. All three men stood up as I arrived, saying nothing, waiting for my request. I was unshaven, sweaty, and caked with mud, but at that moment I felt like I was Lord Grantham, arriving downstairs in servants' quarters without warning. I had entered a fixed role on the mountain, one that had been defined and perfected since the days of Speke and Burton, and is still kept in place by tours, safaris, and trekker organizations.

There would be other challenges, too, that reminded me of earlier expeditions. For seasoned climbers, summiting a 17,000-foot peak—with few technical challenges except for the last day of glacier climbing—is not especially difficult. But I am not a seasoned climber. By the third day of the trek, altitude had made it difficult for me to keep food down. To make matters worse, on my way down from the summit, at 14,500 feet, I awoke in my tent with a sharp pain in my left

Epilogue

kidney. The pain was so severe—a stone, I later learned—that I couldn't stand upright. "I don't think I can go on," I told Kiminywa.

"We can bring up more porters," he said, "but they will take days to get here, then more days to carry you down." He paused. "It's better if you can walk yourself out."

And so, teeth clenched, I kept hiking—without food or sleep, tilted over at a forty-five-degree angle—until we made the next camp eight miles away. It was the most difficult thing I've ever done.

As much as I've spent my career studying—and often critiquing—the adventures of Victorian explorers, I felt as if I had entered the role of one myself. The fact that I spent my days in Uganda looking intently at people's noses, hair, and skin only reinforced this association. However much I feel like a twenty-first-century scholar, critiquing colonialism and its reliance on race science, I felt like I couldn't escape it here. Yet, in a strange way, this was helpful, too. Because it gave me some small understanding of Stanley's feelings of loneliness and isolation in the field: a glimpse of the chasm that, even in a global age of cell phones and social media, still separates Westerners from the rest of the world. It sounds absurd to compare my short trek up the Ruwenzoris with Stanley's three-year gauntlet across Africa, battling for his life against hostile forces, starvation, and endemic diseases. He was out of contact with Europe and the West for years at a time. But it was enough for me to imagine how profoundly these emotions—a craving for contact and the familiar—might shape the encounters of the explorer.

This is not usually how we remember Henry Stanley. History has cast him in different lights: as a pure self-promoter, leveraging his discovery of Livingstone into a lifelong career as celebrity explorer; or as a pawn of empire, doing the bidding of King Leopold in the scramble for Africa; or as a fragmented personality, an emotionally hobbled man, as insecure among his peers as he was intrepid in the field. All of these interpretations have some truth. Yet he was also desperate for contact. Explorers are often defined as self-reliant, aloof, unafraid of being unmoored to the people and places of the wider world. In truth, they seek connection—whether through personal friendships, romantic affairs, or public acclaim—just like the rest of us. What makes them different is not personality but circumstance. Far from home, the traveler feels distance keenly. We talk readily about Victorian explorers' geographical theories, cultural prejudices, and racist assumptions. Yet their encounters with the frightening and the unfamiliar were also filtered through their sense of solitude in the world. Finding the foreign, they grasped for the familiar, any touchstone to the world they left behind.

In this way, "lost" was a term that applied to the explorer as well as the native. Months after he left Gambaragara, Stanley found himself on the Congo—where his expedition suffered most severely. One of his expedition members, an African woman named Amina, lay near death. As Stanley reports it, she told him, "It is a bad world, master, and you have lost your way in it." To her, Stanley was the lost one, not the white tribe that he wrote so much about in his dispatches to the *New York Herald*. The reader can glimpse this in Stanley's giddy description of his meeting with David Livingstone. But in little ways, too, Stanley signaled his profound loneliness and desire for the familiar. In a speech he gave after his return, Stanley admitted that even in the "remote interior of Africa," he had found "startling and truthful silhouettes of European and American friends." He found more than friends, however. "When I first saw Lukongeh, the King of Ukerewe, I was surprised to be reminded of portraits of the great Napoleon; in another I observed a startling resemblance to Daniel Webster, the American orator, and in another I saw a coloured duplicate of President Andrew Jackson. A most prominent statesman of England was faithfully reproduced in a naked native in the jungles of Uregga, and a well-known member of Parliament reminds me of the bald-headed and fine-featured King of Nzabi on the Livingstone River."[5]

All this offers a different reading of Stanley's lost race. Had it only been Stanley, perhaps this idea of finding familiar faces—even familiar races—far from home might seem anomalous. Yet it happened many times. When Vilhjalmur Stefansson reached Victoria Island, he described how the Inuit there saw him as one of their own. So, too, did Victor Mair arriving in Xinjiang, see his brother beneath the glass case. And James Chatters, too, found something marvelous about seeing someone like Patrick Stewart emerging out of the prehistoric past. All these recognitions were undoubtedly inflected by the ideas of race but encounters with the familiar are too common to be explained so easily.

As Europe and North America confronted dwindling birth rates and increased nonwhite migration in the early 1900s, fears of "race suicide" circulated in the West. It is no coincidence that the champions of race migration theories were often those most concerned about the possibility of white culture being swamped by the "colored" cultures of the world. Nor is it surprising that race scientists would so earnestly seek out tribes of Aryans, Caucasians, and Hamites. "Lost white race" takes on a new meaning if, like Amina's declaration to Stanley, it is applied to people of the West, rather than Africa: a description of the troubled, pale-faced inhabitants of New York, London, and Berlin. The search for white tribes was not simply a product of curious physiognomy filtered by racial bias. The intensity of the pursuit and its persistence across the decades of the nineteenth and twentieth centuries point to something lurking beneath the surface of scientific discourse: a lingering insecurity about Western culture in the industrial age, one expressed across a spectrum of writing, from the lost race novels of Haggard to the psychoanalytic writings of Jung. Thus, as much as finding lost tribes represented the research interests of scientists and explorers, it also reflected a deeper, less articulated, concern of the Western world: the desire to find itself.

NOTES

INTRODUCTION

1. Details about the Bond Street interview come from Ker's article "White Africans and the Congo," *New York Times*, December 20, 1885, 6; "The white race of Gambaragara" appears in Stanley's letter to the *Daily Telegraph* and *New York Herald*, November 1, 1876; details about Stanley's stature and demeanor come from Dorothy Tennant's diary, January 10, 1886, MSS 5925, Stanley Archives.
2. The *London Times* coined "The Scramble for Africa" in an article of the same name, September 15, 1884, 8.
3. "White People in Africa," *Hartford Daily Courant*, August 18, 1876, 1; "Central Africa," *Daily Inter Ocean* (Chicago), August 14, 1876, 3; "Stanley's Discoveries in Africa," *Albany Evening Journal*, August 18, 1876, 2; "Geography and Exploration," *American Naturalist* 10 (September 1876): 562; J. A. Grant, "On H. M. Stanley's Exploration of the Victoria Nyanza," *Journal of the Royal Geographical Society* 46 (1876): 27; on Manuel Iradier, see Martin-Márquez, *Disorientations*, 80–84.
4. Ker, *White Africans*, preface; L. E. Neame, "Mysterious White Races," *Chambers's Journal* (London) 8 (February 18, 1905): 188. "Tribe" is a controversial term, now mostly avoided because of its negative and inaccurate connotations. I generally use "clan," "people," and "society" to refer to indigenous groups, but continue to use "tribe" when expressing the views of nineteenth-century explorers and scientists.
5. Geography and exploration literature discussing the "white race" of Gambaragara include Joel Tyler Headley, *The Achievements of Stanley* (Philadelphia: Hubbard Bros., 1878) and Headley's *H. M. Stanley's Wonderful Adventures in Africa* (New York: Union Publishing House, 1886), 462; J. E. Chambliss, *The Life and Labors of David Livingstone* (Philadelphia: Hubbard Bros., 1876), 836; John George Wood, *The Uncivilized Races of Men in All Countries of the World* (San Francisco: J. A. Brainard & Co., 1883), 1530; Robert Brown, *The Story of Africa and Its Explorers* (London: Cassell, 1893), 299; Alexander Hyde and Francis Bliss, *Stanley in Africa* (St. Louis, MO: Columbian Book Co., 1879), 379; Keith Johnston, *Africa* (London, Edward Stanford, 1884), 606; John Geddie, *The Lake Regions of Central Africa* (Edinburgh and New York: T. Nelson and Sons, 1881), 99; James Penny Boyd, *Wonders of the Heavens, Earth, and Ocean* (Philadelphia: International Publishing, 1888), 324.
6. Richard Hall, *Stanley* (London: Collins, 1974), 55; James L. Newman, *Imperial Footprints: Henry Morton Stanley's African Journeys* (Washington, DC: Potomac Books, 2004), xix. No mention is made of Gambaragara or its people in Frank McLynn's

Stanley: The Making of an African Explorer (Chelsea, MI: Scarborough House, 1990), John Bierman's *Dark Safari: The Life Behind the Legend of Henry Morton Stanley* (New York: Knopf, 1990), Byron Farwell's *The Man Who Presumed: A Biography of Henry M. Stanley* (New York: W. W. Norton, 1985), or Tim Jeal's extensively researched *Stanley: The Impossible Life of Africa's Greatest Explorer* (New Haven, CT: Yale University Press, 2007). The few modern references to Gambaragara include Martin-Márquez, *Disorientations*; Gatsinzi Basaninyenzi, "'Dark-Faced Europeans': The Nineteenth-Century Colonial Travelogue and the Invention of the Hima Race," in *Race and the Foundations of Knowledge*, ed. Joseph A. Young and Jana Evans Iraziel (Urbana: University of Illinois Press, 2006), 123.
7. Kennedy, *Spaces*, 220–222.

CHAPTER 1: GAMBARAGARA

1. Stanley describes his encounter with the Gambaragarans in *Through the Dark Continent* (New York: Harpers, 1878), 426–28; *The Exploration Diaries of H. M. Stanley*, ed. Richard Stanley and Alan Neame (New York: Vanguard Press, 1961), 113; *Stanley's Despatches to the New York Herald, 1871–1872, 1874–1877* (Boston: Boston University Press, 1970), 265–67. Stanley quoted from *Despatches*, 266. On skin color of the Ganda people, see Stanley, *Dark Continent*, 197; on explorers in the Lakes Region, see Robert Collins, *Europeans in Africa*, 54–58.
2. On Africa as a place of Western fantasies, see Lorraine Daston and Katharine Park, *Wonders and the Order of Nature, 1150–1750* (New York: Zone Books, 2001), 63–64, 329–63.
3. Stanley quoted in "Stanley in Central Africa," *Thames Advertiser* (London), October 14, 1876, 3. Quotation also appears in E. Chambliss, *The Lives and Travels of Livingstone and Stanley*, (Boston: DeWolfe, Fiske, and Company, 1881), 726.
4. Caesar quoted in Jean Kerisel, *The Nile and Its Masters: Past, Present, and Future* (London: Taylor & Francis, 2001), 8; Eleni Manolaraki, "Nocendi Nilum Cupido: The Nile Digression in Book 10," in *Brill's Companion to Lucan*, ed. Paolo Asso (Leiden: Brill, 2011), 153–56; Francesc Relaño, "Against Ptolemy: The Significance of the Lopes-Pigafetta Map of Africa," *Imago Mundi* 47 (1995): 49–66.
5. Quotation from Baker, *Albert N'yanza*, 308; Kennedy, *Civilized Man*, 93–130.
6. On quest for the Nile's source, see Jeal, *Explorers of the Nile*, 1–17; on Speke's death, ibid., 199–208.
7. On Stanley's trek to Lake Victoria, see Stanley, *Dark Continent*, 88–145.
8. On ivory wars in East Africa, see Oliver and Atmore, *Africa Since 1800*, 94–96; on the trip from Bagamoyo to Lake Victoria, skirmish over milk, and death of Edward Pocock, see Jeal, *Stanley*, 164–68.
9. "Sordid interests…": Stanley, Notebook 15, "A Journey into Africa," Stanley Archives.
10. Dates and locations noted in the appendix of *Dark Continent*, "A Table of Our Wanderings Through Africa, 1874, 1875, 1876, 1877," 528. Quotations from Stanley,

Despatches, 265, 267. reprinted in "Geography and Exploration," *American Naturalist* 10 (November 1876): 695.

11. Twenty-five years later, Harry Johnston would remark, "Sir Henry Stanley would indeed be amazed at the change which has taken place in parts of the forest which some twelve years ago were to him and his expedition more remote from civilization than the North Pole." Johnston, *Uganda Protectorate*, 24.

CHAPTER 2: ANOTHER WORLD

1. Columbus quoted in William D. Phillips and Carla Rahn Phillips, *The Worlds of Christopher Columbus* (New York: Cambridge University Press, 1993), 106; Alvise Cadamosto, *The Voyages of Cadamosto* (London: Hakluyt Society, 1937), 1.
2. Luís de Camões, *The Lusiad; or, the Discovery of India* (London: G. Bell and Sons, 1877), 137.
3. Dee Brown, *Hear That Lonesome Whistle Blow: The Epic Story of the Transcontinental Railroad* (New York: Macmillan, 2001), 222.
4. James Romm, *The Edges of the Earth in Ancient Thought: Geography, Exploration, and Fiction* (Princeton, NJ: Princeton University Press, 1992), 9–44; Barry Cunliffe, *Facing the Ocean: The Atlantic and Its Peoples, 8000 BC–AD 1500* (Oxford: Oxford University Press, 2001), 3–4; Alfred Hiatt, *Terra Incognita* (Chicago: University of Chicago Press, 2008), 65–145.
5. Braude, "The Sons of Noah and the Construction of Ethnic and Geographical Identities in the Medieval and Early Modern Periods," *William and Mary Quarterly* 54 (January 1997): 109, 123, 125–26.
6. Guérin, *Elephant Ivory*, 166–67; Kevin Shillington, *History of Africa* (New York: Palgrave Macmillan, 2012), 54–56.
7. Guérin, *Elephant Ivory*, 159–161.
8. Ibid., 164.
9. Al-Umari, cited in J. F. P. Hopkins and Nehemia Levitzion, *Corpus of Early Arabic Sources for West African History* (Cambridge: Cambridge University Press, 1981), 269–73.
10. Mansa Musa is visible in the 1375 Catalan Atlas at the Bibliothèque Nationale de France: http://expositions.bnf.fr/ciel/catalan/.
11. John Day, "The Great Bullion Famine of the Fifteenth Century," *Past and Present* (May 1978): 11–23, 42; Ronald A. Messier, "The Almoravids: West African Gold and the Gold Currency of the Mediterranean Basin," *Journal of the Economic and Social History of the Orient* 17, no. 1 (March 1974): 31–47.
12. Thomas Benjamin, *The Atlantic World: Europeans, Africans, Indians, and Their Shared History, 1400–1900* (Cambridge: Cambridge University Press, 2009), 79.
13. Matteo Salvadore, "The Ethiopian Age of Exploration: Prester John's Discovery of Europe, 1306–1458," *Journal of World History* 21, no. 4 (2011): 599–608.
14. Michael E. Brooks, "Prester John: A Reexamination and Compendium of the Mythical Figure Who Helped Spark European Expansion," PhD diss., University of Toledo, 2009 (ProQuest, Thesis No. 3394987), 7 and Appendix A, 251.

15. Douglas R. Egerton et al., *The Atlantic World: A History, 1400–1888* (Wheeling, IL: Harlan Davidson, 2007), 10, 58; Alfred W. Crosby, *Ecological Imperialism: The Biological Expansion of Europe, 900–1900* (Cambridge: Cambridge University Press, 2004), 112–15.
16. Gomes Eanes de Zurara, "Crónica da Tomada de Ceuta," in *The Portuguese in West Africa, 1415–1670: A Documentary History*, ed. Malyn Newitt (Cambridge: Cambridge University Press, 2010), 26; Benjamin, *Atlantic World*, 80.
17. Eddy Stols, "The Expansion of the Sugar Market in Western Europe," in *Tropical Babylons: Sugar and the Making of the Atlantic World, 1450–1680*, ed. Stewart B. Schwartz (Chapel Hill: University of North Carolina Press, 2004), 237–88; Sidney W. Mintz, *Sweetness and Power: The Place of Sugar in Modern History* (New York: Penguin, 1985), 19–73.
18. Gomes Eannes de Azurara, *The Chronicle of the Discovery and Conquest of Guinea*, ed. C. R. Beazley and E. Prestage (London: Hakluyt Society, 1896), 1:184; Newitt, *A History of Portuguese Overseas Expansion* (New York: Routledge, 2004), 25.
19. Newett, *Overseas Expansion*, 26; Cadamosto quoted in Hugh Thomas, *The Slave Trade: The Story of the Atlantic Slave Trade, 1440–1870* (New York: Simon & Schuster, 2013), 57.
20. Azurara, *Chronicle*, 2:252–57.
21. Gregory H. Maddox, *Sub-Saharan Africa: An Environmental History* (Santa Barbara, CA: ABC-CLIO, 2006), 84–87.
22. Newett, *Overseas Expansion*, 152–54.
23. Francisco Monclaro, *Records of South Eastern Africa*, ed. George McCall Theal (London: William Clowes and Sons, 1899), 3:202–253; quotation 236.
24. Monclaro, *Records*, 3:251.
25. "White Man's Grave" was popularized by a book of the same name in 1834 by F. Harrison Rankin; K. G. Davies, "The Living and the Dead: White Mortality in West Africa, 1684–1732" in *Race and Slavery in the Western Hemisphere: Quantitative Studies* (Princeton, NJ: Princeton University Press, 1975), 83–98: Philip Curtin, *Disease and Empire: The Health of European Troops in the Conquest of Africa* (Cambridge: Cambridge University Press, 1998), 1–28.
26. Diogo Cao quotation from Bailey W. Diffie and George D. Winius, *Foundations of the Portuguese Empire* (Minneapolis: University of Minnesota Press, 1977), 155; Brooks, "Prester John," 210n47.

CHAPTER 3: EARLY ENCOUNTERS
1. Livingstone and Kirk quoted in Jeal, *Livingstone*, 264 and 265, respectively; on Bennett and the press, see Beau Riffenburgh, *The Myth of the Explorer*, 49–68.
2. Clare Pettitt, *Dr. Livingstone, I Presume? Missionaries, Journalists, Explorers, and Empire* (London: Profile Books, 2007), 71–77; Jeal, *Stanley*, 117–19; Riffenburgh, *Myth*, 49–68.
3. Robinson, *Coldest Crucible*, 25–29.

4. Jeal, *Stanley*, 65; quotation from Stanley, *How I Found Livingstone*, 73.
5. Stanley, *How I Found Livingstone*, quotations from 89–90, 326.
6. Stanley's disintegrating party: Jeal, *Stanley*, 113; "It requires more," Stanley, *How I Found Livingstone*, 308.
7. On the meeting of Stanley and Livingstone: Pettitt, *"Dr. Livingstone,"* 71–77, and Jeal, *Stanley*, 117–19; "vent my joy…": Stanley, *How I Found Livingstone*, 411.
8. "be greeted by everybody…": Stanley, *How I Found Livingstone*, 476.
9. Ibid., 478.
10. Ibid., 495–506.
11. Stanley, Dispatch to NYH, January 16, 1876, *Despatches*, 267. Despite this skepticism, Livingstone told Stanley that he had seen Africans of "a very light color" west of Lake Tanganyika: Stanley, *How I Found Livingstone*, 464.
12. On terminology, see Edwin M. Yamauchi, "The Romans and Meroe in Nubia," in *ItaliAfrica: Bridging Continents and Cultures*, ed. Sante Matteo (Stony Brook, NY: Forum Italicum, 2001), 38–46; Frank M. Snowden, Jr., *Blacks in Antiquity: Ethiopians in the Greco-Roman Experience* (Cambridge, MA.: Harvard University Press, 1970), 1–14.
13. On Labat, see William B. Cohen, *The French Encounter with Africans: White Response to Blacks, 1530–1880* (Bloomington: Indiana University Press, 1980), 27.
14. Stanley, *Despatches*, 267.
15. Boemus quoted in Brooks, "Prester John," 300; representations of Prester John: 197–98.
16. Herman Moll, "Map of Africa," 1710, from online exhibition *To the Mountains of the Moon: Mapping African Exploration, 1541–1880*, http://libweb5.princeton.edu/visual_materials/maps/websites/africa/maps-continent/continent.html. Moll's comments may have come from Andrew Battel who described white Africans—or *negre blancs* as they were called in France—in the 1600s. On this, see Andrew S. Curran, *The Anatomy of Blackness: Science and Slavery in an Age of Enlightenment* (Baltimore: Johns Hopkins University Press, 2011), 87–91, and, by the same author, "Rethinking Race History: The Role of the Albino in the French Enlightenment Life Sciences," *History and Theory* 48 (October 2009): 151–79.
17. Michael Shepard, "A Visit to Zanzibar," in *New England Merchants in Africa: A History Through Documents, 1802–1865*, ed. Norman R. Bennett and George E. Brooks, Jr. (Boston: Boston University Press, 1965), 263.

CHAPTER 4: THE STORY BREAKS
1. Jeal, *Stanley*, 210; Stanley, *Dark Continent*, 2:435–64.
2. "The supplies…": Stanley, *Dark Continent*, 447; "I had to rush," ibid., 460.
3. "hateful…": ibid., 464.
4. "As I looked…": ibid., 462–63.
5. Jeal, *Stanley*, 216–21.
6. Stanley's dispatches discussing Gambaragara in the *New York Herald* include "Stanley. The Great Explorer Heard From After a Year's Silence" (includes

subheading "The Palefaces of Gambaragara"), July 26, 1876, 3; "Stanley's Recent Discoveries," July 27, 1876, 4; "Stanley. Opinions of the Press." July 28, 1876, 5; "Stanley. The Great Explorer's Attempt to Survey the Albert Nyanza," August 11, 1876, 2; "The Sources of the Nile" (map), August 12, 1876, 2.

7. "Central Africa," *Daily Inter Ocean* (Chicago), August 14, 1876, 3; "White Africans," *Maine Farmer*, September 16, 1876, 2; *Hartford Daily Courant*, August 18, 1876, 1; "A Remarkable Mountain and a Race of Pale-Face Africans," *Washington Evening Star* (Washington, DC), July 26, 1876, 1. A sample of press reports include "Discoveries in Africa," *African Repository* 52 (October 1876): 4, 113; "Central Africa," *Duluth Minnesotan-Herald*, September 2, 1876, 3; "Stanley Heard From," *Cincinnati Daily Gazette*, July 28, 1876, 2; "The Wonders of Africa," *Cincinnati Commercial Tribune*, August 14, 1876, 3; [Stanley], *Kalamazoo Gazette*, August 15, 1876, 1; "The Wonders of Africa," *Wheeling Daily Register*, August 16, 1876, 3; "Stanley's Discoveries in Africa," *Albany Evening Journal*, August 18, 1876, 2; "Stanley," *Chicago Daily Tribune*, August 14, 1876, 3; "Stanley Heard From," *New York Observer and Chronicle*, August 3, 1876, 46; "Geography and Exploration," *American Naturalist* 10 (September 1876): 562.

8. "Mr. Stanley and the African Expedition," *Madras Mail* (Madras, India), August 23, 1876, 6; [untitled], *Auckland Star*, November 21, 1876, 2; "La Expedicion de Mr. Stanley," *El Siglo Diez y Nueve* (Mexico City, Mexico), September 20, 1876, 2; [untitled], *Daily Star and Herald* (Panama City, Panama), September 20, 1876, 2.

9. "Notes," *Nature* 14 (July 27, 1876): 279; "Mr. Stanley," *Nature* 17 (February 14, 1878): 298; J. M. Buchan, "Climate and Complexion," *Popular Science Monthly* 17 (May 1, 1880): 3–10; "Geography and Exploration," *American Naturalist* 10 (November 1876): 695–99; "Rapport Sur Les Travaux de la Société," *Bulletin de la Société de géographie* 13 (1877): 400; "Spedizione ai grandi laghi equatoriali," *Annuario Scientifico ed Industriale* (Milan: Fratelli Treves, 1877), 1056; "Die Erforschung des Ukerewe (Victoria-Nyanza) durch Henry M. Stanley u. sein Zug zum Mwutan (Albert-Nyanza)," *Mitteilungen der Kaiserlich-Königlichen Geographischen Gesellschaft*, 19 (1876): 644; "A Geographical Sketch of the Nile and Livingstone (Congo) Basins," *Journal of the Royal Geographical Society* 22 (June 3, 1878): 382–410; J. A. Grant, "On Mr. Stanley's Exploration of the Victoria Nyanza," *Journal of the Royal Geographical Society* 46 (1876): 10–34; Chaillé Long, "Uganda and the White Nile," *Journal of the American Geographical Society of New York* 8 (1876): 285–304.

10. "Boss Tweed" from "All Sorts," *National Republican* (Washington, DC), August 26, 1876, 4.

11. "Facetiae," *London Journal*, October 4, 1879, 222.

12. "The Pale-Faces of Mount Gambaragara," *Dublin University Magazine*, March 1878, 344; Quotation from Manuel Iradier, *Africa: Asociación Euskara La Exploradora* (Bilbao, Spain: Andrés P.-Cardenal, 1901), 37.

13. Stanley, "May," in journal labeled "1874.75.76," Lett's Perpetual Diary, Stanley Archives.

14. Stanley, lecture, "Through the Dark Continent" (first delivered October 1878), 4717, Stanley Archives.
15. "I must...": Stanley, *How I Found Livingstone*, 69.
16. Edward J. Larson, *Evolution's Workshop: God and Science on the Galapagos Islands* (New York: Basic Books, 2002), 15–87.

CHAPTER 5: THE CURSE OF HAM

1. David M. Goldenberg, *The Curse of Ham: Race and Slavery in Early Judaism, Christianity, and Islam* (Princeton, NJ: Princeton University Press, 2003), 1–78.
2. Ibid.
3. Benjamin Braude, "The Sons of Noah and the Construction of Ethnic and Geographical Identities in the Medieval and Early Modern Periods," *William and Mary Quarterly* 54 (January 1997), 103–42.
4. On Alcuin and T-O maps, see Braude, "Sons of Noah," 113.
5. On the puzzling storyline of Gen. 9, see Goldenberg, *Curse of Ham*, 163–66, and Braude, "Sons of Noah," 108. A number of scholars have attributed early Jewish rabbinic sources for forging the link between Noah's curse and black slavery—in short, providing a scriptural justification for racial slavery. More recent scholarship, however, has shown that the evolution of this idea followed more complicated routes, including Christian and Muslim exegesis as well. See David H. Aaron, "Early Rabbinic Exegesis on Noah's Son Ham and the So-Called 'Hamitic Myth,'" *Journal of the American Academy of Religion* 63, no. 4 (Winter 1995): 721–59.
6. David M. Goldenberg, "What Did Ham Do to Noah?" in *"The Words of a Wise Man's Mouth Are Gracious" (Qoh 10,12): Festschrift for Günter Stemberger on the Occasion of His 65th Birthday*, ed. Mauro Perani (Berlin: Walter de Gruyter, 2005), 257–65.
7. On political motives for selecting Canaan for curse, see Aaron, "Rabbinic Exegesis," 730.
8. Goldenberg, *Curse of Ham*, 174; Mandeville, "Travels" (1371), quoted by Braude, "Sons of Noah," 117. On Ham as father of Asia, see Braude, "Sons of Noah," 117–21.
9. On Purchas, see Braude, "Sons of Noah," 135–37.
10. "the curse...": Eannes, *Chronicle* I: 54–55, quoted by Braude, "Sons of Noah," 127–28; "severe curses...": Brigham Young, speech before Joint Session of Utah Legislature, January 23, 1852, in *The Complete Discourses of Brigham Young*, ed. Richard S. Van Wagoner (Salt Lake City, UT: Smith-Pettit Foundation, 2009), 1:473–74.

CHAPTER 6: ORIENTAL JONES

1. "The Persian language...": Jones, *A Grammar of the Persian Language*, ii. Life aboard ship: Jones, The *Letters of Sir William Jones* (Oxford, UK: Clarendon Press, 1970), 2:614.
2. William Jones, "Objects of Enquiry During My Residence in Asia," *Works*, 2:3–4; Urs App, "William Jones's Ancient Theology," *Sino-Platonic Papers* 191 (2009): 3.

3. Jones explained the value of biblical and pagan mythology in his Third Anniversary Discourse to the Asiatick Society, February 2, 1786, "I cannot believe, with *Newton*, that ancient mythology was nothing but historical truth in a poetical dress; nor, with *Bacon*, that it consisted solely of moral and metaphysical allegories; nor, with *Bryant*, that all the heathen Divinities are only different attributes and representations of the Sun or of deceased progenitors; but conceive that the whole system of religious fables rose, like the *Nile*, from several distinct sources" from App, "Ancient Theology," 86.
4. Garland H. Cannon, *The Life and Mind of Oriental Jones Sir William Jone*s, *the Father of Modern Linguistics* (Cambridge: Cambridge University Press, 1990), 195–221; Michael J. Franklin, *'Orientalist Jones': Sir William Jones, Poet, Lawyer, and Linguist, 1746–1794* (New York: Oxford University Press, 2011), 1–42.
5. Robert Clive, quoted in Ramsay Muir, *The Making of British India, 1756–1858* (Manchester, UK: 1915), 76.
6. "to a man resolute...": Nathaniel Halhed, *Code of Gentoo Laws* (London: n.p., 1776), xxxv–xxxvi; Cannon, *Life and Mind*, 230–31. Pandits discussed by Thomas Trautmann, *Aryans and British India* (Berkeley: University of California Press, 1997), 31.
7. Jones to William Pitt the Younger, February 5, 1785, *Letters*, 2:664.
8. Raymond Schwab, *Oriental Renaissance: Europe's Rediscovery of India and the East, 1680–1880* (Columbia University Press, 1984) 51–129. "The bounds...": William Jones, "Preliminary Discourse," *Asiatick Researches: Or, Transactions of the Society Instituted in Bengal, for Inquiring into the History and Antiquities, the Arts, Sciences, and Literature, of Asia* 1 (London, 1801), xi.
9. Cannon, *Life and Mind*, 231.
10. Jones, "Third Anniversary Discourse," reprinted in App, "Ancient Theology," 83–84.
11. As early as the sixteenth century, other Europeans had—albeit less systematically—described linguistic similarities among European and Asian languages. See J. P. Mallory, *In Search of the Indo-Europeans: Language, Archaeology and Myth* (London: Thames & Hudson, 1989), 9–23.
12. "the most ingenious...Scandinavia": William Jones, "Discourse the Ninth," reprinted in App, "Ancient Theology," 115–16.
13. Jones, "Third Anniversary Discourse" in App, "Ancient Theology," 87. On Jones's identification of Sanskrit speakers as descendants of Ham and later rejection of ideas by scholars, see Arvidsson, *Aryan Idols*, 18–19.
14. Cannon, *Life and Mind*, 296–97; Trautmann, *Aryans*, 29.
15. Michael J. Franklin, "Jones, Sir William (1746–1794)," *Oxford Dictionary of National Biography*, ed. H. C. G. Matthew and Brian Harrison (Oxford: Oxford University Press, 2004), online ed., ed. Lawrence Goldman, May 2011, http://www.oxforddnb.com/view/article/15105 (accessed February 12, 2013).
16. "by degrees...": Jones, "Discourse the Ninth," in App, "Ancient Theology," 109. On challenges to biblical chronology, see Martin J. S. Rudwick, *Worlds Before Adam: The*

Reconstruction of Geohistory in the Age of Reform (Chicago: University of Chicago Press, 2010), 253–390.
17. "It may be worthwhile…": Darwin, *Origin of Species*, quoted in Trautmann, *Aryans*, 57; Arvidsson, *Aryan Idols*, 28.
18. "If we possessed…": Darwin, *Origin of Species*, 498; "degenerate…": Jones, quoted in Arvidsson, *Aryan Idols*, 23; "The new theory…": Maine, quoted in Trautmann, *Aryans*, 1.

CHAPTER 7: THE BEAUTIFUL SKULL
1. Blumenbach, quoted in Karl Friedrich Heinrich Marx, "Life of Blumenbach," in *The Anthropological Treatises of Johann Friedrich Blumenbach* (London: Longman, Green, Longman, Roberts, and Green, 1865), 44; Fabian, *Skull Collectors*, 34.
2. M. P. J. Flourens, "Memoir of Blumenbach," in Marx, *Anthropological Treatises*, 50–51; Marx, "Life of Blumenbach," in *Anthropological Treatises*, 28, 35.
3. Peter J. Bowler, *Evolution: The History of an Idea* (Berkeley: University of California Press, 2009), 48–95, 150, 293.
4. A number of scholars—De Maillet, Pierre Louis Moreau de Maupertuis, Buffon—advanced materialistic explanations for the origins of life without relying upon Scriptures, but these did not propose the evolution of all species from a common origin; David N. Livingstone, *Adam's Ancestors: Race, Religion, and the Politics of Human Origins* (Baltimore: Johns Hopkins University Press, 2011), 4–5; Bowler, *Evolution*, 29.
5. Bowler, *Evolution*, 75–78.
6. Blumenbach, "On the Natural Variety of Mankind," in Marx, *Anthropological Treatises*, 269.
7. "for the extreme…," "My beautiful…": Blumenbach, "Contributions to Natural History," in *Anthropological Treatises*, 162, 300; on von Asch, see H. F. Augstein, "From the Land of the Bible to the Caucasus and Beyond: The Shifting Ideas of the Geographical Origin of Humankind," in *Race, Science & Medicine, 1700–1960*, ed. Waltraud Ernst and Bernard Harris (London: Routledge, 1999), 58–79, 63; on aesthetics and Blumenbach, see Schiebinger, *Nature's Body* (Boston: Beacon Press, 1993), 133.
8. C. Rommel quoted in Augstein, "Land of the Bible," 66.
9. "As all the differences…": Blumenbach, "Contributions," in Marx, *Anthropological Treatises*, 303.
10. "curse of Cain…": Blumenbach, "Natural Variety," in Marx, *Anthropological Treatises*, 106.
11. "there were no remains…": Blumenbach, "Observations on Some Egyptian Mummies Opened in London," *Philosophical Transactions of the Royal Society of London* 84 (1794): 181.
12. "which must have been…": ibid., 191.
13. Bruce Baum, *The Rise and Fall of the Caucasian Race: A Political History of Racial Identity* (New York: New York University Press, 2008), 58–117.
14. "repress future exertion…": Thomas Malthus, *An Essay on the Principle of Population* (New York: Dover, 2008 [1798]), 148.

CHAPTER 8: REVISING THE HYPOTHESIS

1. "cut loose...": Josiah Clark Nott, *Two Lectures on the Connection Between the Biblical and Physical History of Man* (New York: Bartlett and Welford, 1849), 7. Some monogenists such as James Cowles Prichard and Sir William Lawrence also departed from biblical chronology; John P. Jackson and Nadine M. Weidman, *Race, Racism, and Science: Social Impact and Interaction* (New Brunswick, NJ: Rutgers University Press, 2005), 37.
2. On polygenism, see John S. Haller, "The Species Problem: Nineteenth-Century Concepts of Racial Inferiority in the Origin of Man Controversy," *American Anthropologist* 72 (1970): 1319–29; Brad D. Hume, "Quantifying Characters: Polygenist Anthropologists and the Hardening of Heredity," *Journal of the History of Biology* 41, no. 1 (Spring 2008): 119–58.
3. Mummy unwrapping described in August B. Granville, "An Essay on Egyptian Mummies; With Observations on the Art of Embalming among the Ancient Egyptians," *Philosophical Transactions of the Royal Society of London* 115 (1825): 269–316; "the *couvrechef*...": 271.
4. "before the building...": ibid, 277.
5. "The celebrated..." and "the *beau idéal*...": ibid, 279. Debates about the racial identity of ancient Egyptians had also been spirited among French scholars during Napoleon's Egyptian campaign. See Melanie Byrd, "The Hamitic Prophesy and Napoleon's Egyptian Campaign," *Consortium on Revolutionary Europe, 1750–1850: Proceedings* 22 (1992): 13–20.
6. "differ[ing] very much": Blumenbach, in Marx, *Anthropological Treatises*, 123.
7. Baum, *Caucasian Race*, 95–103.
8. "Each race was adapted...": Morton quoted in Fabian, *Skull Collectors*, 30.
9. Fabian, *Skull Collectors*, 103–28.
10. "Egyptian, blended...": Morton, *Crania Aegyptiaca*, 12; "I therefore regard...": ibid., 17; "These primeval people...": ibid., 214.
11. Morton, *Crania Aegyptiaca*, xli; Agassiz also argues that Genesis describes the history of the Caucasian race in "The Diversity and Origin of the Human Races," *Christian Examiner* 58 (1850): 110–45.
12. "The valley of the Nile...": Samuel Morton, "Dr. Morton's Craniological Collection," *Transactions of the American Ethnological Society* (New York: Bartlett & Welford: 1848): 220; "three grand divisions...": Gliddon, "A Sketch of the Progress of Archeological Science in America," *Southern Literary Messenger* 11 (July 1845): 8.
13. James Cowles Pritchard, "Anniversary Address for 1848," *Royal Anthropological Institute of Great Britain and Ireland* 2 (1850): 119–49.
14. "By black men...": Arthur de Gobineau, *The Inequality of Human Races* (New York: G. P. Putnam's Sons, 1915), 146; "These are poor words...": Burton, *A Mission to Gelele, King of Dahome* (London: Tinsley Bros., 1864), 2:193; "related the history...": Speke, *What Led to the Discovery of the Source of the Nile* (London: Blackwood, 1864), 340.
15. "The curse of Noah...": Speke, *Journal of the Discovery of the Source of the Nile* (London: Blackwood, 1864), 60; "Ham was cursed...": ibid., xvii.

16. "I think…": Prichard, *Researches into the Physical History of Mankind* (London: John and Arthur Arch, 1813), 384. Stanley also continued to use the term "Hamite" to refer to black Africans even after he adopted the white invasion story put forward by Morton and others: "At their birth the perfect Hamite and the perfect Caucasian are physically equal. But from the instant of his emergence from the womb the Caucasian obtains the advantage." Stanley, speech from 1878, Folder 4718, Stanley Archives.
17. All quotations are from Speke, *Journal*, "Uzinza…": 137; "I admired…": 207; "Ever proud…": 236. Also see 242 for discussion of Hamitic invasion.
18. "the physical…": ibid., 241.
19. Stanley notes Mutesa's knowledge of Ham in *Dark Continent*, 1:271. "I will show…": Mutesa, as reported by Lieut. G. Shergold Smith, in letter of October 6, 1877. Smith continues, "He [Mutesa] tells a quaint story of his descent from Ham, and has promised to give the genealogy complete," *Church Missionary Intelligencer* 3 (April 1878): 212.

CHAPTER 9: KING MUTESA

1. Roland Oliver and Anthony Atmore, *Africa Since 1800* (New York: Cambridge University Press, 2005), 90–102.
2. Apolo Kagwa and Henry Wright Duta Kitakule, "How Religion Came to Uganda," *The Mind of Buganda*, ed. D. A. Low (Berkeley: University of California Press, 1971), 1–2; Oliver and Atmore, *Africa*, 94.
3. Richard Reid, "Images of an African Ruler: *Kabaka* Mutesa of Buganda, ca. 1857–1884," *History in Africa* 26 (1999): 275; "We used to tell…": Kagwa and Kitakule, "Religion," 1.
4. Benjamin C. Ray, *Myth, Ritual, and Kingship in Buganda* (New York: Oxford University Press, 1991), 100.
5. "I left the King…": Linant de Bellefonds, report dated April 27, 1875, reprinted in Low, *Mind*, 3.
6. Neil Kodesh, *Beyond the Royal Gaze: Clanship and Public Healing in Buganda* (Charlottesville and London: University of Virginia Press, 2010), 32–34.
7. Kodesh, *Royal Gaze*, 25–66.
8. "an abridged Protestant Bible…": Stanley, *Dark Continent*, 322; "It is impossible…": ibid., 379.
9. "A mild, human…": Stanley, *Dark Continent*, 345.
10. Smith, *Church Missionary Intelligencer*, 212.
11. "My belief is…": Gordon, letter to Rev. H. Wright, in Kodesh, *Royal Gaze*, 33–34.
12. "The oldest inhabitants…": Arthur Bryan Fisher, "Western Uganda," *Geographical Journal* 24 (September 1904): 251.
13. "personification…": Johnston, quoted in Christopher Wrigley, *Kingship and State: The Buganda Dynasty* (Cambridge: Cambridge University Press, 2002), 112–13.
14. "through the admixture…": C. T. Wilson and R. W. Felkin, *Uganda and the Egyptian Soudan* (London: Sampson Low, Marston, Searle, and Rivington, 1882), 1:196.

15. Kodesh, *Royal Gaze*, 33.
16. On problems with chronology, see Wrigley, *Kingship and State*, 111.
17. Kodesh suggests there was probably a range of opinion among Ganda converts and intellectuals about the location of Kintu's foreign origin. Some may have believed that he came from a place like Mount Elgon outside of Buganda but within East Africa. Personal communication, 2014.
18. "The Batoro…": Fisher, "Western Uganda," 251; on Kigwa and Bimanuka, see Nigel Eltringham, "'Invaders Who Have Stolen the Country': The Hamitic Hypothesis, Race and the Rwandan Genocide," *Social Identities* 12, no. 4 (July 2006) 432–33; "really seems…": Johnston, *Uganda Protectorate*, 2:588–89.
19. Apolo Kagwa, *The Kings of Buganda*, trans. and ed. M. S. M. Kiwanuka (Nairobi: East African Publishing House, 1971), 7; Brian K. Taylor, *The Western Lacustrine Bantu* (London: International African Institute, 1962), 18–19, 42.
20. "I have never…": Stanley, December 27 [1875], Notebook 15, Stanley Archives.

CHAPTER 10: GREAT ZIMBABWE

1. "No further information…": *Carl Mauch, Journals*, 266; D. Munjeri, "Great Zimbabwe: A Historiography and History: Carl Mauch and After: Paper Presented to Mark the 150th Birthday of Carl Mauch," *Heritage of Zimbabwe* 7 (1987): 1–10.
2. "All are absolutely convinced…": Mauch, *Journals*, 267–68.
3. Alcacova and Fernandes quoted in Garlake, *Great Zimbabwe*, 51.
4. "These mines…": de Barros, quoted in Garlake, *Great Zimbabwe*, 52.
5. "a factory…": dos Santos, quoted in Garlake, *Great Zimbabwe*, 53.
6. "the most…": Mauch, quoted in Garlake, *Great Zimbabwe*, 63.
7. "a few beads…": Mauch, letter to August Petermann, September 13, 1871, reprinted in Joseph Forsyth Ingram, *The Land of Gold, Diamonds and Ivory: Being a Comprehensive Handbook and Guide to the Colonies, States and Republics of South and East Africa* (London: W. B. Whittingham, 1893), 107.
8. "The good Lord…": Mauch, *Journals*, 267. On sandalwood, see Garlake, *Great Zimbabwe*, 64.
9. "Geographical Notes," *American Educational Monthly* 9 (1872): 238–39; "The Observatory," *Sunday School Teacher* 5 (1872): 219; Charles Beke, "The Gold Country of Ophir," *Ecclesiastical Observer*, April 1, 1872, 184.
10. "I have tried…": Carl Mauch, *Carl Mauch: African Explorer* (Transvaal, South Africa: C. Struik, 1971), 2.
11. Mauch, *Journals*, 6.
12. "exclusive charge…": the Rudd Concession, quoted in Arthur Keppel-Jones, *Rhodes and Rhodesia: The White Conquest of Zimbabwe 1884–1902* (Montreal: McGill-Queen's University Press, 1983), 78; Blake, *History of Rhodesia* (New York: Knopf, 1978), 42–92.
13. "The names…": James Theodore Bent, *The Ruined Cities of Mashonaland*, 60.
14. "a distinctly Arab…": ibid., 54.
15. "The dreams…": ibid., 33.

16. Garlake, *Great Zimbabwe*, 66–67.
17. "Where did...": Bent, *Ruined Cities*, 188.
18. Bruce Trigger, *A History of Archaeological Thought*, 2nd ed. (Cambridge: Cambridge University Press, 2006), 195–205; Klaus Peter Kopping, *Adolf Bastian and the Psychic Unity of Mankind: The Foundations of Anthropology in Nineteenth Century Germany* (Berlin: LIT Verlag, 2005), 1–6, 126–36.
19. Trigger, *History*, 217–22.
20. Karin R. Andriolo, "Kulturkreislehre and the Austrian Mind," *Man* 14 (1979: 133–44; "[Bent] has proved...": "The Ruins in Mashonaland," *Sun* (New York), February 10, 1892, 3.
21. "There can be left...": David Christiaan De Waal, *With Rhodes in Mashonaland* (Cape Town, South Africa: J. C. Juta and Company, 1896), 276; "Zimbabwe is...": Rhodes, quoted in Garlake, *Great Zimbabwe*, 65.
22. Saul Dubow, *Scientific Racism in Modern South Africa* (Cambridge: Cambridge University Press, 1995), 68–69; "learned nothing...": Theal, *Yellow and Dark-Skinned People of Africa South of the Zambesi* (London: Swan Sonnenschein & Company, 1910), 358.
23. Garlake, *Great Zimbabwe*, 67–72.

CHAPTER 11: AT THE SUMMIT
1. "a peculiar shaped...": Stanley, *In Darkest Africa*, 1:429.
2. Stanley, *Darkest Africa*, 192–206; Jeal, *Stanley*, 354–64.
3. "Self, for the self...": Stanley, *Darkest Africa*, 2:77; Jeal, *Stanley*, 324–42, 354.
4. "Help us..." quoted from Jeal, *Stanley*, 328.
5. Stanley, *Darkest Africa*, 2:139–181; Jeal, *Stanley*, 336–53.
6. Stanley, *Darkest Africa*, 2:317.
7. "I sounded the note...": ibid., 276; W. E. Stairs, "Lieutenant Stairs' Account of His Ascent of Ruwenzori, to a Height of 10,677 Feet Above Sea-Level," *Proceedings of the Royal Geographical Society* 11, no. 12 (December 1889): 729.
8. Jeal, *Stanley*, 378.
9. "What good...": Stanley, "Geographical Results of the Emin Pasha Relief Expedition," *Proceedings of the Royal Geographical Society* 12, no. 6 (June 1890): 327–28.
10. "cold brightness...": Stanley, *Darkest Africa*, 2:332.
11. "What, are they...": ibid., 2:345.
12. "the colour of yellow ivory...": Stanley, "Geographical Results," 320.
13. "I have seen...": Johnston, *Uganda Protectorate*, 25.
14. "whiter than Caucasians...": Serpa Pinto, quoted in "A White Race in Africa," *Stark Democrat* (Canton, OH), July 17, 1879, 1; interview with Zebehr Pasha in "White Natives of Africa," *Belmont Chronicle* (St. Clairsville, OH), September 1, 1887, 4; on white Africans reported by Captain Larrymore, see "Africa's White Race," *Wichita Daily Eagle*, April 14, 1896, 8; "South of Timbuctoo...": *Juniata Sentinel and Republican* (Mifflintown, PA), August 8, 1888, 4.

15. Jeal, *Stanley*, 456.
16. Stanley, *Darkest Africa*, 2:324.
17. Stanley, "The Origin of the Negro Race," *North American Review* 170 (May 1900): 659.
18. "There are many...": Prince Luigi Amedeo of Savoy, *Ruwenzori: An Account of the Expedition of H.R.H. Prince Luigi Amedeo of Savoy, Duke of Abruzzi* (New York: Dutton, 1908), 98–99.

CHAPTER 12: THE DYNASTIC RACE

1. "It may not...": W. M. Flinders Petrie, *Migrations* (London: Anthropological Institute of Great Britain and Ireland, 1906), 5.
2. Petrie, *Medum* (London: David Nutt, 1892), 1.
3. "Could we learn...": Petrie, *Ten Years' Digging in Egypt, 1881–1891* (New York: Religious Tract Society, 1892), 138.
4. "Nothing seemed...": Petrie, *Medum*, 4.
5. "Here is clearly...": Petrie, *Digging*, 146.
6. "A beginner...": Petrie, *Digging*, 161; Sheppard, *Life*, 42–44.
7. Margaret S. Drower, *Flinders Petrie: A Life in Archaeology* (Madison: University of Wisconsin Press, 1995), 135–36.
8. Morton, *Crania Aegyptiaca*, 12.
9. "better to study...": Petrie, *Migrations*, 31.
10. "sympathies becom[e] more tender...": Darwin, *The Descent of Man, and Selection in Relation to Sex* (London: John Murray, 1871), 1:101.
11. "[It] made a marked epoch..." and "I frequently suffered...": Francis Galton, *Memories of My Life* (London: Methuen and Co., 1908), 287, 155.
12. "in order that...": Francis Galton, "Editorial," *Biometrika* 1 (1902):1.
13. Kathleen L. Sheppard, "Flinders Petrie and Eugenics at UCL," *Bulletin of the History of Archeology* 20, no. 1 (May 2010): 16–29.

CHAPTER 13: THE ARYAN TIDAL WAVE

1. "not like niggers...": Friedrich Max Müller, *Auld Lang Syne* (New York: Charles Scribner's Sons, 1899), 2:2–3.
2. "Boys will dream dreams...": ibid., 2:3.
3. Schwab, *Oriental Renaissance*, 131–224; Arvidsson, *Aryan Idols*, 23–26.
4. "that feeling which the digger...": Friedrich Max Müller, *My Autobiography: A Fragment* (New York: Charles Scribner's Sons, 1901), 146.
5. "pure native language...": Francis W. Ellis, "Note to the Introduction," in Alexander D. Campbell, *Grammar of the Teloogoo Language* (Madras, India: The College Press, 1816), 1.
6. "found a rude...": Stevenson quoted in Trautmann, *Aryans and British India*, 157. Original source: *Observations on the Grammatical Structure of the Vernacular Languages of India Journal of the Asiatic Society of Bombay* 3 (1849): 73.

7. "put it beyond all doubt...": Max Müller, "On the Relation of the Bengali to the Arian and Aboriginal Languages of India," *Report of the Seventeenth Meeting of the British Association for the Advancement of Science* (London: John Murray, 1848), 328.
8. "vanquishing, destroying, and subjecting...": ibid., 348.
9. "Aryan tidal-wave...": Edward Tregear, *Aryan Maori* (Wellington, New Zealand: George Didsbury, 1885), 4; Tony Ballantyne, *Orientalism and Race: Aryanism in the British Empire* (New York: Palgrave Macmillan, 2007), 56–82.
10. "more inclining in colour...": Hieronymus de Angelis, quoted in David MacRitchie, *The Aïnos* (New York: E. Steiger & Co., 1892), 6. Alice Lee and Karl Pearson used data from Ainu cephalic indexes to link them racially to Europeans in 1901: "Data for the Problem of Evolution in Man," *Philosophical Transactions of the Royal Society* 196 (1901): 245; the Ainu's Aryan roots were also described by B. Douglas Howard, *Life with Trans-Siberian Savages* (London: Longmans, 1893), 185–86. On Starr, "Been Seeing Japan Close," *Sun* (New York), June 13, 1910, 2.
11. "The small blacks...": Daniel Brinton, "People of the Philippines," *American Anthropologist* 11 (October 1898): 295; "fair-haired aborigines...": Griffith Taylor, "Aborigines in North-West Australia," *Sydney Morning Herald*, March 27, 1925, 10; "long lost brethren...": Herbert Gowen, "Are Hawaiians from Aryan Stock?" *Austin's Hawaiian Weekly*, Honolulu, June 17, 1899, 15; see also W. D. Alexander, "The Origin of the Polynesian Race," *Journal of Race Development* 1 (October 1910): 221–30.
12. "darker peoples," Miles Poindexter, *The Ayar-Incas* (New York: H. Liveright, 1930), x.
13. Taylor, "Climatic Cycles of Evolution," *Geographical Review* 8, no. 6 (December 1919): 312; Taylor, "The Evolution and Distribution of Race, Culture, and Language," *Geographical Review* 11, no. 1 (January 1921): 104.
14. Taylor, "Climatic Cycles," 309–13.
15. "Their faces...": from "Japanese of Mixed Blood," *Mahoning Dispatch* (Ohio), September 12, 1913, 4.
16. "I have declared...": Max Müller, *Biography of Words and the Home of the Aryas* (London: Longmans, 1888), 120.

CHAPTER 14: BLOND ESKIMOS
1. "We are friendly...": Stefansson, *My Life with the Eskimo* (New York: Macmillan, 1913), 190, 192.
2. "had the delicate features...": ibid., 193. Gísli Pálsson, "Hot Bodies in Cold Zones: Arctic Exploration," *The Scholar and Feminist* Online 7, no. 1 (Fall 2008), http://sfonline.barnard.edu/ice/print_palsson.htm.
3. "Neither they...": Stefansson, *The Stefánsson-Anderson Arctic Expedition of the American Museum: Preliminary Ethnological Report* (New York: American Museum of Natural History, 1914), 14:239; "It would be unthinkable...": Rasmussen, quoted in "The 'Blond' Eskimos," *Harpers Monthly Magazine* 156 (1928): 198.
4. The lost Greenland colony was widely discussed in the nineteenth century. For example, see "Account of Danish Discoveries on the East Coast of Greenland in

1829," *Journal of the Royal Geographical Society of London* 1 (1831): 247–52; R. H. Major, "The Site of the Lost Colony of Greenland Determined, and Pre-Columbian Discoveries of America Confirmed," *Proceedings of the Royal Geographical Society of London* 17, no. 5 (1872–73): 312–21.

5. "I wanted…": Stefansson, *My Life*, 1–2. On Fannie Pannigabluk, see Gísli Pálsson, *Writing on Ice: The Ethnographic Notebooks of Vilhjalmur Stefansson* (Hanover, NH: University Press of New England, 2001), 12, 39.
6. *Seattle Times*, September 9, 1912, 1; *Princeton Union*, Sept 19, 1912, 8; "Lost Tribe Discovered," *Vermont Phoenix*, September 13, 1912, 3; "Returns After Four Years from the Far North," *Salt Lake Tribune*, September 10, 1912, 1; *Daily Missoulian*, September 10, 1912, 1; "Arctic Explorer Ends Arctic Search of Four Years," *San Francisco Call*, September 10, 1912, 1. International reports include "L'expédition Stefansson," *Confédéré du Valais* (Switzerland), December 26, 1913, 3; "Crónicas Cosmopolitas," *Vida Marítima* (Madrid), Jan 20, 1912, 1; Ricardo White, "Un Pueblo Desconocido," *La Ilustración Española y Americana* (Madrid), November 8, 1912, 11–13; "Los Esquimales," *Caras y Caretas* (Buenos Aires), December 8, 1916, 16.
7. "the most palpable…": Amundsen, quoted in *As Told at the Explorers Club: More Than Fifty Gripping Tales of Adventure*, ed. George Plimpton (Guilford, CT: Lyons Press, 2005), 116.
8. "the olive color of the Italian…": Jenness, "The 'Blond' Eskimo," *American Anthropologist* 23, no. 3 (July–September 1921), 262.
9. "there is not…": Topinard quoted in Stocking, *Race, Culture, and Evolution*, 58; "natural variation in the complexion": Murdoch quoted in Jenness, "'Blond' Eskimo," 262. On Murdoch's findings, see "Ethnological Results of the Point Barrow Expedition," *Ninth Annual Report of the Bureau of Ethnology* (Washington, DC: U.S. Government Printing Office, 1892).
10. "We should hardly…": Jenness, "'Blond' Eskimo," 265.
11. "From Brazil to Mexico…": Verrill, "Hunting the White Indians," *McClure's Magazine* 43 (July 1924): 48.
12. "I was more…": ibid., 52. "White Indians" were also frequently reported in the nineteenth century. See Harold T. Wilkins, *Secret Cities of Old South America* (Kempton, IL: Adventures Unlimited Press,1998), 88; Kim Hill and A. Magdalena Hurtado, *Ache Life History: The Ecology and Demography of a Foraging People* (Hawthorne, NY: Aldine De Gruyter, 1996), 57–59; Margot Lynn Iverson, "Blood types: A history of genetic studies of Native Americans, 1920—1955," (PhD diss., University of Minnesota, 2007), 1–2.
13. "the enticement…": Arthur Olney Friel, *The River of the Seven Stars* (New York: Harpers, 1924), 34; "blue eyed…": ibid., 397; "it may be a pity…" ibid., 402.
14. "They move…": Alexander Hamilton Rice, quoted in "Explorer Rice Back, Saw White Indians," *New York Times*, July 11, 1925, 6.
15. "prehistoric race…": Ralph Glidden, quoted in Alma Overholt, "Giant White Indian Race Stirs Scientific Research," *Los Angeles Times*, January 26, 1930, F6.

16. "Their almost bare bodies...": Richard Marsh, *The White Indians of Darien* (New York: G. P. Putnam's Sons, 1934), 26.
17. "We saw many more...": ibid., 214–15; "I am disgusted...": Aleš Hrdlička, quoted in James Howe, *A People Who Would Not Kneel: Panama, the United States, and the San Blas Kuna* (Washington, DC: Smithsonian Institution Press, 1998), 242.
18. "I am confident...": Marsh, quoted in Howe, *A People*, 243.
19. "it is pure Aryan...": from Marsh, *The World's Work*, 49 (April 1925), 643; Howe, *A People*, 250–56.

CHAPTER 15: TRIBES OF THE IMAGINATION

1. H. Rider Haggard, *The Days of My Life*, 1: 233; Norman Etherington, *Rider Haggard* (Boston: Twayne Publishers, 1984), 9.
2. "a dunderhead at lessons": Haggard, *Days*, 1: 61; "the picture of weakness and dullness": Etherington, *Haggard*, 1.
3. "creeping over...": Haggard, *Days*, 1:52.
4. Etherington, *Haggard*, 7–30.
5. "drawn by...": Haggard, *King Solomon's Mines* (New York: Longmans, Green, and Company, 1901), 60; "strange mists...": ibid., 70.
6. "I heard...": Haggard, *Days*, 1:242; "designed...": Haggard, *Mines*, 221; "It was...": Haggard, *Mines*, 126.
7. The highest mountain in Botswana is the 4892-foot Otse Hill. In Zimbabwe, it is the 8504-foot Mount Nyangani.
8. "in a white heat...": Haggard, *Days*, 2:245.
9. "Those who are weak...": Haggard, quoted in Etherington, *Haggard*, 47; "It does not appear...": Gosse, quoted in Haggard, *Days*, 245; "fine weird imagination": Stevenson, quoted in Haggard, *Days*, 235.
10. "You should be more careful": Stevenson, quoted in Haggard, *Days*, 235.
11. Fred H. Smith, "Cro-Magnon," in *History of Physical Anthropology*, ed. Frank Spencer (New York: Francis and Taylor, 1997), 1:298–301.
12. Jess Nevins, "Pulp Science Fiction Under German Totalitarianism," http://io9.com/5960383/pulp-science-fiction-under-totalitarian-regimes-part-one-germany, accessed January 15, 2014; Elana Gomel, "Lost and Found: The Lost World Novel and the Shape of the Past," *Genre* 60 (Spring–Summer 2007): 105–10.
13. Everett F. Bleiler and Richard Bleiler, *Science-Fiction, the Early Years: A Full Description of More Than 3,000 Science-Fiction Stories from Earliest Times to the Appearance of the Genre Magazines in 1930* (Kent, OH: Kent State University Press, 1990), 796; Edward James, "Science Fiction by Gaslight: An Introduction to English-Language Science Fiction in the Nineteenth Century," in *Anticipations: Essays on Early Science Fiction and Its Precursors*, ed. David Seed (Syracuse, NY: Syracuse University Press, 1995), 26–45.
14. "It seems to me...": Joseph Conrad, *Heart of Darkness* (New York: Dover Thrift Editions, 1990 [1902]), 24.

15. "At Sakara...": Zebehr Pasha, quoted in "White Natives of Africa," *Belmont Chronicle* (St. Clairsville, OH), September 1, 1887, 4.
16. Etherington, *Haggard*, 109; Terrence Ranger, "The Rural African Voice in Zimbabwe Rhodesia: Archaism and Tradition," *Social Analysis* 4 (September 1980): 100–15; Robert Fraser, "Fiction and the Other Reader: The Reception of Imperial Adventure Romance in Africa," in *Moveable Type, Mobile Nations: Interactions in Transnational Book History*, eds. Simon Frost and Robert W. Rix (Copenhagen: Museum Tusculanum Press, 2010), 99–106. Patrick Brantlinger, "Victorians and Africans: The Genealogy of the Myth of the Dark Continent," *Critical Inquiry* 12 (Autumn 1985): 166–203, 196.
17. "enough to cause...": Haggard, quoted in Etherington, *Haggard*, 36.

CHAPTER 16: THE WHITE PSYCHE

1. Sigmund Freud, *The Interpretation of Dreams* (New York: Macmillan, 1913), 359; Etherington, *Haggard*, 38.
2. "the eternal feminine...": Freud, *Dreams*, 359.
3. Charles De Brosses, *Du culte des dieux fétiches ou Parallèle de l'ancienne religion de l'Égypte avec la religion actuelle de Nigritie* (1760) as quoted in Celia Brickman, *Aboriginal Populations in the Mind: Race and Primitivity in Psychoanalysis* (New York: Columbia University Press, 2003), 37.
4. Richard Noll, *Aryan Christ: The Secret Life of Carl Jung* (New York: Random House, 1997), 98–100.
5. "the sight...": Carl Jung, *Memories, Dreams, Reflections* (New York: Knopf, 2011), 244.
6. "Paul Gauguin," *Dictionary of Modern and Contemporary Art*, eds. Ian Chilvers and John Glaves-Smith (New York: Oxford University Press, 2009), 259–60; Joseph Knowles, *Alone in the Wilderness* (Boston: Small, Maynard and Co., 1913), 144; Tait Keller, "Holy Mountains and Hollow Men: The Search for Sanctuary in the Eastern Alps" (conference talk, American Historical Association annual meeting, January 2011); Petteri Pietikainen, "The Volk and Its Unconscious: Jung, Hauer and the 'German Revolution,'" *Journal of Contemporary History* 35, no. 4 (October 2000): 523–39; "The European...": Jung, *Memories*, 240.
7. "to find...": Jung, *Memories*, 244.
8. "The serious...": ibid., 254; Blake Burleson, *Jung in Africa* (New York: Bloomsbury Academic, 2005), 27–28, 43.
9. "I am not sure...": Ruth Bailey quoted in Burleson, *Jung in Africa*, 75; "Colours rioted...": ibid., 71.
10. "I have the feeling...": Jung, *Memories*, 254.
11. Ibid., 255.
12. "We discovered...": Jung, quoted in Burleson, *Jung in Africa*, 165.
13. "There were no...": Jung, *Memories*, 264.

CHAPTER 17: CRACKS IN THE THEORY

1. "noisy..." and "to undertake...": Gertrude Caton-Thompson, *The Zimbabwe Culture: Ruins and Reactions* (Oxford: Clarendon Press, 1931), 1.

2. On Caton-Thompson's journey to Great Zimbabwe, see Caton-Thompson, *Mixed Memoirs* (New York: Paradigm Press, 1983), 114–18.
3. On Rhodes's collection of artifacts from Great Zimbabwe, see Henrika Kuklick, "Contested Monuments: The Politics of Archeology in Southern Africa," in *Colonial Situations: Essays on the Contextualization of Ethnographic Knowledge*, ed. George W. Stocking, Jr. (Madison: University of Wisconsin Press, 1991), 135.
4. "These objections…": Caton-Thompson, *Zimbabwe Culture*, 4.
5. "contained no germ…": Caton-Thompson, *Memoirs*, 84; "wildernesses…": Caton-Thompson, *Zimbabwe Culture*, 1–2.
6. Robin Derricourt, "The Enigma of Raymond Dart," *International Journal of African Historical Studies* 42, no. 2 (2009): 257–82.
7. "Bantu contamination": Raymond Dart, "The Historical Succession of Cultural Impacts upon South Africa," *Nature* 111, no. 2890 (March 21, 1925): 426.
8. "This alone…": Caton-Thompson, *Memoirs*, 123; "I am quite certain…": ibid., 128; Maund Ruins Plan (plate), *Zimbabwe Culture*, 275.
9. "measures only discover…": Giuseppe Sergi, "My New Principles of the Classification of the Human Race," *Science* 22 no. 564 (November 24, 1893): 290; "The cephalic index…": Flinders Petrie, *Migrations*, 1906, 31; Franz Boas, "Changes in the Bodily Form of Descendants of Immigrants," *American Anthropologist* 14, no. 3 (July–September 1912): 530–62; Elazar Barkan, *The Retreat of Scientific Racism: Changing Concepts of Race in Britain and the United States Between the World Wars* (Cambridge: Cambridge University Press, 1992), 228–78; Robert Wald Sussman, *The Myth of Race: The Troubling Persistence of an Unscientific Idea* (Cambridge, MA: Harvard University Press, 2014), 146–64.
10. "We cannot deny…": Paul Topinard, quoted in George W. Stocking, *Race, Culture, and Evolution: Essays in the History of Anthropology* (Chicago: University of Chicago Press, 1968), 59.
11. "I will allow myself…": Caton-Thompson, *Memoirs*, 131.
12. Press quotations from Caton-Thompson, *Memoirs*, 135–37.
13. "in a tone…": *Cape Times*, ibid., 132.

CHAPTER 18: THE ROOF OF THE WORLD
1. Heather Pringle, *The Master Plan: Himmler's Scholars and the Holocaust* (New York: Hyperion, 2006), 145–76; Christopher Hale, *Himmler's Crusade: The Nazi Expedition to Find the Origins of the Aryan Race* (Hoboken, NJ: John Wiley and Sons, 2003), 154–86. Originally, Schäfer had hoped to reach Tibet by steaming up the Yangtze River in China, but he abandoned this plan after the Japanese invasion of China in July 1937.
2. Pringle, *Master Plan*, 149–51.
3. Andrew D. Evans, *Anthropology at War: World War I and the Science of Race in Germany*, (Chicago: University of Chicago Press, 2010), 61, 82–83.
4. Jon Røyne Kyllingstad, "Norwegian Physical Anthropology and the Idea of a Nordic Master Race," *Current Anthropology* 53, no. S5 (April 2012): S46–S56.
5. On Julius Lehmann and Hans F. K. Gunther, see Hale, *Crusade*, 103–5; Hans H. K. Gunther, *The Racial Elements of European History* (London: Longman, 1928), [ch. 8, part i]; Pringle, *Master Plan*, 155n52.

6. Hale, *Crusade*, 102–8.
7. "long head...": Bruno Beger, quoted in Hale, *Crusade*, 129.
8. "fantastical and surreal": Schäfer quoted by Pringle, *Master Plan*, 162.
9. Hale, *Crusade*, 175.
10. "lunar landscape...": Schäfer quoted by Hale, *Crusade*, 192. Explorer John Wood borrowed the expression "roof of the world," from the Wakhi people of Pakistan who used it to describe the Pamir Mountains at the western edge of the Himalayan range.
11. Léon Poliakov, *The Aryan Myth: A History of Racist and Nationalist Ideas in Europe* (London: Sussex University Press, 1974), 23–28.
12. Hale, *Crusade*, 296–97.
13. David Stahel, *Operation Barbarossa and Germany's Defeat in the East* (Cambridge: Cambridge University Press, 2009), 33–38.
14. Hale, *Crusade*, 325–330.
15. "79 of them...": Beger quoted in Hale, *Crusade*, 362.

CHAPTER 19: COLORED BY WAR

1. "all men belong...": UNESCO "Statement on Race" [1950] in *Four Statements on the Race Question* (Paris: United Nations, 1969), 30; "No Scientific Basis...": *New York Times*, July 18, 1950, 1; Barkan, *Retreat*, 341–47.
2. Carl N. Degler, *In Search of Human Nature: The Decline and Revival of Darwinism in America* (New York: Oxford University Press, 1992), 235–238.
3. Jan T. Gross, *Fear: Anti-Semitism in Poland After Auschwitz* (New York: Random House, 2006), 31–166; John Howard, *Concentration Camps on the Home Front: Japanese Americans in the House of Jim Crow* (Chicago: University of Chicago Press, 2008), 45–64.
4. Cynthia Ann Humes, "Hindutva, Mythistory, and Pseudoarchaeology," *Numen* 59 (2012): 178–201.
5. "The Aryan race...": B. R. Ambedkar quoted in Arvind Sharma, "Dr. B. R. Ambedkar on the Aryan Invasion and the Emergence of the Caste System in India," *Journal of the American Academy of Religion* 73, no. 3 (September 2005): 864; "[The Brahmin] claims to be the representative...": B. R. Ambedkar, quoted in Edwin Bryant, *The Quest for the Origins of Vedic Culture: The Indo-Aryan Migration Debate* (Oxford: Oxford University Press, 2001), 51.
6. Joseph H. Greenberg, "The Classification of African Languages," *American Anthropologist* 50, no. 1 (January–March 1948), 26; Carl Meinhof and Felix von Luschan, *Die Sprachen Der Hamiten* (Hamburg: Friederichsen, 1912).
7. Philip V. Tobias, *The Meaning of Race* (Johannesburg: South African Institute on Race Relations, 1961), 1–21.
8. "not due to...": Batrawi, "The Racial History of Egypt and Nubia: Part II. The Racial Relationships of the Ancient and Modern Populations of Egypt and Nubia," *Journal of the Royal Anthropological Institute of Great Britain and Ireland* 76, no. 2

(1946): 144; Charlotte Roberts, "Ahmed Mahmoud el Batrawi," *The Global History of Paleopathology: Pioneers and Prospects*, ed. Jane Buikstra and Charlotte Roberts (New York: Oxford University Press, 2012), 220–22.
9. "That the Dynastic race...": Reginald Engelbach, quoted in D. E. Derry, "The Dynastic Race in Egypt," *Journal of Egyptian Archaeology* 42 (December 1956): 82; "Crouched...": Frank Addison, *Jebel Moya* (London: Trustees of the late Sir Henry Wellcome, 1949), 51; "the presence...": Derry, "Race," 84; C. G. Seligman, *The Races of Africa* (Oxford: Oxford University Press, 1930); "strongly impregnated...": Dart, quoted in Derricourt, "Enigma," 267.
10. "The pure-bred Fulas...": H. H. Johnston, "A Survey of the Ethnography of Africa: And the Former Racial and Tribal Migrations in That Continent," *Journal of the Royal Anthropological Institute of Great Britain and Ireland* 43 (July–December 1913): 401; J. E. G. Sutton, "Archeology and Reconstructing History in the Kenya Highlands: The Intellectual Legacies of G.W.B. Huntingford and Louis S. B. Leakey," *History in Africa* 34 (2007): 297–320.
11. Robin Law, "The 'Hamitic Hypothesis' in Indigenous West African Historical Thought," *History in Africa* 36 (2009): 293–314.
12. "the Batutsi are superb men...": Rev. L. Classe quoted in Tharcisse Gatwa, *The Churches and Ethnic Ideology in the Rwandan Crises* (Oxford: Regnum Books International, 2005), 70.
13. Mahmood Mamdani, *Victims*, 76–102.

CHAPTER 20: KENNEWICK MAN
1. "This looks...": James C. Chatters, *Ancient Encounters: Kennewick Man and the First Americans* (Simon and Schuster, 2002), 21.
2. Chatters, *Encounters*, 55.
3. "They have...": John Bradbury quoted in Robert E. Bieder, *A Brief Historical Survey of the Expropriation of American Indian Remains* (Bloomington, IN: Native American Rights Fund, 1990), 18.
4. "Thousands...": Armand Minthorn, *Kennewick (WA) Tri-City Herald*, October 27, 1997, D1.
5. "In panic...": Chatters, *Encounters*, 76; on legal controversy of Kennewick man, see Douglas Owsley and Richard L. Jantz, "Kennewick Man—A Kin? Too Distant," *Claiming the Stones, Naming the Bones: Cultural Property and the Negotiation of National and Ethnic Identity*, eds. Elazar Barkan and Ronald Bush (Los Angeles: Getty Publications, 2003), 141–61; *Bonnichsen v. United States*, Court of Appeals, Ninth Circuit, 2004.
6. "He looked...": Victor Mair, quoted in Pringle, *Mummy Congress*, 137.
7. John Noble Wilford, "Mummies, Textiles Offer Evidence of Europeans in Far East," *New York Times*, May 7, 1996, C1.
8. Pringle, "Battle for the Xinjiang Mummies," *Archaeology* 63, no. 4 (July–August 2010), accessed at http://archive.archaeology.org/1007/abstracts/xinjiang.html.

9. Alessandro Rippa, "Re-Writing Mythology in Xinjiang: The Case of the Queen Mother of the West, King Mu and the Kunlun," *China Journal* 71 (January 2014): 43–64; Christopher P. Thornton and Theodore G. Schurr, "Genes, Language, and Culture: An Example from the Tarim Basin," *Oxford Journal of Archaeology* 23, no. 1 (2004): 85.
10. David Hurst Thomas, *Skull Wars: Kennewick Man, Archaeology, and the Battle for Native American Identity* (New York: Basic Books, 2001), xxii.
11. Philip Kohl, review of *The Bronze Age and Early Iron Age Peoples of Eastern Central Asia*, by Victor H. Mair, *American Journal of Archaeology* 103 (July 1999): 549–50.
12. Douglas Preston, "The Lost Man," *New Yorker*, June 16, 1997, 70.
13. Mair quoted in Samuel Hughes, "When West Went East," *Pennsylvania Gazette* 109 (January–February 2011): 44; Thornton and Schurr, *Genes*, 89.
14. Kohl, review of *Bronze Age*, 999.
15. Ibid.
16. Graham Richards, *"Race," Racism, and Psychology: Towards a Reflexive History* (New York: Routledge Press, 1997), 262.

EPILOGUE: WHAT DID STANLEY SEE?
1. Jibril B. Hirbo, "Complex Genetic History of East African Human Populations," PhD thesis, University of Maryland, 2011.
2. Stanley quoted in Ker, *White Africans*, 6.
3. Nina G. Jablonski, *Skin: A Natural History* (Berkeley: University of California Press, 2006).
4. Jean Hiernaux, "Skin Color and Climate in Central Africa: A Comparison of Three Populations," *Human Ecology* 4 (January 1976): 69–73. On the cultural meanings of "lost," see Sumathi Ramaswamy, *The Lost Land of Lemuria: Fabulous Geographies, Catastrophic Histories* (Berkeley: University of California Press, 2004).
5. "When I first saw...": Stanley, unpublished speech no. 4718, "The Dark Continent and Its People, or Africa and the Africans" [1878], Stanley Archives.

SELECT BIBLIOGRAPHY

ARCHIVAL MATERIALS
Dartmouth College (Hanover, NH)
Rauner Special Collections Library: Vilhjalmur Stefansson Collection
Smithsonian Institution (Washington, DC)
National Anthropological Archives: Richard Marsh Collection
Royal Museum for Central Africa (Tervuren, Belgium)
Stanley Archives: Henry Morton Stanley Collection

PUBLISHED MATERIALS
Aaron, David H. "Early Rabbinic Exegesis on Noah's Son Ham and the So-Called 'Hamitic Myth.'" *Journal of the American Academy of Religion* 63 (Winter 1995): 721–59.
Amedeo, Luigi (Prince). *Ruwenzori: An Account of the Expedition of H.R.H. Prince Luigi Amedeo of Savoy, Duke of Abruzzi*. London: Archibald Constable and Co., 1908.
Andriolo, Karin R. "Kulturkreislehre and the Austrian Mind." *Man* 14 (1979): 133–44.
App, Urs. *The Birth of Orientalism*. Philadelphia: University of Pennsylvania Press, 2010.
App, Urs. "William Jones's Ancient Theology." *Sino-Platonic Papers* 191 (2009): 1–125.
Arvidsson, Stefan. *Aryan Idols: Indo-European Mythology as Ideology and Science*. Chicago: University of Chicago Press, 2006.
Augustein, H. F. "From the Land of the Bible to the Caucasus and Beyond: The Shifting Ideas of the Geographical Origin of Humankind." In *Race, Science and Medicine, 1700–1960*, edited by Waltraud Ernst and Bernard Harris, 58–79. London: Routledge, 1999.
Azurara, Gomes Eannes de. *The Chronicle of the Discovery and Conquest of Guinea*. Edited by C. R. Beazley and E. Prestage. 2 vols. London: Hakluyt Society, 1896.
Baker, Samuel White. *The Albert N'yanza; Great Basin of the Nile, and Explorations of the Nile Sources*. London: Macmillan and Co., 1866.
Barkan, Elazar. *The Retreat of Scientific Racism: Changing Concepts of Race in Britain and the United States Between the World Wars*. Cambridge: Cambridge University Press, 1992.
Basaninyenzi, Gatsinzi. "'Dark-Faced Europeans': The Nineteenth-Century Colonial Travelogue and the Invention of the Hima Race." In *Race and the Foundations of Knowledge*, edited by Joseph A. Young and Jana Evans Braziel, 114–26. Chicago: University of Illinois Press, 2006.
Batrawi, Ahmed Mahmood. "The Racial History of Egypt and Nubia: Part II. The Racial Relationships of the Ancient and Modern Populations of Egypt and Nubia." *Journal of the Royal Anthropological Institute of Great Britain and Ireland* 76 (1946): 131–56.
Baum, Bruce. *The Rise and Fall of the Caucasian Race: A Political History of Racial Identity*. New York: New York University Press, 2008.

Select Bibliography

Benjamin, Thomas. *The Atlantic World: Europeans, Africans, Indians, and Their Shared History, 1400–1900*. Cambridge: Cambridge University Press, 2009.
Bent, James Theodore. *The Ruined Cities of Mashonaland*. London: Longmans, 1892.
Bieder, Robert E. *A Brief Historical Survey of the Expropriation of American Indian Remains*. Bloomington, IN: Native American Rights Fund, 1990.
Bleiler, Everett F., and Richard Bleiler. *Science-fiction, the Early Years: A Full Description of More Than 3,000 Science-fiction Stories from Earliest Times to the Appearance of the Genre Magazines in 1930*. Kent, OH: Kent State University Press, 1990.
Blumenbach, Johann Friedrich. *The Anthropological Treatises of Johann Friedrich Blumenbach*. London: Anthropological Society, 1865.
Blumenbach, Johann Friedrich. "Observations on Some Egyptian Mummies Opened in London." *Philosophical Transactions of the Royal Society of London* 84 (1794): 177–95.
Boas, Franz. "Changes in the Bodily Form of Descendants of Immigrants." *American Anthropologist* 14 (July–September 1912): 530–62.
Bowler, Peter J. *Evolution: The History of an Idea*. Berkeley: University of California Press, 2009.
Brantlinger, Patrick. "Victoria and Africans: The Genealogy of the Myth of the Dark Continent." *Critical Inquiry* 12 (Autumn 1985): 166–203.
Braude, Benjamin. "The Sons of Noah and the Construction of Ethnic and Geographical Identities in the Medieval and Early Modern Periods." *William and Mary Quarterly* 54 (January 1997): 103–42.
Brooks, Michael E. "Prester John: A Reexamination and Compendium of the Mythical Figure Who Helped Spark European Expansion." PhD diss., University of Toledo, 2009.
Bryant, Edwin. *The Quest for the Origins of Vedic Culture: The Indo-Aryan Migration Debate*. Oxford: Oxford University Press, 2001.
Burleson, Blake. *Jung in Africa*. New York: Bloomsbury Academic, 2005.
Byrd, Melanie. "The Hamitic Prophesy and Napoleon's Egyptian Campaign." *Consortium on Revolutionary Europe, 1750–1850: Proceedings* 22 (1992): 313–20.
Campbell, Alexander Duncan. *A Grammar of the Teloogoo Language*. Madras, India: College Press, 1816.
Cannon, Garland H. *The Life and Mind of Oriental Jones Sir William Jone*s, *the Father of Modern Linguistics*. Cambridge: Cambridge University Press, 1990.
Caton-Thompson, Gertrude. *Mixed Memoirs*. New York: Paradigm Press, 1983.
Caton-Thompson, Gertrude. *The Zimbabwe Culture: Ruins and Reactions*. Oxford: Clarendon Press, 1931.
Chatters, James C. *Ancient Encounters: Kennewick Man and the First Americans*. New York: Simon and Schuster, 2002.
Collins, Robert. *Europeans in Africa*. New York: Knopf, 1971.
Conrad, Joseph. *Heart of Darkness*. New York: Dover Thrift Editions, 1990.
Crosby, Alfred W. *Ecological Imperialism: The Biological Expansion of Europe, 900–1900*. Cambridge: Cambridge University Press, 2004.
Cunliffe, Barry. *Facing the Ocean: The Atlantic and Its Peoples, 8000 BC–AD 1500*. New York: Oxford University Press, 2001.
Curran, Andrew S. *The Anatomy of Blackness: Science and Slavery in an Age of Enlightenment*. Baltimore: Johns Hopkins University Press, 2011.

Select Bibliography

Curran, Andrew S. "Rethinking Race History: The Role of the Albino in the French Enlightenment Life Sciences." *History and Theory* 48 (October 2009): 151–79.
Curtin, Philip. *Disease and Empire: The Health of European Troops in the Conquest of Africa*. Cambridge: Cambridge University Press, 1998.
Dart, Raymond. "The Historical Succession of Cultural Impacts upon South Africa." *Nature* 115 (March 21, 1925): 425–29.
Darwin, Charles. *The Descent of Man, and Selection in Relation to Sex*. London: John Murray, 1871.
Darwin, Charles. *On the Origin of Species*. London: John Murray, 1859.
Daston, Lorraine, and Katharine Park. *Wonders and the Order of Nature, 1150–1750*. New York: Zone Books, 2001.
Davies, K. G. "The Living and the Dead: White Mortality in West Africa, 1684–1732." In *Race and Slavery in the Western Hemisphere: Quantitative Studies*, edited by Stanley L. Engerman and Eugene D. Genovese, 83–98. Princeton, NJ: Princeton University Press, 1975.
Day, John. "The Great Bullion Famine of the Fifteenth Century." *Past and Present* 79 (May 1978): 3–54.
Degler, Carl N. *In Search of Human Nature: The Decline and Revival of Darwinism in America*. New York: Oxford University Press, 1992.
Derricourt, Robin. "The Enigma of Raymond Dart." *International Journal of African Historical Studies* 42 (2009): 257–82.
Derry, D. E. "The Dynastic Race in Egypt." *Journal of Egyptian Archaeology* 42 (December 1956): 80–85.
Drower, Margaret S. *Flinders Petrie: A Life in Archaeology*. Madison: University of Wisconsin Press, 1995.
Dubow, Saul. *Scientific Racism in Modern South Africa*. Cambridge: Cambridge University Press, 1995.
Egerton, Douglas, Alison Games, Jane G. Landers, Kris Lane, and Donald R. Wright. *The Atlantic World: A History, 1400–1888*. Wheeling, IL: Harlan Davidson, 2007.
Eltringham, Nigel. "'Invaders Who Have Stolen the Country': The Hamitic Hypothesis, Race and the Rwandan Genocide." *Social Identities* 12, no. 4 (July 2006): 425–46.
Etherington, Norman. *Rider Haggard*. New York: Twayne, 1984.
Evans, Andrew D. *Anthropology at War: World War I and the Science of Race in Germany*. Chicago: University of Chicago Press, 2010.
Fabian, Ann. *The Skull Collectors: Race, Science, and America's Unburied Dead*. Chicago: University of Chicago Press, 2010.
Franklin, Michael J. *"Orientalist Jones": Sir William Jones, Poet, Lawyer, and Linguist, 1746–1794*. New York: Oxford University Press, 2011.
Fraser, Robert. "Fiction and the Other Reader: The Reception of Imperial Adventure Romance in Africa." In *Moveable Type, Mobile Nations: Interactions in Transnational Book History*, edited by Simon Frost and Robert W. Rix, 99–106. Copenhagen: Museum Tusculanum Press, 2010.
Freud, Sigmund. *The Interpretation of Dreams*. New York: Macmillan, 1913.
Galton, Francis. *Memories of My Life*. London: Methuen and Co., 1908.
Garlake, Peter S. *Great Zimbabwe*. London: Thames and Hudson, 1973.
Gatwa, Tharcisse. *The Churches and Ethnic Ideology in the Rwandan Crises*. Bletchley, UK: Regnum Books International, 2005.

Geddie, John. *The Lake Regions of Central Africa*. Edinburgh: T. Nelson and Sons, 1881.
Gobineau, Arthur Comte de. *The Inequality of Human Races*. New York: G. P. Putnam's Sons, 1915.
Goldenberg, David M. *The Curse of Ham: Race and Slavery in Early Judaism, Christianity, and Islam*. Princeton, NJ: Princeton University Press, 2003.
Goldenberg, David M. "What Did Ham Do to Noah?" In *The Words of a Wise Man's Mouth Are Gracious (Qoh 10, 12): Festschrift Gunter Stemberger on the Occasion of his 65th Birthday*, edited by Mauro Perani, 257–65. Berlin: Walter de Gruyter, 2005.
Gomel, Elana. "Lost and Found: The Lost World Novel and the Shape of the Past." *Genre* 60 (Spring–Summer 2007): 105–10.
Granville, August B. "An Essay on Egyptian Mummies; With Observations on the Art of Embalming among the Ancient Egyptians." *Philosophical Transactions of the Royal Society of London* 115 (1825): 269–316.
Greenberg, Joseph H. "The Classification of African Languages." *American Anthropologist* 50 (January-March, 1948): 24–30.
Gross, Jan T. *Fear: Anti-Semitism in Poland After Auschwitz*. New York: Random House, 2006.
Guérin, Sarah M. "Avorio d'ogni ragione: The Supply of Elephant Ivory to Northern Europe in the Gothic Era." *Journal of Medieval History* 36 (2010): 156–74.
Gunther, Hans H. K. *The Racial Elements of European History*. London: Methuen, 1928.
Haggard, H. Rider. *The Days of My Life*. 2 vols. London: Longmans, 1926.
Hale, Christopher. *Himmler's Crusade: The Nazi Expedition to Find the Origins of the Aryan Race*. Hoboken, NJ: John Wiley and Sons, 2003.
Haller, John S. "The Species Problem: Nineteenth-Century Concepts of Racial Inferiority in the Origin of Man Controversy." *American Anthropologist* 72 (1970): 1319–29.
Hiatt, Alfred. *Terra Incognita: Mapping the Antipodes Before 1600*. Chicago: University of Chicago Press, 2008.
Hirbo, Jibril B. "Complex Genetic History of East African Human Populations." PhD thesis, University of Maryland, 2011.
Howard, Benjamin Douglas. *Life with Trans-Siberian Savages*. London: Longmans, 1893.
Howard, John. *Concentration Camps on the Home Front: Japanese Americans in the House of Jim Crow*. Chicago: University of Chicago Press, 2008.
Howe, James. *A People Who Would Not Kneel: Panama, the United States, and the San Blas Kuna*. Washington, DC: Smithsonian Institution Press, 1998.
Hume, Brad D. "Quantifying Characters: Polygenist Anthropologists and the Hardening of Heredity." *Journal of the History of Biology* 41 (Spring 2008): 119–58.
Humes, Cynthia Ann. "Hindutva, Mythistory, and Pseudoarchaeology." *Numen* 59 (2012): 178–201.
Jablonski, Nina G. *Skin: A Natural History*. Berkeley: University of California Press, 2006.
Jackson, John P., and Nadine M. Weidman, *Race, Racism, and Science: Social Impact and Interaction*. New Brunswick, NJ: Rutgers University Press, 2005.
James, Edward. "Science Fiction by Gaslight: An Introduction to English-Language Science Fiction in the Nineteenth Century." In *Anticipations: Essays on Early Science Fiction and Its Precursors*, edited by David Seed, 26–45. Syracuse, NY: Syracuse University Press, 1995.

Select Bibliography

Jeal, Tim. *Explorers of the Nile: The Triumph and Tragedy of a Great Victorian Adventure.* New Haven, CT: Yale University Press, 2011.
Jeal, Tim. *Livingstone.* New York: Putnam, 1973.
Jeal, Tim. *Stanley: The Impossible Life of Africa's Greatest Explorer.* New Haven, CT: Yale University Press, 2007.
Jenness, Diamond. "The 'Blond' Eskimo." *American Anthropologist* 23 (July–Sept. 1921): 257–67.
Johnston, Harry Hamilton. "A Survey of the Ethnography of Africa: And the Former Racial and Tribal Migrations in That Continent." *Journal of the Royal Anthropological Institute of Great Britain and Ireland* 43 (July–December 1913): 375–421.
Johnston, Harry Hamilton. *The Uganda Protectorate.* 2 vols. London: Hutchinson and Co., 1902.
Jones, William. *A Grammar of the Persian Language.* London: W. and J. Richardson, 1771.
Jones, William. *The Works of Sir William Jones.* 13 vols. London: John Stockdale, 1807.
Jung, Carl Gustav. *Memories, Dreams, Reflections.* New York: Pantheon, 1963.
Kagwa, Apolo. *The Kings of Buganda.* Translated and edited by M. S. M. Kiwanuka. Nairobi: East African Publishing House, 1971.
Kennedy, Dane. *The Last Blank Spaces: Exploring Africa and Australia.* Cambridge, MA: Harvard University Press, 2013.
Kennedy, Dane. *The Highly Civilized Man: Richard Burton and the Victorian World.* Cambridge, MA: Harvard University Press, 2005.
Keppel-Jones, Arthur. *Rhodes and Rhodesia: The White Conquest of Zimbabwe 1884–1902.* Montreal: McGill-Queen's University Press, 1983.
Kodesh, Neil. *Beyond the Royal Gaze: Clanship and Public Healing in Buganda.* Charlottesville: University of Virginia Press, 2010.
Kopping, Klaus Peter. *Adolf Bastian and the Psychic Unity of Mankind: The Foundations of Anthropology in Nineteenth Century Germany.* Berlin: LIT Verlag, 2005.
Kuklick, Henrika. "Contested Monuments: The Politics of Archeology in Southern Africa." In *Colonial Situations: Essays on the Contextualization of Ethnographic Knowledge,* edited by George W. Stocking, Jr., 135–69. Madison: University of Wisconsin Press, 1991.
Kyllingstad, Jon Røyne. "Norwegian Physical Anthropology and the Idea of a Nordic Master Race." *Current Anthropology* 53 (April 2012): S46–S56.
Larson, Edward J. *Evolution's Workshop: God and Science on the Galapagos Islands.* New York: Basic Books, 2002.
Law, Robin. "The 'Hamitic Hypothesis' in Indigenous West African Historical Thought." *History in Africa* 36 (2009): 293–314.
Livingstone, David N. *Adam's Ancestors: Race, Religion, and the Politics of Human Origins.* Baltimore: Johns Hopkins University Press, 2011.
Low, D. A. *The Mind of Buganda: Documents of the Modern History of an African Kingdom.* Berkeley: University of California Press, 1971.
MacRitchie, David. *The Aïnos.* New York: E. Steiger & Co., 1892.
Major, R. H. "The Site of the Lost Colony of Greenland Determined, and Pre-Columbian Discoveries of America Confirmed." *Proceedings of the Royal Geographical Society of London* 17 (1872–1873): 312–21.
Mallory, J. P. *In Search of the Indo-Europeans: Language, Archaeology and Myth.* London: Thames & Hudson, 1989.

Mamdani, Mahmood. *When Victims Become Killers: Colonialism, Nativism, and the Genocide in Rwanda*. Princeton, NJ: Princeton University Press, 2001.

Marsh, Richard. *The White Indians of Darien*. New York: G. P. Putnam's Sons, 1934.

Martin-Márquez, Susan. *Disorientations: Spanish Colonialism in Africa and the Performance of Identity*. New Haven, CT: Yale University Press, 2008.

Mauch, Carl. *The Journals of Carl Mauch: His Travels in the Transvaal and Rhodesia*. Edited by E. E. Burke. Salisbury: National Archives of Rhodesia, 1969.

Mauch, Carl. *Karl Mauch: African Explorer*. Edited and translated by F. O. Bernhard. Transvaal, South Africa: C. Struik, 1971.

Max Müller, Friedrich. *Auld Lang Syne*. New York: Charles Scribner's Sons, 1899.

Max Müller, Friedrich. *Biography of Words and the Home of the Aryas*. London: Longmans, 1888.

Max Müller, Friedrich. *My Autobiography: A Fragment*. New York: Charles Scribner's Sons, 1901.

Max Müller, Friedrich. "On the Relation of the Bengali to the Arian and Aboriginal Languages of India." In *Report of the Seventeenth Meeting of the British Association for the Advancement of Science*. London: J. Murray, 1848, 319–50.

Meinhof, Carl and Felix von Luschan. *Die Sprachen Der Hamiten*. Hamburg: L and R Friederischsen, 1912.

Messier, Ronald A. "The Almoravids: West African Gold and the Gold Currency of the Mediterranean Basin." *Journal of the Economic and Social History of the Orient* 17 (March 1974): 31–47.

Morton, Samuel George. *Crania Aegyptiaca*. Philadelphia: John Penington, 1844.

Morton, Samuel George. "Dr. Morton's Craniological Collection." *Transactions of the American Ethnological Society* 2 (1848): 215–22.

Munjeri, D. "Great Zimbabwe: A Historiography and History: Carl Mauch and After: Paper Presented to Mark the 150th Birthday of Carl Mauch." *Heritage of Zimbabwe* 7 (1987): 1–10.

Newman, James L. *Imperial Footprints: Henry Morton Stanley's African Journeys*. Washington, DC: Potomac Books, 2004.

Noll, Richard. *Aryan Christ: The Secret Life of Carl Jung*. New York: Random House, 1997.

Oliver, Ronald, and Anthony Atmore. *Africa Since 1800*. Cambridge: Cambridge University Press, 2005.

Owsley, Douglas W., and Richard L. Jantz. "Kennewick Man—A Kin? Too Distant." In *Claiming the Stones, Naming the Bones: Cultural Property and the Negotiation of National and Ethnic Identity*, edited by Elazar Barkan and Ronald Bush, 141–61. Los Angeles: Getty Publications, 2003.

Pálsson, Gísli. "Hot Bodies in Cold Zones: Arctic Exploration" In "Gender on Ice," special issue, The Scholar and Feminist Online 7, no. 1 (Fall 2008), http://sfonline.barnard.edu/ice/print_palsson.htm.

Pálsson, Gísli. *Writing on Ice: The Ethnographic Notebooks of Vilhjalmur Stefansson*. Hanover, NH: University Press of New England, 2001.

Petrie, W. M. Flinders. *Medum*. London: David Nutt, 1892.

Petrie, W. M. Flinders. *Migrations*. London: Anthropological Institute of Great Britain and Ireland, 1906.

Petrie, W. M. Flinders. *Ten Years' Digging in Egypt, 1881–1891*. New York: Religious Tract Society, 1892.

Select Bibliography

Pettitt, Clare. *Dr. Livingstone, I Presume? Missionaries, Journalists, Explorers, and Empire.* London: Profile Books, 2007.

Pietikainen, Petteri. "The Volk and Its Unconscious: Jung, Hauer and the 'German Revolution.'" *Journal of Contemporary History* 35 (October 2000): 523–39.

Poindexter, Miles. *The Ayar-Incas.* New York: H. Liveright, 1930.

Poliakov, Léon. *The Aryan Myth: A History of Racist and Nationalist Ideas in Europe.* Sussex, UK: Sussex University Press, 1974.

Pringle, Heather. "Battle for the Xinjiang Mummies." *Archaeology* 63 (July/August 2010): 30–34.

Pringle, Heather. *The Master Plan: Himmler's Scholars and the Holocaust.* New York: Hyperion, 2006.

Pritchard, James Cowles. "Anniversary Address for 1848." *Royal Anthropological Institute of Great Britain and Ireland* 2 (1850): 119–49.

Pritchard, James Cowles. *Researches into the Physical History of Mankind.* London: John and Arthur Arch, 1813.

Ramaswamy, Sumathi. *The Lost Land of Lemuria: Fabulous Geographies, Catastrophic Histories.* Berkeley: University of California Press, 2004.

Ranger, Terrence. "The Rural African Voice in Zimbabwe Rhodesia: Archaism and Tradition." *Social Analysis* 4 (September 1980): 100–115.

Ray, Benjamin C. *Myth, Ritual, and Kingship in Buganda.* New York: Oxford University Press, 1991.

Reid, Richard. "Images of an African Ruler: *Kabaka* Mutesa of Buganda, ca. 1857–1884." *History in Africa* 26 (1999): 269–98.

Relaño, Francesc. "Against Ptolemy: The Significance of the Lopes-Pigafetta Map of Africa," *Imago Mundi* 47 (1995): 49–66.

Richards, Graham. *"Race," Racism, and Psychology: Towards a Reflexive History.* New York: Routledge Press, 1997.

Riffenburgh, Beau. *The Myth of the Explorer: The Press, Sensationalism, and Geographical Discovery.* London: Belhaven Press, 1993.

Rippa, Alessandro. "Re-Writing Mythology in Xinjiang: The Case of the Queen Mother of the West, King Mu and the Kunlun." *China Journal* 71 (January 2014): 43–64.

Robinson, Michael. *The Coldest Crucible: Arctic Exploration and American Culture.* Chicago: University of Chicago Press, 2006.

Romm, James. *The Edges of the Earth in Ancient Thought: Geography, Exploration, and Fiction.* Princeton, NJ: Princeton University Press, 1992.

Rudwick, Martin J. S. *Worlds Before Adam: The Reconstruction of Geohistory in the Age of Reform.* Chicago: University of Chicago Press, 2010.

Salvadore, Matteo. "The Ethiopian Age of Exploration: Prester John's Discovery of Europe, 1306–1458." *Journal of World History* 21 (2011): 593–627.

Sanders, Edith R. "The Hamitic Hypothesis: Its Origins and Functions in Time Perspective." *Journal of African History* 10 (1969): 521–32.

Schwab, Raymond. *Oriental Renaissance: Europe's Rediscovery of India and the East, 1680–1880.* New York: Columbia University Press, 1984.

Seligman, C. G. *The Races of Africa.* Oxford, UK: Oxford University Press, 1930.

Sergi, Giuseppe. "My New Principles of the Classification of the Human Race." *Science* 22 (November 24, 1893): 290.

Sharma, Arvind. "Dr. B. R. Ambedkar on the Aryan Invasion and the Emergence of the Caste System in India." *Journal of the American Academy of Religion* 73 (September 2005): 843–70.
Sheppard, Kathleen L. "Flinders Petrie and Eugenics at UCL." *Bulletin of the History of Archeology* 20 (May 2010): 16–29.
Sheppard, Kathleen L. *The Life of Margaret Alice Murray: A Woman's Work in Archaeology.* Plymouth, UK: Lexington Books, 2013.
Speke, John Hanning. *Journal of the Discovery of the Source of the Nile.* London: Blackwood, 1864.
Speke, John Hanning. *What Led to the Discovery of the Source of the Nile.* London: Blackwood, 1864.
Stahel, David. *Operation Barbarossa and Germany's Defeat in the East.* Cambridge: Cambridge University Press, 2009.
Stairs, W. E. "Lieutenant Stairs' Account of His Ascent of Ruwenzori, to a Height of 10,677 Feet Above Sea-Level." *Proceedings of the Royal Geographical Society* 12 (December 1889): 726–30.
Stanley, Henry M. *The Exploration Diaries of H. M. Stanley.* Edited by Richard Stanley and Alan Neame. New York: Vanguard Press, 1961.
Stanley, Henry M. "Geographical Results of the Emin Pasha Relief Expedition." *Proceedings of the Royal Geographical Society* 12 (June 1890): 313–31.
Stanley, Henry M. *How I Found Livingstone: Travels, Adventures, and Discoveries in Central Africa.* London: Sampson Low, Marston, Low, and Searle, 1872.
Stanley, Henry M. *In Darkest Africa.* 2 vols. London: Sampson Low, Marston, Searle, and Rivington, 1890.
Stanley, Henry M. "The Origin of the Negro Race." *North American Review* 170 (May 1900): 656–65.
Stanley, Henry M. *Stanley's Despatches to the New York Herald, 1871–1872, 1874–1877.* Boston: Boston University Press, 1970.
Stanley, Henry M. *Through the Dark Continent.* New York: Harpers, 1878.
Stefansson, Vilhjalmur. "The 'Blond' Eskimos," *Harpers Monthly Magazine* 156 (1928): 191–98.
Stefansson, Vilhjalmur. *My Life with the Eskimo.* New York: Macmillan, 1913.
Stefansson, Vilhjalmur. *The Stefánsson-Anderson Arctic Expedition of the American Museum: Preliminary Ethnological Report* 14. New York: American Museum of Natural History, 1914.
Stocking, George W. *Race, Culture, and Evolution: Essays in the History of Anthropology.* Chicago: University of Chicago Press, 1968.
Sussman, Robert Wald. *The Myth of Race: The Troubling Persistence of an Unscientific Idea.* Cambridge, MA: Harvard University Press, 2014.
Sutton, J. E. G. "Archeology and Reconstructing History in the Kenya Highlands: The Intellectual Legacies of G.W.B. Huntingford and Louis S. B. Leakey." *History in Africa* 34 (2007): 297–320.
Taylor, Brian K. *The Western Lacustrine Bantu.* London: International African Institute, 1962.
Taylor, Griffith. "Climatic Cycles and Evolution." *Geographical Review* 8, no. 6 (December 1919): 289–328.

Taylor, Griffith. "The Distribution of Future White Settlement: A World Survey Based on Physiographic Data." *Geographical Review* 12 (July 1922): 375–402.

Taylor, Griffith. "The Ecological Basis of Anthropology." *Ecology* 15 (July 1934): 223–42.

Taylor, Griffith. "The Evolution and Distribution of Race, Culture, and Language." *Geographical Review* 11, no. 1 (January 1921): 54–119.

Taylor, Griffith. "The Nordic and Alpine Races and Their Kin: A Study of Ethnological Trends." *American Journal of Sociology* 30 (July 1931): 67–81.

Theal, George McCall. *Yellow and Dark-Skinned People of Africa South of the Zambesi.* London: Swan Sonnenschein & Company, 1910.

Thornton, Christopher P., and Theodore G. Schurr. "Genes, Language, and Culture: An Example from the Tarim Basin." *Oxford Journal of Archaeology* 23 (2004): 83–106.

Tobias, Philip V. *The Meaning of Race.* Johannesburg: South African Institute on Race Relations, 1961.

Trautmann, Thomas R. *Aryans and British India.* Berkeley: University of California Press, 1997.

Tregear, Edward. *Aryan Maori.* Wellington, New Zealand: George Didsbury, 1885.

Trigger, Bruce. *A History of Archaeological Thought*, 2nd ed. Cambridge: Cambridge University Press, 2006.

Waal, David Christiaan De. *With Rhodes in Mashonaland.* Cape Town, South Africa: J. C. Juta and Company, 1896.

Wilson, C. T., and R. W. Felkin, *Uganda and the Egyptian Soudan.* London: Sampson Low, Marston, Searle, and Rivington, 1882.

Wrigley, Christopher. *Kingship and State: The Buganda Dynasty.* Cambridge: Cambridge University Press, 2002.

INDEX

Abraham, Medi, 97
Abyssinians, 92–93
Acaxumo, 110
Account of the Polynesian Race (Fornander), 153
Acoreus, 15
acquired characteristics, inheritance of, 142
Across the Dark Continent (Stanley), 127
Addison, Frank, 230
aesthetics
    "Beauty of Xiaohe" and, 243
    Granville on perfect Caucasian and, 87
    skulls and, 79–80
Africa. *See also* African origin stories; North Africa
    allure for conquest of, 3
    Christianity's beginnings in, 26
    colonialism and independence of, 8, 233
    European currency needs with gold from, 28–29
    European explorers and "point of no return" in, 30
    European ignorance on interior of, 19, 21–22, 34
    European interests with slavery in, 24
    Europeans noting racial diversity in, 43–44
    geological compared to anthropological interest in, 42–43
    gold in, 14, 28
    Haggard inspired by, 176–77
    Hamitic theory supported by linguistics in, 228–29
    Ham's story learned by, 96
    Islam spreading throughout, 27
    Jones on genealogy and race links of Indians and, 71
    Jung searching for European primitivity in, 196–97
    map adjustments for discoveries from, 23
    map of, *12*
    maps of, in early 1400s, 25–26
    maps with fantasy and fact in depictions of, 15
    philosophy adjustments with discoveries from, 23–24
    Portugal's trading post strategy in, 33
    slavery fought by, 32
    slowness of discovery in, 24
    Speke on slavery origins and, 91–92
    Stanley on geological history of, 106
    Stanley's expeditions and bloodshed in, 7, 49
    trading forts along coast of, 33–34
    Western fantasies with, 14–15
    as "White Man's Grave," 33
African Americans, Jim Crow and, 226
African Association, 33
African origin stories
    Biblical time frame and, 130
    changing nature of, 105
    as fantasy and historical, 105–6
    Hamitic hypothesis and Caucasian invasions in, 104–5
    lost white tribes in, 105–6
Agassiz, Louis, 89
Age of Discovery (1400-1600), 24
Ahmad, Muhammad, 122
Ainu, 152–53, 160
Akurias, 170
Albany Evening Journal, 4
albinism, 172–73, 249–50
Alcuin of York, 59
Allan Quatermain (Haggard), 175, 179, 186–87
Ambedkar, B. R., 227–28
Amedeo, Luigi, 131
American Anthropologist, 153
American Education Monthly, 112
American Geographical Society, 51

Index

American museums, Indian remains
  interests of, 237
AMT. *See* Aryan migration theory
Amundsen, Roald, 166
Anderson, Rudolph, 166
Arab traders
  European explorers compared to, 96–97
  Ham's story told by, 98
  Islam promoted by, 97
  Mutesa and impact of, 97–98
  slavery and, 97
Arbo, Carl Oscar Eugen, 214
archaeologists
  Great Zimbabwe damaged by, 118–19, 204
  Hamitic hypothesis disputed by, 229
  public fascination with discoveries of, 180–81
  sites damaged by, 140
Aristotle, 23
The Art of Travel (Galton), 145
Aruwimi River, 120–22
Aryan invasion theory, 9–10, 64, 208, 248. *See also* Nordic race theory
  AMT growing out of, 227
  broad appeal of, 154, 156
  controversy of, 154
  Copper Inuit and, 163
  Darwin's theory of evolution as basis for, 158
  early migration theories woven into, 156
  empathy and, 160
  Gunther and nobility in, 217
  Hamitic hypothesis compared to, 9–10
  Himmler and, 213
  Himmler's expansion plans for quests for, 219
  interest in, despite World War II, 226–27
  Japan and, 152–53
  Jones's beliefs contrasting with, 213
  lost white tribes explained by, 160–61
  Müller on division caused by, 160
  Müller's work giving rise to, 147, 212–13, 216–17
  Nazism tainting, 222
  New Zealand and, 152
  Pacific Rim application of, 153–54
  pre-historic America and, 154
  problems with, 158, *159*, 160
  racial advancement and, 156, 158
  Sanskrit origins of, 150
  Schäfer and, 213
The Aryan Maori (Tregear), 152
Aryan migration theory (AMT), 227–28
Asatru Folk Assembly, 244
Asia, European trade deficit with, 28
Asiatick Researches, 71
Asiatick Society, 68–71, 212–13
Atlantis: The Antediluvian World (Donnelly), 180
Auld Lang Syne (Müller), 147–48
Auschwitz, 220–21
The Ayar-Incas (Poindexter), 154

Bachwezi, 104–5, 127
Baer, John L., 171–72
Bahutu, 233–34
Bailey, Ruth, 197–98
Baker, Florence, 16
Baker, Samuel, 16
Bakonjo people, 123–24
Bakonzo people, 251–52
Balegga, 127
Bambaras, 43
Bankole people, 127–28
Banks, Joseph, 75
Bantu, 118
Barreto, Francisco, 32–33
Barth, Justus, 214
Bastian, Adolf, 116
Batchelor, John, 153
Batoro, 104
el Batrawi, Ahmed Mahmoud, 229–30
Batutsi, 127, 233–34
Bavira, 127
Bazigaba, 104
"Beauty of Xiaohe," 243
Beger, Bruno, *212*
  Auschwitz and live subjects work of, 220–21
  German Caucasian expedition and, 221–22
  racial research of, 216
  test subject challenges and strategies of, 217
  World War II and tainted image of, 225
Beira, 199–201
Belgium, 3
Benares (Varanasi), 148–49
Bennett, James Gordon, 38
Bent, James Theodore, *109*, 202

diffusionist views of, 117
on Egyptian gold origins, 115–16
Great Zimbabwe origin story skepticism of, 114
Great Zimbabwe's foreign influence and discoveries of, 115–17
Berbice River, 170
Bevwa, 126
Bible. *See also* Ham; Hamitic hypothesis
 Blumenbach's theory and, 83–84
 Caucasian origin story and, 90
 Caucasus and origins in, 80
 dynastic race theory challenging time in, 140
 as fantasy and fact, 105
 Flood in, 57–60, *58*
 genealogy and, 54, 59
 Genesis in, 56–62, 84, 90, 263n5
 geography in, 57–59, *58*
 human ancestry and, 55
 Noah in, 57–60, *58*, 70, 263n5
 polygenists challenging, 86, 151–52, 276n1
 race and, 56, 59
 slavery justification with, 62–63, 103
 Stanley's gift to Mutesa of special, 100
 time frame of, 130–31
 T-O maps and, 59
Bierman, John, 257n6
Bimanuka, 104
biogenetic law, 193
biometrics, 144–45, 207
Biometrika, 144–45
"The 'Blond' Eskimo," 168
"Blond Eskimos." *See* Copper Inuit
"blond Maquiritares," 170
Blue Nile, 16
Blumenbach, Johann Friedrich, 85, 93, 140–41, 156, 158, 243
 Bible and theory of, 83–84
 on Caucasians and human ancestry, 78–80
 on climate and race, 81–82, 88
 degeneration theory of, 78
 Georgians skulls of, *79*, 79–80
 Granville influenced by, 87–88
 Granville on race compared to, 88
 liberal humanism of, *222*
 on migration of original Caucasians, 80
 Morton's theory on racial differences compared to, 90
 mummies studied by, 82–83
 racial theory of, 81–84
 recognition and support for theories of, 83–84
 skull collection of, 75–76
 on skulls for human ancestry and race, 75
 travel aversion of, 76
Boas, Franz, 207, 210, 237
Boemus, Johannes, 45
Boma, 48–49
Bombay, Sidi Mabarak, 91
Bopp, Franz, 149
Botswana, 273n7
Bradbury, John, 237
Brazil, 170–71
Breder, Charles, 171
Brinton, Daniel, 153
British Association for the Advancement of Science, 17, 200–201, 208–9
British East India Company, 67
British South African Company, 114
broken pyramid of Meidum, *138*, 138–39
Buffon, La Comte de, 77
Buganda, 3, 18
 Bunyoro relations with, 20
 Christianity and origin of, 104
 Christianity's growth in, 103
 Ham and origin of, 99–100
Bugishu Psychological Expedition, 194–98
Bunyoro, 52, 104. *See also* Uganda
 Buganda relations with, 20
Burroughs, Edgar Rice, 185
Burton, Richard, 16–17, 37, 41, 46, 145
 on race terminology, 91
Burundi, 42

Cadamosto, Alvise, 23–24, 32–33
Caesar, Julius, 15
Calamares, 173
Calcutta. *See* Kolkata
Canaan, 57–58. *See also* Bible
 political motives of curse of, 263n5
 race and curse of, 61
 slavery and, 60–61
Canary Islands, 31
Cao, Diogo, 260n26
Cape Bojador, 30–31

Index

Cape Times, 209
Carnegie, Andrew, 181
Case White. *See Fall Weiss*
caste
  discrimination from, 228
  Hamitic hypothesis and, 232–33
  race and, 217–18
  Rwandan genocide and, 233–34
Catalina Island, 171
Caton-Thompson, Gertrude, *200*
  career prestige and methodologies of, 203–4
  cyclone delaying travel of, 201
  Dart criticizing work of, 210
  Great Zimbabwe expedition of, 199–201
  on Great Zimbabwe's construction, 209
  Hamitic hypothesis faults revealed by, 205–6, 209
  Maund Ruins excavation of, 205, *206*
  Maund Ruins findings and presentation of, 208–9
  press reaction to work of, 209
Caucasians
  Bible and origin story of, 90–91
  Blumenbach on human ancestry and, 78–80
  Blumenbach on migration of original, 80
  Granville on aesthetics of perfect, 87
  Hamites as, 91
  Hamitic hypothesis and African origin stories of invasions by, 104–5
  Kintu portrayed as, 101–3, *102*
  Morton's version of Hamitic hypothesis and, 90–91
  as racial signifier, 83
  Speke on Wahuma connections to, 92–93
Caucasus, 78
  Biblical origins in, 80
  Hitler's invasion goals with, 219–20
  Jones references to, 80
Central America, 171–73
cephalic index, 163, 207
Cetywayo and His White Neighbors (Haggard), 177
Chaillé-Long, Charles, 51
Chatters, James, 235–36, 238, 254
Cherchen Man, 238–40, 242–43
Chicago Inter Ocean, 50

children, primitive peoples as, 191–92
China, Cherchen Man discovery in, 238–40, 242–43
Christianity
  Africa and beginnings of, 26
  Buganda and growth of, 103
  Buganda's origin and, 104
  European and Ethiopian alliances and, 29–30
  Livingstone's missionary challenges with, 36
  Mutesa embracing, 95, 101
  North Africa battles between Islam and, 27
Chucunaque River, 172
Church Times, 209
civilization, religion as marker of, 190–91
Clark, William, 241
class, Stanley's insecurities with, 20. *See also* caste
climate
  Blumenbach on race and, 81–82, 88
  Darwin on, 142
  migration and change in, 249
  Morton on race and, 89
Clive, Robert, 67
Code of Gentoo Laws (Halhed), 68
Colebrooke, Henry Thomas, 150
"collective unconscious," Jung and, 116, 194, 197–98
colonialism
  Africa's independence from, 8, 233
  Hamitic hypothesis and, 232
  India and, 151
  modern remains of, 253
  native peoples resistance to, 122–23
  primitive peoples and governing strategies of, 192
Columbus, Christopher, 23, 33
Comparative Grammar (Bopp), 149
competition, ethics and, 143
Comte, Auguste, 116
Congo, 1, 3, 120, 125, 129–30, 185
Congo River, 21, 34, 48–49
conquest, evolution as, 143. *See also* racial conquest theory
Conrad, Joseph, 185–86
Copper Inuit
  alternate origin theories of, 166
  Aryan invasion theory and, 163
  homogeneity assumptions with, 168–69

lost Franklin expedition and, 163–64
map showing distribution of, *167*
physical traits of, 162–63
press on discovery of, 165–66
Stefansson receiving criticism on theory of, 166, 168–69
Stefansson's discovery of, 162
Stefansson's Scandinavian heritage theory of, 164–67
Crania Aegyptiaca (Morton), 89–91
Crania Americana (Morton), 88–89, 237
craniology, 206–7
Crocodile, 64–66, 71
"Cushite," 43
Cuvier, Georges, 83, 88

Da Asia (de Barros), 110
Daily Inter Ocean, 4
Daily Missoulian, 166
Daily Telegraph, 17, 50
Dark Safari: The Life Behind the Legend of Henry Morton Stanley (Bierman), 257n6
Dart, Raymond
    academic career of, 203–4
    Caton-Thompson's work criticized by, 210
    Great Zimbabwe research of, 204
    skull discovery of, 203
Darwin, Charles, 53, 77, 142, 181
    Aryan invasion theory basis in evolution theory of, 158
    on climate, 142
    on evolution, 142–43, 192
    on language and human ancestry, 73
    race and, 143–44
    Stanley's impact on work of, 247
Davis, John, 165
Dawn (Haggard), 177
de Alcaçova, Diogo, 110
de Angelis, Hieronymus, 152
de Azurara, Gomes Eannes, 62
de Barros, Joao, 110
de Bellefonds, Ernest Linant, 99
De Brosses, Charles, 192
de Camões, Luís Vaz, 24
de Gama, Vasco, 24
degeneration, evolution through, 78, 83, 158
Demerara River, 170

de Montaigne, Michel, 182
de Quatrefages, Armand, 153
Derry, D. E., 230
The Descent of Man (Darwin), 142, 247
De Waal, D. C., 118
de Zurara, Gomes Eanes, 31
Diffie, Bailey W., 260n26
diseases. *See also* malaria
    European explorers and, 32–33, 47
    Livingstone enduring, 37
Donnelly, Ignatius, 180
dormant genetic traits, 170
dos Santos, Joao, 110–11
dreams, Freud analyzing *She*, 188–89
Dublin University Magazine, 51–52
dynastic race theory. *See also* Aryan invasion theory; Nordic race theory
    Biblical time challenged by, 140
    criticisms of, 229–30
    Hamitic hypothesis compared to, 137
    Petrie developing, 137, 202, 207
    problems with, 207–8
    proof of, 137–38, 141, 145
    scientific data for, 145
    skull measurements and, 141–42

Eanes, Gil, 31
East African Standard, 197
Ecclesiastical Observer, 112
Egypt, 229–30. *See also* dynastic race theory
    Bent on origins of gold in, 115–16
    debates on race of ancient, 276n5
    "invasion theory" of, 137
    mummies from, 82–83, 86–87
    Petrie's interests with, 138
Elgonyi people, 198
Ellis, Francis Whyte, 150
Emin Pasha
    Mahdist rebellion and, 122–23
    serious injury of, 124
    slavery opposed by, 120
    Stanley finding, 123
    Stanley's rescue mission for, 120–23
Emin Pasha Relief Fund, 123
Engelbach, Reginald, 230
Erickson, Leif, 164–66
An Essay on Human Understanding (Locke), 183
ethics, competition and, 143

Ethiopia, 45, 91
    Christianity and European alliances with, 29–30
"Ethiopians," 43
Ethiopia Oriental (dos Santos), 111
Europe. *See also* explorers, European
    Africa and slavery interests of, 24
    African interior and ignorance of, 19, 21–22, 34
    African racial diversity noted by, 43–44
    Asian trade deficit with, 28
    Boma's residents from, 48–49
    Christianity and Ethiopian alliances with, 29–30
    gold from Africa and currency needs of, 28–29
    gold's scarcity in, 28
    India's impact on thought in, 73
    Jung on escaping, 195, 198
    Jung searching Africa for primitivity of, 196–97
    Nile's mysteries for, 26
    North Africa's familiarity with, 25–26
    slavery banned by, 97
    Stanley's return to, 49
evolution. *See also* human ancestry
    Aryan invasion theory basis in Darwin's theory of, 158
    biogenetic law and, 193
    children and, 191–92
    as conquest, 143
    as cultural phenomenon, 116
    Darwin on, 142–43, 192
    degeneration and, 78, 83, 158
    early theories of, 77–78, 265n4
    family-tree models in language and, 72–74
    fixed stages of, 191
    Freud's beliefs on, 193
    Haeckel's theory of, 192–93
    lost race literature on racial, 182
    "out-of-Africa" theory of, 231–32
    "out-of-Asia" theory of, 231
    social, 191
    Taylor's tree of human, *159*
La Exploradora, 52
explorers, European
    accuracy and half-discoveries of, 53
    African "point of no return" for, 30
    Arab traders compared to, 96–97
    bias and emotions of, 17

    diseases and, 32–33, 47
    human ancestry traced by, 53–54
    imagination of, 17
    Jung as, 196
    loneliness of, 253–54
    motivations of, 254–55
    Nile's source and quest of, 15–16
    public fascination with, 38

Fairchild, Herman L., 171
Fall Weiss (Case White), 219
family-tree models, in evolution and language, 72–74
fantasy. *See also* lost race literature
    African origin stories as historical and, 105–6
    Bible as fact and, 105
    lost white tribes as, 7
    maps of Africa highlighting fact and, 15
    Stanley's concerns regarding, 15
    Western notions of Africa and, 14–15
    "white race of Gambaragara" as, 7
Farwell, Byron, 257n6
Felkin, Robert, 103
Ferrer, Jaume, 30
Fisher, A. B., 101–2
Flood, in Bible, 57–60, *58*
Foolahs, 129
Fornander, Abraham, 153
France, 3
Franco-Prussian War of 1871, 214
Franklin, John, 38
    Copper Inuit and lost expedition of, 163–64
    death of, 164
French Revolution, 81
Freud, Sigmund, 198
    evolution beliefs of, 193
    Haggard's appeal to, 188
    "primitive mind" and, 194
    primitive peoples and interests of, 189–90
    She dreams analyzed by, 188–89
    unconscious mind and, 193–94
Friel, Arthur Olney, 170
fundamentalist Hinduism, 228

Galton, Francis, 144–45, 186, 208
Gambaragara, 196. *See also* Ruwenzori Mountains; "white race of Gambaragara"

Index
295

accessibility of, 21–22
allure of, 21, 34
climbing challenges of, 252–53
landscape and mountain features of, 14, 20, 35
press on, 50–52
renaming of, 131
Stanley's essay on, 52
Stanley's expedition in, 13–14, *14*
Stanley's first impression of, 20, 34
Stanley's return to, 120
Ganges River, 66, 148
Garlake, Peter, 232
Garthshore, Maxwell, 82
Gauguin, Paul, 195
genealogy, 251. *See also* human ancestry; race
Bible and, 54, 59
Flood and, 57
Jones on links of Indians and Africans with, 71
native peoples and, 53–54
Generalplan Ost (General Plan for the East), 219
Generelle Morphologie der Organismen (Haeckel), 192
Genesis, in Bible, 56–62, 84, 90, 263n5
Genesis Rabbah, 58
genetic traits, dormant, 170
Gentlemen's Magazine, 71
Georgians, skulls of, *79*, 79–80, 87
German Caucasian expedition, 221–22
Germania (Tacitus), 214
German Tibet expedition, *212*
arrival of, 217
goal of, 211
Himmler on success of, 218
return of, 218
weather challenges of, 216
Germany, 3. *See also* Aryan invasion theory; Nordic race theory
language unifying, 149–50
Poland invaded by, 219, 225
World War II defeat of, *222*
Gibbon, Edward, 143
Giza pyramids, 138–39
Glidden, Ralph, 171
Gliddon, George, 89, 91, 137, 140–41, 151, 207

gold
in Africa, 14, 28
Bent on origins of Egyptian, 115–16
European currency use and rising demand of African, 28–29
European scarcity of, 28
trans-Saharan trade of, 29
Gordon, C. E., 101
Gordon, Charles George, 120, 122
Gosse, Edmund, 180
Gowen, Herbert, 153–54
Graebner, Fritz, 117
A Grammar of the Persian Language (Jones), 65
Grant, James, 51
Granville, Augustus, 140–41
on aesthetics of perfect Caucasian, 87
Blumenbach on race compared to, 88
Blumenbach's influence on, 87–88
mummies examined by, 86–87
grave robbing, Native American concerns with, 237–38
Great Britain, 3
Great Zimbabwe, *109*, 178, 231, 248
archaeologists damaging, 118–19, 204
Bantu founding theory of, 118
Bent's discoveries of foreign influence at, 115–17
Bent's skepticism on origin theory of, 114
Caton-Thompson on construction of, 209
Caton-Thompson's expedition to, 199–201
Dart's research on, 204
Hamitic hypothesis and, 202
Mauch's first look at, 108
Mauch's foreign building theory of, 199
Mauch traveling to, 111–12
Maund Ruins at, 205, *206*, 208–9
Mediterranean invaders theory for building of, 112
press on discovery of, 112–13
Randall-MacIver on origins of, 201–2
Rhodes' foreign builder theory on, 202–3
Rhodes traveling to, 118
rumors and myths of, 109–10
Greely, Adolphus, 166
Greenberg, Joseph, 229
Greenland, 164–65, 271n4

Guanches, 31
Guiana, 169–70
Guineas, 43
Gunther, Hans H. K.
    on Aryan invasion theory and nobility, 217
    at Jena University, 215
    on Nordic race theory, 214–15
    on Nordic race theory and invasion routes, *215*, 215–16

Haeckel, Ernst, 192–93
Haggard, H. Rider, *176*, 183, 228, 255. *See also*; *King Solomon's Mines*; *She*
    Africa inspiring, 176–77
    early novels of, 177
    education and job failures of, 176
    Freud and appeal of, 188
    as lawyer, 177
    lost white tribes in fiction of, 179
    psychology in work of, 187
    skills of, 179–80
    success of, 175, 186–87
    translations of work of, 186–87
    weaknesses of work of, 180
Hajj, 27, 56
Halhed, Nathaniel, 67–68
Hall, Richard, 6, 118–19, 203
Ham, 57. *See also* Bible
    Africans learning story of, 96
    Arab traders telling story of, 98
    Buganda's origin and, 99–100
    as Caucasian invader, 91
    Islam and, 98
    Jones on migration of sons of, 70–71
    Jones on power of, 74
    migration of sons of, 58–59, 70–71
    Mutesa captivated by story of, 99–100, 267n19
    Mutesa on Kintu as, 101
    Noah's anger provoked by, 60
    power of, 61–62
    race and curse of, 61–63
    slavery justification with curse of, 62–63
Hamite, terminology and category of, 71, 91–93, 267n16
Hamitic hypothesis
    African linguistics support of, 228–29
    archaeologists disputing, 229
    caste and, 232–33
    Caton-Thompson revealing faults in, 205–6, 209
    Caucasians invasions in African origin stories and, 104–5
    colonialism and, 232
    craniology problems and, 206–7
    decline in popularity of, 84, 85
    durability and appeal of, 10, 230–31, 248–49
    dynastic race theory compared to, 137
    Great Zimbabwe and, 202
    Kintu and issues with, 103–4
    on lost white tribes, 8
    Morton's Caucasian version of, 90–91
    Mutesa's acceptance of new, 94, 95
    origins of, 8–9
    "out-of-Africa" evolution theory's toll on, 231–32
    polygenists and new, 86
    race and, 63
    race as category problems with, 208
    Rwandan genocide and, 233–34
    Speke's interpretation of, 92–93, 99
    Stanley's impact on, 248
    twentieth century expansion of, 230–31
    Victorian age contradictions with, 93
    "white race of Gambaragara" explained by, 63, 85
"hard heredity," 142
Harding, Warren, 154
Harrington, J. P., 173
Hartford Courant, 4, 50
Hastings, Warren, 67
Hawara Pyramid, 141
Heart of the World (Haggard), 189
Hearts of Darkness (Conrad), 185–86
Henrique, Infante Dom (Henry the Navigator), 30–31, 44–45
Henry the Navigator. *See* Henrique, Infante Dom
Herodotus, 43
Hicks, William, 122
Hiernaux, Jean, 250
Himmler, Heinrich, 211, 215, 216
    Aryan invasion theory and, 213
    Aryan invasion theory quests and expansion plans of, 219
    on German Tibet expedition's success, 218

Hinduism, 66–67
    fundamentalist, 228
Hinton, Walter, 171
Hitler, Adolf, 211, 218
    Caucasus invasion goals of, 219–20
    defeat of, 222
    Nordic race theory and aims of, 220
Hobbes, Thomas, 143
Hooghly River, 66
Hook, Raymond, 231
Hough, Walter, 171–72
How I Found Livingstone (Stanley), *40*
Hrdlička, Aleš, 172–73
human ancestry. *See also* evolution; genealogy
    Bible and, 55
    Blumenbach on Caucasians and, 78–80
    Blumenbach's study on skulls for race and, 75
    Darwin on language and, 73
    European explorers tracing, 53–54
    Jones using language to trace, 64, 69–70, 72–73
    Linnaeus' hierarchical categories and, 76–77
    lost white tribes discovery and theories of race and, 4–5
    Morton on racial differences and, 88–89
    mystery of, 9
    polygenists theories of, 85
human variation, 251
Huntingford, G. W. B., 231
Huxley, Thomas, 142
hybridity, racial data and, 168

Ibn-Battuta, 27
Al Idrisi, Mohammed, 27
Imperial Footprints (Newman), 6
The Impossible Life of Africa's Greatest Explorer (Jeal), 257n6
In Darkest Africa (Stanley), *121*, 125–26
India
    AMT and, 227–28
    British East India Company's lawlessness in, 67
    colonialism and, 151
    European thought and impact of, 73
    Jones arrival in, 66–67
    Jones on genealogy and race links of Africans and, 71

    Müller on origins of, 151–52
    Müller's fascination with, 147–49
    Sanskrit and laws of, 67
Indo-European theory, 64, 84, 149–50
"Indomania," 149
inheritance of acquired characteristics, 142
The Interpretation of Dreams (Freud), 188–89
Iradier, Manuel, 4, 52
Iraqw clan, 233
Irving, Washington, 30
Islam
    Africa and spread of, 27
    Arab traders promoting, 97
    Ham and, 98
    Mutesa learning, 98
    North Africa battles between Christianity and, 27

Japan, 152–53
Japanese-Americans, internment of, 226
Japhetic race, 151
Jeal, Tim, 257n6
Jebel Moya, 230
Jefferson, Thomas, 78, 237
Jena University, 215
Jenness, Diamond, 166, 168–69
Jephson, A. J. Mounteney, 102, *102*
Jerusalem, 29
Jim Crow, 226
John, Prester, 29–30, 44–45, 110
Johnson, Floyd, 235–36, 238
Johnston, Harry, 105, 127, 259n11
Johnston, H. H., 230–31
Jones, William, 85, 93, 149, 158
    on African and Indian genealogy and race links, 71
    on ancient mythology, 264n13
    Aryan invasion theory contrasting with beliefs of, 213
    Asiatick Society and, 68–71
    Caucasus referenced by, 80
    death of, 72
    Eastern cultures and interests of, 66
    on Ham as powerful, 74
    India arrival of, 66–67
    language tracing human ancestry in work of, 64, 69–70, 72–73
    legacy of, 72–73
    on migration of Ham's sons, 70–71

Jones, William (*continued*)
  "Orientalism" as accepted scholarship with, 71–72
  Persian language studied by, 65
  projects and interests of, 65–66
  on Sanskrit and common heritage, 69–70, 150
  Sanskrit learned by, 68–69
Journal of the Discovery of the Source of the Nile (Speke), 92
Jung, Carl, 224, 255
  Africa used for European primitivity search of, 196–97
  Bugishu Psychological Expedition and primitive peoples search of, 194–98
  "collective unconscious" and, 116, 194, 197–98
  on escaping Europe, 195, 198
  as explorer, 196
  "personal unconscious" and, 194

Kabba Rega, 20, 35
Kampala University, 245, 252
Kangxin Han, 239, 243
Katikiro, 98
Katukula, 98
Kennewick Man
  dating of, 236
  discovery of, 235–36
  migration theories for, 236
  Native American reactions to, 236–38
  public debate over, 244
  racial sensitivity with, 242–44
  skull of, 235–36
  tests on, 240
Kenyon, Kathleen, 204
Ker, David, 126
  lost race literature of, 184
  Stanley interviewed by, 3–5
  on Stanley's appearance, 1
Kigwa, 104
Kiminywa, William, 251–53
King Solomon's Mines (Haggard), 175, *178*
  inspiration for, 178–79
  popularity of, 184
  Stanley's influence on, 179
  story of, 177–78
  translations of, 187
Kintu, *102*
  Caucasian portrayal of, 101–3, 102f

Hamitic hypothesis issues with, 103–4
Mutesa on Ham as, 101
origin story of, 99–100, 268n17
Stanley on, 100–101
Kirk, John, 36
Knowles, Joseph, 195
Kohl, Philip, 241, 243
Kolkata (Calcutta), 66–67, 69
Komnenos, Manuel I, 29
Koran, 56
Krapf, Johann, 196
Krishingar, 68–69
Kuna Indians, 172–73

Labat, Jean-Baptist, 43
Lady Alice, 18, 48, 246
Lake Albert, 19, 122–23
Lake Bangweulu, 16
Lake Edward, 20, 246
Lake Tanganyika, 16, 19, 21, 39–40, *40*, 46, 49
  Livingstone and Stanley exploring, 41–42
Lake Victoria, 46
  as Nile's source, 19, 21, 49
  size of, 19
  Speke's discovery of, 16
  Stanley surveying, 18–19
Lamarck, Jean, 72
language. *See also* linguistics; Sanskrit
  Darwin on human ancestry and, 73
  family-tree models in evolution and, 72–74
  Germany unified by, 149–50
  Jones tracing human ancestry with, 64, 69–70, 72–73
  Persian, 65, 68
  PIE, 84
Lartet, Louis, 181
Lawrence, William, 83, 276n1
Leakey, Louis, 200, 231
Ledyard, John, 33
Lehmann, Julius, 214
Lepsius, Karl Richard, 91
Lettsome, John, 82
Lewis, Meriwether, 241
Lincoln, Abraham, 241
linguistics, 64, 73–74. *See also* language
  Hamitic theory supported by African, 228–29
  rise of, 84

Linnaeus, Carolus, 76–77
Livingstone, David, 1, *37*, 113, 247, 251, 254, 261n11
 Christian missionary challenges of, 36
 diseases endured by, 37
 disposition of, 36
 explorations of, 36–37
 Lake Bangweulu discovery of, 16
 Lake Tanganyika explored by Stanley and, 41–42
 Lualaba River hypothesis of, 38
 malaria and death of, 44
 Nile's source sought by, 37–38, 42–43
 Stanley finding, 3, 17, *40*, 40–41
 Stanley's exploration intents compared to, 41
 Stanley's quest to find, 38–40
Lobengula, King, 114
Locke, John, 182–83
London Journal, 51
London Times, 3
Lost Among White Africans (Ker), 5, 184
lost race literature
 of Conrad, 185–86
 of Ker, 184
 modernity critiqued in, 184–85
 "noble savage" and, 182–83
 origins of, 184
 popularity of, 175, 183–84, 186–87
 racial evolution in, 182
 translations of work of, 186–87
 Western fascination with, 180
lost white tribes. *See also* "white race of Gambaragara"
 in African origin stories, 105–6
 albinism and, 172–73, 249–50
 Aryan invasion theory explaining, 160–61
 on Catalina Island, 171
 end of search for, 224
 as fantasy, 7
 Friel's stories of, 170
 global discovery of, 9–10
 in Haggard's fiction, 179
 Hamitic hypothesis on, 8
 historical accounts of, 44–46
 history redefined by, 8
 human ancestry, race and discovery of, 4–5
 influential claims of, 247–48
 Mauch on, 109

 Moll's account of, 45
 motivations for discovery of, 254–55
 Nazism tainting search for, 222
 novels inspired by, 5
 of Panama, 171–73
 Shepard's account of, 45–46
 Verrill on encounters with, 169–70
 West Africa and, 45
 Western fascination with, 180–81
 in Western imagination, 173–74
 World War II impact on search for, 224–25
Louisiana Purchase Exposition, 153
Lualaba River, 19, 21
 Livingstone's hypothesis on, 38
Lucas, Simon, 33
"The Lusiads," 24
Lyell, Charles, 72, 142

Maasi, 233
Mackinnon, William, 123
Macrobius, 25, *25*
Madoc, 241
Mahabharata, 149
Mahdist rebellion, 122–23
Maine, Henry Summer, 73
Maine Farmer, 50
Mair, Victor, 238–39, 254
malaria, 32
 Livingstone's death by, 44
 Stanley and, 39, 42
Malthus, Thomas, 84, 143
Mandan tribe, 241
Mandeville, John, 61–62
Mansa Musa, 28
The Man Who Presumed: A Biography of Henry M. Stanley (Farwell), 257n6
maps
 Africa, fantasy and fact in, 15
 of Africa, *12*
 Africa discoveries and adjustments for, 23
 of Africa in early 1400s, 25–26
 of Copper Inuit distribution, *167*
 of Macrobius, 25, *25*
 Tabula Rogeriana, 27
 of Taylor on racial migration, *155*, 163
 T-O, 59
Marsh, Richard, 171–73, 249

Mashonaland, 108, 111, 114. *See also* Great Zimbabwe
Mauch, Carl, 117, 178, 184, 199
    death of, 113
    Great Zimbabwe as first seen by, 108
    Great Zimbabwe foreign building theory of, 199
    Great Zimbabwe journey of, 111–12
    on lost white tribes, 109
    press struggles of, 113
    Stanley's self-promotion abilities compared to, 113
Maund Ruins, at Great Zimbabwe, 205, *206*, 208–9
McLynn, Frank, 257n6
Mecca, 27
Medieval Rhodesia (Randall-MacIver), 201–2, 203
Meidum pyramid, *138*, 138–39
Meinhof, Carl, 229
Memories, Dreams, Reflections (Jung), 195
Merensky, Alexander, 111
Michaelis, Johann David, 80
migration
    Aryan invasion theory weaving together theories on, 156
    Blumenbach's theory of original Caucasians and, 80
    climate change and, 249
    Ham's sons and patterns of, 58–59, 70–71
    Jones on Ham's sons and, 70–71
    Kennewick Man theories of, 236
    Taylor's map on racial, *155*, 163
Migrations (Petrie), 137
Milton, John, 111
Minthorn, Armand, 237–38
Missionary Travels and Researches in South Africa (Livingstone), 37
Moll, Herman, 45, 261n16
Monclaro, Francisco, 32–33
Monomotapa (Wilmot), 118
Monthly Review, 71
Morgan, Lewis, 116
Morton, Samuel George, 93, 137, 140–41, 151, 207, 237
    Blumenbach's theory on racial differences compared to, 90
    Caucasian version of Hamitic hypothesis from, 90–91
    polygenists supported by findings of, 90
    on race and climate, 89
    on racial differences and human ancestry, 88–89
    skull collection of, 88
    skull study flaws of, 89–90, 141
mound builders, Native Americans and controversy over, 241
Mount Elgon, 198
Mount Gordon Bennett, 124
Mount Nyangani, 273n7
Mount Stanley, 131, 196, 252–53. *See also* Gambaragara
Mukabya. *See* Mutesa, King
Mukamba, 42, 44
Müller, Max, *148*
    Aryan invasion theory and work of, 147, 212–13, 216–17
    on Aryan invasion theory causing division, 160
    India fascination of, 147–49
    on Indian origins, 151–52
    Rg Veda translation and commentary of, 150–52, 160
    Sanskrit studied by, 149–50
mummies
    bandaging of, 87
    Blumenbach studying, 82–83
    Granville examining, 86–87
    unwrapping, 276n2
    verification of studies on, 140–41
Munich Agreement of 1938, 218
Murdoch, John, 168
museums, Indian remains interests of American, 237
Mutapa, 32–33
Mutesa, King, 3, *96*, 232, 246
    Arab traders making impact on, 97–98
    childhood of, 97–98
    Christianity embraced by, 95, 101
    Ham's story captivating, 99–100, 267n19
    Islam learned by, 98
    on Kintu as Ham, 101
    new Hamitic hypothesis' acceptance in, 94, 95
    rise of, 98
    royal heritage of, 95
    Speke's depiction of, 18
    Stanley assisted by, 18–19, 44
    Stanley giving special Bible to, 100

Mwanga, 123
My Life with the Eskimo (Stefansson), 165

NAGPRA. *See* Native American Graves Protection and Repatriation Act
Nambi, 99–100, *102*
Namionju, Prince, 44
Natal, 176–77
National Geographic Magazine, 166, *167*
Native American Graves Protection and Repatriation Act (NAGPRA), 238, 240
Native Americans
  grave robbing concerns of, 237–38
  Kennewick Man reactions of, 236–38
  mound builders controversy with, 241
  scientists and historical concerns of, 240–42
native peoples. *See also* primitive peoples
  colonialism resisted by, 122–23
  history and genealogy of, 53–54
  slavery of, 54
Nature, 204
Nazi Schutzstaffel (SS), 211, 216
Nazism, Aryan invasion theory tainted by, 222
Neame, L. E., 5
Neanderthal discoveries, 181
Negritos, 158, *159*, 183, 191
"Negro," 43
Nehru, Jawaharlal, 227
Newman, James, 6
New Stanley Hotel, 196–97
New Testament, 56. *See also* Bible
New Yorker, 242
New York Herald, 4, 17, 34, 38, 41, 50, 113, 261n6
New York Sun, 166
New York Times, 5, 171, 226
New Zealand, 152
Nietzsche, Frederick, 181–82
Nile
  arguments over source of, 16–17
  European explorers and quest for source of, 15–16
  Europeans and mysteries of, 26
  Lake Victoria as source of, 19, 21, 49
  Livingstone seeking source of, 37–38, 42–43
  Stanley's expedition of, 17–18
Noah, in Bible, 57–60, *58*, 70, 263n5
"noble savage," lost race literature and, 182–83
Nordic race theory (*nordische Gedanke*). *See also* Aryan invasion theory
  dismissal of, 226–27
  Gunther on, 214–15
  Gunther on Nordic invasion routes and, *215*, 215–16
  Hitler's aims and, 220
  origins of, 214
  Tibetan nobility and, 217
Die nordische Rasse bei den Indogermanen Asiens (Gunther), *215*, 215–16
Norie, Dorothy, 204
North Africa, 61, 80. *See also* Africa
  European familiarity with, 25–26
  Islam and Christianity battles in, 27
North American Review, 129
Nyamwezi, 18, 39

Obruchev, Vladimir, 182
Operation Barbarossa, 219, 222
Ophir, 111–12, 199
"Orientalism," 71–72
Origin of Species (Darwin), 73, 142–43, 144, 158, 181, 247
"The Origin of the Negro Race," 129–31
Orinoco River, 170
Ortelius, Abraham, 111, 190, *190*
Oto, 250
Otse Hill, 273n7
"out-of-Africa" evolution theory, 231–32
"out-of-Asia" evolution theory, 231

Pacific Rim, Aryan invasion theory applied to, 153–54
Pamir Mountains, 276
Panama, 171–73
Pannigabluk, Fannie, 165
Paradise Lost (Milton), 111
Parima River, 170–71
Pennsylvania Gazette, 243
Persian language, 65, 68
"personal unconscious," Jung and, 194
Petermann, Augustus, 112–13

Index

Petrie, Flinders, 131, 186. *See also* dynastic race theory
   on cephalic index problems, 207
   dynastic race theory developed by, 137, 202, 207
   Egyptian interests of, 138
   Galton collaborating with, 145
   on Meidum pyramid's structure, *138*, 138–39
   race and science challenges acknowledged by, 208
   skeleton discoveries of, 139–40
   skull measurement techniques of, 141–42
philology, 64
PIE. *See* "proto Indo-European"
Pike, Alice, 49
Pinto, Serpa, 128, 251
Pitt, William, 68
Plato, 69, 180
Plutonia (Obruchev), 182
Pocock, Edward, 18
Poindexter, Miles, 154
Poland
   anti-Jewish riots in, 226
   Germany's invasion of, 219, 225
polygenists
   Bible challenged by, 86, 151–52, 276n1
   human ancestry theories of, 85
   Morton's findings as pillar for, 90
   new Hamitic hypothesis and, 86
   on race as fixed, 143
   on racial commonality, 117
Portugal, 23, 28, 30
   African trading post strategy of, 33
   slavery raids of, 31–32
Posselt, Willi, 117
"pre-Adamites," 90
pre-historic America, Aryan invasion theory and, 154
Prehistoric Rhodesia (Hall), 203
press. *See also specific publications*
   on Caton-Thompson's work, 209
   on Copper Inuit discovery, 165–66
   on Gambaragara, 50–52
   on Great Zimbabwe discovery, 112–13
   Mauch struggling to gain, 113
   public fascination with explorers understood by, 38
   Stanley finding Livingstone in, 41
   on "white race of Gambaragara," 4, 35, 50–52, 127–29
Preston, Douglas, 242
Prichard, James Cowles, 91–92, 276n1
"primitive mind," Freud and, 194
primitive peoples. *See also* native peoples
   as children of nature, 191–92
   colonialism strategies for governing, 192
   Freud interests in, 189–90
   Jung's Bugishu Psychological Expedition searching for, 194–98
   as living relics, 191
Princeton Union, 166
"proto Indo-European" (PIE), 84
"psychic unity," 116
Ptolemy, 15, 34, 110
Purchas, Samuel, 62
Purchas His Pilgrimage (Purchas), 62
Pygmies, 158, 191
Pythagoras, 69

race. *See also* Aryan invasion theory; dynastic race theory; genealogy; Nordic race theory; slavery
   of ancient Egyptians debated, 276n5
   Aryan invasion theory and advancement of, 156, 158
   Beger's research on, 216
   Bible and, 56, 59
   Blumenbach on climate and, 81–82, 88
   Blumenbach's study on skulls for human ancestry and, 75
   Blumenbach's theory of, 81–84
   Burton on terminology for, 91
   Canaan's curse and, 61
   caste and, 217–18
   Caucasians as signifier for, 83
   cephalic index and, 163, 207
   craniology and identification of, 206–7
   Darwin's work and, 143–44
   Europeans noting Africa's diversity of, 43–44
   French Revolution impact on theories of, 81
   Galton's theories on, 144–45
   Granville compared to Blumenbach on, 88
   Hamitic hypothesis and, 63
   Hamitic hypothesis and problems with category of, 208
   Ham's curse and, 61–63
   historical terminology for, 43
   hybridity and data on, 168
   Jones on links of Indians and Africans with, 71

Index

Kennewick Man and sensitivity with, 242–44
lost race literature on evolution and, 182
lost white tribes discovery and theories of human ancestry and, 4–5
Morton on climate and, 89
Morton on human ancestry and differences of, 88–89
Morton's theory compared to Blumenbach's on differences of, 90
Petrie and challenges of science and, 208
polygenists on commonality of, 117
polygenists on fixed types of, 143
Rwandan genocide and, 233–34
as scientific concept, 142
slavery and distinctions of, 43
"soft heredity," "hard heredity" and, 142
Taylor's lava flow analogy on global distribution of, 156, *157*
Taylor's map on migration and, *155*, 163
terminology for, 132, 144
underground discussions of, 226–27
World War II impact on scientific attitudes towards, 225–26
Race Division, SS, 216
"The Race Question," 225–26
The Races of Africa (Seligman), 230
"race suicide," 254–55
racial conquest theory, 145–46
The Racial Ethnology of the German People (Gunther), 214
"racial hygiene," 214, 220–21, 225
The Racial Lore of the German Volk (Gunther), 214
radiocarbon dating, 231, 236
Ramlochan, Pandit, 69
Randall-MacIver, David, 201–4
Rankin, F. Harrison, 260n25
Rasmussen, Knud, 164
Ratzel, Friedrich, 117
Rebmann, Johannes, 196
Records of South-Eastern Africa (Theal), 118
religion, as civilization marker, 190–91
Render, Adam, 112
Rg Veda, 150–52, 160
Rhodes, Cecil, 114
  expedition artifacts obtained by, 117–18, 275n3
  Great Zimbabwe and foreign builder theory of, 202–3
  Great Zimbabwe expedition of, 118
Rhodesia, 119, 201–2, 210, 232

Rhodesia Ancient Ruins Ltd., 118
Rice, Alexander Hamilton, 170–71
Richards, Graham, 244
The River of the Seven Stars: Searching for the White Indians on the Orinoco (Friel), 170
Rommel, C., 80
Rousseau, Jean-Jacques, 182–83
Royal Geographical Society, 16, 51, 123, 129
Royal Museum of Central Africa, 245
The Ruined Cities of Mashonaland (Bent), *109*, 117
Rusizi River, 41–42
Ruwenzori Mountains, *121*, 123, *128*, 223. *See also* Gambaragara
  expeditions from 1889-1906, 127
  race to summit, 129
  Stanley and Stairs climbing, 124
  Stanley's lecture and writings on, 125–26
  sunlight around, 250
Rwandan genocide, 233–34

Sahara
  gold trade across, 29
  historical trade routes through, 26–27
  imposing barrier of, 26
Said, Seyyid, 97
Sanikov Land Kraft der Pfadfinder (Obruchev), 182
Sanskrit, 147, 264n13
  Aryan invasion theory origins in, 150
  Indian laws in, 67
  Jones finding common heritage in texts in, 69–70, 150
  Jones learning, 68–69
  Müller studying, 149–50
  Persian translations of, 68
Sara, 250
Schäfer, Ernst, 212, 216
  Aryan invasion theory and, 213
  German Caucasian expedition and, 221–22
  Sven Hedin Institute for Inner Asian Research work of, 220
  Tibet entered by, 217
  Tibet mission goal of, 211
  Tibet travel route plan of, 275n1
Schleicher, August, 84
Schliemann, Heinrich, 100
Schopenhauer, Arthur, 149
scurvy, 47

Seattle Times, 165
Sekajugu, Colonel, 14, 20
Selassie, Sahela, 92
self-discipline, Stanley and, 21
Seligman, C. G., 230
Sella, Vittorio, *128*
Semliki River, 123–24
Seneferu, Pharaoh, 139
Senegambians, 43
Sergi, Giuseppe, 207
She (Haggard), 175, 180, 195
    Freud's dreams of, 188–89
    story of, 179
    translations of, 187
Shepard, Michael, 45–46
Shepstone, Theophilus, 177
skulls. *See also* Cherchen Man; Kennewick Man
    aesthetics and, 79–80
    Blumenbach's collection of, 75–76
    Blumenbach's study of human ancestry, race and, 75
    craniology and, 206–7
    Dart's discovery of, 203
    dynastic race theory and measurements of, 141–42
    of Georgians, *79*, 79–80, 87
    of Kennewick Man, 235–36
    Morton's collection of, 88
    Morton's flaws in studies on, 89–90, 141
    mummies and, 82–83
    Petrie's measurement techniques for, 141–42
    as records of past, 76
slavery, 8
    African's fighting against, 32
    Arab traders and, 97
    Bible as justification for, 62–63, 103
    Canaan and, 60–61
    Emin Pasha's opposition of, 120
    European ban of, 97
    European interests in Africa and, 24
    Ham's curse and justification for, 62–63
    of native peoples, 54
    Portugal and raids for, 31–32
    racial distinction and, 43
    Speke on Africa and origins of, 91–92
    Young defending practice of, 63
Smith, G. S., 101
Smith, Samuel Stanhope, 83

social Darwinism, 143, 181
social evolution, 191
Sofala, 110
"soft heredity," 142
South America, 169–70
Spain, 23, 27
Speke, John Hanning, 37, 41, 46, 145, 251
    on caste and race, 218
    death of, 17
    Hamitic hypothesis interpretation of, 92–93, 99
    Lake Victoria discovery of, 16
    Mutesa as depicted by, 18
    on slavery origins and Africa, 91–92
    on Wahuma and Caucasian connections, 92–93
Spencer, Herbert, 181
Die Sprachen Der Hamiten (Meinhof), 229
SS. *See* Nazi Schutzstaffel
Stairs, William, 124, 126
Stalin, Joseph, 219
Stanley (Hall), 6
Stanley, Henry Morton, 2, *121*, 184, 224, 250–51
    accent of, 1
    African expeditions and bloodshed caused by, 7, 49
    on African geological history, 106
    Aruwimi River challenges of, 121–22
    Biblical time frame and, 130–31
    biographies on, 6–7
    class insecurities of, 20
    Congo conquest of Belgium and, 3
    Darwin's work influenced by, 247
    Emin Pasha found by, 123
    Emin Pasha rescue mission of, 120–23
    Europe return of, 49
    fame of, 44, 113
    fantasy concerns of, 15
    foreign nature of, 1–2
    Gambaragara and first impression of, 20, 34
    Gambaragara essay of, 52
    Gambaragara expedition of, 13–14, *14*
    Gambaragara return of, 120
    Hamitic hypothesis and impact of, 248
    health problems of, 129
    Ker on appearance of, 1
    Ker's interview of, 3–5
    King Solomon's Mines and influence of, 179

Index

on Kintu, 100–101
Lake Tanganyika explored by Livingstone and, 41–42
Lake Victoria surveyed by, 18–19
legacy of, 247, 253–54
Livingstone found by, 3, 17, *40*, 40–41
Livingstone rescue mission of, 38–40
Livingstone's exploration intents compared to, 41
loneliness of, 254
malaria and, 39, 42
Mauch's self-promotion issues compared to, 113
modern journey retracing steps of, 245–47, *246*
Mutesa assisting, 18–19, 44
Mutesa receiving Bible from, 100
Nile expedition of, 17–18
"The Origin of the Negro Race" essay of, 129–31
origins and upbringing of, 19–20
reputation and credibility concerns of, 52–53
Ruwenzori Mountains climbed by, 124
Ruwenzori Mountains lecture and writing of, 125–26
self-discipline and, 21
starvation fought by, 47–48
truth stretched by, 44, 52
"white race of Gambaragara" and initial reaction of, 42
"white race of Gambaragara" encountered by, 3–4, 13–14
"white race of Gambaragara" focus of, 34–35, 126–27, 129–31
"white race of Gambaragara" idea abandoned by, 131
Stanley: The Making of an African Explorer (McLynn), 257n6
Starr, Frederick, 153
Stead, William Thomas, 118
Stefansson, Vilhjalmur, 254
  Copper Inuit and discovery of, 162
  Copper Inuit Scandinavian heritage theory of, 164–67
  criticism of Copper Inuit theory of, 166, 168–69
  physical measurements used by, 168
Stevenson, John, 151

Stevenson, Robert Louis, 177, 180, 187
St. Louis World's Fair, 153
Stories Told in An African Forest (Jephson), 102, *102*
Suna II, 97–99
Sunday School Teacher, 112
Sven Hedin Institute for Inner Asian Research, 220
Symbaoe, 111
System of Nature (Linnaeus), 76–77

Tabula Rogeriana map, 27
Tacitus, 214
Tanzania, 233
Tarim Basin, 239–40, 243
Tarzan of the Apes (Burroughs), 185
Taylor, Griffith, 153
  global distribution of race and lava flow analogy of, 156, *157*
  human evolution tree of, *159*
  racial migration map of, *155*, 163
Theal, George McCall, 118
Theatrum Orbis Terrarum (Ortelius), 190, *190*
Thornton, Richard, 36
Through the Dark Continent (Stanley), 4, *14*, 49–50, 100
Tibet. *See also* German Tibet expedition
  Nordic race theory and nobility of people of, 217
  Schäfer entering, 217
  Schäfer's goal in mission to, 211
  Schäfer's travel route plan for, 275n1
Tilak, B. G., 227
The Time Machine (Wells), 182
T-O maps, 59
Topinard, Paul, 168, 208
"torrid zone," 23
To the Mountains of the Moon: Mapping African Exploration, 1541–1880, 261n16
The Travels of Sir John Mandeville (Mandeville), 61–62
Treasure Island (Stevenson, Robert Louis), 177, 180
Tregear, Edward, 152, 156
"tribe," terminology of, 257n4
Tristam, Nuno, 32
Twa, 250
Tweed, William, 51
Tylor, Edward Burnett, 116

Übermensch (Nietzsche), 182
Uganda, 100, 231–32, 245–46, 253. *See also* Bunyoro
Ugarit, 60
Uighurs, 239–40
Ujiji, 39–40
ultraviolet radiation (UVR), 250
Al-Umari, 28
Umatilla, 237–38
unconscious mind, Freud and, 193–94
Underwood, John J., 165
UNESCO Constitution, 225
United Nations Charter, 225
Universal Declaration of Human Rights, 225
Upanishads, 149
Ussher, James, 77
UVR. *See* ultraviolet radiation
Uzige, 126–27

Varanasi. *See* Benares
Verrill, Alpheus Hyatt, 169–70
Victoria Islanders. *See* Copper Inuit
Vivaldi brothers, 30
Vogenitz, Paul, 173
Völkisch movement, 195
von Asch, Georg Thomas, 79
von Humboldt, Alexander, 83
von Sömmerring, Samuel, 76

Wahuma, 92–93
Wakhi people, 276
Wallace, Alfred Russell, 142
Wangoni, 196
Wanyavingi tribe, 126
Washington Evening Star, 50
Wells, H. G., 182
West Africa, 28, 128, 230–32
    lost white tribes and, 45
Wheeler, Mortimer, 227
"White Man's Grave," 260n25
White Nile, 16
white race. *See* Aryan invasion theory; Caucasians; lost white tribes; Nordic race theory
"white race of Gambaragara." *See also* lost race literature; lost white tribes

albinism and, 249–50
as anthropological fact, 5
appearance of, 13
communication with, 13–14
credibility concerns with, 52–53
fading interest in, 5–6
fame of, 50–52
as fantasy, 7
Hamitic hypothesis explaining, 63, 85
history redefined by, 8
lifestyle of, 14
press on, 4, 35, 50–52, 127–29
Stanley abandoning idea of, 131
Stanley encountering, 3–4, 13–14
Stanley's focus on, 34–35, 126–27, 129–31
Stanley's initial reaction to, 42
uniqueness of, 19
UVR and, 250
witnesses of, 44
whites-going-native literature, 184
whites-in-captivity literature, 184
Wilmot, Alexander, 118
Wilson, C. T., 103
Wilson, G. E. H., 231
Winius, George D., 260n26
Wissler, Clark, 173
The Witch's Head (Haggard), 177
Wood, John, 276
The World as Will and Representation (Schopenhauer), 149

Xinjiang, 239

Yellow and Dark-Skinned People of Africa South of the Zambesi (Theal), 118
Young, Brigham, 63, 263n10
Young, Thomas, 149

Zanzibar, 39, 45–46
Zebehr Pasha, 128, 186
Zimbabwe, 32, 249, 273n7. *See also* Great Zimbabwe
Zulu, 177